04

004

805

'005

05

D0453066

Postmodern Cities and Spaces

Postmodern Cities and Spaces

Edited by
Sophie Watson
and
Katherine Gibson

BLACKWELL
Oxford UK & Cambridge USA

First published 1995
Reprinted 1995

Blackwell Publishers Inc.
238 Main Street
Cambridge, Massachusetts 02142
USA

Blackwell Publishers Ltd
108 Cowley Road
Oxford OX4 1JF
UK

Library of Congress Cataloging-in-Publication Data
Postmodern cities and spaces / edited by Sophie Watson and Katherine Gibson.
    p.   cm.
  Includes bibliographical references (p.   ) and index.
  ISBN 0–631–19403–7 (acid-free paper). – ISBN 0–631–19404–5 (pbk,: acid-free paper)
  1. Cities and towns.   2. Postmodernism – Social aspects.
3. Sociology, Urban.   I. Watson, Sophie.   II. Gibson, Katherine.
HT155.P67   1995
307.76 – dc20   94–15841
                                                                                CIP

British Library Cataloguing in Publication Data
A CIP catalogue record for this book is available from the British Library.

Typeset in 9½ on 12 pt Bembo
by Best-set Typesetter Ltd., Hong Kong
Printed in Great Britain by Hartnolls Limited, Bodmin, Cornwall

This book is printed on acid-free paper

Contents

Part II   Postmodern Cities

Part III   Postmodern Politics

Contributors

Diane J. Austin-Broos is Associate Professor of Anthropology, University of Sydney.

John Connell is Associate Professor of Geography, University of Sydney.

Alexander Cuthbert is Professor of Town Planning, University of New South Wales.

Benjamin Genocchio is a Tutor in the Department of Fine Arts, University of Sydney.

Katherine Gibson is Director of the Centre for Women's Studies and a Senior Lecturer in the Department of Geography and Environmental Science, Monash University, Melbourne.

Elizabeth Grosz is Associate Professor of Women's Studies, Philosophy, Comparative Literature and Critical Theory, Monash University, Melbourne.

John Lea is Associate Professor of Urban and Regional Planning, University of Sydney.

John Lechte is a Lecturer in Sociology, Macquarie University, Sydney.

Alan Mabin is a Senior Lecturer in Planning, University of the Witwatersrand.

Peter Marcuse is Professor of Urban and Regional Planning, Columbia University, New York.

Jim Masselos is a Senior Lecturer in History, University of Sydney.

Paul Patton is a Senior Lecturer in Philosophy, University of Sydney.

Edward W. Soja is a Professor in the Department of Urban Planning, University of California, Los Angeles.

Gillian Swanson is a Lecturer in Cultural and Women's Studies, Griffith University.

Sophie Watson is a Professor in the Department of Urban and Regional Planning, University of Sydney.

Elizabeth Wilson is Professor of Media Studies, University of North London.

Oren Yiftachel is a Senior Lecturer in Geography, Ben-Gurion University of the Negev, Beer-Sheva, and a Senior Lecturer in the School of Architecture, Curtin University, Perth.

ACKNOWLEDGEMENTS

We are very grateful to Robin Connell for her support and enthusiasm for this project and Qingsheng Zhou for his excellent assistance with the production of this edition at various stages. Our thanks also to Simon Prosser, with whom it has been a delight to work. Finally, we would like to thank Peter Marcuse and Edward Soja for their terrific generosity of spirit during their visit to Sydney, when some of the ideas for this book were first aired.

Copyright for individual chapters remains with the author(s) of those chapters.

Elizabeth Grosz's chapter first appeared in the 'Architecture and the Feminine: Mop-up Work' issue of *ANY*, January/February 1994.

Edward W. Soja's chapter 'Heterotopologies' first appeared in *Strategies*, 3: 6–39, 1990.

Elizabeth Wilson's chapter first appeared in *New Left Review*, 191: 90–110, 1992.

1. Postmodern Spaces, Cities and Politics: An Introduction

Katherine Gibson and Sophie Watson

Discourses of the postmodern are having profound effects on a range of urban practices, from philosophy to planning. It would seem that, whether we like it or not, the postmodern is here to stay. The last few years have seen rapid growth in debate about the relationships between a *postmodern aesthetic* (and its influence upon architectural, artistic and cultural styles), a *socioeconomic 'condition' of postmodernity* (overlaid upon a global economic restructuring of space), and a *postmodern paradigm of knowledge* (heavily influenced by poststructuralism) (Frow 1991). This book looks at the influences of discourses of the postmodern on thinking about spatiality, contemporary cities and questions of power in urban life.[1]

The essays collected here can be seen as excursions in and around the two antithetical discourses of the postmodern – that which constitutes the postmodern as an era or socioeconomic period, and that which elaborates a postmodern science or way of thinking and knowing. While both postmodern discourses problematize discontinuity, disjuncture and transformation, their subjects are radically different. For the first it is reality, the city, or more specifically late capitalist urban space, that is the subject of transformation and disjuncture. For the second, it is a type of knowledge, thinking and representation which is discontinuous with what went before.

The chapters are organized into three parts which focus in turn upon space, cities and politics. It is tempting to portray those chapters which concentrate upon the postmodern as period and which relate stories about concrete places and events as the 'empirical' pieces. We might then be enticed to describe the other pieces, concerned with abstract arguments, philosophical elaboration and the postmodern as an intervention in knowledge practice, as the 'theoretical' ones. But what would be the purpose and effect of such a binary structuring except to reaffirm modernism and reduce by half the number of chapters that any one reader might be drawn to? This book is not concerned with boundary making, with defining the postmodern, or with adjudicating precisely who is truly postmodern and who is not.[2]

Our collection brings together an exciting group of scholars from a wide range of disciplines (philosophy, planning, geography, history, feminism, anthropology, sociology and cultural studies), each situated differently with respect to the postmodern in its contradictions; some in sympathy, some in antagonism, some in apprehension, some in praise. The tensions between these positions could be elaborately mapped onto a terrain marked by borders and divides. However, we prefer to offer a different cartography, more of a route map, which charts a course through the collection taking pleasure in the oppositions, the boundary crossings and the differently textured fabrics of the discursive landscapes to follow.

As we pass through neighbourhoods of difference in the cities and spaces of the postmodern contained here, the juxtaposition of distinctively different methods and subjects may, we hope, generate a disturbing pleasure and encourage an openness to otherness. But, at the outset of our journey, a warning – our tour will not evince the pleasure of the famed strolling *flâneur*, whose pace and dalliances would allow the observation of lingering detail. Picture us, on this introductory excursion not 'walking in the city'[3] but more appropriately (or is it postmodernistly?) seated in a tour bus speeding along a motorway with scenes of recognition and disarray flashing through the tinted glass. Given time and space, only the occasional side track will be made off the highway and into the urban labyrinth for the succour and relief of a momentary pit-stop.

The book begins with considerations on postmodern spatiality. In part I: Postmodern Space authors reflect upon how we think, represent, live in, and create space. It is, perhaps, appropriate that the work of Michel Foucault is the starting point for this excursion. His speculations on the suppression of space and spatiality in modern social theory, with its preoccupation with time, history and forward-thrusting narrative, have excited many to rethink accepted modes and suppositions of enlightenment analysis. In 'Of Other Spaces', a lecture given in 1967, Foucault outlined his most explicit views on space. Here he introduced a space he called *heterotopia*, or places which are 'outside of all places, even though it may be possible to indicate their location in reality', places which are 'absolutely different from all sites that they reflect and speak about' (1986: 24). In 'Heterotopologies: A Remembrance of Other Spaces in the Citadel-LA'[4] Edward Soja uses the concept of heterotopia to provide an alternative reading of the structure and meaning of contemporary and past urban spaces.

Soja has elsewhere taken Foucault's scattered statements about space and argued most persuasively for the 'reassertion of spatiality' in critical social theory (1989). His project has been to collapse modern(ist) history into postmodern geography by countering the persistent residual historicism of urban and social analysis, creating in his own work on Los Angeles what he calls a 'rebalanced spatio-temporal narrative'. His essay in this book takes the form of a tour around an exhibition, held at UCLA in 1989, dedicated to the 200th anniversary of the French Revolution. In it, the heterotopias of Paris and Los Angeles 1789/1989 have been displayed/constructed as artworks. In Soja's piece the reader becomes a companion on his metaphorical stroll around the exhibition space, viewing the works he describes. His commentary provides many points of reference which are revisited in subsequent chapters of this book. He mentions, in passing, the Arche de La Défense and Parc de la Villette, two of the examples of Parisian postmodern architecture which Lechte discusses in detail in chapter 7; he touches on the meanings of 'civitas' and 'polis', which Patton takes up in discussing notions of the urban community in chapter 8; he draws attention to the diachronomania of those interested in mapping modernism and postmodernism onto the right set of historical coordinates (Davis's (1990) 'true temporalities'), something that is taken up in part II.

Indeed, Soja provides a very contemporary version of the *flâneur's* narrative, one which muses on a set of literal, 'real' heterotopias he helped to marshal in the exhibition – Biddy Mason's memorial place, the remembrances of the Bastille, the Bastaventure entrancement, the Citadel-LA, the cultural Acropolis, the El Pueblo palimpsest, the Panopticon prisons. There is a desire in this multimedia text to reveal the postmodern geography of 'other spaces' lurking within modern history and modern cities. At the end of his tour Soja acknowledges that this desire has been created by his pre-postmodern hankering for a way of seeing which does not abandon emancipation, political commitment and the deep need for communication. In a final moment of self-disclosure he confesses his reluctance to put on Baudrillard's lenses, through which he might see 'places where images bear no relation to any reality whatever, where good and bad appearances have dis-appeared, where the real and its representations are not what they used to be'.

Some insight into the disquiet with which Soja's commentary ends is offered by Benjamin Genocchio in his very different reflections on Foucault's 'other spaces'. In 'Discourse, Discontinuity, Difference: The Question of "Other" Spaces' he draws upon another reference to heterotopia, in Foucault's preface to *The Order of Things* (1970), where this concept is defined as 'absolutely differentiated discursive spaces' rather than actual, extra-discursive locations. Placing this definition next to the one offered in Foucault's lecture, mentioned above, Genocchio locates any collective desire to promote 'new forms of conceiving social space' as an impossibility, an unrealizable goal which sets a limit to Western systems of thought. In the face of this recognition, he argues that the impossibility of thinking 'other spaces' has, nevertheless, enabling effects on existing discourse and practice. Whereas Soja's heterotopias seem to offer him a revealing viewpoint, Genocchio argues for the impossibility of seeing in just this way. His piece ends not with a tone of resignation and paralysis but with an exciting sense of tension and possibility.

Within feminist thought the enabling moments which have arisen from the very impossibility of thinking 'other' have produced a dizzying number of new and challenging theoretical texts.[5] Metaphors of spatiality are curiously central to much poststructuralist feminist thinking with its interest in location, position, site, dwelling, inhabitation and locale. In 'Women, *Chora*, Dwelling' Elizabeth Grosz examines Plato's notion of *chora*, an inherently spatial concept which has been elaborated by Jacques Derrida, Julia Kristeva and (indirectly) Luce Irigaray. Grosz argues that *chora*, Plato's space between being and becoming, or the 'space in which place is made possible', contains many of the characteristics which masculinist knowledge has expelled, characteristics which can be attributed to the feminine, and which are the very conditions of existence of 'men's self-representation and cultural production'. She explores a feminist reconceptualization of space and spatiality by tracing the parallels between the 'enclosure of women in men's physical space' and the 'enclosure of women in men's conceptual universe'.

Constantly moving from the architectural and physical to the epistemological and ontological, Grosz argues that an understanding of the ways in which women occupy space is predicated upon an exploration of the appropriation and disenfranchisement of femininity within dominant knowledge systems. Any projects towards dwelling in new spaces or new bodies (for both men and women) must acknowledge the invaded and occupied nature of spaces and bodies as we currently know them.

In posing initial questions such as 'Where are women in the modernist city, in public space, in urban representations and language, and in the space of knowledge?' feminists have developed a keen sense of the many discursive and extra-discursive spaces of exclusion which limit women's urban lives and a female urban imaginary. Elizabeth Wilson, in her recent book *The Sphinx in the City*, has taken up the feminist challenge to think about new ways of inhabiting city space. Rejecting the construction which places women in a necessary relation of fear of, and oppression within, the city, she writes of reclaiming the urban as a place in which women can formulate and enact positive visions. In 'The Invisible *Flâneur*' Wilson provides an entertaining analysis of the situation of women in those representations of the modernist city (by writers such as Kracauer, Benjamin, Simmel, Baudelaire) which have become the foundational texts upon which postmodernist representations of the city are being written.

Importantly, Wilson turns our attention to the crucial influence of sexuality in spatial structure, regulation and behaviour. The male gaze of the modernist *flâneur* eroticized life in the city, sexualizing the spaces it viewed. This gaze enabled a mapping of the dangerous influences of sexuality exclusively onto women and the spaces they inhabited. That the figure of the prostitute was perturbingly problematic to these male writers is of interest to Wilson. As an accepted part of street life in the modern city, the prostitute colonized the public role for women in the city, rendering 'respectable' women's movements in urban space a subject for strict regulation.

In chapter 5 Wilson's strategy is to deflate the masculine power modernist theorists gave to the *flâneur*, a power which was projected from urban subject to urban society in a sleight of hand which left women relatively invisible in public urban space, denied civic subjectivity and urban sociality. Gillian Swanson takes this feminist critique of modernist urban analysis further into the realms of economic space and consumption in chapter 6. She shows how women have been excluded from an active role in civic association through their denigrated public role as shoppers.

In 'Drunk with the "Glitter": Consuming Spaces and Sexual Geographies' Swanson shows how contemporary models of consumption and exchange which underpin accepted notions of civility and urbanism have drawn upon highly gendered concepts of individuality, desire and sexual difference. A discourse of consumption which adheres to notions of women as the sexualized, the desiring, the uncontrolled and passionate acts to derogate again women's position in the space (especially the civic and public space) of the city. For Swanson, a recasting of consumption will be part of the process of inhabiting new (postmodern) space.

John Lechte brings us back, in '(Not) Belonging in Postmodern Space', to *chora*, arguing that this notion might play an instructive role in the 'postmodern paradigm of knowledge' Lyotard discusses in *The Postmodern Condition* (1984). Emphasizing the status of indeterminacy associated with *chora* (especially in Kristeva's usage), Lechte argues that postmodern science takes us to the 'limits of knowledge and the beginning of chance'. Perhaps we are back where Genocchio left us with heterotopia – with the realization of the impossibility of knowledge of other spaces, only the possibility of their non-knowledge? In chapter 7 Lechte writes us on a walk in the kind of space that is 'constitutive of the postmodern city'. This is the city of indetermination which resides within the modern city. *Chora* now denotes the space or relationship between the determinate and indeterminate and is illustrated with reference to two explicitly postmodern Parisian monuments, La Grande Arche at La Défense and Tschumi's follies in the Parc de la Villette. Again we see a committed intervention into established systems of knowledge and the use of writing as an enabling (and avowedly indeterminate) act.

In the last essay of this part on postmodern space, 'Imaginary Cities: Images of Postmodernity', Paul Patton discusses the different senses in which postmodern cities are 'imaginary' in the work of Jameson, Raban, Harvey and Young. He notes that much postmodern discourse on the city addresses the 'experience of postmodernity' in ways very consistent with the celebrations and doubts about the 'experience of modernity' elaborated by the 'great' *fin de siècle* urban commentators Wilson takes on. Urbanism, with its confusions about who is who, its opportunities for individuals to take on many roles, and the dangers of losing oneself, provokes similar worries for those imagining cities, whether modern or postmodern. These worries centre on the effect of urban experience on the self, especially the self as an active and effective agent.

Patton draws our attention to the ways in which imaginary cities are written with respect to 'reality'. For some writers real conditions of urban existence underlie the signs they describe, for others there is no distinction between the imaginary and the real. What is of concern in chapter 8 is the possibility that a reading of cities (the production of further signs, or urban imaginaries), rather than the excavation of a foundational real city (the decoding of the urban imaginary), might enhance our capacity to live in urban relations which are unoppressive. This chapter can be used as an interesting lens through which the essays in the next part of the book can be viewed. For in part II: Postmodern Cities a number of actual cities are, to varying degrees, 'read' or 'decoded', with differing enabling effects.

If one thinks of postmodernism and the city it is most likely that certain cities, such as Los Angeles, will come to mind. Certainly, the urban discourse on postmodernism has been largely contained within analyses of key or 'paradigmatic' postmodern places (Soja 1989). In the light of such a designation, the cities discussed in part II represent a curious mix of the paradigmatic and the non-paradigmatic. Alongside a discussion of Los Angeles are placed discussions of Hong Kong, Kingston, Jamaica and the cities of Melanesia. No attempt at comprehensiveness or systematicity has been made in this selection of places. In a sense, their juxtaposition undermines the essentialism embodied in the very notion of a paradigm place. If we live in a 'postmodern era' all cities are postmodern places. If we employ a 'postmodern discourse of analysis' any city can be our object. In this part we see four different attempts to constitute the postmodern with respect to four very different urban places.

LA, host and home to Disneyland where utopia becomes reality (Baudrillard 1993), is represented as the city which, while ignored as 'the crowning moment of twentieth century urban modernity' (Soja 1989: 2), has become the focus and inspiration for characterizations of what is postmodern about contemporary city life (see for example the work of Harvey 1989; Jameson 1984). Like many others, Soja is both attracted and repelled by the utopian dreams and dystopian nightmares he conjures in the name of LA.

In 'Postmodern Urbanization: The Six Restructurings of Los Angeles', Edward Soja continues his study of LA and its restructurings, creating a picture of the interweaving of many different processes which have come together to unravel modernism, ushering in something else, perhaps the postmodern. What he sees as remarkable in the emergence of 'postmodern critical urban studies' is a renewed interest in the specificities of the urban. In his own work this means an attentiveness to the interrelationships between urban form, the geography of production, global–local links, social polarization, social control and the urban imaginary. Gone is the presumption that urban political economy is the key to understanding contemporary cities. Soja's analysis gives weight (although perhaps not equal weight) to the non-economic as well as to the economic in the process of urban change.

The six restructuring processes Soja describes are contained within two historical markers – the Watts riots of 1968 and the Rodney King riots of 1992. These two climactic moments of urban upheaval, action and destruction are represented as marking the beginning of a period of crisis-generated restructuring (in the late 1960s) and the beginning of a period of restructuring-generated crisis (in the early 1990s). His claim is that such events have raised popular consciousness of the very nature of the urbanization process.[6] His belief is that from this consciousness can grow a more progressive future.

Another epochal account of urban change is given in chapter 10 by Alexander Cuthbert in his discussion of Hong Kong, business jewel in the economic crown of the Pacific Rim. This island city/state is poised at an extremely vulnerable moment in its history, anticipating the eruption which may or may not occur when China finally takes possession in 1997. In 'Under the Volcano: Postmodern Space in Hong Kong', Cuthbert describes a distinctive set of restructuring processes shaping the urban political and cultural economy. He shows how important groundings for what might occur in 1997 are being laid by the Hong Kong state, as it negotiates the influences and dictates of Confucianism–Taoism, British law, and the Chinese Communist Party. Whether we will see the volcano erupt into violent fireworks, silencing and blanketing dust storms or benign rumblings, Cuthbert does not predict, though he does indicate that all are possible.

The urgency and anticipation of the post-colonial moment has passed in Jamaica, but the legacy of centuries of colonialism lives on in this Caribbean island. Kingston, Jamaica, could not be further from Hong Kong in its positioning in a world economic system. In 'Gay Nights and Kingston Town: Representations of Kingston, Jamaica', Diane Austin-Broos documents the colonial economic history of this island shaped by the global trade in labour, bananas, tourists, bauxite and music. In her discussion of musical representations of Kingston Town, Austin-Broos argues that the shift in content and style from the erotic otherness of Harry Belafonte's calypsoes, to the hopeful survivalism of Jimmy Cliff's songs, to the transgressive transcendentalism of Bob Marley's reggae mirrors changes in the political economic circumstances of the city and, more particularly, its poor.

In Kingston, the ghetto is both intensely local and international, a site of unique cultural production, at the same time as it is networked globally through international migration and flows of commodities, especially music. Austin-Broos describes Kingstonians as a postmodern people, implying that they have never succumbed to the ideals and emancipatory promises of modernist politics or economic strategies. While the postmodern may be mapped in terms of cultural and economic forms onto Jamaica, she sees its people as always already transnational, transgressive, in short 'postmodern'.

John Connell and John Lea take up this issue of a postmodern people in a similar way in their discussion of urban life in contemporary Papua New Guinea, 'Distant Places, Other Cities? Urban Life in Contemporary Papua New Guinea'. Melanesia is, perhaps, the most recently urbanized part of the world. With no premodern cities to build upon, colonialism brought urbanization, with most urban development being a very recent product of the post-World War II era. The now post-colonial cities of Melanesia are characterized by Connell and Lea in terms of a lack of cohesion, disarray, divisions and the absence of true 'urbanites' severed wholly from their rural roots. What is so interesting in this representation of Papua New Guinea (PNG) is its emphasis upon fluidity, directionlessness, collision and juxtaposition. While history remains the backdrop to this tale of post-colonial urbanization, the narrative avoids the temptation to weave the processes it describes too tightly together.

The place described by Connell and Lea is one in which a postmodern politics is in active process. The inability of any semblance of mass-party politics to take root in and have relevance to Papua New Guinean society is patently obvious. Here the political agenda is not shaped by a romantic attachment to bygone days of political unity and mobilization by big groups around big issues. Instead, political diversity, based upon small group identity, is a daily reality which quite frequently produces violent conflict. Any politics in PNG is destined to be a politics of difference, indeed, a postmodern politics.

In LA the challenges of a postmodern urban politics are posed in the frightening context of race riots, urban destruction and the breakdown of urban order. In PNG these challenges are similarly accompanied by violence and inter-ethnic rivalry, but the breakdown is that of an imposed colonial order. Perhaps it is from the perspective of the 'periphery' and post-coloniality that some of the more positive insights into what postmodernism brings to contemporary urban politics can be gained. Certainly in part III: Postmodern Politics three of the four essays discuss post-colonial contexts (Johannesburg, Bombay and Israel's Galilee region) in which an everyday postmodern politics starkly confronts one of the legacies of modernism – urban planning (particularly segregation), which has long been used as a form of political control. In each place the confrontation between new urban social movements and modernist planning regimes is engendering the distinctive use of space in political action.

In 'On the Problems and Prospects of Overcoming Segregation and Fragmentation in Southern Africa's Cities in the Postmodern Era', Alan Mabin vividly describes perplexing aspects of the political moment which faces South Africa, especially those young leaders of community-based organizations (the 'civics') which were so influential in the successful movement to oppose and overthrow apartheid. Born of a modernist politics of emancipation, these leaders are now faced with a charter to rebuild, develop and change the social order (not the smallest part of which are the cities and townships) using a politics which can no longer suppress difference, even if it wanted to. How can apartheid be destroyed by the active intervention of planners and social policy makers? What room for movement is there?

In this essay we see the need for a coming together of the insights generated by analyses of the postmodern as an era and those of the postmodern as a science. While traces of most of the restructuring processes Soja identifies in LA can be seen to be affecting the urban system of South Africa, Mabin argues that within the interstices of this spatial (re)ordering can be glimpsed moments of political opportunity. In a sense, he directs our gaze to catch heterotopic flashes, not of developed 'other spaces/places', but of potentialities that lie within, perhaps impossible to know fully or to give birth to, but there nevertheless.

In South Africa, where the challenge is to overcome the fragmentation wrought by colonialism and modernist planning, the possibility of postmodern fragmentation poses less a threat than an opportunity for building new ways of administering a less oppressive, less polarized, but still heterogeneous community. In India, the fragmentations exacerbated by British colonialism and papered over by Indian nationalism erupted in Bombay in January 1993 in the worst riots the city has seen since independence. In 'Postmodern Bombay: Fractured Discourses' Jim Masselos tells how the pre-eminent business and financial capital of India was fractured by religion-based violence, killing and destruction of property. Unlike past riots in which fighting took place on the edges of territories identified with particular communities of interest, the pattern of conflict in the January riots was diffuse, disordered and indeterminate. Masselos puts this down to the three-dimensional structuring of social space in Bombay and the influence of a national, if not global, politicization of religion which overrides local attachments and values. In this mix of political influences what is modern, what is postmodern and what is premodern is unclear, leading one to wonder about the use of such a classification. What is clear is that the task of attaining political stability and just city management in the postmodern here and now requires thought and innovation, certainly not a return to the modernist politics of functional and cultural segregation and the hopes of peaceful (but always economically exploitative) co-existence.

Oren Yiftachel confronts the 'dark side of modernist planning' in his essay on Israel's control of ethnic minorities in the Galilee. In chapter 15 he highlights the ways in which urban and regional planning, a seemingly benevolent and reformist form of intervention, has been used as an effective and insidious form of social control in many deeply divided societies. The history of the planning of Majd el Krum illustrates the micro-relations of power and control embedded in rather mundane planning actions which, taken in isolation, might not be seen as controversial or unjust, but, taken together, add up to the enactment of systematic surveillance, segregation and control of the Arab community by the Israeli government. Yiftachel's essay is about the repression and fragmentation enforced by modernism in the name of reform. His instructive and critical reflection upon established and accepted urban orders and practices has been enabled by discourse on and of the postmodern.

Our penultimate word on postmodern politics is offered by Peter Marcuse. In 'Not Chaos but Walls: Postmodernism' and the Partitioned City' he sets out the many ways in which walls of exclusion and inclusion are being shaped in contemporary US cities, particularly New York. Differences are accentuated, in his view, by walls of a physical, socio-economic and cultural nature. 'Walls' – or bounded spaces occupied by specific groups – may offer protection or places of resistance. These may be necessary for minorities to establish themselves. But even these spaces can quickly shift into places open to attack or abuse or lack of opportunity. Walls can also represent exclusion and domination – bounding spaces where those with power exclude those without. So walls or bounded spaces can have different meanings which shift all the time. This chapter highlights how these different meanings are constituted spatially and across time. Marcuse concludes with a plea for urban planners and progressive urbanists to keep up the attempt to pull down barricades of all types and to erect in their place welcoming, sheltering walls.

There is a wistful quality to this concluding plea. Marcuse holds quietly to an ideology of progress, to some notion of the better good, to the idea that cities can be made better and that outcomes might be knowable. These beliefs, vestiges of a modernist politics of emancipation that they are, are not something that all those interested in the postmodern might want to give up. But the question must be asked: could the new walls we might erect 'in the better good' do anything but encompass spaces which once again suppress the differences liberated by a discourse of the postmodern? This is a question raised in many different ways throughout this collection, and one which we return to in 'Postmodern Politics and Planning: A Postscript' at the end of the book.

NOTES

1 Some of the chapters of the book are based on papers given at a conference on postmodern cities held in Sydney in 1993; others have been contributed by those who were not able to attend.

2 The Postmodern Cities Conference (held in April 1993 at the University of Sydney), at which many of these chapters were initially presented as papers, was similarly characterized by a refreshing absence of adjudication between disciplinary perspectives and postmodern 'positions'.

3 Who has the time to walk in the city any more?
4 Reprinted from *Strategies: A Journal of Theory, Culture and Politics*: Special Issue: In the City, 1990, 3: 6–34, with kind permission of the editors.
5 Indeed, many of the new theorists of social space have drawn upon, in acknowledged and unacknowledged ways, concerns and insights which feminist thinking has developed in recent years.
6 An alternative set of readings of the most recent LA riots is offered in Gooding-Williams (1993).

REFERENCES

Baudrillard, J. 1993: 'Hyperreal America', trans. D. Macey, *Economy and Society*, 22, 2: 243–52.
Davis, M. 1990: *City of Quartz: Excavating the Future in Los Angeles*, London: Verso.
Foucault, M. 1970: *The Order of Things: An Archaeology of the Human Sciences*, London: Tavistock.
Foucault, M. 1986: 'Of Other Spaces', *Diacritics*, Spring: 22–7.
Frow, J. 1991: *What was Postmodernism?*, Sydney: Local Consumption Publications.
Gooding-Williams, R. (ed.) 1993: *Reading Rodney King: Reading Urban Uprising*, London: Routledge.
Harvey, D. 1989: *The Condition of Postmodernity*, Oxford: Blackwell.
Jameson, F. 1984: 'Postmodernism, or the Cultural Logic of Late Capitalism', *New Left Review*, 146: 53–92.
Lyotard, J.-L. 1984: *The Postmodern Condition: A Report on Knowledge*, Minneapolis: University of Minnesota Press.
Soja, E. 1989: *Postmodern Geographies*, London: Verso.
Wilson, E. 1991: *The Sphinx in the City*, London: Virago.
Young, I.M. 1990: 'The Ideal of Community and the Politics of Difference', in L.J. Nicholson (ed.), *Feminism/Postmodernism*, New York and London: Routledge.

Part I

POSTMODERN SPACE

2. Heterotopologies: A Remembrance of Other Spaces in the Citadel-LA

Edward W. Soja

Let me draw again on Michel Foucault (with just a little help from Jean Baudrillard) to set the scene for another interpretive look at the 'spatial text' of contemporary Los Angeles.[1] My focus here is on the sites and sights which compose the Citadel-LA, the urban fortress found in the controlling center of the Los Angeles region. The Citadel-LA is remembered as it was commemorated, alongside the Place de la Bastille, in a mnemonic exhibition I helped to organize at UCLA in 1989 to celebrate the bicentennial of the French Revolution. As I have done before, this contextual reading, this remembrance of 'other spaces,' will be used to open up and explore a post-Foucauldian 'interpretive analytics' located in the rebalanced conjuncture of space and time, spatiality and historicity.

Behind this abbreviated introduction is another scene-setting intonation from Foucault that begins the first chapter of my *Postmodern Geographies* (1989). Looking back at a century in which time and the making of history were privileged in critical discourse over space and the making of geography, he asks: 'Did it start with Bergson or before? Space was treated as the dead, the fixed, the undialectical, the immobile. Time, on the contrary was richness, fecundity, life, dialectic.' The present essay begins with an assumed contemporary erosion of these privileging distinctions.

HETEROTOPOLOGIES

Foucault's writing is perfect in that the very movement of the text gives an admirable account of what it proposes: on one hand, a powerful generating spiral that is no longer a despotic architecture but a filiation en abyme, *coil and strophe without origin (without catastrophe either), unfolding ever more widely and rigorously; but on the other hand, an interstitial flowing of power (where the relations of power and seduction are inextricably entangled). All this reads* directly *in Foucault's discourse (which is* also *a discourse on power). It flows, it invests and saturates, the entire space it opens.*

Baudrillard, *Forget Foucault*

I don't deny history. It's an immense toy.

Baudrillard, *Forget Foucault*

A whole history remains to be written of spaces — *which would at the same time be the history of* powers *(both these terms in the plural) — from the great strategies of geopolitics to the little tactics of the habitat.*

Michel Foucault, 'The Eye of Power'

Just before his death, an old batch of lecture notes prepared by Foucault in 1967 were released into the public domain for an exhibition in Berlin. These notes, generated in part by an invitation from a group of architects to do a 'study of space,' were never reviewed for publication by Foucault and thus were not recognized as part of the official body of his works until their appearance, under the title 'Des Espaces Autres', in the French journal *Architecture–Mouvement–Continuité* in 1984. Subsequently published in English as 'Of Other Spaces' in the Texts/Contexts section of *Diacritics* (Spring 1986; translation by Jay Miskiewic), they contain a collection of insite-full ideas on how to interpret human geographies as texts and contexts, how to see the 'other spaces' hidden in the more obvious and diverting multiplicity of real-world sights and situations. I propose here to celebrate their rediscovery.

Foucault's compass pointed to what he called *heterotopias*, real existing places that are 'formed in the very founding of society,' as part of the presuppositions of social life. He saw them as 'something like counter-sites, a kind of effectively enacted utopia in which the real sites, all the other real sites that can be found within the culture, are simultaneously represented, contested, and inverted' (1986: 24). These combinatorial, microcosmic, concretely abstract heterotopias were placed in contrast not only to the 'real sites' themselves but also to their apparent reflections in *utopias*, sites with no real place, nowhere lands, fundamentally unrealized spaces which present society in either a perfected form or else turned upside down. Foucault qualifies the opposition between utopias and heterotopias through a lateral glance into the *mirror*. The mirror represents both 'in a sort of mixed, joint experience,' at once a placeless, virtual, unreal place in which I see myself where I am not, over there where I am absent (utopia); and a real, counteracting space in which I discover my absence from the place where I am since I see myself over there, a realization that makes me come back toward myself, to reconstitute myself there where I am (heterotopia).[2]

These 'curious' sites are socially constructed but they simultaneously recreate and reveal the meaning of social being. Conventional formal descriptions of them, as empirical geometries or as sites for the storage, circulation, marking, classification and encoding of areally differentiated human elements (the characteristic template of the spatial scientists), tend to miss their meaning, to hide the revealing tensions and contradictions that exist between them and all other real sites. The brilliant illuminations of Bachelard and the spatial phenomenologists opened to view the heterotopias of internal space, 'the space of our primary perception, the space of our dreams and that of our passions' (Foucault 1986). But this too was not quite the space Foucault had in mind. For Foucault (1986: 23), heterotopias represent 'the space in which we live, which draws us out of ourselves, in which the erosion of our lives, our time and our history occurs, the space that claws and gnaws at us'. To get to these 'other' spaces requires a different way of seeing, a different interpretive analytics.

Heterotopias are thus *des espaces autres*, those 'other' spaces and places that are often obscured from view by excessive emphasis on their empirical opaqueness or their ideational transparency. To help us discover and find meaning in this hidden and revealingly 'different' human geography, Foucault casually invents a new knowledge, *heterotopology*, and outlines, with examples, some of its principles.

First: heterotopias are found in all cultures, every human group, although they take varied forms and no single one is ever universal. Two broad categories, however, are identified by Foucault for our particular attention, one consisting of privileged, sacred, or forbidden spaces reserved for individuals who are in some way in a state of stressful personal transition ('crisis' heterotopias such as the nineteenth-century boarding school, military service facilities, the 'honeymoon hotel'); the other outlining more modern heterotopias of 'deviation,' such as rest homes, psychiatric hospitals, and ('of course,' he adds) prisons. Tracing the historical, 'modernizing' transitions between heterotopias of crisis and those of deviation has, of course, been central to nearly all of Foucault's major works.

Second: heterotopias can change in function and meaning over time, according to the particular 'synchrony of the culture' in which they occur. The example given is the 'strange heterotopia' of the cemetery, until the late eighteenth century placed at the heart of the city next to the church and still deeply associated with sacred resurrection and the immortality of the soul, later removed to the suburbs in 'bourgeois appropriation' aimed at improved health and the individualization of the dead, with each family possessing its dark resting place in 'the other city.' Each heterotopia thus carries with it a revealing genealogy to go along with its revealing geography.

Third: the heterotopia is capable of juxtaposing in one real place several different spaces, 'several sites that are in themselves incompatible' or foreign to one another. Here Foucault looks at places where many spaces converge and become entangled, using as a model the rectangular stage of the theatre and the cinema screen as well as the oriental garden, the smallest parcel of the world that, since antiquity, has been designed to represent the terrestrial totality. It is this complex juxtaposition and cosmopolitan simultaneity of differences in space that charges the heterotopia with social and cultural meaning and connectivity. Without such a charge, the space would remain fixed, dead, immobile, undialectical.

Fourth: heterotopias are typically linked to slices of time, termed *heterochronies* 'for the sake of symmetry.' This intersection and phasing of space and time, this periodization of spatialities, allows the heterotopia 'to function at full capacity' within a trackable historical geography. In the modern world, many specialized sites exist to record these crossroads of time and space. Foucault argues, for example, that museums and libraries have become 'heterotopias of indefinitely accumulating time,' specialized spaces of all times that appear themselves outside of time and its ravages. In contrast, there are also more fleeting, transitory, precarious spaces of time, such as festival sites, fairgrounds, and vacation and leisure villages. In a foresighting of a more Disneyed world, Foucault sees both forms increasingly converging in compressed, packaged environments that seem to both abolish and preserve time and culture, that appear somehow to be both temporary and permanent.

Fifth: heterotopias always presuppose a system of opening and closing that simultaneously makes them both isolated and penetrable. Entry and exit are regulated in many ways: by compulsion (the prison, the army barracks), by rites and purifications (the Muslim *hammam*, the Scandinavian sauna); or by illusions of freedom (the supposedly open-to-all bedrooms of the great farms of Brazil, the famous American motel rooms for adulterous sex), where more subtle boundary disciplines are imposed. Here the heterotopia takes on the qualities of human territoriality, with its surveillance of presence and absence, its demarcation behaviors, its protective definition of the inside and the out. Implicit in this regulation of opening and closing are the workings of power, of disciplinary technologies.

Last: heterotopias have a function in relation to all the space that remains, an 'external' almost wraparound function that 'unfolds' between two extreme poles:

> *Either their role is to create a space of illusion that exposes every real space, all the sites inside of which human life is partitioned, as still more illusory (perhaps that is the role that was played by those famous brothels of which we are now deprived). Or else, on the contrary, their role is to create a space that is other, another real space, as perfect, as meticulous, as well arranged as ours is messy, ill constructed, and jumbled. This later type would be the heterotopia, not of illusion, but of compensation, and I wonder if certain colonies have not functioned somewhat in this manner. In certain cases, they have played, on the level of the general organization of terrestrial space, the role of heterotopias. (Foucault 1986: 27)*

Here the spaces extend from the body and the boat to all the widening scales that range from the 'little tactics of the habitat' to the 'great strategies of geopolitics.'[3] In each arena the occupant is tugged by the simultaneous pleasures of accentuated illusion and delusion.

These musings on heterotopology remained virtually unseen by Foucauldian scholars, yet they flow through all his major works as a subtle but persistently spatializing undercurrent. In *Postmodern Geographies*, I tried to explain the near invisibility of Foucault's critical spatialization (and the parallel projects of Henri Lefebvre, John Berger, and others) as a product of a persistent residual historicism that continues to blinker contemporary critical social theory to the emancipatory insights embedded in the construction of human geographies. To recapture these arguments, I re-present here some passages from Foucault's introduction to 'Of Other Spaces,' where he is most straightforward about the contemporary interplay between the historical and geographical imaginations.

The great obsession of the nineteenth century was, as we know, history: with its themes of development and suspension, of crisis and cycle, themes of the ever-accumulating past, with its preponderance of dead men and the menacing glaciation of the world . . . The present epoch will perhaps be above all the epoch of space. We are in the epoch of simultaneity: we are in the epoch of juxtaposition, the epoch of the near and far, of the side-by-side, of the dispersed. We are at a moment, I believe, when our experience of the world is less that of a long life developing through time than that of a network that connects points and intersects with its own skein. One could say that certain ideological conflicts animating present-day polemics oppose the pious descendants of time and the determined inhabitants of space.

Foucault continues at this point with an interesting aside on structuralism as a means of effectively spatializing history and historiography.

Structuralism, or at least that which is grouped under the slightly too general name, is the effort to establish, between elements that could have been connected on a temporal axis, an ensemble of relations that makes them appear as juxtaposed, set off against one another, in short, as a sort of configuration.[4] *Actually structuralism does not entail a denial of time; it does involve a certain manner of dealing with what we call time and what we call history.*

He concludes his notes with a cautious admission.

In any case I believe that the anxiety of our era has to do fundamentally with space, no doubt a great deal more than with time. Time probably appears to us only as one of various distributive operations that are possible for the elements that are spread out in space.

Foucault thus brings us up to date in space and time, enabling this narrative emplotment to proceed to another field of geographical remembrances.

1789/1989, PARIS/LOS ANGELES: THE CITY AND HISTORICAL CHANGE

In spring 1989, a heterotopological exhibition of sorts took place within the spaces of the Graduate School of Architecture and Urban Planning at UCLA as part of the school's participation in a multi-year celebration on campus of the bicentennial of the French Revolution. Associated with the exhibition were a series of public lectures and a colloquium, both of which featured interventions by Jean Baudrillard and other ex- plorations of the nexus of place and power in Paris and Los Angeles over the past two centuries.[5] No catalogue for the exhibition was ever prepared. In its place, I will reconstruct some pictures of the exhibition while finding both the time and space to explore further the heterotopology of the Citadel-LA.

From the Power of Place to the Places of Power

All things were changed; all those places that were so well known to me presented a different fact, and appeared to be recently embellished; I lost myself amidst grand and beautiful streets, that were built in straight lines; I entered a spacious square, formed by the termination of four streets, where there reigned such perfect order, that I found not the least embarrassment, nor heard any of those confused and whimsical cries that formerly rent my ears; I saw no carriages ready to crush me . . . the city had an animated aspect, but without trouble and confusion.

Louis-Sebastien Mercier, *Memoirs of the Year 2440*

It is interesting, if not useful, to consider where one would go in Los Angeles to have an effective revolution of the Latin American sort. Presumably, the place would be in the heart of the city. If one took over some public square, some urban open space in Los Angeles, who would know? A march on City Hall would be inconclusive. The heart of the city would have to be sought elsewhere.

Charles Moore, quoted in Von Eckardt, *A Place to Live: The Crisis of the Cities*

Opposite a wall embedded with a great rectangular chunk of Louis Sullivan's masterful ornamental façade for the old Gage building in Chicago is a glassed-in display cabinet containing a mini-exhibit of 'The Power of Place,' the name and restorative aim of a non-profit, design-oriented, memory-preserving organization whose most recent accomplishment is the recreation of Biddy Mason's Place in the history and geography of Los Angeles.[6] Biddy Mason was a midwife and nurse, an ex-slave who became a founder of the first Black church in Los Angeles (in 1972) and was the first Black woman to own property in the city. Her old place is now redesigned as a designated urban mnemonic, an architectural madeleine for a very particular *recherche du temps perdu.*

The Power of Place project locates its remembrances not only at the intersection of space and time but also at the crossroads of several movements shaping the looks of downtown Los Angeles and other American cities: the promotional development of Art in Public Places provided much of the funding, the now well-established efforts to preserve the historical and cultural heritage of the city helped empower the project, and the struggle for more visible representation of the under-represented (mainly workers, women and minorities) gives it force and direction. Its memorial orientation arises from the revelatory existentialism of the question *What Time is This Place?*, the title of an evocative book by the urban designer, Kevin Lynch, author of *The Image of the City* (1960), and a conceptual source for the radical political aesthetic of 'cognitive mapping' that features so prominently in the recent work of Fredric Jameson, to whom we will shortly return in our circuit around the exhibition.

From the boxed-in window, visually displaying the creative plans for the reconstitution of Biddy Mason's particular place, is inflected a fretwork of additional lines of more general inquiry about the curious concatenation of space and time, spatiality and historicity: Whose history is to be preserved in these acts of commemoration? In what places is this history most appropriately encased? What forms shall the memories take? How can choosing a past help us to construct a future? Through preserving urban history, can we help explain the current design of the city and its political economy? Can such historical understanding enable us to change the design and political economy in significantly beneficial ways?

Other questions can also be asked: By redesigning the built environment can we, must we, reinterpret the past? Given what Foucault called the synchrony of culture, is what we construct now only a false representation of history, a simulation that accrues to itself only its own immediate contemporary meaning? Can we ever recapture and preserve an historical site when its set of relations to other real sites has been erased by time? What is it that we are preserving when we engage in cultural and historical preservation? Would not a deeper understanding of the contemporary dynamics of urban design and political economy serve us better than exploring the past in constructing a better future?

These two sets of questions differentially privilege history and geography, the past and the present. They emanate from two different ways of looking at places and spaces, the first informed by an emancipatory sense of the power of archeology and genealogy, by an emplotment within a meaningful historical narrative; the second by an emancipatory sense of the cartography and heterotopology of power, an emplotment within a meaningful interpretive geography. Both can be described as spatio-temporal perspectives, but one (the first and most familiar) historicizes geography while the other (more difficult to grasp) spatializes history. Keep this difference in mind as we turn the corner into the second sight of the exhibition, 'Remembering the Bastille, 1789–1989.'

Here a long illuminated wall guides the viewer through a chronological corridor picturing the richly heterotopic site of the Place de la Bastille, from its revolutionary storming to its various commemorative redesigns and monumental punctuations (including a short-lived *papier-maché* elephant of gargantuan proportions) to the newly completed Opera House, where the photo-narrative peaks in a spectacular videotape presentation (auteured by Robert Maniquis) set opposite to a huge hanging satellite reproduction of 'Los Angeles – From Space,' a semi-permanent fixture in the central open enclosure of the building. It is a heady walk along this bridge of sights, from that translucent moment when the fourteenth-century fortress disappeared brick by brick, through its many different preservational reappearances, each in different ways trying to recapture the past in the present. Today, all the memories boggle as a freshly commodified fortress of culture replaces and reconstitutes the historical site as one of several spectacular bicentennial implantations into the space of Paris.[7]

The video screen provides both immediacy and transition, juxtaposing in one place several sights and sites that are themselves incompatible. Nostalgic music plays as the just-seen photo-narrative blends into old cinematic representations of the revolutionary Bastille (complete with a hell-hag Madame La Farge) to retrace the transformation of historical memory into heroic (and anti-heroic) modern imagery. Then, as we listen to the fulsome contemporary debates over the Opera House and its leadership – and see what has been happening elsewhere around the Place – we suddenly begin to realize at the video's end (just before the rolling tape beings at the beginning again) that even the familiar modernist images are themselves being displaced by an entirely new set of time-eroding simulations, forcing the past into the heterochrony of the present. As Foucault noted, 'the heterotopia begins to function at full capacity when men arrive at a sort of absolute break with their traditional time' (1986: 26). Perhaps this is also when the power of place is neutralized or inverted (again, Foucault's words) into places of power; and, writ larger, when nearly all of modern history is forcefully collapsed into a contemporary, postmodern geography.

Places of Power: Symbolizing the Citadel in Los Angeles

This is the end of art 'as we know it'. It is the end of the art of art history. It is the end of urban art with its dialectical struggles. Today this simulated art takes place in cities that are also doubles of themselves, cities that only exist as nostalgic references to the idea of city and to the ideas of communication and social intercourse. These simulated cities are placed around the globe more or less exactly where the old cities were, but they no longer fulfill the function of the old cities. They are no longer centers; they only serve to simulate the phenomenon of the center. And within these simulated centers, usually exactly at their very heart, is where this simulated art activity takes place, an activity itself nostalgic for the reality of activity in art.

Peter Halley, 'Notes on Nostalgia'

We arrive now at the central place of the exhibition, the center of centers, moving just beyond the video monitor into the entrance to a small gallery, where a spotlit bird of paradise (the city's official flower)[8] announces present-day Los Angeles.[9] At this point the narrative breaks down into a cluster of revealing emplotments in imitation of the splintered labyrinth that is set before us. Each tells its own story. They should be read simultaneously but, alas, this is not possible.

Entrancement

To tell you where you have been as well as where you are going, a massive sculptural form dominates the gallery space and powerfully catches your eye. Half of it rises from a billowy base of matted brown butcher paper to the crenellated turrets of a simulated Bastille. The other half sits atop a slightly cracked bunker of grey concrete upholding the gleaming bronzed-glass towers of the Bonaventure Hotel, the chosen microcosmos of postmodernized Los Angeles. The two sides of the soaring sculpture, dubbed the 'Bastaventure,' blend into one another in brilliantly executed adjacencies that highlight the epochal transition between crumbling old fortress and resurgent new citadel.[10]

The Bonaventure Hotel symbolizes and simulates the geographical experience of postmodernity just as the Bastille symbolizes and simulates the historical experience of the French Revolution. This is made most clear when the Bonaventure (or, for that matter, the Bastille) is seen as a contemporary heterotopia, as an evocative 'counter-site' in which all other (and absolutely different) real sites within the synchronous culture are 'simultaneously represented, contested, and inverted.' Like most other heterotopias, it functions at full capacity within a specifically periodized slice of time and after a break with historical tradition. Architectural stylists might label it Late Modern (and it can be 'read' as such), but its life-space and its relation to all other real sites, its simultaneities and juxtapositions, signify a noticeable departure from the modernist traditions of the past century.

Jameson (1984: 53–92) was the first to read the Bonaventure heterotopologically, as a figurative con-text of postmodernism's most absorbing cultural logic, and his global reading of the shining site has stirred extensive controversy, especially from more local readers.[11] For Jameson, this 'populist insertion into the city fabric' has become a 'hyperspace' of both illusion and compensation, a new kind of cultural brothel and colony (combining Foucault's separate allusions) that exposes such archetypical postmodern conditions as depthlessness, fragmentation, the reduction of history to nostalgia, and, underlying it all, the programmatic decentering of the subject, the rattling awareness that the individual human body has been losing 'the capacity to locate itself, to organize its immediate surroundings perceptually, and cognitively map its position within a mappable external world' (1984: 83). Seen through the 'real pleasures' of the Bonaventure is a mutated cityscape of seductive simulations, a built environment in which an aesthetic becomes politically anaesthetic, enticing both the subject and object of history under a numbing amnesiac blanket of exact copies for which no original ever existed.

In the bunkered fortress of the Bonaventure, entrance and exit ways are curiously unmarked and appear at many different levels, as if 'some new category of closure [was] governing the inner space of the hotel itself' (Jameson 1984). Inside and out, one is lost in a 'placeless dissociation,' an 'alarming disjunction between the body and the built environment' that Jameson compares (and links) to the experience of Los Angeles itself and, even more pointedly, to the increasing incapacity of our minds to cognitively map another hyperspace, 'the great global multinational and decentered communicational network in which we find ourselves caught as individual subjects.' I have covered similar tracks in my own depiction of the Bonaventure, written some time after strolling through the microcosmopolois with Jameson and Henri Lefebvre.

> Like many other Portman-teaus which dot the eyes of urban citadels in New York and San Francisco, Atlanta and Detroit, the Bonaventure has become a concentrated representation of the restructured spatiality of the late capitalist city: fragmented and fragmenting, homogeneous and homogenizing, divertingly packaged yet curiously incomprehensible, seemingly open in presenting itself to view but constantly pressing to enclose, to compartmentalize, to circumscribe, to incarcerate. Everything imaginable appears to be available in the micro-urb but real places are difficult to find, its spaces confuse an effective cognitive mapping, its pastiche of superficial reflections bewilder coordination and encourage submission instead. . . . Once inside . . . it becomes daunting to get out again without bureaucratic assistance. (Soja 1989: 243–4)

Jameson's intentionally spatializing interpretation of the Bonaventure Hotel has occupied the eye of a still-unsettled storm of historical criticism that vividly illustrates those present-day polemics and ideological conflicts Foucault predicted would arise between 'the pious descendants of time and the determined inhabitants of space' (1986: 22), between the historicizers of geography and the spatializers of history. Given the continuing hegemony of historicism in contemporary critical studies, even sympathetic critics of Jameson, who themselves have been struggling with spatiality in their own writings, have tended to be perplexed by Jameson's assertively spatialized new agenda for history and criticism, seeing its Bonaventure-ous interpretations as blithely ahistorical or worse, as anti-history. Characteristically, the response of these critics is an almost nostalgic defense of the nineteenth-century privileges of historicism.

Thus Mike Davis, in an otherwise illuminating interpretation of the 'decadent tropes' of modernism in Los Angeles, berates Jameson for presenting a present 'deprived of historical coordinates.' To find them, Davis (1985) seeks what he calls the 'true temporalities' that can be read from the spatial text of Bunker Hill and the Bonaventure Hotel (which Jameson incorrectly identified as 'Beacon Hill' and the 'Bonaventura' in 1984). Jameson's stated attempt at establishing historical coordinates, derived from the heterochronies of Mandel, is then criticized for missing the right dates and thereby for misapprehending the politically correct meaning of the urban 'renaissance' of downtown Los Angeles. Davis's alternative reading is brilliantly executed and much more directively and confidently political than Jameson's. But it remains strait-jacketed by a lingering diachronomania drawn too uncritically from that most historicist of epistemes, '*post hoc, ergo propter hoc.*' With the present so unproblematically a product of the past, the possibility that postmodernity poses a new challenge to radical discourse and politics virtually disappears.[12]

In the inaugural issue of *Strategies*, Donald Preziosi (1988) approaches Jameson's Bonaventure from an entirely different point of view. Turning Davis's critique upside down, he blames Jameson for not escaping enough from historicism, for being 'supremely historical,' for never moving outside 'that grand master narrative plot,' that 'commonplace, totalizing historicism central to art historical discourse since the nineteenth-century institutionalizations on both sides of the Atlantic.' Here a sort of exochronomania reigns, demanding that we 'position ourselves *outside* or beyond not simply 'postmodernism' itself, but outside of time, space, and *history.*' Rather than Jameson's 'rhetorical overcomplications of the relatively simplistic Bonaventure Hotel,' we are ultimately guided to 'metacommentary on architectonic representation itself,' wherein all the devilish faults of 'the historical canon(s)' have already been sublimely exorcised. History is thus stripped of its problematics and becomes little more than what Baudrillard called it: 'an immense toy.'

Moving in opposite directions, both Davis and Preziosi, despite interesting forays of their own, miss the meaning of the marked spatial turn that was signified in – and indeed instigated by – Jameson's discoveries in the Bonaventure. By entering the debate on postmodernism and the city, Jameson became absorbed in a new and different project that he himself was not at first fully aware he had entered. Neither a total denial nor a fulsome celebration of historicism, this new spatialized project began with just the metacommentary on the architectonics of representation that Preziosi applauds. But it did not stop there, for the windows of the Bonaventure opened onto more challenging possibilities for the construction of a rebalanced spatio-temporal narrative, a reconfigured critical historiography and political aesthetic that is simultaneously and inseparably a geography.

The Jamesonian shift was clumsy at first and perhaps leaned too much on the Lynchian proxy rather than the more profound inspiration of Henri Lefebvre. After all, it was Lefebvre more than anyone else who made the author of *The Political Unconscious* (1981) change his mind about the slogan that is proclaimed in the book's first words as the 'one absolute and . . . "transhistorical" imperative of all dialectical thought': *Always historicize!* In the continuing debate on the theorization of the contemporary, the Bonaventure deserves to be remembered as the site which, with Lefebvre's assistance, landmarked Jameson's first published reflections on a new dialectic: *Always spatialize as you historicize!* In other words, the plot thickens!

Centropolis

Everything else at the exhibition of heterotopological symbols converges around the Citadel-LA, the expanded civic center of Los Angeles that is colorfully mapped on the gridded main wall of the gallery. Amidst the dense clustering of footprints (gold for government buildings, bright red-orange for cultural structures), a boldly written placard announces another reading of the spatial text of Los Angeles:

> *The first cities appeared with the simultaneous concentration of commanding symbolic forms, CIVIC CENTERS designed to announce, ceremonialize, administer, acculturate, discipline, and control. In and around the institutionalized locale of the CITADEL (literally, a 'little city') adhered people and their spatially focussed social relations, creating a CIVIL SOCIETY and an accordingly built environment.*
>
> *The city continues to be organized through two interactive processes, surveillance and adherence, looking out from and in towards the citadel and its panoptic eye of POWER. To be urbanized means to adhere, to be made an adherent, a believer in a collective ideology and culture rooted in the extensions of polis (politics, policy, polity, police) and civitas (civil, civic, civilian, citizen, civilization).*

The Citadel-LA, the little city at the civic center of the sprawling, polynucleated Los Angeles region, is at first glance an unremarkable site: a rectangular band of buildings just minutes away from the Elysian fields, where the city is being born again.[13] Surely the centralized powers described in the proclamations above no longer apply here, of all places, the world's most symbolic space of urban decentralization, of dissociated neighborhoods, of the decentered idiocy of urban life.[14] Yet the centrality of the citadel exists, in part as an historical residual (lest we forget, this has been the center of the region for more than two hundred years) but also as an imposing contemporary accretion of the powers associated with new modes of urban surveillance and adherence. Even as things fall apart, the center holds.

A few details: Nowhere else outside the federal citadel in Washington, DC, is there a larger concentration of government offices and employees. The County Board of Supervisors, a fiefdom of five white males for as long as anyone can remember, deliberates here over a constituency of more than eight million, the largest local government unit in the country. The County Courthouse is reputed to be the busiest anywhere, churning incessantly to feed the country's largest urban prison system, with more inmates than New York City and Cook County (Chicago) combined. The City Hall complex administers the second largest city and projects its Dragnet-image televisually all over the world. Its imagery is bolstered by the nearby Parker Center, headquarters of the Los Angeles Police Department, which makes up for its relatively limited manpower with a vast arsenal of crack-house ramming tanks and other special-ized weaponry. If one looks hard enough, a revealing inscription can be read on the facade of City Hall: 'The city came into being to preserve life, it exists for the good life.'

Bumping up against the government fortresses north of First Street (many of which are arrayed around an old Beaux Arts backbone) are additional centers of effulgent power. The burgeoning and now mostly foreign owned financial center reaches to global heights, inviting the prediction that it will surpass all others in the new millennium. Now the only major daily newspaper, the *Los Angeles Times* already dominates its urban information field like no other metropolitan news source. Not far away from its press rooms, the first estate looms large: St Vibiana's Cathedral rules over four million adherents in one of the world's largest Catholic archdioceses. It presses up against Skid Row, the absolute inversion of empowerment, with its concentrated encampments of the homeless, reputed to be larger than in any other American city. Moving ever outward around the center, a procession of cellular ethni-cities contains residential populations from nearly everywhere, building into the fabric of the inner city the world's largest theme park of urbanized cultures, obediently employed to make everything work smoothly and cheaply. And there is still more to be seen in this centropolis of surveillance and adherence, especially when its second surface is explored.

Cultural Crown

Across from the citadel wall is a futurist scene. On the ground sits what the architects call a massing model for the newest jewel to be added metonymically to the 'cultural crown' of downtown Los Angeles, the Walt Disney Concert Hall, competitively designed by the current king of California architects, Frank Gehry. In the background is posted a collection of working drawings and promotional text dreaming the tomorrows of the contemporary Acropolis, the 'topmost city' of the Citadel-LA, the fortress of fine arts that has put Bunker Hill squarely in the center of the map of American urban imagineering.

Compared with the new Opera House in the Place de la Bastille, Disney Hall (future headquarters for the Los Angeles Philharmonic Orchestra) is meant to be primordially indigenous, Cali-casually informal, a sort of vegetative climax perfectly adapted to local conditions, a celebration of home-grown inhabitants and heroes. The glassed-in foyer is described as 'the city's living room' open to the mixed use of the masses, the sprawling plazas are the 'culmination' of the city's public space, the plants and trees celebrate the locale – no exotics here. Even the most Pritzkerly prestigious outsiders (Böhm of Cologne, Hollein of Vienna, Stirling of London) did not have a chance against the indigenous competition.

A more symbolic pairing than Gehry and Disney is scarcely imaginable. Together, their dreamworlds will complete the reconstitution of Bunker Hill from the 'old town, lost town, crook town' described by Raymond Chandler to what the archly anarchic architect Arthur Erikson predicted would be a 'center of centers of the western world.' A series of placards around the future site of the Walt Disney Hall on the citadel wall traces this transformation. First there is Chandler from *The High Window*:

Bunker Hill is old town, lost town, crook town . . . In the tall rooms haggard landladies bicker with shifty tenants. On the wide cool front porches, reaching their cracked shoes into the sun, and staring at nothing, sit the old men with faces like lost battles . . . Out of the apartment houses come women who should be young but have faces like stale beer, men with pulled-down hats and quick eyes that look the street over behind the cupped hand that shields the match flame; who look like nothing in particular and know it, and once in a while even men that actually go to work. But they come out early, when the wide cracked sidewalks are empty and still have dew on them.

Erasing this past, literally sheering it off, has been an avalanche of developments down Grand Avenue, from the Music Center complex that first injected culture into the rectangular Citadel-LA in the 1960s to the vast, mixed-use California Plaza project that now contains the celebrated Museum of Contemporary Art (MOCA), skyscraping office towers, pockets of good and bad (appropriately capitalized) Public Art, and the site of the future Disney–Gehry extravaganza of performance spaces.[15]

The Music Center is the cultural crown of Southern California, reigning over orchestral music, vocal performance, opera, theatre and dance . . . It tops Bunker Hill like a contemporary Acropolis, one which has dominated civil cultural life since it was inaugurated in 1964. (Extract from a pictorial map of downtown Los Angeles produced by Unique Media Incorporated)

Walt Disney Hall will capture the axis of the old Music Center buildings and bend it directly towards architect Arata Isozaki's understated Hollywood bonsai.

[The Museum of Contemporary Art is] a temple . . . in which the gods cavort, amuse, and delight, even as they inspire . . . [Its] ambience invokes the power and wonder of the Roman Pantheon, though Isozaki has replaced cylinder and dome with cube and pyramid. The result is an equally uplifting space whose awesome splendor invites contemplation and joy . . . Isozaki's design embodies the exquisite shape and proportion of Marilyn Monroe – classic, voluptuous, and sensuously draped to enhance and tantalize . . . [just as] Frank Gehry's Temporary Contemporary [his nearby prelude to MOCA] proclaims the inimitable bone structure of a Katherine Hepburn, magnificently lean and rugged yet indisputably regal, even in work clothes . . . Two goddesses of a very different sort – yet both cast an aura that transcends mere physical presence and hovers somewhere closer to the realm of pure energy. (Sherry Geldin, MOCA's Associate Director)[16]

California Plaza on Bunker Hill will become the center for all these other centers [of culture, government, commerce, ethnic life]. Los Angeles [can thus] express what is unique about itself and at the same time begin to fulfill its future role as a center of centers of the western world. (Arthur Erikson, architect)

Looking up, a floating sky of chicken-wire netting can be seen linking up the entire exhibition. From it dangles a collection of volunteered symbols of Los Angeles 1989:

surfboards, palm trees, bumper stickers, cameras, the Hollywood sign, traffic signals, insignia from past Olympics, signposts saying 'Trespassers Will Be Shot,' and other signatures on the contemporary landscape donated for commemoration by faculty and students in the Architecture and Urban Planning Programs. The cloud of symbols infects the space with a hovering sense of unity that is both temporary and contemporary. One can look forward to the Gehry display and back to the citadel map, reflecting all the time upon the curiously revealing and concealing juxtapositions that compose the contemporary cultural Acropolis.

Palimpsest

Another wall in the exhibition has been created to carry the burden of history on its surface. There is a space behind it that has not yet been explored, for the wall is actually a partitioning of the gallery constructed purposefully to conceal. On the surface facing what we have already seen is a giant replica of the French tricolor, flag of the revolution, tall columns of blue, white, and red across which a time-line moves eventfully in a dated path of francophonic turning points: 1789–1830–1848–1871–1889–1914–1940–1968–1989. The historical display runs from right to left, synchronically and symbolically reconnecting Paris and Los Angeles via the story of El Pueblo de Nuestra Senora la Reina de Los Angeles, the Urban birthplace of the regional metropolis and now an historic park, state monument, and tourist mecca. The rising time-line ends in an arrow pointing to the current site of El Pueblo on the map of the Citadel-LA, where it fittingly belongs.

There are many histories and heterotopologies to be plumbed at El Pueblo, for it is as deeply and deceptively charged with cultural and political meaning as any other place in the region. The Yang-Na greeted the first Spanish explorers here (as did several small earthquakes, one of which Father Crespi reportedly described as 'half as long as an ave maria'). In 1781, 44 settlers (more than half with some African blood) built willow-reed huts around a common plaza, constructed the first irrigation ditch, and officially established (Afro?) Spanish Los Angeles. By the time of the French Revolution, *ranchos* had been allocated to soldiers guarding the thriving agricultural settlement and trading center, and a Christianized Indian was appointed as the first mayor.

In 1830, El Pueblo was part of the Republic of Mexico and the era of the Californios had begun, centered on the new plaza and Catholic church built at their present-day sites and dominated by families whose names echo still in the contemporary landscape: Pico, Sepulveda, Carillo. After years of resistance and struggle between Yankees and Californios, bandits and thugs, the Californios were defeated in 1848 and the victors brought 'Hell Town' into the Union to begin a new era of extraordinary violence, lawlessness, and interracial conflict. This 'vile little dump,' as it was called, averaged a murder a day as it was Americanized by Yankee hustlers and cattle thieves, hispanophobic vigilante groups and lynch mobs, and the armed force of the Los Angeles 'Rangers.'

In the year of the Paris Commune (1871), El Pueblo broke into world headlines for perhaps the first time, as a rampaging mob of 500 capped the Americanization of Los Angeles by slaughtering more than 20 Chinese along the Calle de los Negros leading in to the Plaza. Little is remembered of these events, for the site of El Pueblo was afterwards left behind in space and time. A new Citadel-LA was constructed just to the south and the past was romantically reconstructed to fit the mythology of *Romona*, Helen Hunt Jackson's idyllic novel and play of early Los Angeles, still performed in revival meetings today to reassure forgetfulness. By 1889, when the French were celebrating the revolution's centennial, the Calle de los Negros had been renamed Los Angeles Street and the decaying El Pueblo was recreated as the City's first official facility of the just created Parks and Recreation (sic) Department.

Over the next century, the Plaza and the La Placita church, along with the few remaining sites of the Californios, functioned like Foucault's mirror in the formation of urban consciousness, a sort of mixed, joint experience, at once utopia and heterotopia. Until the onset of the Great Depression, the Plaza sheltered free-speech rostrums that spawned Mexican revolutionaries struggling against dictatorship in their homeland and American socialist workers fighting for empowerment closer by. Today, La Placita provides sanctuary for the homeless and for political refugees from Central America, resisting growing efforts to expel them from the center of the city. El Pueblo thus survives as a residual gathering space for political and cultural assertion, commemorating not so much the original colony as a much larger expressive heritage that continues to be eaten away by the explosive growth of the metropolis around it.

Intertwined with this continuity, however, is another, even more resilient, tradition, drawing selectively upon the past to crack open and invert the heritage that is preserved at other local sites and spaces. As a counter-site, El Pueblo has maintained and innovatively reinforced its ability to Americanize the un-American and destroy undesirable alien images, thus serving the traditional aims of the citadel to 'ceremonialize, administer, acculturate, discipline, and control.' It was a focal point for the 'repatriation movement' that aimed to deport Mexicans around the time of the 1932 Olympic games and a primary 'nativist' hunting ground during the anti-*pachuco* Zoot Suit riots of World War II, when the United Services Organization occupied a central place in the plaza. It has also memorably served the ideological state apparatus in another way, by being among the first testing grounds for a new kind of heterotopia created around a combination of cultural simulation and dissimulation (pretending to have what one has not while simultaneously pretending not to have what one really has).

In 1926, a dedicated woman, Christine Sterling, approached Harry Chandler, kingpin of the *Los Angeles Times*, with an inspired plan to rejuvenate the seedy El Pueblo along the lines of the City Beautiful movement that was then cosmetically refacing the Citadel-LA. Four years later, a little urban 'theme park' was opened to the public, ostensibly built as a monument to the founding of Los Angeles and represented in the form of 'an important Latin American trade and social center.' Along Olvera Street (cleaned up and lowered three feet by gangs of prison labor provided by the City), a 'picturesque Mexican market place' provided the appropriate commodification. With amendments over the years, this reconstituted space (located in between the now similarly reconstituted spaces of Chinatown and Little Tokyo) attracts three million visitors a year.[17]

Looking back, El Pueblo has been the primordial urban palimpsest of the City of Angels, prepared from its origins to be written upon and erased over and over again in the evolution of public consciousness and civic imagination.[18] In Foucauldian terms, it resembles that 'new kind of temporal heterotopia' which combines the fleeting time of the festival site or vacation village with the indefinitely accumulating time of the museum or library. As such, like its Disneyfied descendants, it simultaneously serves to abolish history and culture and to discover them anew in 'other spaces.'[19]

Panopticon

Our final stop in the exhibition need not take long, for its rudiments have already been sighted, sited, and cited. It is an attempt to evoke in a more direct way the carceral city that underlies all urban histories and geographies, that everywhere concentrates and projects the citadel's powers of surveillance and adherence. We enter it through the time-line wall where it approaches the plotted Citadel-LA, a map which extends inward from roughly the site of El Pueblo to display the enclosures containing the largest urban prison population in the country, sites which violently intrude upon the unbarred *barrio* of East Los Angeles, where another form of spatial enclosure is practiced.

A takeaway fact sheet provides you with some information: 18,000 inmates fill four county jails, including Men's Central and Sybil Brand, the nation's largest women's prison. In 1988, another 23,000 'non-threatening' prisoners were released early to free up space, provoking Governor Deukmejian (who is determined to build more prisons in this downtown wedge against the resistance of its other residents) to proclaim that criminals are Los Angeles's 'principal export.' A newspaper headline tells of neo-Nazi and Ku Klux Klan terrorism within Men's Central aimed at intimidating Black deputies and inmates alike with cross-burnings, gang-baiting taunts, and Nazi memorabilia. One is never free from the legacy of racism in Los Angeles, even when behind bars.

By now, you are in a dark, cell-like room lit by a bare red bulb. The chicken-wire cloud that floats Gehrishly over the rest of the gallery spills into the enclosure and tightly meshes an interior wall. On all sides are ominous photographs of the newest addition to the obviously carceral city, the Metropolitan Detention Center, a federal 'administrative' facility squeezed into the Citadel-LA near the Federal Building and US Courthouse, just across the freeway from El Pueblo.[20] The only visible bars are hung on the outside of the building in a perfect dissimulation of the carceral, feigning not to have what it most certainly has.

The obvious allusions are referenced in bold-faced lettering in a quotation adapted from Gwendolen Wright and Paul Rabinow, 'Spatialization of Power: A Discussion of the Work of Michel Foucault,' published in *Skyline* (1982).

For Foucault, SPACE is where the discourses about POWER and KNOWLEDGE are transformed into actual relations of power. Here, the knowledge in the forefront is that of aesthetics, of an architectural profession, of a science of planning. But these 'disciplines' never constitute an isolated field. They are of interest only when one looks to see how they mesh with economics, politics, or institutions. Then both architecture and urban planning offer privileged instances for understanding how power operates.

The PANOPTICON, Jeremy Bentham's proposal for radially planned institutional buildings, is by now the most famous instance of a concretization of power applied through architecture. Foucault came upon Bentham's 1787 plan while studying reforms in eighteenth-century hospital and prison architecture, and took it as the paradigmatic example of the interworkings of SPACE, POWER and KNOWLEDGE in disciplinary society. The PANOPTICON is the 'diagram of a mechanism of power reduced to its ideal form', a combination of abstract schematization and very concrete applications.

Every city is a carceral city, a collection of surveillant nodes designed to impose a particular model of conduct and disciplinary adherence on its inhabitants. This agglomeration of the spatial means of social control, these centers of power, is what differentiates the urban from the rural, adherents from the not yet adherent, *polites* from *idiotes*. But one must not assume that urban incarceration operates simply and directly along the extended visual lines of Bentham's Panopticon or that its disciplinary technologies and heterotopologies remain constant over time. Too much happens in the city for this to be true.

In the modern world, the primary scale of surveillance and adherence, of *citizenship* and *politics*, shifted dramatically from the city to the state, recentering the locus of power outside the direct gaze of the citadels and into a more invisible process of 'normalization' that pervades patriotic allegiance and representative rather than participatory democracy. It is no surprise then to find modern political theory and critical social science abandoning its roots in the polis and denying the specificity of the city, its centrality as an object of knowledge. The discourses on power and knowledge in the constitution of society continued to acknowledge that things took place *in* cities (an unavoidable though inconsequential coincidence) but were not (or no longer) *of* cities, directly imbricated in the urban. For the past century at least, the urban become epiphenomenal to the constitution of modern societies and the making of modern histories.

Foucault and, in his parallel project, Henri Lefebvre both capped this modern discourse in the late 1960s and significantly turned it around by rekindling attention to the specificity of the urban via an explicitly spatializing strategy. For both, socially produced space (which at least since the rise of industrial capitalism has been an imperatively urbanized space) is where the discourses about power and knowledge are transformed into actual relations of power (to re-use Wright and Rabinow's words). In this view, the modern state (national and local) thus does not reduce the city's social power as much as it expands and extends it in scale and scope, preserving the urban as a contested space for a politics that is simultaneously based on the reproduction of state and society and on its potentially revolutionary transformation *in situ*.[21]

This assertive emplacement simultaneously inscribes the interworkings of space, power, and knowledge into both a socio-spatial and an historico-geographical dialectic, a meshing of ontological and epistemological fields that were kept apart for most of the past century in what I have described as the subordination of space in critical social theory. In the spatializing strategies, the incipient postmodern geographies of Foucault and Lefebvre, the city is brought back into focus through the 'eye of power' that sees not only the past but also the present revolving around the politically charged spatiality of social life. Seeing the city as carceral is only the beginning.

Retrospective?

What has been pictured at the exhibition is teasingly incomplete and preliminary, only a few small steps into the debates on postmodernity, a mere tweaking here and there of the lingering pretensions of High Modernist historiography, cultural criticism, and critical social theory. Merely remembering Foucault's spatial turn (and Jameson's) is not enough to be fully convincing about the importance of postmodern geographies or the insights to be derived in learning from Los Angeles. And it all sounds so modernist in the end, does it not, especially to those categorical umpires who chalk off the foul lines of discourse? To postmodernize more effectively what has been pictured in the exhibition, it is ultimately necessary to remember Baudrillard.

In Biddy Mason's memorial place, the remembrances of the Bastille, the Bastaventure entrancement, the Citadel-LA, the cultural Acropolis, the El Pueblo palimpsest, the Panopticon prisons, there are contained the seeds of a contextual deconstruction that reverses the tapestry of modernist interpretation by attempting something new and different, a decidedly post-marked exploration of 'other spaces.' Neither Foucault nor Lefebvre succeeded in getting there himself, although they brilliantly demonstrated a way out of the dishevelled discourses of late modernity. To explore the spaces of postmodernity another map is needed, one that is marked by a new legend and requires new viewfinders to help explain the meanings of being there, *être*-LA.

I conclude therefore by briefly commemorating Baudrillard for his s(t)imulating 'post'-enlightenment. And, as with so much that has been commemorated here, I will do so in quick strokes that punctuate rather than elaborate the argument. The scene with which I leave the text is one that requires three sets of lenses to be seen, each envisioning a different mode of epistemic representation, a way of looking at and learning from the relation between thoughtful image and empirical reality, or if you prefer the signified and the signifier.

The first lenses focus on a picture that has dominated (for good reason) western philosophy and science since the beginnings of the Enlightenment, a picture of the mind as a great *mirror–map* of 'good appearances,' of potentially accurate representations of reality that must be sifted through methodically to separate the good from the bad. What is seen is an empirically discoverable, accurately mappable life-world. These time-worn lenses, even today, remain in constant use, albeit with slightly different disciplinary tints. Many have never used any other.

A second, 'corrective' pair of lenses has allowed us to see through the *masking map* of appearances, many of which Baudrillard argues are perceived as 'evil,' to discover a whole new life-world filled with generative essentials, hidden signifiers, and deeper meaning. Exploration and epistemology here take on the representational task of unmasking, demystifying, exposing this second semiological surface. Various forms of structuralism have searched the territory most methodically, but it has also been revealingly explored for its emancipatory potential by virtually every branch of modern critical thought. Creative artists were probably there in the first place, individually probing behind the scenes and the seen, but the space became most densely occupied after the various modern movements in the human sciences that arose in the late nineteenth and early twentieth centuries.

Foucault's heterotopology provides a brilliant guidebook to unmasking the 'other spaces' concealed in this modernist landscape of hidden signifiers. But he also had on order another set of lenses that he never really wore. Baudrillard filled his prescription with wild new spectacles that did not simply invert the images but introduced a radically different way of seeing. Through these lenses, images no longer either reflected or masked a basic reality; they revealed instead its protracted absence in a postmodern, poststructuralist landscape of absorbing simulations and hyperrealities. Then, in a delirious optical allusion, Baudrillard bifocalized the lens to allow the possibility of seeing an emerging fourth life-world of 'pure' simulacra, filled with places where images bear no relation to any reality whatever, where good and bad appearances have dis-appeared, where the real and its representations are not what they used to be. In this life-world, we can no longer test pretence against reality for we cannot tell which is which. We thus approach becoming eye-less, I-less, and aye-less.

I have tried to peek through Baudrillard's lenses in looking with him at Los Angeles, but I still do not know how to describe what I saw or to know that I saw it. He smiled and nodded at my efforts in the Bicentennial symposium at UCLA to see the postmodern world through his eyes, but later claimed, still smiling, that what I saw was still intrepidly pre-postmodern, insufficiently hyperrealistic. Is there really (or hyperreally) another way that we can see to engage in a politically committed critique of postmodernity that is itself thoroughly postmodernized? Can we create an effective postmodernism of resistance that involves more than bovine immobility or sitting on the fences like parodic Humpty Dumpties playing with words? In the end, I do not know – but neither, I think, does Baudrillard. Meanwhile, let us not forget Foucault.

NOTES

1 For some earlier contextual readings, see Soja (1989, 1990). Also worthwhile looking at is Michael Shapiro and Deane Neubauer (1989).

2 These brief, essentially ontological reflections on objectification, subjectification, and emplacement illuminate with some new twists the interesting debate on the existential spatiality of being. See Soja (1989: 131–7).

3 Foucault ends his lecture with a passionate tribute to the boat, a floating piece of space, a place without a place, the greatest reserve of the footloose imagination. 'In civilizations without boats,' he writes, 'dreams dry up, espionage takes the place of adventure, and the police take the place of the pirates.' One wonders what Foucault would have thought about the now rigidly docked *Queen Mary*, spectacularly placed in Long Beach harbor alongside the equally grounded *Spruce Goose* (Howard Hughes's enormous folly and still the largest airplane ever built). Today, filled with dried up dreams of mobility, both are unmovingly imagineered by the Disney Company, their present owners.

4 I emphasize the term *configuration* to trigger a connection with the essentially historicizing use of the same term, adapted from Ricoeur (in White 1987), and in other creative attempts to defend critical historiography against its critics. Although cognizant of the

importance of space and 'geography' (as he sees it) in history and in the narrative, White persistently misses the point being made by Foucault (and perhaps by Ricoeur as well?) that such concepts as 'configuration' and 'emplotment' demand a profound and iconoclastic spatial turn to the writing of history, an explicit spatialization of the narrative rather than just a celebration of its explanatory historicity.

5 The public lectures included James Leith (Queen's University, Canada), 'La Bastille and Paris: 1789 to 1989'; Dora Weiner (UCLA), 'Sacred and Secular Space: Transformations of Religious into Medical Buildings, 1789 to 1820'; Jean Baudrillard (University of Paris IX), 'Revolution and the End of Utopia'; and Josef W. Konvitz (Michigan State University), 'Spatial Change and the Centralization of Power: Paris Before and After the Revolution.' The colloquium featured Richard Lehan (UCLA), 'The City and Literature: Pre-modern Paris and Post-modern Los Angeles, Cities at the End of Time'; James Leith, 'Planning for the Louvre: A Case for the *Longue Durée*'; Dolores Hayden (UCLA), 'The Power of Place Project: Planning for the Preservation of the Urban History of Los Angeles;' Edward Soja (UCLA), 'Taking Los Angeles Apart: Fragments of a Postmodern Geography'; Jean Baudrillard, 'From Beaubourg to the Arche de la Défense: Architecture, Urban Space, and the Power of Simulacra: A Commentary.' All the events were organized through the auspices of the UCLA Bicentennial Program and its chair, Robert Maniquis, with financial assistance from the National Institute for the Humanities.

6 The organization is the brainchild of Dolores Hayden. For an introduction to its aims, see Hayden (1988: 5–18). The small exhibition of its recent work was curated by Donna Graves.

7 Others include the intrusively imposing Arche de la Défense, the wackily postmodern Parc de la Villette (with its planned garden designed jointly by Peter Eisenmann and Jacques Derrida), and the Pei-emplaced pyramid puncturing through the heart of the Louvre. Will Paris – or the French Revolution – ever be the same again?

8 Floreal was also the eighth month of the French Revolutionary (Republican) Calendar. It extended from April 20 to May 19, coinciding almost exactly with the UCLA exhibition.

9 Many people helped to put together this portion of the exhibition with me, but there from the beginning to end were Taina Rikala de Noriega and Iain Borden.

10 The sculptors of the Bastaventure are Ali Barar and James Kaylor.

11 See Fredric Jameson (1984: 53–92). See also the critical responses from Mike Davis (1985: 106–13) and Donald Preziosi (1988: 82–99).

12 Davis's subsequent essays on Los Angeles and his recent book *City of Quartz* (1990) are much more successful in avoiding this diachronomaniacal historicism. See Davis (1987, and 1990).

13 At the North Broadway entrance to Elysian Park, a monument marks the first white sighting of Los Angeles, the place where Gaspar de Portola and Father Juan Crespi made camp on August 2, 1769, during the first European expedition through California. By the time of the French Revolution, the indigenous Yang-Na Indians had virtually disappeared without a trace of commemoration from what were once their primary hunting grounds and water source. Nearly two centuries later, the nearby Chavez Ravine was cleared of its rebellious residents – many distant descendants of the old Californios – to make room for Dodger Stadium, one of the most profitable sports sites in the world. Elysian Park today

also contains California's first botanic garden, filled with exotics from all over the world, and the much more domestic Los Angeles Police Academy, where young recruits are taught contemporary hunting and gathering skills.

14 Such idiocy derives from the Greek root *idios*, one's own, private, separate, apart, as in 'idiosyncratic,' acting in a way peculiar to oneself; originally, unlearned in the way of the traditional *polis*, as in the 'idiocy of rural life.'

15 The largest of the performance plazas will eventually span across Olive Street in a dramatically ambivalent public space. A giant water fountain designed by WET, the company responsible for the water fantasies of both Disneyland and Walt Disney World, will dialogue with the public, at times flooding the plaza with its wet tricks, at other times parching it to permit spectacular displays of local ethnic artistry. Good timing will be necessary.

16 Quoted in Berelowitz (n.d.). For more on MOCA, see Berelowitz 1990.

17 A celebration was held at the Plaza in 1989 to commemorate the centennial of the Recreation and Parks Department (which changed its name to put recreation first during the same year). As reported in the local press, there were performances by the Asian American Ballet, the Xipe Totec Aztec Indian dancers, and Somebody Special, Inc., 'a drill team of teen-age girls who boogie to Motown sounds.' A time capsule was also buried under Olvera Street containing representative ethnic arts and crafts, feathers from the endangered California condor, a preserved grunion, and park-sponsored T-shirts.

18 Today the area is again a center of controversial re-evaluation, as competing redevelopers eye its prime location and dream of alternative land uses as the Central City bulges northward.

19 Plans abound to construct a symbolic 'gateway' extravaganza surmounting the freeway at this precise spot to commemorate Los Angeles's extraordinary pull as an immigrant entrepôt – a local and very contemporary version of Ellis Island and the Statue of Liberty rolled into one. The winning plan proposed a 'steel cloud' grill-work filled with restaurants, museums, gift shops, and aquaria floating above the traffic below and set between the prison and the Pueblo. Whether it will be built is still up in the air.

20 I waved back once, after entering a fern-filled atrium that is just to the right of the main entrance. Out of nowhere, guards appeared to shoo me away from such open communication with the one-armed inhabitants. Despite its location and its involvement in such sensitive local issues as immigration control and financial fraud, the Metropolitan Detention Center was built with remarkably little local awareness and even today few law-abiding downtown workers or visitors know of its existence.

21 Foucault and Lefebvre problematized revolution spatially around the politics of the urban, the struggles for power over the governing of space and territory that are centered in cities but extend well beyond them into the 'urbanized' countrysides and peripheries. For Lefebvre, see *Le droit à la ville* (1968) and *La Revolution urbaine* (1970) (forthcoming as *Writings on Cities* (1994)), as well as *La survie du capitalisme* (1973) and *La production de l'espace* (1974). No one has yet explored in detail the fascinating similarities and differences in the spatializing projects of Lefebvre and Foucault, in part because few have been able to comprehend their expanded vision of the urban and their politicized views of the 'making of geographies,' or what Lefebvre was the first to call *spatial praxis*.

REFERENCES

Baudrillard, J. 1987: *Forget Foucault*, New York: Semiotext(e).

Berelowitz, J.-A. 1990: 'A New Jerusalem: Utopias, MOCA, and the Redevelopment of Downtown Los Angeles', *Strategies*, 3: 202–26.

Berelowitz, J.-A. (n.d.) 'The Jewel in the Crown: Bunker Hill, MOCA, and the Ideology of Urban Redevelopment', unpublished manuscript.

Davis, M. 1985: 'Urban Renaissance and the Spirit of Postmodernism', *New Left Review*, 151: 106–13.

Davis, M. 1987: 'Chinatown, Part Two? The "Internationalization" of Downtown Los Angeles', *New Left Review*, 164: 65–86.

Davis, M. 1990: *City of Quartz: Excavating the Future in Los Angeles*, London: Verso.

Foucault, M. 1986: 'Of Other Spaces', *Diacritics*, Spring: 22–7.

Hayden, D. 1988: 'The Power of Place: A Proposal for Los Angeles', *The Public Historian*, 10: 5–18.

Jameson, F. 1981: *The Political Unconscious*, London: Routledge.

Jameson, F. 1984: 'Postmodernism, or the Cultural Logic of Late Capitalism', *New Left Review*, 146: 53–92.

Lefebvre, H. 1973: *La survie de la capitalisme*, Paris: Anthropos.

Lefebvre, H. 1974: *La production de l'espace*, Paris: Anthropos.

Lefebvre, H. 1994: *Writings on Cities*, eds E. Kofman and E. Lebas, Oxford and Cambridge, MA: Blackwell.

Lynch, K. 1960: *The Image of the City*, Cambridge, MA: MIT Press.

Lynch, K. 1972: *What Time is This Place?*, Cambridge, MA: MIT Press.

Preziosi, D. 1988: 'La Vi(ll)e en rose: Reading Jameson Mapping Space', *Strategies*, 1: 82–99.

Shapiro, M. and Neubauer, D. 1989: 'Spatiality and Policy Discourse: Reading the Global City', *Alternatives*, 14: 301–25.

Soja, E. 1989: 'Taking Los Angeles Apart: Towards a Postmodern Geography', ch. 9 in *Postmodern Geographies: The Reassertion of Space in Critical Social Theory*, London: Verso.

Soja, E. 1990: 'Inside the Orange County Exopolis: A Contemporary Screen-Play', in M. Sorkin (ed.), *Variations on a Theme Park: Scenes from the New American City*, New York: Pantheon.

White, H. 1987: *The Content of the Form: Narrative Discourse and Historical Representation*, New York: Johns Hopkins.

3. Discourse, Discontinuity, Difference: The Question of 'Other' Spaces

Benjamin Genocchio

Ah, bear in mind this garden was enchanted!

Edgar Allan Poe

I

Accompanying the much celebrated demise of the authority of Western metaphysics, it is now evident that there has been a marked opening up of the processes of social, political and cultural transformation in post-industrial societies to forms of spatial analysis. So much so, in fact, that many writers have observed that this shift in critical emphasis has caught the attention of theorists from a variety of disciplines, some of which have formerly eschewed spatial modes of inquiry.[1] In general, however, the 'reassertion' of space into postmodern theory has led to widespread critical attention being given to emergent spatial transformations in our everyday lives as the loci of our coming into experience and collective social action.

In a recent article entitled 'Mapping Power: Cartography and Contemporary Cultural Theory', Elizabeth Ferrier has suggested that most contemporary theorizations of space are built around the assumption of a declining Cartesian spatial order.[2] This is a spatiality associated with Western metaphysics and its tribe of grids, binaries, hierarchies and oppositions. As this conception of a fixed, ordered space begins to give way to views imbued with more 'flexible and equitable organizations', so what can loosely be described as 'postmodernist' discourse has largely come to be associated with a critique of Cartesian space. When it comes, however, to considering its replacement, opinions are fundamentally diverse.

On the basis of a brief survey, critical positions concerning the hybridized spatial order that sits poised to take us into the next millennium can, for the most part, be divided into two categories. On the one hand, theorists of the Jean Baudrillard genus continue to chant their millenarian credo of gloom and doom, convinced that the bastard child of Cartesian space threatens to eclipse all semblance of the 'real' in a series of simulated orgies in Disney-style dystopias. Variations on this theme(park?) can also be found within the work of Paul Virilio, an ambivalent David Harvey and a nostalgic Fredric Jameson.[3] On the other hand, theorists such as Foucault, Bourdieu, de Certeau, Deleuze and Guattari have insisted upon hidden but unmistakably clear possibilities for both active and constructive intervention.[4] Yet despite subtle or obvious differences of opinion, what all these theorists have in common is a collective desire to promote new forms of conceiving social space in an attempt to account for an eclectic occupation and engagement with an increasingly segregated, oppressively functionalist and electronically monitored everyday reality.

In view of the complexity of these ideas and concerns, what I want to concentrate upon in this article is just one such conception of our heterogeneous and contested social space, that of the work of Michel Foucault. More specifically, from among the many and varied things to be found in the body of work that bears his name, a minor discursive/ theoretical 'invention', that of the heterotopia.[5]

Now my reasons for this perhaps marginal task are three-fold. In the first place, over the last few years Foucault's notion of heterotopias – absolutely Other and differentiated social spaces such as brothels, prisons, asylums – has received a great deal of critical attention. In particular, many of the so-called 'new theorists of social space' have used and extended the term to reveal the possibility of socially constructed counter-sites embodying a form of 'resistance' to our increasingly surveyed, segregated and simulated socio-spatial order. Yet the majority of these appropriations provide little critical engagement with Foucault's texts, simply calling up the heterotopia as some theoretical *deus ex machina*. Secondly, despite its attractions, Foucault's notion of heterotopias is fundamentally problematic. Lastly, I believe a more patient reading of Foucault's remarks on heterotopias enables us to restore a complexity and profundity to his work that has been so sorely lacking in the myopic sociological functionalism that has obscured the insight of this thinker over the past few years.

II

Shortly before his death in 1984, Michel Foucault released into the public arena, for a showing of his work in Berlin, the text of a lecture which he had prepared and presented in 1967. Never edited for publication, this lecture was only recognized as part of his official oeuvre after its appearance in late 1984 in the French journal *Architecture–Mouvement–Continuité* under the title 'Des Espaces Autres'. Subsequently published in English as 'Of Other Spaces', it constitutes a short treatise on the theme of heterotopias.[6]

In contrast to the 'internal' spaces so meticulously explored by Gaston Bachelard, Foucault defined heterotopias as absolutely Other, 'external' spaces that are to be found, in all societies, in some given social spaces whose functions are different or even opposite to all others. Although these ideas around what Foucault dubbed 'heterotopology' remained shelved for almost twenty years, the term had previously appeared in a somewhat different context in the preface to *The Order of Things* (1980). The two uses of the term, however, bear a strange inconsistency.

In 'Of Other Spaces', Foucault describes the heterotopia as a 'heterogeneous site' capable of juxtaposing in a 'single real place' several spaces that are in themselves incompatible. In *The Order of Things*, heterotopias are defined as the coexistence in an 'impossible' space of a large number of fragmentary, possible, though incommensurable orders or worlds. The difference is essentially that in *The Order of Things* the juxtaposition of heterogeneous elements is so incongruous and disruptive to our normal sense of order that we are unable to realize such perversity within a coherent and familiar domain.

Now in spite of this discrepancy, it would appear that the difference stems simply from the fact that, in *The Order of Things*, Foucault's discussion of heterotopias centres upon a discursive/linguistic site in contrast to, in the first instance, an examination of actual extra-discursive locations. Moreover, in each case the distinguishing feature of the heterotopia is its purported status as a form of spatially discontinuous ground; a status which, in turn, gives each the ability to transgress, undermine and question the alleged coherence or totality of self-contained orders and systems.

III

Insisting that space itself has a history within Western experience, Foucault begins 'Of Other Spaces' by claiming that the present spatial epoch is one in which the use, function and structure of space take the form of 'relations among sites'. As the characteristic space of post-industrial life, the site is defined by 'relations of proximity between points or elements'. Indebted to the spatial descriptions of phenomenologists such as Heidegger and Husserl, Foucault suggests that our experience of space thus takes the form of relations of proximity, propinquity between points or elements which can be mathematically or scientifically described.[7] For Foucault, we live inside sets of 'irreducible relations that delineate sites'.

Among all the sites that go together to make up a particular community – something which presupposes a commonality of belief in a shared experience or understanding of a particular spatiality – Foucault was interested, in 'Of Other Spaces', in describing certain ones that are not only visibly excluded, but also: 'have the curious property of being in relation to all the other sites in such a way as to suspect, neutralise or invert the set of relations that they happen to designate, mirror or reflect' (Foucault 1986: 24). These absolutely singular spaces whose functions are 'different or even opposite to' all others are, he suggests, of two main types: utopias and heterotopias.

In general, utopias can be defined as models or critiques premised on their fictional nature. As their name literally suggests, they are sites without any actual locality. For Foucault, however, they are also sites that have a general relation of 'direct or inverted analogy' with the 'real' space of society in that, beginning with Sir Thomas More's brave new island world, they have projected the vagaries of imagination, possibility and hope. On the other hand, heterotopias were sketched out as 'real' existing places of difference that are variably constituted and formed, over and against a homogeneous and shared spatiality, in the very founding of all societies as part of the 'presuppositions of social life'.

Acting as counter-sites, spaces in contestation of, or contrast or opposition to (but also within which and depending upon for their difference), all the other real sites that can be found in a culture, heterotopias hold a general relation to all other places. Furthermore, Foucault suggests that heterotopias, as heterogeneous collections of several spatio-temporal sites and the relations between them, have a different and important function in relation to all the other space that remains:

> This function unfolds between two extreme poles. Either their role is to create a space of illusion that exposes every real space, all the sites inside of which human life is partitioned, as still more illusory. . . . Or else, on the contrary, their role is to create a space that is other, another real space, as perfect, as meticulous, as well arranged as ours is messy, ill constructed, and jumbled. This type would be the heterotopia not of illusion, but the heterotopia of compensation. (Foucault 1986: 25/27)

Differentiated from all other sites, heterotopias were thus conceived as spaces that are outside of all other places even though it may be possible to indicate their position 'in reality'. For Foucault, heterotopias constitute a discontinuous but socially defined spatiality, both material and immaterial at the same time. To outline this other spatiality, six principles were tentatively given, backed up by a dizzying array of examples: brothels, churches, hotel rooms, museums, libraries, prisons, asylums, Roman baths, the Turkish *hammam*, the Scandinavian sauna. One could no doubt add to this list similar spaces of 'extra-territorial' heterogeneity such as fairs and markets, sewers, amusement parks and shopping malls. Scripted as spaces of both repugnance and fascination, they also function as powerful sites of the imaginary.

Yet despite the persuasive commentary and seductive prose, a question immediately presents itself: how is it that we can locate, distinguish and differentiate the essence of this difference, this 'strangeness' which is not simply outlined against the visible? More specifically, how is it that heterotopias are 'outside' of or are fundamentally different to all other spaces, but also relate to and exist 'within' the general social space/order that distinguishes their meaning as difference? In short, how can we 'tell' these Other spaces/stories?

Noel Gray has articulated this very dilemma under the aegis of what he sees as a 'coherency problem' in Foucault's argument within 'Of Other Spaces'.[8] Gray points out that as heterotopias are intended to act in general as counter-sites, then it follows that for Foucault to retain coherency in his claim that heterotopias are 'outside' of, or are fundamentally different to, all other spaces but also relate to and exist 'within' the general social space/order, his notion of differentiation depends upon him clearly differentiating the disordered and discontinuous 'internal' character of these sites. In short, Foucault's argument is reliant upon a means of establishing some invisible but visibly operational difference which, disposed against the background of an elusive spatial continuum, provides a clear conception of spatially discontinuous ground. Crucially, what is lacking from Foucault's argument is exactly this.[9]

While Foucault's wondrous description of heterotopic sites remains both instructive and useful, the implication of this omission is, to my mind at least, two-fold. Firstly, Foucault's argument regarding the differentiation of absolutely 'Other' spaces must be assumed to be incomplete. Secondly, it would appear that the entire notion of spatially discontinuous ground is bound up in a wider set of complex philosophical questions; in particular, those regarding the impossibility of transcending or transgressing the metaphysics of presence.

One of the most contentious but fundamental insights to be found in the work of Jacques Derrida is his repeated insistence on the ineluctable character of what he has called 'logocentrism' or the metaphysics of presence (Derrida 1978: 279–80). In *Of Grammatology*, a text centrally concerned with, among other things, the difficulties associated with the articulation of 'difference', Derrida insists that as we cannot hope to escape from, or think 'outside' of, that which underlies all of our knowledge and thought; 'there is nothing outside the text'; we must undertake a critique of it from within (Derrida 1976: 158). Any attempt to do otherwise, he convincingly illustrates, is doomed to become caught up in the very terms, structures and language it seeks to evade.

While it is perhaps obvious that the complexity of spatial questions cannot simply be reduced to the implied categories of an either/or, there is no doubt that this powerful theoretical argument has widespread implications for *all* attempts to define and differentiate notions of Other, absolutely different, resistant or transgressive space. In brief, this is the case in that in any attempt to mobilize the category of an outside or absolutely differentiated space, it follows logically that the simple naming or theoretical recognition of that difference always to some degree flattens or precludes, by definition, the very possibility of its arrival as such.

Although Foucault never returned to the substance of his argument in 'Of Other Spaces', much has been made of this short piece by a host of critics and commentators.[10] While on the one hand there would appear to be cause for some celebration here, on the other, almost all of these critical applications are characterized by a (more or less) literal reading of the text. In short, 'Of Other Spaces' is invariably called up (within a simplistic 'for/against' model of conventional politics) to provide the basis for some 'alternative' strategy of spatial interpretation which might be applied to any 'real' place. Scouring the absolute limits of imagination, the question then becomes: what cannot be designated a heterotopia? It follows that the bulk of these uncritical applications of the term as a discontinuous space of impartial/resistant use must be viewed as problematic.

IV

In contrast to the previous attempt to define and differentiate actual extra-discursive locations, Foucault's second conception of heterotopias is primarily concerned with the possibility of articulating absolutely differentiated discursive space. Foucault begins the preface to *The Order of Things*, undoubtedly written after the text, by announcing his overwhelming fascination with a flaw in the glass, a flaw derived from a now famous passage in an essay by Jorge Luis Borges, 'The Analytical Language of John Wilkins'.

A fanciful flight into the fantastic, Borges's essay recalls apocryphally the 'remote pages' of a certain Chinese encyclopedia, dubiously entitled 'Celestial Emporium of Benevolent Knowledge', in which it is written that all animals are divided into:

> a) belonging to the Emperor, b) embalmed, c) tame, d) sucking pigs, e) sirens, f) fabulous, g) stray dogs, h) included in the present classification, i) frenzied, j) innumerable, k) drawn with a fine camel-hair brush, l) et cetera, m) having just broken the water pitcher, n) those that from a long way off look like flies. (Borges 1988: 103)

This passage is so fascinating for Foucault because the thing that he perceives as freely demonstrated by its 'exotic charm' is no less than the very limitation of our own system of thought; in short, 'the stark impossibility of thinking that' (Foucault 1980: xv). Foucault thus views Borges's imaginary bestiary as a symbol of 'absolutely Other' patterns of categorization in that it points to an incommensurable system of the ordering of things.

Yet Foucault is far from content just to cite this impossible site of unthinkable ordering. Examining the fable, he begins to question the very nature of this impossibility by posing two paradoxical if not absurd questions. First, what is it impossible to think about this taxonomy? Secondly, what kind of impossibility are we faced with here?

In answer to the first question, Foucault's reply is clear; 'what is impossible is not the propinquity of the things listed, but the very site upon which their propinquity would be possible' (Foucault 1980: xvi). What is impossible to imagine then is a coherent space which could ever contain such a classificatory scheme; a space where the categories listed in the taxonomy could ever meet. Certainly, there is no other place than the 'non-place' of language itself, a space without an immediate location.

This wonderment of taxonomy, however, refuses to sit quietly at the foot of language either. Although the taxonomy is to be found within language, 'which serves up the categories before us', it can only do so in an 'unthinkable' space. This is the case in that, because the incommensurable categories do not allow one any recourse to an ordering principle 'outside' of the fable itself, it is impossible to designate any continuous or common ground, 'that which enables thought to operate on the entities of our world', upon which it is possible for these categories to be juxtaposed. Foucault writes:

> The central category of animals 'included in the present classification' . . . is indication enough that we shall never succeed in defining a stable relation of contained to container between each of these categories and that which includes them all: if all animals divided up here can be placed without exception in one of the divisions of this list, then aren't all the other divisions to be found in that one division too? And then again, in what space would that single, inclusive category have its existence? Absurdity destroys the 'and' of the

enumeration by making impossible the 'in' where the things enumerated would be divided up. (Foucault 1980: xvii)

So what kind of impossibility are we faced with here? Borges's bizarre and incommensurable bestiary leads Foucault to the suspicion that there exists a worse kind of disorder than the unexpected juxtaposition of extremely disparate objects and entities occurring in an otherwise familiar location; a type of disorder, as Georges Teyssot has suggested, that makes the radical incongruence of an alphabetical series as revealed when a dictionary is 'read as if it were a novel' look like a mere inconvenience (Teyssot 1980: 81). After all, a dictionary could be described as heterogeneous, while the incommensurability found in Borges's catalogue, where fragments of a great number of possible though exclusive and inconsistent orders coexist in a space 'without law or geometry', a space in which the structure no longer defines any common centre of classification or coherent locus of residence beneath the categories, can only be defined as heterotopic. What other space could possibly accommodate such hopeless confusion, akin, as Foucault suggests, to the profound distress of a frenzied aphasiac?[11]

Yet as a discontinuous montage of obsessive assemblage, Foucault claims that the heterotopia has a subversive function in that it runs against the grain of the order/ language that both defines and limits it. A redefinition follows:

[Heterotopias] make it impossible to name this and that . . . because they shatter or tangle common names, because they destroy syntax in advance, and not only the syntax with which we construct sentences but also that less apparent syntax which causes words and things (next to but opposite to one another) to 'hold together' . . . heterotopias (such as those to be found so often in Borges) desiccate speech, stop words in their tracks, contest the very possibility of language at its sources; they dissolve our myths, sterilize the lyricism of sentences. (Foucault 1980: xviii)

Like the 'invisible' cities that populate the empire of the Great Khan in Italo Calvino's surreal novel (1979), the impossible multiplicity of the heterotopia designates a structure of both anti-utopian and anti-discursive space (McHale 1989: 44). Its real power would thus appear to lie in its ability to both question and undermine the limits of the alleged coherence and totality of self-contained linguistic and spatial systems. Yet can the language of reason itself ever really hope to speak the difference of such a madness?

In order to call an existing order into question, Foucault's incommensurable structures must, as we have seen, remain outside (absolutely differentiated from) that order while at the same time relate to and be able to be defined within it. Yet the familiar problem with this is, as Steven Connor points out, that once such a space of incommensurable difference has been sighted ('Of Other Spaces'), cited (*The Order of Things*) and re-cited on the pages transcribing it, it is no longer the lacuna that it once was, in that even as an 'impossible' or 'unthinkable' space it is none the less operational as such. To quote Connor: 'Once such a heterotopia has been named . . . it is no longer the conceptual monstrosity which it once was, for its [absolute] incommensurability has been in some sense bound, controlled and predicatively interpreted, given a centre and illustrative function' (Connor 1989: 9).

While Foucault never explicitly returned to the ideas inspired by Borges's bizarre bestiary, much has again been made of his use of the term by a variety of critics and commentators; in particular, 'postmodern' architectural and literary theorists.[12] Yet the problem with the majority of these critical appropriations is that they simply adopt the mildly incongruent aspect of Foucault's inviting description. The heterotopia is invariably reified as a handy marker for a variety of centreless structures or an elastic postmodern plurality. Not only do such appropriations avoid questions concerning the coherency of Foucault's argument, but in so doing, they lose the disruptive, transient, contradictory and transformative implications of what remains a far more fluid idea.

V

Although Foucault gives no apparent answer to the difficulties in either of his texts, simply to write off his conception of heterotopias as incoherent seems less than prudent. So what then is the critical value of the term? Moreover, what implications does it have for any possible politics of space? In order to answer such questions we must first return to the role of the heterotopia within Foucault's own discourse.[13]

There is no doubt that we can locate a substantial critical oversight within 'Of Other Spaces'. Yet while it would appear that in *The Order of Things* Foucault retains the problematic conception of the heterotopia as an absolutely differentiated space, I would suggest that he mobilizes the term not so much to insist upon an operational notion of that difference as, by virtue of its discursive demonstration as a limitation to Western systems of thought, to name and manifest his own uneasiness but also fascination with the entire proposition. In short, the heterotopia does represent a space of exclusion within his writings, but, knowing full well the impossibility of its realization, it comes to designate not so much an absolutely differentiated space as the site of that very limit, tension, impossibility. Somewhat incidentally, Foucault shows himself to be fully aware of the problems connected with the articulation of spatially discontinuous ground on more than one occasion, most notably in an interview with the Lycéens when he remarked rather gravely, 'even to imagine another order/system is to extend our participation in the present one' (Megill 1987: 198).

One could say then that through the heterotopia Foucault acknowledges the impossibility of the move to absolutely differentiated and contestory spaces. At the same time, however, he also discovers that the very possibility of knowing this impossibility is in turn operational as such, acting back upon the circumstances in which knowing itself takes place. The heterotopia would thus appear to function within Foucault's discourse as a radical site/space of irreconcilable tension with the hermeticism of inescapable binary terms. As such, it cannot simply be dismissed as just an-Other excess, negativity or even marker for the desire for an outside/beyond, which Derrida found latent in Foucault's thought along with that of his contemporaries.[14]

Acting as points of a kind of mediatory enablement rather than fencing off any discontinuous ground, Foucault's descriptions suggest that we scrutinize and question the implications and possibilities of the slips, exceptions, oddities lurking at the very limits of the system that defines for us what is thinkable, sayable, knowable. The heterotopia is thus more of an idea about space than any actual place. It is an idea that insists that the ordering of spatial systems is subjective and arbitrary in that we know nothing of the initial totality that it must presuppose. It is an idea which consequently produces/ theorizes space as transient, contestory, plagued by lapses and ruptured sites. In this capacity it coincides with the ambitions of those writers and artists who over the past few years have turned to multivalent public installation projects in an attempt to call into question the increasingly functionalist, repetitively replicated and electronically moni- tored spatial experience that constitutes post-industrial city life.

One recent example of such a juxtaposition of artistic forms and spaces was that of Australian artist Denis del Favero's environmental installation and mystery-thriller 'Un- dercover'.[15] Designed by Eamon D'Arcy and Derek Nicholson for platforms 5 and 6 of the Wynyard underground station in Sydney, this installation of interviews, radio- broadcasts, images, text and soundwork provided an ambitious use of the space of the subway as a site from which to articulate issues as to its occupation and experience. The importance of this project with respect to heterotopias, however, lies in recognizing, as Michel de Certeau has suggested, that the 'non-place' of the modern subway system is in essence an accretion of powers associated with disciplinary modes of surveillance and control (de Certeau 1984: 111–14). In this respect, the most interesting aspect of the whole installation was the fact that the sound-track was repeatedly silenced by the railway police for unspecified 'security' reasons.

As a site of incongruent representations and conflicting desires, public installations such as 'Undercover' capture an unpredictable nexus of imagination, ideology and power. Embracing an emporium of knowledges in a weave of media, artistic forms, experiences, representations and practices, they are at once sites of displacement and contradiction. With a strangely secular magic they are thus able to inscribe instability into a given spatial order, and in turn generate the potential for shaking the very foundations of that order by temporarily effacing the accepted relationships which define and limit it. Not only then do public installations like 'Undercover' force us to confront and examine that which we take for granted through the collective spatial experience implicit within habitual, everyday uses, acts and perceptions; but in celebrating both the disruptive and transformative powers of incongruence and eclecticism they insist, like the heterotopia, that social space is polysemous and contestory, made from a woven thread of some still enchanted fabric which must always be questioned, fought over, altered and most of all, unravelled.

NOTES

1 In particular, historiography. On this point see Soja (1989). An earlier version of this article appeared in the architectural journal *Transition*, 41 (1993), 2–11.

2 In the general remarks on space that follow I am indebted to this wide-ranging article.

3 Baudrillard (1983), Jameson (1984), Virilio (1986), Harvey (1989).

4 de Certeau (1984), Bourdieu (1985), Deleuze and Guattari (1987), Foucault (1990).

5 Hetero-topia: derived from the Greek words 'topos' meaning place and 'heteros' meaning other or different.

6 Foucault (1986). For the above 'biographical' remarks I am grateful to Soja (1990).

7 This is not just another structuralist reassertion of space into critical theory. Foucault's more innovative conception of an 'operational' space/time bears a greater similarity to Martin Heidegger's conception of 'lived' spatiality (Heidegger 1975).

8 I refer here to Noel Gray's commentary on 'Of Other Spaces' in his introduction to the Art Association of Australia Conference session, 'Heterotopias and Other Spaces', 28th of September 1990. I am drawing on his remarks reproduced in Best (1991).

9 It would appear that the problems connected with Foucault's notion of absolutely differentiated spaces can be understood, in part, by a consideration of the theoretical pedigree of the idea. The spatial ordering of heterotopias bears a fundamental affinity with George Bataille's crucial split between restricted and general economics. Briefly, Bataille's distinction is based upon an interchange between a restricted economy, in which there is nothing which cannot be made to make sense, is not useful/reasonable, and a general economy which affirms and upholds that which exceeds use, meaning (Bataille 1988). More importantly, however, Bataille reworks this distinction in a derivative relationship between the worlds of homogeneous and heterogeneous spaces, bodies and forms, in an essay entitled 'The Psychological Structure of Fascism' (Bataille 1985). Witness then Bataille on the heterogeneous: 'the very term heterogeneous indicates that it concerns elements that are impossible to assimilate. . . . In summary, compared to everyday life, [the spaces of] heterogeneous existence can be represented as something other, as incommensurate' (pp. 140, 143). While Foucault's early and well-known interest in Bataille (in particular his understanding of transgression) has been remarked upon elsewhere, the connection here is further strengthened by the fact that both make a bid to universalize the production of these 'sacred' sites as a generalized anthropological principle. I would thus argue that Bataille's insistence on the absolute necessity for the creation of spaces of unproductive expenditure in turn become Foucault's heterotopic sites of contestation. I thank Susan Best for this suggestion.

10 Perhaps the most obvious and ambitious critical appropriation of Foucault's remarks in 'Of Other Spaces' is to be found in the work of Soja (1989, 1990). Other examples include Ruddick (1990), Hanna (1991).

11 Numerous medical studies of schizophrenic thought patterns have also examined the similarities between the process of classification and identification found in Borges's taxonomy and the way in which schizophrenics form categories (Sass 1992).

12 For example, McHale (1989) and Benitez-Rojo (1992). With specific reference to architecture, see Tafuri (1987, 1990), Teyssot (1980), Porphyrios (1982).

13 Moreover, it might well be that a clearer conception of the specific use and function of the heterotopia within Foucault's writings can help us to clarify or redefine other, related areas within his work. For example, Foucault's understanding of specific disciplinary logics, primarily concerned with the way in which power structures unfold in institutional practices, clearly underwrote a conception of resistance reliant upon the discovery of

localized sites, knowledges and strategies of contestation. Derek Gregory has astutely suggested that the heterotopia would appear to be intimately involved with this process (Gregory 1990).

14 For Derrida's critique of Foucault, see Derrida (1978: 31–63). For Foucault's reply, see Foucault (1979).

15 'Undercover' was produced as part of an Artspace project, curated by John Barrett-Lennard, on art in public spaces, entitled 'Working in Public', March 27 to April 26, 1992.

REFERENCES

Bataille, G. 1985: *Visions of Excess*, Minneapolis: Minnesota University Press.

Bataille, G. 1988: *The Accursed Share, An Essay on General Economy: Vol. 1. Consumption*, New York: Zone.

Baudrillard, J. 1983: *Simulations*, New York: Semiotext(e).

Benitez-Rojo, A. 1992: *The Repeating Island: The Caribbean and the Postmodern Perspective*, London: Duke.

Best, S. 1991: 'Window Dressing Up as Art', *Transition*, 35: 21–31.

Borges, J.L. 1988: *Other Inquisitions*, Austin: Texas University Press.

Bourdieu, P. 1985: *Distinction: A Social Critique of the Judgement of Taste*, London: Routledge.

Calvino, I. 1979: *Invisible Cities*, London: Picador.

de Certeau, M. 1984: *The Practice of Everyday Life*, Berkeley: University of California Press.

Connor, S. 1989: *Postmodernist Culture: An Introduction to Theories of the Contemporary*, Oxford: Blackwell.

Deleuze, G. and Guattari, F. 1987: *A Thousand Plateaus*, Minneapolis: Minnesota University Press.

Derrida, J. 1976: *Of Grammatology*, Baltimore: Johns Hopkins.

Derrida, J. 1978: *Writing and Difference*, Chicago: University of Chicago Press.

Ferrier, E. 1990: 'Mapping Power: Cartography and Contemporary Cultural Theory', *Antithesis*, 4, 1: 35–49.

Foucault, M. 1979: 'My Body, This Paper, This Fire', *Oxford Literary Review*, 4, 1: 9–28.

Foucault, M. 1980: *The Order of Things*, New York: Vintage.

Foucault, M. 1986: 'Of Other Spaces', *Diacritics*, Spring: 22–7.

Foucault, M. 1990: *The History of Sexuality Vol. 1: An Introduction*, London: Penguin.

Gregory, D. 1990: 'Chinatown, Part Three? Soja and the Missing Spaces of Social Theory', *Strategies*, 3: 40–104.

Hanna, B. 1991: 'Green Valley: Sameness and Difference in Suburbia', *West*, 3, 1: 6–13.

Harvey, D. 1989: *The Condition of Postmodernity*, Oxford: Blackwell.

Heidegger, M. 1975: *Poetry, Language, Thought*, New York: Harper and Row.

Jameson, F. 1984: 'Postmodernism, or the Cultural Logic of Late Capitalism', *New Left Review*, 146: 53–92.

McHale, B. 1989: *Postmodernist Fiction*, London: Routledge.

Megill, A. 1987: *Prophets of Extremity*, Berkeley: University of California Press.

Porphyrios, D. 1982: *Sources of Modern Eclecticism: Studies on Alvar Aalto*, London: Academy Editions.

Ruddick, S. 1990: 'Heterotopias of the Homeless', *Strategies*, 3: 184–202.

Sass, L.A. 1992: *Madness and Modernism: Insanity in the Light of Modern Art, Literature, and Thought*, New York: HarperCollins.

Soja, E. 1989: *Postmodern Geographies*, London: Verso.

Soja, E. 1990: 'Heterotopologies: A Remembrance of Other Spaces', *Strategies*, 3: 6–39 [reprinted as ch. 2 in this volume].

Tafuri, M. 1987: 'Ceci n'est pas une Ville', *Lotus International*, 13.

Tafuri, M. 1990: *The Sphere and the Labyrinth*, Cambridge, MA: MIT Press.

Teyssot, G. 1980: 'Heterotopias and the History of Spaces', *Architecture and Urbanism*, 121: 79–100.

Virilio, P. 1986: 'The Overexposed City', *Zone*, 1/2: 15–31.

4. Women, *Chora*, Dwelling

Elizabeth Grosz

Language is the house of Being. In its home man dwells.

Martin Heidegger, 'Letter on Humanism'

The house of language in which man dwells to protect himself from his original dereliction can become a prison for both sexes.

Margaret Whitford, *Luce Irigaray*

You supplant that horizon by the home and its institutions. Instead of ties which are always developing, you want fixed bonds. You only encounter proximity when it is framed by property . . .

Everywhere you shut me in. Always you assign a place to me. Even outside the frame that I form with you . . . You set limits even to events that could happen with others . . . You mark out boundaries, draw lines, surround, enclose. Excising, cutting out. What is your fear? That you might lose your property. What remains is an empty frame. You cling to it, dead.

Luce Irigaray, *Elemental Passions*

There are many different approaches a feminist might take in exploring the theme of women and architecture. For the purposes of this brief exploration, I will remain silent regarding most of them, leaving undiscussed the sometimes crucial issues of sexism and the often manifest discrimination against women in architectural training, apprenticeship and practice. Such issues are best discussed and understood by those actively involved in the profession, who not only have first-hand experience of the operations of such discriminatory practices, but have insights into the internal exigencies of the system in which they work, and an understanding of the various strategies pragmatically at hand in architectural institutions, to transform them into sites of contestation. My concern here is with a series of narrower and more theoretical issues which link the very *concept* of architecture with the phallocentric effacement of women and femininity; that is, the cultural refusal of women's specificity or corporeal and conceptual autonomy and social value.

I wish to make some very indirect and rather tenuous connections between architecture, deconstruction and feminist theory, forging some rudimentary connections, and pointing out some of the rather awkward points of dis-ease between these various concerns. My goal here will be to present an initial exploration of the cultural origins of notions of spatiality in the writings of the Classical period, most notably in Plato, who in the *Timaeus* invokes a mythological bridge between the intelligible and the sensible, mind and body, which he calls *chora*. *Chora* has been the object of considerable philosophical reflection, especially in contemporary French philosophy, having taken on the status of a master term in the writings of Julia Kristeva, in her understanding of the stabilization and destabilization of the speaking subject; and more recently in the writings of Jacques Derrida, particularly in his various theoretical exchanges with architecture, in his commentaries on and contributions to the work of the architects and architectural theorists Bernard Tschumi and Peter Eisenman. *Chora*, which Derrida insists must be understood without any definite article, has an acknowledged role at the very foundations of the concept of spatiality and placing: it signifies, at its most literal level, notions of 'place', 'location', 'site', 'region', 'locale', 'country': but it also contains an irreducible, yet often overlooked, connection with the function of femininity, being associated with a series of gender-aligned terms – 'mother', 'nurse', 'receptacle' and 'imprint-bearer'. Derrida is interested in this term, in keeping with the larger and more general features of 'deconstructive reading', which always seek out terms that disturb the logic, the *logos*, of the text under examination, in order to show that it exceeds and cannot be contained by the logic, explicit framework and overt intentions of the text. Derrida continually seeks out these terms, terms impossible to assimilate into the text's logic, but which are nevertheless necessary for it to function, and are thus fundamentally ineliminable from the text's operations, terms which exert a disruptive force, an aporetic effect, on the apparent claims and concerns of the text in question. *Chora* thus follows a long line of deconstructively privileged terms in Derrida's texts, from 'writing', 'trace', 'pharmakon', 'dissemination', 'supplement' and 'parergon', in his earlier writings, to 'cinders', 'ghost', 'remainder' and 'residue' (among others) in his more recent texts. These terms each designate and locate a point of indeterminacy or undecidability, a point at which the text's own writing exceeds its explicit goals and logic, where the text turns in on itself and ties itself into a strategically positioned knot.

It will be my argument here, reading Plato and Derrida on *chora*, that the notion of *chora* serves to produce a founding concept of femininity whose connections with women and female corporeality have been severed, producing a disembodied femininity as the ground for the production of a (conceptual and social) universe. In outlining the unacknowledged and unrepayable debt that the very notion of space, and the built environment that relies on its formulation, owe to what Plato characterizes as the 'femininity' of the *chora* (a characterization he both utilizes and refuses to commit himself to), I will develop some of the insights of the French feminist, philosopher, linguist and psychoanalyst, Luce Irigaray, in her critical analysis of the phallocentric foundations of western philosophy. Irigaray's reading of the history of philosophy as the erasure or covering over of women's specificity has served to demonstrate that even where women and femininity are not explicitly mentioned or evoked in philosophical and architectural texts, none the less they, and concepts associated with them, serve as the unconscious, repressed or unspoken foundations of and guarantee for philosophical value. This chapter may be understood as the confrontation of one strand of contemporary architectural theory, represented by Derrida's relatively small and admittedly oblique contributions to architectural writing and planning, and Irigaray's sweeping analysis of the investment that all modes of knowledge have in perpetuating the secondary and subordinate social positions accorded to women and femininity. Irigaray *contra* Derrida in the domain of the dwelling: where and how to live, as whom and with whom?

DWELLING: BETWEEN THE INTELLIGIBLE AND THE SENSIBLE

Timaeus represents Plato's attempt to produce a basic explanation of the universe as we know it – a *modest* attempt on the part of a philosopher who believed that only philosophers were fit to rule the well-ordered *polis* – an explanation of the divine creation of the cosmos and the earth. In an age where myth is not yet definitively separated from science or philosophy, Plato presents an account of the genesis of the universe from divine and rational metaphysical principles (for a much more detailed discussion of the philosophical and architectural context of Plato's thought, see Bergren 1992). He sets up a series of binary oppositions which would henceforth mark the character of western thought: the distinctions between being and becoming, between the intelligible and the sensible, the ideal and the material, the divine and the mortal, which may all be regarded as versions of the distinction between the (perfect) world of reason and the (imperfect) material world.

This opposition between what is intelligible and unchanging, being (the world of Forms or Ideas), and what is sensible (which Plato describes as visible) and subject to change, becoming, seems relatively straightforward; but it is difficult to use as an explanatory model, a ground of ontology, unless there is the possibility of some mediation, some mode of transition or passage from one to the other. Plato complicates and indeed problematizes and undoes this opposition by devising a third or intermediate category whose function is to explain the passage from the perfect to the imperfect, from the Form to the reality – *chora*. This intermediate category, it is claimed, shares little with either term in the opposition. Plato does suggest at some points that it shares in the properties of both the Forms and material reality; yet at other points, he claims that it has nothing in common with either. He rather enigmatically and impossibly suggests both that it has no attributes of its own; and that it shares some of the attributes of the Forms: 'we shall not be wrong if we describe it as invisible and formless, all-embracing, possessed in a most puzzling way of intelligibility, yet very hard to grasp' (Plato 1977: 70). Somehow, in a 'puzzling way', it participates in intelligibility yet is distinct from the intelligible; it is also distinct from the material world in so far as it is 'invisible and formless', beyond the realm of the senses. It dazzles the logic of non-contradiction, it insinuates itself between the oppositional terms, in the impossible no-man's land of the excluded middle. This is already enough to indicate to Derrida, no less than to Irigaray, that there is something odd at stake here, something that exceeds what Plato is able to argue legitimately using his own criteria.

Plato cannot specify any particular properties or qualities for *chora*: if one could attribute it any specificity it would immediately cease to have its status as intermediary or receptacle and would instead become an object (or quality or property). It is thus by definition impossible to characterize. It is the mother of all qualities without in itself having any – except its capacity to take on, to nurture and to bring into existence any other kind of being. Being a kind of pure permeability (in many ways, Freud's concept of the infinitely permeable neuronal structures constituting perception, as outlined in the *Project for a Scientific Psychology* (1895), provides a modern analogue for the pure impressionability of *chora*), infinitely transformable, inherently open to the specificities of whatever concrete it brings into existence, *chora* can have no attributes, no features of its own. Seeped in paradox, its quality is to be quality-less, its defining characteristic that it lacks any defining feature. It functions primarily as the receptacle, the storage point, the locus of nurturance in the transition for the emergence of matter, a kind of womb of material existence, the nurse of becoming, an incubator to ensure the transmission or rather the copying of Forms to produce matter which resembles them. Matter bears a likeness to the Forms. This relation of resemblance (like the paternal bond between father and son) depends on the minimalized contributions of the receptacle/space/mother in the genesis of becoming. Moreover, it becomes less clear as the text proceeds whether something like *chora* is necessary for the very genesis of the Forms themselves – that is, whether *chora* can be conceived as a product or copy of the Forms – or, contrarily, whether the Forms are themselves conditioned on *chora*:

> *It can always be called the same because it never alters its characteristics. For it continues to receive all things, and never itself takes a permanent impress from any of the things that enter it, making it appear different at different times. And the things which pass in and out of it are copies of the eternal realities, whose form they take in a wonderful way that is hard to describe. (Plato 1977: 69)*

Chora can only be designated by 'its', by 'her', function: to hold, nurture, bring into the world. Neither an 'it' nor a 'she', *chora* has neither existence nor becoming. *Not* to procreate or produce – this is the function of the father, the creator, god, the Forms – but to nurse, to support, surround, protect, incubate, to sort, or engender – the worldly offspring of the Forms. Its function is a neutral, traceless production, a production that leaves no trace of its contributions and thus allows the product to speak indirectly of its creator without need for acknowledging its incubator. Plato explicitly compares the Forms to the role of the male, and *chora* to the role of the female according to Greek collective fantasies: in procreation, the father contributes all the specific characteristics to the nameless, formless incubation provided by the mother:

> *We may indeed use the metaphor of birth and compare the receptacle to the mother, the model to the father, and what they produce between them to their offspring; and we may notice that, if an imprint is to present a very complex appearance, the material on which it is to be stamped will not have been properly prepared unless it is devoid of all the characters which it is to receive. For if it were like any of the things that enter it, it would badly distort any impression of a contrary or entirely different nature when it receives it, as its own features would shine through. (Plato 1977: 69)*

Neither something nor yet nothing, *chora* is the condition for the genesis of the material world, the screen onto which is projected the image of the changeless Forms, the space onto which the Form's duplicate or copy is cast, providing the point of entry, as it were, into material existence. The material object is not simply produced by the Form(s) but also resembles or is a copy of the original, a copy whose powers of verisimilitude depend upon the neutrality, the blandness, the lack of specific attributes of its 'nursemaid'.

This peculiar receptacle which is *chora* functions to receive, to take in, to possess without in her turn leaving any correlative impression of what she receives. She takes in without holding onto: she is unable to possess for she has no self-possession, no self-identity. She supports all material existence with nothing to support her own. Though she brings being into becoming she has neither being nor the possibilities of becoming: both the mother of all things and yet without ontological status, she designates less a positivity than an abyss, a crease, perhaps a pure difference between being and becoming, that space that produces their separation and thus enables their co-existence and interchange.

Plato slips indifferently into a designation of *chora* as space itself, the condition for the very existence of material objects (it is no accident that Descartes takes the ability to occupy space as the singular defining characteristic of material objects). Space is a third kind of 'entity' that is apprehended neither by the senses nor by reason alone, being understood only with difficulty, in terms of a 'spurious reason', 'in a kind of a dream', in a modality that today, following Kant, may be described as apperception. Plato is here describing a space

> *which is eternal and indestructible, which provides a position for everything that comes to be, and which is apprehended without the senses by a sort of spurious reasoning and so is hard to believe in — we look at it indeed in a kind of dream and say that everything that exists must be somewhere and occupy some space, and that what is nowhere in heaven or earth is nothing at all. (Plato 1977: 71–2)*

Chora then is the space in which place is made possible, the chasm for the passage of spaceless Forms into a spatialized reality, a dimensionless tunnel opening itself to spatialization, obliterating itself to make others possible and actual. It is the space that engenders without possessing, that nurtures without requirements of its own, that receives without giving, and that gives without receiving, a space that evades all characterization including the disconcerting logic of identity, of hierarchy of being, the regulation of order. It is no wonder that *chora* resembles the characteristics the Greeks, and all those who follow them — including the most postmodern — have long attributed to femininity, or rather, have expelled from their own masculine self-representations and accounts of being and knowing and have thus *de facto* attributed to the feminine. Moreover, this femininity not merely is itself an abstract representation of generic features (softness, nurturance, etc.) but is derived from the attributes culturally bestowed on women themselves, and in this case, particularly the biological function of gestation. While *chora* cannot be directly identified with the womb — to do so would be to pin it down naively to something specific, convert it into an object rather than the condition of existence of objects — none the less it does seem to borrow many of the paradoxical attributes of pregnancy and maternity.

DERRIDA: BETWEEN WRITING AND ARCHITECTURE

Derrida has written a good deal on Greek philosophy and has devoted considerable words to unravelling the texts of Plato. He has done so not only because Plato's work functions at the cultural horizon of the inauguration of western philosophy (such an approach would remain tied to the history of ideas), but because the platonic tradition has established basic frameworks, assumptions and methods that have guided not only philosophy, but western reason, ever since. It is thus not entirely surprising that for his two contributions written explicitly for an architecturally literate public, Derrida has again chosen to write on, with or around Plato, and the *Timaeus*. As I understand him, Derrida's work is neither architectural in itself (although no doubt it possesses its own 'architectonic') nor devoid of any architectural relevance. He challenges, not architecture itself, but a series of assumptions, categories and terms by which architecture is, as are all *writing* practices – and architecture is clearly a mode of writing in the Derridean sense – implicated in and governed by metaphysics: he challenges architecture with its own irreducibly written traces, its own self-undoing, just as his work in turn is challenged with its own modes of textuality, its obliteration of spatiality and materiality (for further, see Bergren 1992).

Derrida's reading of *chora* is ingenious: he shows how the counter-logic or a-logic of the *chora* as concept–term in Plato's writings infects the other apparently unrelated claims of the *Timaeus*, its explanation of the origins of the universe and the ways in which political, physical and biological factors are rendered explicable. Moreover, it also seeps into Plato's own self-conception, the position he accords to Socrates in his texts. The peculiar functioning of *chora* cannot be readily contained in a self-identical place for it seeps into all that it contains, into all the oppositions and metaphysical assumptions that depend on it for their existence: the Forms, the material world and their interrelations remain inexplicable except in terms of the mediation produced by *chora*. The world of objects, material reality in all its complexity, is in fact infiltrated by the very term whose function is to leave no imprint, no trace. *Chora* is interwoven throughout the fabric of Plato's writing. It effectively intervenes into Plato's accounts of ontology, of political rulership, of the relations between heavenly bodies (his cosmology) and the organization of the human body – of all that makes up the world: these other relations all exhibit an 'abyssal and analogous reflexivity' (Derrida 1993) with what Plato says about *chora*. Moreover, and more importantly for the purposes of this argument, it is interwoven into the very *economy* of the architectural project itself.

It is significant that 'economy' is derived from the Greek term *oikos*, meaning 'home' or 'house', 'residence' or 'dwelling'. An economy is the distribution of material (cultural, social, economic, representational, libidinal) goods in a system of production and circulation. An architectural economy consists not only in the distribution of bricks, stone, steel and glass, but also in the production and distribution of discourses, writings, including the bodily traces of a building's occupants, and its divisions of space, time and movement, as well as the architectural plans, treatises and textbooks that surround and infuse building. Derrida's goal seems not to be to destroy, to deconstruct (in a more pedestrian sense), to problematize and render architecture's assumptions unworkable, but rather to see whether it is possible to build–write according to a different economy, to reroute and transform the logic which distinguishes between space and time, form and matter, the intelligible and the sensible, theory and practice, so that it functions in different ways, with unexpected and unpredictable results, innovating different modalities of construction, both conceptual and material. His goal has always been to upset pregiven categories, to demonstrate the textual contortions that such categories entail, to show their cost and to effect some sort of rupture or transformation in their operations. His contributions to architecture remain of the same order: to open other possibilities for rethinking space, time, dwelling, the built environment and the operative distinctions with which such concepts function.

Derrida does not intervene *as such* into architectural practice. He reserves a different role for himself: in effect, providing some kind of validation of the writing and building experiments of others (most notably, Eisenman and Tschumi), who themselves challenge the prevailing assumptions of functionalism, form and measure in their attempts to think, and to produce, what might be considered a 'radical architecture', an architecture of transgression. In this sense, *chora*, and the reconceptualization of space that a deconstructive reading of this concept entails, require rethinking the requirements of those oppositions that have structured architecture to the present: figure and ground, form and function, ornament and structure, theory and practice; and most particularly, both architectural consumerism (whose function is to subordinate materiality to the consumer's will or desire – a fundamentally impossible project, given the inherent open-endedness of desire, its fundamentally volatile and ever-changing nature) and architectural functionalism (whose goal is to subordinate subjects' desires to the exigencies of function – an increasingly impossible project, particularly in the era of increasingly rapid transformation of technological and corporate functions). One of his goals remains to contest the intervention into architectural practices of the exigencies of either aestheticism (the demands of beauty) or functionalism (the requirements of dwelling). Not that these requirements can be dispensed with, or must be abandoned: rather they need to be rethought in terms of their role as internal or constitutive factors, factors which function according to a different economy:

> you have to reinscribe *these motifs [the hegemony of the aesthetic and the useful] within the work. You can't (or you shouldn't) simply dismiss those values of dwelling, functionality, beauty and so on. You have to construct, so to speak, a new space and a new form, to shape a new way of building in which those motifs or values are reinscribed, having meanwhile lost their external hegemony.* (Norris 1987: 73)

This reconceptualization of space and spatiality that Derrida signals without specifying, and which he indicates is at the heart of both philosophical and architectural reflection, is, I believe, a concern he shares with feminist theory, particularly with feminists involved in architectural theory and practice. It is also one of the major areas of concern in the writings of Irigaray, who, like Derrida, concentrates primarily on philosophical texts, but particularly on those which also have some direct relevance to understanding the built environment.

I do not want to suggest that Derrida's work is directly compatible with the interests of feminist theory: quite the contrary. Whatever relations may exist between Derridean deconstruction and feminist theory have yet to be forged and explored in thorough detail, although it is today clear that a number of feminist theorists (among them, Gayatri

Spivak, Drucilla Cornell, Barbara Johnson, Peggy Kamuf), with whatever reservations they may individually have regarding the feminist validity of Derrida's work, none the less are interested in and have worked with Derridean texts and concepts for various feminist projects. It seems clear to me that while Derrida's work is neither feminist nor anti-feminist, it retains both feminist and anti-feminist elements. His work is fundamentally ambivalent. Making it relevant to feminist concerns is a matter of considerable negotiation: his writings always contain an unassimilable residue that is not only problematic in feminist terms, but always tilts his writings into an uneasy and ambiguous alliance with other interests and issues (for example, his relations to the writings of Martin Heidegger and Paul de Man on the question of fascism have always remained undecidable, much to the frustration of those who want clear-cut alignments and an easily readable or transparent political position).

FEMINIST REOCCUPATIONS OF SPACE

Conceptions of spatiality and temporality have rarely been the explicit object of feminist reflection: they have always appeared somehow above the more mundane concerns of day-by-day politics, too abstract, too neutral and self-evident to take as an object of critical feminist analysis (although this is now increasingly being revised in the work of some feminists working in the area of architecture, for example, Bergren 1992, Bloomer 1992 and Colomina 1992). It has, however, become increasingly clear that the organization and management of space – the projects of architecture and regional planning, among others – have very serious political, social and cultural impact, and in a sense cannot but be of concern to feminists. Among the more interesting writings on (philosophical notions of) space and spatiality are Irigaray's, whose works, while perhaps less well known in the area of architectural theory, have had considerable impact on Anglo-American feminist theory and philosophy, and through them on the ways in which space, time, subjectivity and corporeality are currently considered.

While I cannot here outline her claims regarding the opposition between space and time – which she discusses with reference to Kant in *Ethique de la différence sexuelle* (1984) – I would like to use elements of her work to counterpose to the Derridean reading and use of the Platonic *chora* and to show the ways in which a feminist reading of *chora* may be able to reappropriate the maternal dimension implied by the term, and thus to reorient the ways in which spatiality is conceived, lived and used.

Irigaray's writings on the dwelling are based largely on her readings of a number of philosophical texts, most particularly those of Kant, Heidegger and Levinas. But more particularly, like Derrida and a whole history of western philosophers, she relies heavily on metaphors of dwelling, inhabitation, building, unearthing, tombs, ruins, temples, homes, caves, prison. Like Derrida's, her work remains indirect in its relation to architectural practice. But, like his, her writing may be readily appropriated by architectural practices in the hope of transforming men's and women's relations to space. Her concerns are directed towards the establishment of a *viable* space and time for women to inhabit as women. The ways in which space has been historically conceived have always functioned either to contain women or to obliterate them. She makes it clear that a reconceptualization of the relations between men and women – as is required for an autonomous and independent self-representation for women and femininity – entails the reconceptualization of the representations of space and time: 'In order for [sexual] difference to be thought and lived, we have to reconsider the whole problematic of *space* and *time* . . . A change of epoch requires a mutation in the perception and conception of *space-time*, the *inhabitation of place* and the *envelopes of identity*' (Irigaray 1984: 15).

Irigaray claims that masculine modes of thought have performed a devastating sleight of hand: they have obliterated the debt they owe to the most primordial of all spaces, the maternal space from which all subjects emerge, and which they ceaselessly attempt to usurp. Here Irigaray is not talking about specific men, or even a general tendency in men (although this may in fact be appropriate), but rather, a tendency in phallocentric thought to deny and cover over the debt of life and existence that all subjects, and indeed all theoretical frameworks, owe to the maternal body, their elaborate attempts to fore-close and build over this space with their own (sexually specific) fantasmatic and paranoid projections. The production of a (male) world – the construction of an 'artificial' or cultural environment, the production of an intelligible universe, religion, philosophy, the creation of true knowledge and valid practices of and in that universe – is implicated in the systematic and violent erasure of the contributions of women, femininity and the maternal. This erasure is the foundation or ground on which a thoroughly masculine universe is built: 'He can only touch himself from the outside. In order to recapture that whole sensation of the inside of a body, he will invent a world. But the world's circular horizon always conceals the inner movement of the womb. The imposition of distinc-tions is the mourning which their bodies always wear' (Irigaray 1992: 15).

Men produce a universe built upon the erasure of the bodies and contributions of women/mothers and the refusal to acknowledge the debt that they owe to the maternal body. They hollow out their own interiors and project them outward, and require women as supports for this hollowed space. Women become the guardians of the private, the interpersonal, while men build conceptual and material worlds. This appropriation of the right to a place or space is correlative with men's seizure of the right to define and utilize a spatiality that reflects their own self-representations. Men have conceived of themselves as self-made, and, in disavowing this maternal debt, have left themselves, and women, in dereliction and in homelessness. The question of the dwelling, of where and how to live, is thus a crucial one both in the production of the male domination of women's bodies, and in women's struggles to acquire an autonomous space they can occupy, and live in as women. In seeking to take up all (social) space themselves, in aspiring to occupy not only the territory of the earth, but also that of the heavens, in seeking a dominion from the earth to the sky, men have contained women in a death-like tomb, which Irigaray sometimes refers to as a 'sepulchre' (1985: 143–4). In a rigid containment or mortification of women's explorations of their own notions of spatiality (and temporality), men place women in the positions of being 'guardians' of their bodies and their spaces, the conditions of both bodies and space without body or space of their own: they become the living representatives of corporeality, of domesticity, of the natural order which men have had to expel from their own self-representations in order to construct themselves as above the mundane, beyond the merely material. To sustain this fantasy of auto-production and pure self-determination in a systematic way, men have had to use women as the delegates of men's materiality. This containment within the (negative) mirror of men's self-reflections strips women of an existence either autonomous or symmetrical with men's: it relegates women to the position of support or precondition of the masculine – precisely the status of *chora* in the platonic tradition: 'I was your house. And, when you leave, abandoning this dwelling place, I do not know what to do with these walls of mine. Have I ever had a body other than the one which you constructed according to your idea of it? Have I ever experienced a skin other than the one which you wanted me to dwell within?' (Irigaray 1992: 49).

The containment of women within a dwelling which they did not build, which indeed was not even built for them, can only amount to a homelessness within the very home itself: it becomes the space of duty, of endless and infinitely repeatable chores which have no social value or recognition, the space of the affirmation and replenishment of others at the expense and through the erasure of the self, the space of domestic violence and abuse, the space which harms as much as it isolates women. It is as if men are unable to resist the temptation to colonize, to appropriate, to measure, to control and to instrumentalize all that they survey, reducing the horizon (the horizon of becoming, the measure and reflection of positionality) into the dwelling, as Irigaray claims in the quotation opening this essay. But this manipulation and containment of women and space always has its costs: in appropriating the body of the other, man must lose access to his own. In succumbing to the inducements of the phallus, and the paternal privilege it entails, he gives up the rest of his body for the phallus. In exchange for the body he has had to sacrifice (the polymorphous pleasures of the pre-oedipal period) he is granted access to the bodies of women, women whose bodies replace the place from which he came (the maternal womb). Women's bodies are the socially guaranteed compensation for men's acquisition of phallic status, the repositories of men's own lost corporeality, and the guardians of men's mortality. It is not surprising, given the massive disavowal necessary to sustain men's vicarious containment of and living from women's energies, that it is steeped in hostility, resentment and aggression. Dwelling becomes the domain of hatred and murderous control: 'He passes from the formlessness of his relationship with his mother to the measureless excess of male power . . . He enters into paternal power, to keep within him the life he drinks from the other. But enclosed within that form, she dies' (Irigaray 1992: 53–4). This enclosure of women in men's physical space is not entirely different from the containment of women in men's conceptual universe either: theory, in the terms in which we know it today, is also the consequence of a refusal to acknowledge that other perspectives, other modes of reason, other modes of construction and constitution are possible. Its singularity and status, as true and objective, depend on this disavowal.

For women to be able to occupy another space, or to be able somehow to occupy this space in a different way, it is clear for Irigaray that several major transformations need to be effected. Most particularly, a series of upheavals in the organization of personal life (transformations in the way the mother–daughter relation is both conceived and mediated, changes in the ways in which female subjectivity and sexuality are structured according to the privileges of phallic subjectivity and sexuality, changes in the ways in which the two sexes relate to and exchange with each other), in the ways in which women's relations to what is larger than them (the divine, the environment and nature) are conceived, and in the ways in which theory, and cultural production more generally, are regarded (for further detail, see Whitford 1991). This interconnected cluster of issues cannot be readily untangled or easily resolved: these are more directions in which feminists must now turn rather than issues to be solved and eliminated. One thing remains clear, though: unless men can invent other ways to occupy space, unless space (as territorialized, as mappable or explorable) gives way to place (occupation, dwelling and being lived in), until space is conceived in terms other than according to the logic of penetration, colonization and domination, unless they can accord women their own space, and negotiate the occupation of shared spaces, unless they no longer regard space as the provenance of their own self-expression and self-creation, unless they respect spaces and places which are not theirs, entering only when invited, and accepting this as a gift, they cannot share in the contributions that women may have to offer in reconceiving space and place.

While Irigaray, to my knowledge, does not explicitly refer to *chora* in any of her writings, none the less her work seems to confirm that its disruptive 'logic' is everywhere at work, even today, in the production of phallocentric discourses and patriarchal modes of domination. *Chora* emblematizes a common manoeuvre used to maintain this domination: the silencing and endless metaphorization of femininity as the condition for men's self-representation and cultural production. This is no less true of Derrida than it is of Plato: their various philosophical models and frameworks depend on the resources and characteristics of a femininity which has been disinvested of its connections with the female, and especially the maternal, body and made to carry the burden of what it is that men cannot explain, cannot articulate or know, that unnameable recalcitrance that men continue to represent as an abyss, as unfathomable, lacking, enigmatic, veiled, seductive, voracious, dangerous and disruptive but without name or place. *Chora* may well serve as one of the earliest models of this appropriation and disenfranchisement of femininity.

The project ahead, or one of them, is to return women to those places from which they have been dis- or re-placed or expelled, to occupy those positions – especially those which are not acknowledged as positions – partly in order to show men's invasion and occupancy of the whole of space, of space as their own and thus the constriction of spaces available to women, and partly in order to be able to experiment with and produce the possibility of occupying, dwelling or living in new spaces, which in their turn help generate new perspectives, new bodies, new ways of inhabiting.

REFERENCES

Antonopoulos, A. 1992: 'Feminism's Other: On the Politics and Poetics of Domesticity in Postmodern Texts', unpublished paper presented at the Canadian Society for Women and Philosophy, Toronto: York University.

Battersby, C. 1992: 'Hermaphrodites of Art and Vampires of Practice: Architectural Theory and Feminist Theory', *Journal of Philosophy and the Visual Arts*, 3.

Bergren, A. 1992: 'Architecture, Gender, Philosophy', in J. Whiteman, J. Kipnis and R. Burdett (eds), *Strategies in Architecture*, Cambridge, MA: MIT Press.

Bloomer, J. 1992: 'Abodes of Theory and Flesh: Tables of Bower', *Assemblage*, 17: 7–29.

Colomina, B. (ed.) 1992: *Sexuality and Space*, Princeton, NJ: Princeton Architectural Press.

Cornell, D. 1992: *Beyond Accommodation*, New York: Routledge.

Deleuze, G. 1991: 'Postscript on the Societies of Control', *October*, 59, Winter: 3–7.

Derrida, J. 1983: 'The Principle of Reason: The University in the Eyes of its Pupils', *Diacritics*, Fall: 3–20.

Derrida, J. 1985: 'Point de folie – maintenant l'architecture', in B. Tschumi (ed.), *La case vide la vilette*, London: Architectural Association.

Derrida, J. 1986: 'Architecture "Where Desire May Live"', *Domus*, 671, April: 17–24.

Derrida, J. 1988: 'Why Peter Eisenman Writes Such Good Books', *Threshold* (Journal of the School of Architecture, University of Illinois at Chicago), 4: 99–105.

Derrida, J. 1991: ' "Eating Well", or the Calculation of the Subject: An Interview with Jacques Derrida', in E. Cadava, P. Connor and J.-L. Nancy (eds), *Who Comes After the Subject?*, New York: Routledge.

Derrida, J. 1993: 'Chora', in J. Kipnis (ed.), *Choral Works: A Collaboration between Peter Eisenman and Jacques Derrida*, New York: Rizzoli Architectural Press.

Douglas, M. 1991: 'The Idea of a Home: A Kind of Space', *Social Research*, 46, Spring: 287–307.

Freud, S. 1895: *Project for a Scientific Psychology*, Standard Edition of the Complete Psychological Works of Sigmund Freud, Oxford: Hogarth Press, Vol. 1.

Heidegger, M. 1978: 'Letter on Humanism', in D.F. Krell (ed.), *The Basic Writings from Being and Time (1927) to The Task of Thinking (1964)*, London: Routledge and Kegan Paul.

Irigaray, L. 1983: 'Comment et où habiter?', *Cahiers du Grif*, 26, Mars.

Irigaray, L. 1984: *Ethique de la différence sexuelle*, Paris: Minuit.

Irigaray, L. 1985: *Speculum of the Other Woman*, trans. Gillian C. Gill, New York: Cornell University.

Irigaray, L. 1985/6: 'Language, Persephone and Sacrifice: An Interview', *Borderlines*, Winter: 30–2.

Irigaray, L. 1992: *Elemental Passions*, New York: Routledge.

Irigaray, L. 1993: *Je, tous, nous: Toward a Culture of Difference*, New York: Routledge.

Martin, L. 1990: 'Transpositions: On the Intellectual Origins of Tschumi's Architectural Theory', *Assemblage*, 11: 23–35.

Plato 1977: *Timaeus and Critias*, trans. D. Lee, Harmondsworth: Penguin.

Spivak, G. 1987: *In Other Words*, New York: Routledge.

Tschumi, B. 1983: 'Illustrated Index: Themes from the Manhattan Transcripts', *Architectural Association Files*, 4, July: 65–74.

Whitford, M. 1991: *Luce Irigaray: Philosophy in the Feminine*, London: Routledge.

Wigley, M. 1987: 'Postmortem Architecture: The Taste of Derrida', *Perspecta*, 23: 158–72.

Wigley, M. 1989: 'The Translation of Architecture: The Production of Babel', *Assemblage*, 8: 7–21.

5. The Invisible *Flâneur*

Elizabeth Wilson

The relationship of women to cities has long preoccupied reformers and philanthropists.[1] In recent years the preoccupation has been inverted: the Victorian determination to control working-class women has been replaced by a feminist concern for women's safety and comfort in city streets. But whether women are seen as a problem of cities, or cities as a problem for women, the relationship remains fraught with difficulty. With the intensification of the public/private divide in the industrial period, the presence of women on the streets and in public places of entertainment caused enormous anxiety, and was the occasion for any number of moralizing and regulatory discourses. In fact, the fate and position of women in the city was a special case of a more general alarm and ambivalence which stretched across the political spectrum. It is true that some – predominantly liberals – expressed an optimistic and excited response to the urban spectacle. Perhaps not surprisingly, those who stood to gain most from industrial urbanization were the ones that praised it most strongly: the new entrepreneurs, the rising bourgeois class. For them the cities – above all the great city, the metropolis – offered an unprecedented and astonishing variety of possibilities, stimuli and wealth. The development of a consumer and spectacular society on a scale not previously known represented opportunities for progress, plenty and a more educated and civilized populace.[2]

Hostility to urbanization was more likely to come from opposite ends of the political spectrum. On the Left, Engels was deeply critical not only of the slum and factory conditions in which the majority had to survive, but equally of the indifference and selfishness with which people behaved in crowds where no one knew anyone else. By contrast with an implied natural order of things, the new urban forms of human interaction had about them 'something repulsive, something against which human nature rebels'. Urban life encouraged 'the brutal indifference, the unfeeling isolation of each in his private interest' (Engels 1962: 56). The utopian socialist William Morris hated the dirt and poverty of the industrialized town, and advocated a return to medieval village architecture and ways of life – a life in which women would be once more safely ensconced in the domestic sphere (Morris 1986: 234–5). That Morris is still so popular on the Left (especially with the men), and received so uncritically, is an index of the strength of left-wing romantic anti-urbanism.

Right-wing critics of urban life equally harked back to an organic rural community. They feared the way in which the break-up of tradition in cities led to the undermining of authority, hierarchy and dignity. The menace of the cities was not only disease and poverty; even more threatening were the spectres of sensuality, democracy and revolution. One particular cause for alarm was the way in which urban life undermined patriarchal authority. Young, unattached men and women flocked to the towns to find more remunerative work. There, freed from the bonds of social control, they were in danger of succumbing to temptations of every kind; immorality, illegitimacy, the breakdown of family life and bestial excess appeared to threaten from all sides. Perhaps worse was that, in the rough and tumble of the city street and urban crowd, distinctions of rank of every kind were blurred.

PUBLIC WOMEN

In particular, female virtue and respectability were hard to preserve in this promiscuous environment. 'Who are these somebodies whom nobody knows?' famously enquired William Acton (1968) in his survey of prostitution, published in 1857; and prostitution was the great fear of the age. Evangelical reformers in the Britain of the 1830s and 1840s wrote impassioned tracts in which they described this, the 'great social evil', as a plague that was rotting the very basis of society, and they campaigned for its eradication. Significantly, they often linked prostitution to the ideals of the French Revolution. Prostitution, then, was not only a real and ever-present threat; it was also a metaphor for disorder and the overturning of the natural hierarchies and institutions of society. Rescue, reform and legislation were to rid the cities of this frightful evil (Walkowitz 1980).

The pioneer of investigations into prostitution was the French bureaucrat, Alexandre Parent-Duchtelet, whose survey of the problem appeared in 1836. He favoured a regulatory regime of the kind Foucault has documented, arguing that each prostitute must have her dossier, and that the more information that could be gathered about each individual – the better she was known by the state – the easier would become the task of surveillance.[3] Alain Corbin has studied Parent-Duchtelet's work in other areas of hygiene, his investigations of slaughter houses, for example, and has drawn out the way in which his writings articulate a contradictory ideology of prostitution. In this ideology the prostitute's body is putrefying, and infects the social body with corruption and death; yet at the same time it is a drain which siphons off that which would otherwise corrupt the whole of society. In order to effect this, bourgeois surveillance and regulation were to bring the brothel within a utilitarian regime of control (Corbin 1986).

Parent-Duchatelet's perspective was distinct from that of the British evangelical clergymen and philanthropists, and his stance closer to that of the physician William

Acton. By the 1850s Acton was arguing for the regulation of prostitution from a worldly and cynical perspective far different in tone from that of evangelicals (Acton 1968).

In Britain an intense struggle developed between those who favoured more stringent regulation and those who objected to it. The regulation of prostitutes could all too easily shade over into the regulation of all − or at least all working-class − women. Josephine Butler undertook her campaign against the Contagious Diseases Acts (from 1864) on civil-liberties grounds, and partly because women who were not prostitutes could so easily fall foul of the new ordinances and find themselves subject to arrest and humiliating examination (Butler 1896). Judith Walkowitz has argued that the very existence of these Acts served to separate prostitutes more clearly from other women − and that therefore the regulation of prostitutes in a sense almost created and certainly exacerbated the evil it was intended to contain (Walkowitz 1980).

The prostitute was a 'public woman', but the problem in nineteenth-century urban life was whether every woman in the new, disordered world of the city − the public sphere of pavements, cafés and theatres − was not a public woman and thus a prostitute. The very presence of unattended − unowned − women constituted a threat both to male power and to male frailty. Yet although the male ruling class did all it could to restrict the movement of women in cities, it proved impossible to banish them from public spaces. Women continued to crowd into the city centres and the factory districts.

The movements of middle-class women were more successfully restricted. The development of the bourgeois suburb as a haven of privacy was particularly marked in Britain, serving to 'protect' middle-class women from the rough-and-tumble of the urban street. And these women, even in such a city as Paris, where the exodus to the suburbs did not occur in the same way, were closely guarded. In British society it was the young marriageable woman under thirty years of age who was most rigorously chaperoned; married women, governesses and old maids had a little more − if hardly flattering − freedom (Davidoff 1973).

AMBIVALENCE AND MARGINALITY: EXPERIENCING THE URBAN SPECTACLE

Bourgeois men, by contrast, were free to explore urban zones of pleasure such as − in Paris especially − the Folies Bergères, the restaurant, the theatre, the café and the brothel, where they met working-class women. (In London they were perhaps as likely to visit the masculine haunt of the Pall Mall clubs.) The proliferation of public places of pleasure and interest created a new kind of public person with the leisure to wander, watch and browse: the *flâneur*, a key figure in the critical literature of modernity and urbanization. In literature, the *flâneur* was represented as an archetypal occupant and observer of the public sphere in the rapidly changing and growing great cities of nineteenth-century Europe. He might be seen as a mythological or allegorical figure who represented what was perhaps the most characteristic response of all to the wholly new forms of life that seemed to be developing: ambivalence.

The origins of the word *flâneur* are uncertain; the nineteenth-century *Encyclopaedia Larousse* suggests that the term may be derived from an Irish word for 'libertine'. The writers of this edition of *Larousse* devoted a long article to the *flâneur*, whom they defined as a loiterer, a fritterer away of time. They associated him with the new urban pastimes of shopping and crowd watching. The *flâneur*, *Larousse* pointed out, could exist only in the great city, the metropolis, since provincial towns would afford too restricted a stage for his strolling and too narrow a field for his observations. *Larousse* also commented that although the majority of *flâneur*s were idlers, there were among them artists, and that the multifarious sights of the astonishing new urban spectacle constituted their raw material.[4]

The earliest citation given by *Larousse* comes from Balzac, and the *flâneur* is normally discussed in the context of mid-nineteenth-century Paris. However, at least one discussion of this form of urban individual dates from 1806. An anonymous pamphlet published in that year describes a day in the life of M. Bonhomme, a typical *flâneur* of the Bonaparte era; and clearly set out there are all the characteristics later to be found in the writings of Baudelaire and Benjamin (Anon. n.d.).[5] No one knows, states the anonymous author of this description, how M. Bonhomme supports himself, but he is said to be a rentier, seemingly set free from familial, landowning or mercantile responsibilities to roam Paris at will. The *flâneur* spends most of his day simply looking at the urban spectacle; he observes in particular new inventions; for example, he stops in the place Louis XV 'to examine the signals of the marine telegraph, although he understands nothing about them', and he is fascinated by the many new building works then under way. Public clocks and barometers serve to regulate his day – an indication of the growing importance of precise time-keeping, even for one who was under no regime of paid labour – and he passes the hours by shopping or window-shopping, looking at books, new fashions, hats, combs, jewellery and novelties of all kinds.

A second feature of M. Bonhomme's day is the amount of time he spends in cafés and restaurants; and, significantly, he chooses establishments frequented by actors, writers, journalists and painters – that is, his interests are predominantly aesthetic. During the course of the day, he picks up gossip about new plays, rivalries in the art world, and projected publications, and several times he mentions his eager anticipation of the salon exhibitions of painting. Thirdly, a significant part of the urban spectacle is the behaviour of the lower ranks of society – for example, he watches soldiers, workers and 'grisettes' at an open-air dance. Fourthly, he is interested in dress as a vital component of the urban scene. Fifthly, women play but a minor role in his life. He notices an attractive street vendor, and implies that she may be engaged in prostitution on the side, but there is no indication that he enjoys an active sexual life of his own. On the other hand, a woman painter is mentioned, and the shouts of the manageress of the restaurant he frequents are an indicator of her role as overseer. (Women painters were still quite numerous at this period, while women played an important role in the catering trade, possibly partly because of the conscription of male cooks, bakers and waiters.)

Particularly striking is M. Bonhomme's marginality. He is essentially a solitary onlooker, activated, like Edgar Allan Poe's *Man of the Crowd*, by his fleeting, but continuous and necessary, contact with the anonymous crowd. In his resolution 'to keep a little diary recording all the most curious things he had seen or heard during the course of his wanderings, to fill the void of his nocturnal hours of insomnia' is the germ of the *flâneur*'s future role as writer; it also hints at the boredom and ennui which seem inescapably linked to the curiosity and voyeurism that are so characteristic.

Here, then, is the mid-nineteenth-century *flâneur* rising fully formed in the much earlier context of post-Revolutionary Parisian society, and this first appearance indicates his class location. He is a gentleman; at this period he has retained at least some private wealth, yet he is subtly *déclassé*, and above all he stands wholly outside production.

COMMODIFIED SPACES

Siegfried Kracauer (1937) and Walter Benjamin (1973) – both, of course, Marxist writers associated with the Frankfurt School – wrote of the emergence of the *flâneur* in terms very similar to each other. Kracauer, however, emphasized more strongly the economic determinants of the role. He argued that the 1830s and early 1840s saw the age of 'classic bohemia' in Paris. The bohemian was a student, living in his garret while planning to become a great writer or artist. Many of these students formed relationships and lived with young women from a humbler background – the grisettes. Kracauer (1937) argues that the bohemians came from the lower middle class or petty bourgeoisie of artisans and clerks. Bohemia went into decline, he tells us, with the development of industrial capitalism, when this class was squeezed out as factories replaced workshops and the world of Louis-Philippe was replaced by the Second Empire of Napoleon III, the ultimate society of the spectacle.

For Kracauer, the student bohemian was to be distinguished from the *flâneur* of a later date. Also distinct were the dandies, who in the 1830s and 1840s took possession of the Maison D'Or and Caf' Tortoni in the Boulevarde des Italiens. This street was the centre of fashionable public life, and along it loitered the dandies, the bohemians and the courtesans – but also the population at large. 'Innumerable curious sightseers strolled through these streets on Sundays', writes Siegfried Kracauer: 'All classes of the population received a common and uniform education in the streets . . . their real education. Workers, laughing grisettes, soldiers, the petty bourgeoisie, who have few opportunities for strolling and gazing at shop windows during the week . . . all took the opportunity of gazing their fill on Sundays' (Kracauer 1937: 23).

This special form of public life was played out in a zone that was neither quite public nor quite private, yet which partook of both; the cafés, the *terrasses* and the boulevards, likewise Benjamin's arcades, and, later, the department store and the hotel[6] – these were commodified spaces in which everything was for sale, and to which anyone was free to come, yet they endeavoured to create the atmosphere of the salon or the private house. Here, the glamorous section of society *was* at home; the crowds came to stare at but also to mingle with them. The society which thus constituted itself as a spectacle was a society of outsiders, and the boulevards and cafés offered, as Kracauer puts it, a homeland for these individuals without a home.

Like Benjamin, Kracauer emphasizes the commercialization and commodification of two areas: writing and sexuality. Urban industrial life generated a demand for new forms of writing – the feuilleton, the magazine article. It gave birth to a new kind of literature, a journalistic record of the myriad sights, sounds and spectacles to be found on every corner, in every cranny of urban life. This was every bit as much the case in Britain as in France. It was a literature that was inquisitive, anecdotal, ironic, melancholy, but above all voyeuristic (M. Wolff and Fox 1973). As George Augustus Sala wrote in the London context: 'The things I have seen from the top of an omnibus! . . . Unroofing London in a ride . . . varied life, troubled life, busy, restless, chameleon life . . . Little do you reck that an [observer] is above you taking notes, and, faith, that he'll print them!'[7]

Kracauer tells us that in Paris, 'newspapers had hitherto been purely political organs, with circulations restricted to small groups of readers sharing the same views. Small circulations meant high subscriptions rates, and newspapers had to charge their readers 80 francs a month in order to be able to exist at all.' In the 1830s, however, came the commercialization of the press. Kracauer credits Emile de Girardin, publisher of *La Presse*, with initiating this revolution. Girardin charged only forty francs, but accepted far more advertising, which was easily obtained because of the growing circulation of his paper. This, though, had the further result that the papers became less political, catering rather to a demand for entertainment – amusing articles about everyday life, gossip and, before long, the serialized novel. These developments in turn increased the demand for journalists (Kracauer 1937: 66–7).

Kracauer describes the coming together on the boulevards and in the cafés of upper-class dandies and the new journalists, arguing that these groups were in many ways similar. Both rejected conventional society, yet both were financially dependent upon it, and as a result their attitude towards society was cynical or ironic rather than passionately and committedly oppositional. Their 'blasé attitude' – the attitude which Georg Simmel saw as so characteristic of urban life – was the attitude of men who have been bought: while critical of and opposed to the philistinism of bourgeois society, they were paid to entertain it.

Kracauer argues that sexuality was also commercialized as the grisettes, who had simply lived as unmarried partners with their lovers, were replaced by the *lorettes* (so called because they lived in the Notre Dame de Lorette district), who exchanged sex for money on a less emotionally committed basis. 'Although it was necessarily only the favoured few who succeeded in scaling the giddy heights to which the great courtesans belonged, there were nevertheless a number of honourable intermediary stages, and those who belonged to the boulevards' rank and file had climbed quite a considerable portion of the ladder' (Kracauer 1937: 72). Women who lived by their wits and their sexuality played an important role in the Second Empire, often acting as negotiators, Kracauer claims, in the orgies of speculation and stock-market madness characteristic of Louis Napoleon's reign.

During the Second Empire the decline of bohemia in no way prevented Paris from becoming an even more dazzling spectacle than it had been in the 1830s, and in this Paris the *flâneur* replaced the bohemian. At first sight, the *flâneur* appears as the ultimate ironic, detached observer, skimming across the surface of the city and tasting all its pleasures with curiosity and interest. Walter Benjamin writes of the way in which the *flâneur*-as-artist 'goes botanizing on the asphalt' (Benjamin 1973: 26). He is the naturalist of this unnatural environment. (Marcel Proust had already developed the metaphor of the naturalist, comparing the eponymous narrator of *A la recherche du temps perdu*, Marcel, to a botanist. This comparison is made on the occasion when Marcel observes a chance encounter between two homosexuals. This he likens to the conjunction of a rare kind of bee with the orchid which needs its visit in order to be fertilized. The scene when the two men – both known to Marcel, but strangers to each other and from utterly different walks of life – meet is said by Proust to be 'stamped with a strangeness, or if you like a naturalness, the beauty of which steadily increased' (Proust 1981: 627)). This is just how the *flâneur* viewed the multitudinous encounters that occurred every day and thousands of times over in the streets of the great city – and of course the growth of urban life in itself is held to have made possible the very emergence of the 'homosexual identity'.[8]

WOMEN, IDEOLOGY AND THE NEW PUBLIC SPHERE

It is this *flâneur*, the *flâneur* as a man of pleasure, as a man who takes visual possession of the city, who has emerged in postmodern feminist discourse as the embodiment of the 'male gaze'. He represents men's visual and voyeuristic mastery over women. According to this view, the *flâneur*'s freedom to wander at will through the city is essentially a masculine freedom. Thus, the very idea of the *flâneur* reveals it to be a gendered concept. Janet Wolff argues that there could never be a female *flâneur*: the *flâneuse* was invisible (J. Wolff 1985). Griselda Pollock writes of the way in which women – middle-class at least – were denied access to the spaces of the city, even a successful painter such as Berthe Morisot mostly taking as her subject-matter interiors and domestic scenes instead of the cafés and other sites of pleasure so often painted by her male colleagues (Pollock 1988).

Just how did women experience nineteenth-century urban space? Griselda Pollock and Janet Wolff concede that some women at least were permitted access to certain parts of the essentially masculine public domain, but argue that 'the ideology of women's place in the domestic realm permeated the whole of society' (J. Wolff 1985: 37). Yet we cannot automatically accept the nineteenth-century ideological division between public and private spheres on its own terms. For one thing, in practice the private sphere was – and is – also a masculine domain; although the Victorians characterized it as feminine, it was organized for the convenience, rest and recreation of men, not women, and it has been an important part of feminism to argue that the private sphere is the *workplace* of the woman. In addition, the bourgeois home was not in practice a safe haven, least of all for working-class women – domestic servants – confined within it. On the contrary, it was an 'ideal location' for sexual attacks across class boundaries: 'In the attics, basements and backstairs of the Victorian home, that haven of peace and security, housemaids were in permanent contact with a male population whose intentions were often bad . . . while the mistress was at church or on a walk, the big houses of the rich murmured with illicit desires and furtive ambushes' (Barret-Ducrocq 1991: 47, 49–50).

Janet Wolff argues that women *were* wholly excluded from the public sphere:

> *The experience of anonymity in the city, the fleeting, impersonal contacts described by social commentators like Georg Simmel, the possibility of unmolested strolling and observation first seen by Baudelaire, and then analysed by Walter Benjamin, were entirely the experiences of men. By the late nineteenth century, middle-class women had been more or less consigned (in ideology if not in reality) to the private sphere. The public world of work, city life, bars, and cafés was barred to the respectable woman . . . (By the end of the nineteenth century shopping was an important activity for women, the rise of the department store and of the consumer society providing a highly legitimate, if limited, participation in the public sphere. But of course, the literature of modernity . . . [was] not concerned with shopping.) (J. Wolff 1990: 58)*

To substantiate her view, Janet Wolff relies on the theories of Thorstein Veblen, who viewed bourgeois women as vehicles for 'conspicuous consumption', and as the chattels of their husbands. The amazingly elaborate way in which they dressed, in particular, he felt, constructed them as 'signs' for their husbands' wealth. Writing in 1899, however, Veblen was already out of date. He had been influenced by the arguments of the growing dress-reform movement, which rejected fashionable dress entirely, believing it to be ugly as well as unhygienic, unhealthy and restricting – but by 1900 or thereabouts, these radical ideas were beginning to influence mainstream fashion. Women's fashions were following those of men: just as men had converted sporting wear into an urban uniform at the beginning of the nineteenth century, so now women were adopting the 'coat and skirt' for city wear, a style adapted from the riding habit. (In the twentieth century, Chanel and others were to work this style into a universally accepted fashion for women.) In any case, Veblen's wholesale rejection of fashion totally disregarded its role in urban life as communicative text as well as source of pleasure, and ignored the inevitable and necessary function of clothing as the visible form taken by the body in culture. As Theodor Adorno has pointed out, Veblen's analysis is very economistic, and displays a defective understanding of the role played by cultural institutions and representations in general.[9]

It is not always clear whether Janet Wolff perceives the *flâneur* as a gendered concept, or as a descriptive account – or is it both? Is it appropriate to counter this interpretation of an ideology by recourse to empirical fact? Alain Corbin suggests that such a strategy is not legitimate: 'Images and schemas rather than collections of monotonously repeated arguments or denotative discourses should be our object of study' (Corbin 1986: 210) – that is, we are confronted with representations, and these are impossible to counter by means of material evidence, trapped as we are in 'the ultimate labyrinth – history' (Buci-Glucksmann 1986: 220). Yet the distinction Janet Wolff draws between 'ideology' and 'reality' raises serious problems. Ideology, it is implied, bears absolutely no relation to 'reality', and conceivably all women could venture out on to the streets, yet still be, 'in ideology', confined to the home. Ideology thus becomes a rigid and monolithic monument of thought. By an inversion of 'reflectionist' theories of ideology, instead of ideology mirroring reality, reality becomes but a pale shadow of ideology, or even bears no relation to it at all. This approach is unhelpful to the political cause of feminism, since it creates such an all-powerful and seamless ideological system ranged against women, and one upon which they can never make an impact. Griselda Pollock insists on a similar radical division between the 'mental map' of ideology and the 'description of social spaces', although there 'was none the less an overlap between the purely ideological maps and the concrete organisation of the social sphere' (Pollock 1988).

Mary Poovey's approach is more fruitful. Writing of mid-nineteenth-century England, she states:

> *Representations of gender constituted one of the sites on which ideological systems were simultaneously constructed and contested; as such . . . representations of gender . . . were themselves contested images, the sites at which struggles for authority occurred, as well as the locus of assumptions used to underwrite the very authority that authorized these struggles . . .*

> *To describe an ideology as a 'set' of beliefs or a 'system' of institutions and practices conveys the impression of something that is internally organised, coherent and complete . . . Yet . . . what may look coherent and complete in retrospect was actually fissured by competing emphases and interests . . . The middle-class ideology we most often associate with the Victorian period was both contested and always under construction; because it was always in the making it was always open to revision, dispute, and the emergence of oppositional formations. (Poovey 1989: 2–3)*

Janet Wolff's account is, of course, also an ideological and/or representational construction, but I believe its inaccuracies do matter. She states, for example, that middle-class women had 'more or less' been consigned to the home by the closing years of the nineteenth century, yet this was the very period when, in England, they were emerging more and more into the public spaces of the city.

With the growth of white-collar occupations for women, there was a need, for example, for eating establishments where women could comfortably go on their own. The lack of these in London had long been felt. In 1852, one observer had noted that working-class women did frequent public houses – places in which no middle-class person of either sex felt comfortable. By the 1870s guidebooks were beginning to list 'places in London where ladies can conveniently lunch when in town for a day's shopping and unattended by a gentleman' (Thorne 1980: 25, quoting the *Women's Gazette*, 1876). Restaurants as we know them were much commoner in Paris than in London, but by the 1860s were springing up in the British capital too. Crosby Hall, Bishopsgate, opened in 1868, employed waitresses instead of waiters, and 'made special provisions to ensure that women felt comfortable there' (Thorne 1980: 41). These included ladies' lavatories with female attendants. Thereafter the number of eating establishments grew rapidly, with railway-station buffets, refreshment rooms at exhibitions, ladies'-only dining rooms, and the opening of West End establishments such as the Criterion (1874), which specifically catered for women. At the end of the century Lyons, the ABC tearooms, Fullers' tearooms, vegetarian restaurants and the rest rooms and refreshment rooms in department stores had all transformed the middle- and lower-middle-class woman's experience of public life (Thorne 1980: 41). While it is arguable that these provisions precisely indicate the extent of the problem, they hardly support the view that women were 'invisible'.

Nor is it the case that shopping was 'invisible' in the literature of modernity. Quite the contrary: the commodification of which Benjamin wrote was very much to do with shopping, the availability of goods to buy; Emile Zola, Proust, Dickens and many other writers record this aspect of urban life, and, as we saw, shopping and/or window-shopping were a key element in the identity of the *flâneur* as far back as 1806.

The high point of the nineteenth-century shopping revolution was the creation of the department store. Like the arcades, the boulevard and the café, this was an environment half-public, half-private, and it was a space that women *were* able to inhabit comfortably. Although one could argue that shopping was for many women – perhaps the majority – a form of work rather than pleasure, at least for the leisured few it provided the pleasures of looking, socializing and simply strolling – in the department store, a woman, too, could become a *flâneur* (M. Wolff and Fox 1973; Wilson 1985).

THE MALE GAZE: THE WORLD TURNED UPSIDE DOWN?

In her discussion of 'Modernity and the Spaces of Femininity', Griselda Pollock is concerned with representations in the modernist art of Edouard Manet and his contemporaries of a proletarian or *demi-mondaine* female sexuality, by painters who predominantly came from a superior social class. Many of the locations they recorded were sexualized public places in which lower-class women sold their bodies in one way or another to bourgeois men. Respectable middle-class women were, of course, rigidly excluded from such locations. Griselda Pollock writes from within a theoretical tradition that has emphasized the importance of the 'male gaze': the gaze of the *flâneur* articulates and produces a masculine sexuality which in the modern sexual economy enjoys the freedom to look, appraise and possess (Pollock 1988).

This theoretical position derives from the psychoanalysis of Jacques Lacan. Feminist theoreticians influenced by Lacanian psychoanalysis

> *have been particularly concerned with how sexual difference is constructed . . . through the Oedipal process . . . For Lacan, woman cannot enter the world of the symbolic, of language, because at the very moment of the acquisition of language, she learns that she lacks the phallus, the symbol that sets language going through a recognition of difference; her relation to language is a negative one, a lack. In patriarchal structures, thus, woman is located as other (enigma, mystery), and is thereby viewed as outside of (male) language. (Kaplan 1984: 321)*

The male gaze is constructed as voyeuristic, but it does not simply represent conscious desire and potential mastery; its unconscious significance is to 'annihilate the threat that woman (as castrated, and possessing a sinister genital organ) poses' (Kaplan 1984: 323).

This position offers little in the way of a theory of change; yet although many feminists approach it with at best ambivalence,[10] it has gained a perhaps surprising domination over feminist art history, film theory and literary criticism. The use of a Lacanian perspective represented, among other things, a reaction against the 'vulgar reflectionism' of seeing art as a mirror of reality. The result has been, however, not merely to agree that our knowledge of reality is always constructed through discourse and representation, but to render 'reality' a pathetically naive misunderstanding, as the authoritarianism of Lacanian discourse annihilates opposition by rendering it meaningless. Ironically, a theoretical position derived from Lacan, who argued that subjectivity was split and unstable (Eagleton 1991: 144), has resulted in the creation of a theoretical Medusa's head, whose gaze petrifies everything: women are stuck forever in the straitjacket of otherness, struck down and turned to stone by the Male Gaze.[11] We might have expected an emphasis on signifying practices and representations to result in a fluid universe of shifting meanings (rather like the urban spectacle itself). Instead, the opposite has happened, and thus in a curious way the Lacanian discourse replicates or reinforces the ideology it was meant to deconstruct.

Debates and disagreements among feminists seem often to begin as differences in emphasis and end as polarized antagonisms. Although we know that the world is turned upside down when viewed through a gendered lens, by this time we also know that not every feminist sees the same scene through her spectacles, and indeed not every feminist has the same prescription.[12] Janet Wolff, Griselda Pollock and I would all agree, I imagine, that women were exploited and oppressed in the nineteenth-century city, and my points of difference are partly matters of emphasis, although there are two more fundamental underlying disagreements: whether Lacan provides the most helpful available source of theory for feminists; and whether urban space is structured at some fundamental level by gender difference, or whether such constructions are contradictory and shifting.

BLURRING THE LINES OF DEMARCATION

To look at the issue from a slightly different angle, it is a matter for emphasis whether one insists on the dangers or rather the opportunities for women in the cities. It depends on the comparison. Then and now, opportunities were very much according to class and race; yet if we compare the life of urban working-class women with what they had left behind in the countryside, we may well conclude that they were better off in the town. One study of divorce in France at the end of the eighteenth century suggests that the reason divorce was more common in cities was because women had a wider choice of alternative forms of financial support (that is, paid work) and a wider range of alternative housing than in the rural areas (Phillips 1980).[13] Their financial position notwithstanding, women's independence does seem to have increased when they lived in towns. Nevertheless, they certainly remained badly off by comparison with men of their own class. The majority of women led insecure lives at best, and often they existed in conditions of grinding poverty – according to one study there were 60 per cent more pauper women than men in Paris (Leroy-Beaulieu 1873). Yet most became wage labourers, and this offered a minimum of freedom denied the rural worker embedded in the family economy.

There were intermediate zones inhabited by women of indeterminate class and who often escaped the rigid categories into which society tried to force them. The women of the English Pre-Raphaelite circle provide examples of such women, although it is important to remember that they were not typical of Victorian society. Elizabeth Siddall figures in Pre-Raphaelite legend as Dante Gabriel Rossetti's 'Muse' and the epitome of a style of feminity celebrated by the group. In fact, she too was a painter, although her attempts to succeed in this male-dominated calling were fraught with difficulty. Both Rossetti and Ruskin supported her, yet their 'help' and patronage were in different ways ambivalent. The wife and daughter of William Morris worked in subordination to him, assisting his family business, which was his design workshop. The lives of the women of the Pre-Raphaelite circle were not easy, and they were certainly not typical of the period; on the other hand, their lives bear no very close correspondence to the accepted picture of a society in which women were at all times rigidly policed and controlled, or one in which a departure from convention was irreversible and disastrous in terms of respectable society at the time. Indeed William Acton himself acknowledged that outright prostitution was but a passing phase in the lives of many women, and one that by no means usually ended in disaster and death. Annie Miller, at one time associated with Holman Hunt (although probably not his mistress), later married an infantry officer related to the aristocracy (Marsh and Nunn 1989; Marsh 1985). Thus, while it would be unwise to generalize from the varying fates of these women, the feminist analysis of Pre-Raphaelite representations of them in art at the very least underplays or misses a whole range of inconsistencies and contradictions. No matter how carefully these are acknowledged, the psychoanalytic study of 'regimes of meaning' dependent upon largely unconscious processes – the study of 'woman as sign' – too often ends with the *reduction* of woman to sign.[14]

'Femininity' seems to have rested even more uneasily on working-class women. In what is also, of course, a series of literary representations, the philanthropists and reformers of the nineteenth century characterized them as violent, wild and bestial. They were insolent and defied the observers' codes of morality. 'Their carelessness, their frivolity, their audacious impudence are tirelessly catalogued. These indomitable, intoxicated furies seem to fear nothing and nobody' (Barret-Ducrocq 1991: 31). Having in many cases almost no 'private sphere' to be confined to, they thronged the streets – this was one of the major threats to bourgeois order – and to read the journalism of the mid- and late nineteenth century is to be struck by their *presence* rather than their absence.

Nor was it the case that female advancement could only be by means of prostitution in one form or another. There were *flâneuses* in the sense that there were women journalists and writers. George Sand is the most famous example (famous, among other things, for wearing male dress on occasion in order to roam the streets in freedom – a clear indication of the limitations on that freedom); Delphine Gay, who married Emile de Girardin, the newspaper proprietor mentioned earlier, was a most successful novelist, playwright and poet, and had been long before her marriage. Her mother, Sophie Gay, was also an independent woman who supported herself and her daughter by writing, after her husband, a Napoleonic functionary, had fallen from grace. Mme de Girardin wrote in her husband's papers under a male pseudonym, but her biographer states that this was an open secret (D'Heilly 1869), and she wrote under her own name in other publications. Thus, the fact that women writers were forced to take on a male identity indicates the narrow parameters of their freedom; but the convention was also one form of the resistance that too intense an emphasis on ideological discourse occludes.

The feminist accounts I have discussed overemphasize the passivity and victimization of women, and assume too readily that the very clear line of demarcation which the nineteenth-century bourgeoisie attempted to draw between public and private, as between the virtuous and the fallen woman, was actually as clear as it was meant to be. Ideological discourse, ranging from Hegel right through to Mrs Beeton's *Book of Household Management*, constantly reworked this ideology, so that philosophy itself must be described as gendered; yet in attaching so much weight to these constructions we may lose sight of women's own resistance to, and reworkings of, these systems of thought.[15]

THE PROSTITUTE AS METAPHOR

Could not the prostitutes themselves be seen, ultimately, as the *flâneuses* of the nineteenth-century city? Such a suggestion may seem mere romanticism, and no feminist should ever romanticize the prostitute's lot in the way that men have so often done. Certainly, prostitutes, 'women of the streets', never inhabited the streets on the same terms as men (Buck-Morss 1986). Yet to be a prostitute was not inevitably to be a victim – this notion was, and is, a feminist as well as a male romance of prostitution.

Prostitution became, in any case, a metaphor for the whole new regime of nineteenth-century urbanism. Both Baudelaire (1955) and Benjamin (1973) view the metropolis as the site of the commodity and of commodification above all else. Prostitution comes to symbolize commodification, mass production and the rise of the masses, all of which phenomena are linked:

> *Prostitution opens up the possibility of a mythical communion with the masses. The rise of the masses is, however, simultaneous with that of mass production. Prostitution at the same time appears to contain the possibility of surviving in a world in which the objects of our most intimate use have increasingly become mass produced. In the prostitution of the metropolis the woman herself becomes an article that is mass produced. (Benjamin 1985: 40)*

Feminists might condemn Benjamin for equating women with sexuality, and for identifying women as the 'problem' of urban space. He certainly takes as his starting point Baudelaire's assumption that woman is the site of sexuality. In Baudelaire's writings, women represent the loss of nature, which appeared as a key feature of urbanization. The androgynous woman, the lesbian, the prostitute, the childless woman, all indicate new fears and new possibilities, raising questions – even if they do not provide answers – as to the eroticization of life in the metropolis. Benjamin is well aware that Baudelaire 'never once wrote a prostitute poem from the perspective of the prostitute' (Benjamin 1985: 42). Adrienne Monnier, he points out, believed that women readers dislike Baudelaire, whereas men enjoy his work because 'to the men he represents the depiction and transcendence of the lewd side of their libidinal life, or redemption of certain sides of their libidinal life' (Benjamin 1985: 44). On the other hand, we may discern a nostalgia for lost naturalness also in Benjamin's observations – for example, that it is the artificial disguise of cosmetics that renders women 'professional'; we may feel that to write of the lesbian as unnatural, sterile, masculine, is a simple stereotype (Benjamin sees her 'heroic' masculinity as a protest, itself 'modern', against technological urban civilization). As Susan Buck-Morss (1986: 122) has pointed out, Benjamin as much as Baudelaire objectifies the prostitute, and in emphasizing the 'heroism' of 'unnatural' types of urban womanhood, surrounds them with the isolating aura of bourgeois tragedy. For him, as for Baudelaire, the prostitute remains the 'other'. Yet Baudelaire is more than a misogynist (J. Wolff 1985), and it pays to read the Benjamin/Baudelaire commentary, flawed as it may be from a feminist point of view, as an attempt to confront just what this new urban life meant in terms of sexual relations.

Certainly the interpretation of the *flâneur* as masterful voyeur underplays the financial insecurity and emotional ambiguity of the role. While this role was open to one narrow segment of the population only, educated men (and was thus a class-bound concept as well as a gendered one, as Griselda Pollock acknowledges), it, too, often led to poverty and obscurity. An excessive emphasis on 'the Gaze' occludes – ironically – the extent to which the *flâneur* was actually *working* as he loitered along the pavement or delved into the underworld of the 'marginals'. It also prevents us from discerning the enormous anxiety which the discourse on the *flâneur* expresses.

Some writers romanticized the *flâneur* as a tragic figure. Jules Valls (1969), for example, himself a Communard and more politically unambiguous than most of his fellow writers, commented upon the romantic yet fated calling of these new men of the crowd. For him they were the 'Réfractaires' – the refractory ones, the rebels, the refuseniks:

There is . . . a race of men who . . . have sworn to be free; who, instead of accepting the place in life to which they were destined, have wanted to make a place for themselves by dint of their own efforts alone, whether by audacity or talent . . . who have cut across the fields instead of keeping to the main road and who now . . . make their way along the gutters of Paris . . .

The professor who has sold his gown, the officer who has exchanged his tunic . . . the lawyer who has become an actor, the priest who takes up journalism . . . [They are those who] have a mission to complete, a sacred trust to carry out, a flag to defend.

He is a refractory whoever has no roots in life, who has no profession, no standing, no skill . . . whose only baggage . . . is the obsession he makes of art, literature, astronomy,

*magnetism, chiromancy, or who dreams of founding a bank, a school or a religion. (Valls
1969: 148–9)*

And indeed, the *flâneur* characteristically appears as a marginal. Baudelaire aligned himself
with all the marginals of society – with the prostitutes, the ragpickers, the drunkards. It
is not unusual for a rebel of his class to identify with the 'lumpen' part of society; yet
there was more to it than that. Baudelaire anticipated Kracauer and Benjamin in
interpreting the society in which he lived in terms of an overwhelming process of
commodification. The whole society was engaged in a sort of gigantic prostitution;
everything was for sale, and the writer was one of the most prostituted of all since he
prostituted his art. We might say that, as unpleasant as it may be to live out your life as
a hack writer, it is worse to sell your body; and that Baudelaire had more choice – he
voluntarily appropriated the place of the prostitute, and took on that identification rather
than having it thrust upon him by brute necessity.[16] Yet this, to some extent, is to
overlook the desperation which motivates the wanderings of the *flâneur*.

'THE HOME OF THE HESITANT'

For Benjamin the metropolis is a labyrinth. The overused adjective 'fragmentary' is
appropriate here, because what distinguishes great city life from rural existence is that we
constantly brush against strangers; we observe bits of the 'stories' men and women carry
with them, but never learn their conclusions; life ceases to form itself into epic or
narrative, becoming instead a short story, dreamlike, insubstantial or ambiguous (although
the realist novel is also a product of urban life, or at least of the rise of the bourgeoisie
with which urban life is bound up). Meaning is obscure; committed emotion cedes to
irony and detachment; Georg Simmel's 'blasé attitude' is born. The fragmentary and
incomplete nature of urban experience generates its melancholy – we experience a sense
of nostalgia, of loss for lives we have never known, of experiences we can only guess at.

It is Baudelaire's obsession with 'spleen' that Benjamin takes as pointing towards the
deeper meanings of the urban spectacle and the *flâneur*'s apparently inconsequential
existence. At the heart of Benjamin's meditation on the *flâneur* is the ambivalence towards
urban life already mentioned, a sorrowful engagement with the melancholy of cities. This
melancholy seems to arise partly from the enormous, unfulfilled promise of the urban
spectacle, the consumption, the lure of pleasure and joy which somehow seem destined
to be disappointed, or else are undermined by the obvious poverty and exploitation of
so many who toil to bring pleasure to the few.

Benjamin's critique identifies the 'phantasmagoria', the dream world of the urban
spectacle, as the false consciousness generated by capitalism. We may look but not touch,
yet this tantalizing falsity – and even the very visible misery of tramps and prostitutes –
is aestheticized, 'cathected' (in Freudian terms), until we are overcome as by a narcotic
dream. Benjamin thus expresses a utopian longing for something *other than* this urban
labyrinth. This utopianism is a key theme of nineteenth- and twentieth-century writings

about 'modern life'. In Max Weber, in Marxist discourse, in the writings of postmodernism, the same theme is found: the melancholy, the longing for 'the world we have lost' – although precisely what we have lost is no longer clear, and, curiously, the urban scene comes to represent utopia and dystopia *simultaneously*.[17]

There is, however, a further theme in Benjamin's exploration of urban life: that of the sexual life generated by capitalist relations. The city is a labyrinth, and the *flâneur* an embodiment of it. The labyrinth has a specific sexual meaning: male impotence. It is, suggests Benjamin, 'the home of the hesitant. The path of someone shy of arrival at a goal easily takes the form of a labyrinth. This is the way of the (sexual) drive in those episodes which precede its satisfaction' (Benjamin 1985: 40). Voyeurism and commodification lead to the attenuation and deferral of satisfaction. Related to this is Baudelaire's 'spleen'. This mood or temperament determines his vision of the city. Gambling, wandering and collecting are all activities, suggests Benjamin, waged (or wagered) against spleen. And yet the routines of the *flâneur* are entirely monotonous, and Benjamin observes ominously: 'For people as they are today there is only one radical novelty, and that is always the same: death. Petrified unrest is also the formula for the image of Baudelaire's life, a life which knows no development' (Benjamin 1985: 40). The repetitive monotony of the *flâneur*'s regime of strolling is an instance of 'eternal recurrence' – the eternal recurrence of the new, which is 'always ever the same'. And the monster at the heart of the labyrinth is the Minotaur, the monster waiting to kill. Baudelaire's spleen is also a kind of death: 'male impotence – the key figure of solitude' (Buci-Glucksmann 1986: 226).

From this perspective, we might say that there could never be a female *flâneur*, for this reason: that the *flâneur* himself never really existed, being but an embodiment of the special blend of excitement, tedium and horror aroused by many in the new metropolis, and the disintegrative effect of this on the masculine identity. The *flâneur* does indeed turn out to be like Poe's *Man of the Crowd* – a figure of solitude, he is never alone; and, when singled out, he vanishes. He is a figure to be deconstructed, a shifting projection of angst rather than a solid embodiment of male bourgeois power. Benjamin likens him to 'the idler whom Socrates engaged as his partner in discussion in the Athenian market place . . . Only there is no longer a Socrates and so he remains unengaged. And even the slave labour has come to an end which guaranteed him his idleness' (Buci-Glucksmann 1986: 226). He floats with no material base, living on his wits, and, lacking the patriarchal discourse that assured him of meaning, is compelled to invent a new one.

WRENCHING HEROISM FROM DEFEAT

The *flâneur* represented not the triumph of masculine power, but its attenuation. A wanderer, he embodies the Oedipal under threat. The male gaze has failed to annihilate the castrate, woman. On the contrary, anonymity annihilates *him*. The *flâneur* represents masculinity as unstable, caught up in the violent dislocations that characterized urbanization. Christine Buci-Glucksmann suggests that in Baudelaire desire is polarized between perversity and a 'mystical consummation' – a split we still consider the key to Victorian sexuality, and which remains with us in one form or another. The split between the two is constitutive of male impotence; and the metaphors of stone and petrification in Baudelaire's poetry hint at this ruin of desire (and also suggest, she says, a partial convergence of Benjamin's analysis of Baudelaire with Lacanian thought) (Buci-Glucksmann 1986: 226).

The turbulent industrial city is a 'transgressive' space, which 'dislocates established frontiers and forces apparent opposites together in thought' (Buci-Glucksmann 1986: 221; Petro 1989). Such is the *mise en scène* of this disintegration of masculine potency. It is an agoraphobic, giddy space, productive of hysteria, terror. The image of the labyrinth conceals this other way of experiencing the threat of urban space – as too open, causing whomsoever ventures into it to become totally destabilized. Agoraphobic space tempts the individual who staggers across it to do anything and everything – commit a crime, become a prostitute. The only defence against transgressive desire is to turn either oneself or the object of desire to stone. One such attempt may be the representation of women in art as petrified, fixed sexual objects. Unfortunately, women, the 'mass produced' of urban space, always rise up again.

In the labyrinth the *flâneur* effaces himself, becomes passive, feminine. In the writing of fragmentary pieces, he makes of himself a blank page upon which the city writes itself. It is a feminine, placatory gesture – yet he is still endangered. The Minotaur of some horrible love object – a decayed prostitute, an androgyne – still waits round every corner. And in the long run he, too, becomes sinister and dangerous; the *flâneur* himself becomes the Minotaur, Peter Lorre's 'M', a forerunner of the serial killer with which contemporary popular culture is so preoccupied. Clearly Hannibal Lecter, in the film *The Silence of the Lambs*, does represent the Minotaur. He eats his victims, and he is, like the Minotaur, trapped at the centre of a labyrinth (although this is but the latest reworking of a founding cliché of the horror film).

It is, then, the *flâneur*, not the *flâneuse*, who is invisible. He dissembles the perversity and impossibility of his split desires, attempting an identification with their object, and wrenching his 'heroism' out of this defeat: 'The pageant of fashionable life and the thousands of floating existences – criminals and kept women – which drift about in the underworld of a great city... prove to us that we have only to open our eyes to recognise our heroism' (Baudelaire 1955: 128). The heroism – for both sexes – is in surviving the disorientating space, both labyrinthine and agoraphobic, of the metropolis. It lies in the ability to discern among the massed ranks of anonymity the outline of forms of beauty and individuality appropriate to urban life. The act of creating meaning, seemingly so arbitrary, becomes heroic in itself.

Today we are still preoccupied with a devastating new series of changes wrought on our cities by further developments in capitalist relations. It is important for us to take note of the ways in which renewal may create new forms of gendered space, based on the attempt to recall conceptions of difference appropriate to a time long gone (Wilson 1991). Many planners attempted this in the late nineteenth and early twentieth centuries, striving to bring back the lost village, the garden city, the rural family. The question that remains unanswered today – and indeed it was seldom posed with absolute directness by the reformers – is whether sexuality is being or has been entirely commodified by capitalism; whether urban reform could prevent or has prevented this; and what, really, we think about it.

Ultimately more truthful than the zeal of the reformer was the disturbed glance of the *flâneur*, recording with stoicism the challenge to patriarchal thought and existence made by the presence of women in cities. Contemporary debates concerning rape, pornography and sexual harassment testify that we have not solved these problems; nor have they gone away.

NOTES

1 The theme of this article is touched on in Wilson (1991). The immediate stimulus for it was the 'Cracks in the Pavement' (Women and City Spaces) conference organized by Lynne Walker and the Design Museum in April 1991. I am much indebted to all those who participated in the lively discussions that took place on that occasion, and my especial thanks to Lynne Walker for inviting me.

2 See, for example, Robert Vaughan (1843); Andrew Lees (1985) discusses at length attitudes towards urbanization in Europe and the United States.

3 Alexandre Parent-Duchtelet (1836: 366–7, 370) writes: 'Public women, left to their own devices and free of surveillance during the anarchy of the first years of the first revolution, abandoned themselves to all the disorders which, during this disastrous period, were favoured by the state of the society; soon the evil became so great that it excited universal outrage, and . . . in 1796 the municipal authorities ordered a new census . . . registration was always considered the most important means of arresting the inevitable disorder of prostitution. Is it not in fact necessary to get to know the individuality of all those who come to the attention of the police?'

4 *Larousse* heads the entry *flâneur/flâneuse*, but refers to the *flâneur* as masculine throughout. The entry also notes a second meaning for *flâneuse*, as the name of a kind of reclining chair, of which there is a line illustration. It looks like an extended deck chair, and welcomes its occupant with womanly passivity.

5 I am very grateful to Tony Halliday for his generosity in giving me this reference, and for sharing his knowledge of the period with me.

6 There exists an extensive literature on the department store. See, for example, Miller (1981), Williams (1982) and Bowlby (1985).

7 See Sala (1971: 220). In Paris, women were not allowed to ride on the tops of buses (Buck-Morss 1986).

8 This view has been developed by McIntosh (1968). See also Bray (1982), D'Emilio (1984), and Duberman, Vicinus and Chancey (1990).

9 See Adorno (1981); Veblen (1957). For a further, and most insightful, commentary on fashion as representation, see Kaja Silverman (1986).

10 Feminist criticism of the Lacanian tradition has often been from within an alternative psychoanalytic perspective (Sayers 1986; Ryan 1991; Hamer 1990).

11 As Susan Buck-Morss (1986) has pointed out, the image of the Medusa's head is frequently used to refer to the castrating potential of the urban woman, and especially the

woman of the revolutionary crowd. See Neil Hertz (1983). There is a feminist tradition of the subversion of this image; see Hélène Cixous (1980).

12 Ocular imagery is a contested issue, and much postmodern discourse has criticized the overvaluation of the visual – the visual terrorism of modernism being held to be one of its major problems. Doreen Massey (1991: 45), for example, writes: 'It is now a well-established argument, from feminists, but not only from feminists, that modernism both privileged vision over the other senses and established a *way* of seeing from the point of view of an authoritative, privileged, and male, position . . . the privileging of vision impoverishes us through deprivation of other forms of sensory perception.' Luce Irigaray made a similar point in *Speculum de L'Autre Femme* (1974). Martin Jay, however, writes, in the context of a discussion of the work of Michel Foucault, of 'a discursive or paradigm shift in twentieth-century French thought in which the denigration of vision supplanted its previous celebration'. He suggests that 'it may be time to begin probing the costs as well as benefits of the anti-ocular counter-enlightenment. Its own genealogy needs to be demystified, not in order to restore a naive faith in the nobility of sight, but rather to cast a little light on the manifold implications of its new ignobility.' See Martin Jay (1986). The feminist critique of visualism thus becomes part of a new problem, rather than the solution of an old one.

13 My thanks to Tony Halliday for this reference.

14 Griselda Pollock (written in collaboration with Deborah Cherry), 'Woman as Sign in Pre-Raphaelite Literature: The Representation of Elizabeth Siddall', in Pollock, *Vision and Difference*. This is not to deny the very sensitive analysis of representations of Elizabeth Siddall in its own terms.

15 The feminist literature on this subject is too vast to cite, but for an interesting discussion of some of the issues, see Rosaldo (1980).

16 My thanks to Christine Battersby for this suggestion – part of the discussion at the 'Cracks in the Pavement' conference (see note 1).

17 This is a theme pursued, for example, in Jameson (1984); see also Kroker and Cook (1986); Kroker and Kroker (1988); and Alex Callinicos suggests some reasons for the aestheticization of the contemporary urban scene (Jameson's 'hallucinatory euphoria') in 'Reactionary Postmodernism?' (Boyne and Rattansi 1990).

REFERENCES

Acton, W. 1968: *Prostitution*, ed. P. Fryer, London: MacGibbon and Kee.

Adorno, T. 1981: 'Veblen's Attack on Culture', in *Prisms*, trans. S. and S. Weber, Cambridge, MA: MIT Press.

Anon. n.d. (1806): *Le Flaneur au Salon, ou M. Bonhomme, Examen Joyeux des Tableaux, Ml de Vaudevilles*, Paris.

Barret-Ducrocq, F. 1991: *Love in the Time of Victoria*, trans. J. Hower, London: Verso.

Baudelaire, C. 1955: 'The Salon of 1846', in *The Mirror of Art: Critical Studies by Charles Baudelaire*, London: Haldon.

Benjamin, W. 1973: *Charles Baudelaire: A Lyric Poet in the Era of High Capitalism*, trans. H. Zohn, London: New Left Books.

Benjamin, W. 1985: 'Central Park', *New German Critique*, 34, Winter: 32–58.

Bowlby, R. 1985: *Just Looking: Consumer Culture in Dreiser, Gissing and Zola*, London: Methuen.

Boyne, R. and Rattansi, A. (eds) 1990: *Postmodernism and Society*, Basingstoke: Macmillan Education.

Bray, A. 1982: *Homosexuality in Renaissance England*, London: Gay Men's Press.

Buci-Glucksmann, C. 1986: 'Catastrophic Utopia; The Feminine as Allegory of the Modern', *Representations*, 14: 124–52.

Buck-Morss, S. 1986: 'The *Flâneur*, the Sandwichman and the Whore: The Politics of Loitering', *New German Critique* (second special issue on Walter Benjamin), 39, Fall: 99–140.

Butler, J. 1896: *Memories of a Great Crusade*, London.

Cixous, H. 1980: 'The Laugh of the Medusa', in E. Marks and I. de Courtivron (eds), *New French Feminisms*, Brighton: University of Massachusetts Press.

Corbin, A. 1986: 'Commercial Sexuality in Nineteenth Century France: A System of Images and Regulations', *Representations* (special issue on the body), 14: 153–78.

Davidoff, L. 1973: *The Best Circles: Society, Etiquette and the Season*, London: Croom Helm.

Duberman, M.B., Vicinus, M. and Chancey, G., Jr (eds) 1990: *Hidden From History: Reclaiming the Gay and Lesbian Past*, Harmondsworth: Penhuin.

Eagleton, T. 1991: *Ideology: An Introduction*, London: Verso.

D'Emilio, J. 1984: 'Capitalism and Gay Identity', in A. Snitow, C. Stansell and S. Thompson (eds), *Desire: The Politics of Sexuality*, London: Virago.

Engels, F. 1962: *The Condition of the Working Class in England in 1844*, Moscow: Progress.

Hamer, D. 1990: 'Significant Others', *Feminist Review*, 34: 134–51.

D'Heilly, G. 1869: *Madame E. de Girardin (Delphine Gay): Sa Vie et Ses Oeuvres*, Paris.

Hertz, N. 1983: 'Medusa's Head: Male Hysteria under Political Pressure', *Representations*, I, 4: 179–210.

Irigaray, L. 1974: *Speculum de l'autre femme*, Paris.

Jameson, F. 1984: 'Postmodernism, or the Cultural Logic of Late Capitalism', *New Left Review*, 146: 53–92.

Jay, M. 1986: 'In the Empire of the Gaze: Foucault and the Denigration of Vision in Twentieth Century French Thought', in D.C. Hoy (ed.), *Foucault: A Critical Reader*, Oxford: Blackwell.

Kaplan, E.A. 1984: 'Is the Gaze Male?', in A. Snitow, C. Stansell and S. Thompson (eds), *Desire: The Politics of Sexuality*, London: Virago.

Kracauer, S. 1937: *Offenbach and the Paris of his Time*, trans. G. David and E. Mosbacher, London: Constable.

Kroker, A. and Cook, D. 1986: *The Postmodern Scene: Excremental Culture and Hyper-aesthetics*, Basingstoke: St Martin's Press.

Kroker, A. and Kroker, M. (eds) 1988: *Body Invaders: Sexuality and the Postmodern Condition*, Basingstoke: Macmillan Education.

Lees, A. 1985: *Cities Perceived: Urban Society in European and American Thought, 1820–1940*, Manchester: Manchester University Press.

Leroy-Beaulieu, P. 1873: *Le Travail des Femmes au XIX Siècle*, Paris.

Marsh, J. 1985: *The Pre-Raphaelite Sisterhood*, New York: Quartet.

Marsh, J. and Nunn, P.G. 1989: *Women Artists and the Pre-Raphaelite Movement*, London: Virago.

Massey, D. 1991: 'Flexible Sexism', *Society and Space*, 9, I: 300–7.

McIntosh, M. 1968: 'The Homosexual Role', *Social Problems*, 16: 182–92.

Miller, M. 1981: *The Bon Marché: Bourgeois Culture and the Department Store, 1869–1920*, London: Princeton University Press.

Morris, W. 1986: *News From Nowhere, and Selected Writings and Designs (1890)*, Harmondsworth: Hamilton.

Parent-Duchtelet, A. 1836: *De La Prostitution Dans La Ville de Paris*, Paris.

Petro, P. 1989: *Joyless Streets: Women and Melodramatic Representation in Weimar Germany*, Princeton, NJ: Princeton University Press.

Phillips, R. 1980: *Family Breakdown in Late Eighteenth Century France: Divorces in Rouen, 1792–1803*, Oxford: Clarendon Press.

Pollock, G. 1988: 'Modernity and the Spaces of Feminity', in *Vision and Difference: Femininity, Feminism and the Histories of Art*, London: Routledge.

Pollock, G. with Cherry, D. 1988: 'Woman as Sign in Pre-Raphaelite Literature', in *Vision and Difference: Femininity, Feminism and the Histories of Art*, London: Routledge.

Poovey, M. 1989: *Uneven Developments: The Ideological Work of Gender in Mid-Victorian England*, London: Virago.

Proust, M. 1981: 'Cities of the Plain', Part One, *Remembrance of Things Past*, Vol. 2, trans. C.K. Scott Moncrieff and T. Kilmartin, London: Chatto and Windus.

Rosaldo, M.Z. 1980: 'The Uses and Abuses of Anthropology', *Signs*, 5, 3: 100–2.

Ryan, J. 1991: 'Letter', *Feminist Review*, 38: 118–20.

Sala, G.A. 1971 (1859): *Twice Around the Clock*, Leicester: Leicester University Press.

Sayers, J. 1986: *Sexual Contradictions: Psychology, Psychoanalysis and Feminism*, London: Tavistock Publications.

Silverman, K. 1986: 'Fragments of a Fashionable Discourse', in T. Modleski (ed.), *Studies in Entertainment: Critical Approaches to Mass Culture*, Bloomington: Indiana University Press.

Thorne, R. 1980: 'Places of Refreshment in the Nineteenth Century City', in A.D. King (ed.), *Buildings and Society: Essays on the Social Development of the Built Environment*, London: Routledge and Kegan Paul.

Valls, J. 1969 (1857) 'Les Réfractaires', in *Oeuvres Complètes*, Vol. II, Paris.

Vaughan, R. 1843: *The Age of Great Cities*, London.

Veblen, T. 1957: *The Theory of the Leisure Class*, London: Unwin.

Walkowitz, J. 1980: *Prostitution and Victorian Society: Women, Class and the State*, Cambridge: Cambridge University Press.

Williams, R. 1982: *Dream Worlds: Consumption in Late Nineteenth Century France*, Berkeley: University of California Press.

Wilson, E. 1985: *Adorned in Dreams: Fashion and Modernity*, London: Virago.

Wilson, E. 1991: *The Sphinx in the City*, London: University of California Press.

Wolff, J. 1985: 'The Invisible *Flâneuse*: Women and the Literature of Modernity', *Theory, Culture and Society*, 2, 3: 37–46.

Wolff, J. 1990: 'Feminism and Modernism', in *Feminine Sentences: Essays on Women and Culture*, Berkeley: University of California Press.

Wolff, M. and Fox, C. 1973: 'Pictures from the Magazines', in H.J. Dyos and M. Wolff (eds), *The Victorian City*, Vol. II, London: Routledge and Kegan Paul.

6. 'Drunk with the Glitter': Consuming Spaces and Sexual Geographies

Gillian Swanson

Narratives of nineteenth-century urban development discussed in this chapter tell of women pressing themselves into the spaces of modern city life, contributing to a spatial recasting of the metropolis. While these may seem to contradict a common contemporary view that women were – and are – absent from city space, that the city has been inhospitable to them and their interests, the concerns voiced in nineteenth-century culture over the impact of such transformations nevertheless equally confirm a conception that the feminine and public life are antipathetic.[1] Women are perceived as *intruding* in the public spaces of city life when they use them as a domain of social presence.

As Natalie Zemon Davies points out in her study of the growing cities of sixteenth-century France, women had played diverse economic and social parts in urban life well before the period dealt with in this essay, even if they were restricted in their entry into particular arenas, such as the political domain (Zemon Davies 1987: 68–71). The extent to which – and the forms by which – women are seen to 'enter' or 'intrude' is indicative of a new scrutiny accorded to them due to changed patterns and conditions of participation, rather than evidence of an actual prior absence from public life. My concern is with the reasons that women and their activities are singled out – at particular moments and under particular circumstances – as a sign of the disintegration of legitimate categories and demarcations of social arrangement, and in those spaces and activities which are understood in terms of the preservation or erosion of sexual difference.

For as lines demarcating public and private were redrawn in the changing geographies of the nineteenth-century metropolis, the feminine became used as a motif of instabilities considered to be distinctive and symptomatic of modern city life. The sexual was identified as a key aspect of the dangers inherent in new social relations. The association between the feminine and the sexual thus provided the conditions for the woman in city space, the public woman, to be used as a sign of urban pathology.

The identification of the consuming woman towards the end of the nineteenth century shows the meanings of the sexualized, public woman being extended to new sites and inscribed upon a newly modernized femininity, formed from the development of commerce and the commodified entertainments of urban centres. The idea that women's public presence is disruptive has depended upon a conception of an unruly feminine desire to consume, which, following the escalation of the consumption industries from the mid-nineteenth century, has been used to testify to the 'inauthenticity' of city life. In medico-moral writings as well as social commentary on the modern city, the female consumer became indicative of the impact of new economic relations on both social and sexual life. In such urban commentaries, women were figured as insufficiently in command of the disciplines by which a public subjectivity may be achieved, too close to the corporeal to be coherently featured in narratives of a rational urban presence; hence they came to stand for the derogation of modern consumer culture.

As nineteenth-century urban culture transformed the relations of spaces and bodies in geographies of sexual difference, consumption was used as a means of addressing the public management of individuals. I will examine the history of these awkward and revealing alliances, the historical pressure of our conception of activities of consumption and its connection to the feminine, and their impact on the way we understand the relation of women and the city. The purpose here is to redraw the relation of the individual and the social, sexual difference and social management and the relation of women and consumption. I will suggest that to do so we need to resist models that assume a dichotomized sexual identity that is aligned with a divide between public and private spaces and identities; instead we may use an ethical model of consumption to focus on the forms of exchange conducted in civic life.

SHOCKS AND EXCITATIONS: PATHOLOGIES OF FEMININITY

In the last half of the nineteenth century and the first part of the twentieth, the technologies of urban life, mass consumption and commodified entertainments restructured perceptual and experiential contexts and recast the spatialization of contemporary subjectivity (Petro 1987). As the redrawing of lines between the public and the private challenged the boundaries of dichotomized sexual difference, so the feminine was used a motif for the instabilities associated with the transformation of social life.

The legacy of woman's relation to pleasure, her susceptibility to passion, was seen in eighteenth-century liberal contract theory to prevent her gaining a mastery of rational forms of self-discipline and justice. It was a corporeal susceptibility to passion, the emotions and sentiment that constituted women's difference and justified her containment within the domestic sphere (Pateman 1989; Laqueur 1987).[2] It was also used to explain her relation to derogated forms of cultural activity, specifically the popular novel in its connection to sentiment. As her 'untutored, "primitive" psyche' rendered her susceptible to the corrupting effects of 'flights of fancy', the draining sensuality that novel-reading represented could be marked in the nineteenth century by images of

Victorian women 'who spent much of their middle-class girlhoods prostrate on chaises-longues with their heads buried in "worthless novels"' (Douglas 1977, cited in Modleski 1986: 41). A development from this can be seen in debates over the development of the 'sensation novel' in the 1880s and 1890s. The development, and popularity, of this form of writing were seen as a symptom of the potential of modern urban life to irritate and excite emotion and senses, thereby draining the subject of the moral capacity for self-regulation and instigating 'morbid addictions', calling on the metaphor of a pathological feminine body which posed a threat for both public and private life (Bourne-Taylor 1988: 1–7, 30–9). The coupling of inertia with the threat of an uncontrollable and irrational force is made in a language used to address both the dangers of women's sensuality and those of the voracious mob, thirsty for pleasure, liable to surge lawlessly forth (Kaplan 1986: 44).

A reciprocal association between the working-class mob and feminine sensuality is made according to a prerequisite; the development of city life and its particular forms of social contact and public movement. This is what allows such an association to impact upon a concept of public urban femininity that is more generalized than the visibility offered to working-class female sexuality in the figure of the prostitute. For as I will show, in the second half of the nineteenth century an exchange develops between the meanings of prostitution – embodying working-class urban femininity – and those of the middle-class female consumer, establishing the two ends of a spectrum of pathological sexuality whereby women in general become identified as a disturbance to public life.[3]

Among other things, the different relations between public and private that are constituted within the city and newly developing forms of mobility offer a 'promiscuous sociability'.[4] As the development of train travel in the middle of the century offers connections between sights conventionally held apart by the time and space of pre-modern travel, the connection between this technology's reorganization of the subject in space and the development of modern forms of perception are also evident in the restructuring of city space (Shivelbusch 1979). The *flâneur*, as much as the train passenger, is constituted in terms of a modern sensibility whose moral and social character is endangered by the 'shocks' of modern life, shocks whose other side is evident in a fascination with the sensations offered by new forms of mobility and spatial horizons.[5] This refiguration of perception is harnessed to the development of a panoramic gaze; a mobile gaze, collapsing the relations of space and time. As objects are removed from their immediate and unique spatiality, their arrangement around the motion of train travel or the wandering of the *flâneur* robs them of authenticity. This different mode of encountering objects, drawn from exotic and dispersed locations, also characterizes the organization of the display of commodities in the department store from the 1850s (Shivelbusch 1979).

One of the most disturbing aspects noted in the development of this 'panoramic' perception was its elimination of difference as individual views were merged in a panoramic world that stretched around the subject's viewpoint in an ever-changing succession of tableaux. The collapse of boundaries that located the subject in an authoritative relation to space was linked to an altered moral sensibility that it was feared would undermine 'family sentiments' (Shivelbusch 1979: 71). Such moral questions were also evident in proscriptions identifying the dangers associated with women travelling by train.

In the modern city, it was the *flâneur* who was put in touch with an expansive city space and its sights as he strolled through the crowd, a private subject who, in Susan Buck-Morss's words, 'dreamed himself out into the world' in an 'abstracted' imaginary relation that was seen as endemic to urban culture's newly diverse stimuli, always on the border of engulfing the individual and rendering (him) passive (1986: 103). The perceptual attitude the *flâneur* represented was one constitutively linked to a phase in the development of a modern experience. As the earlier arcades were superseded by crowded pavements, the individualized spatial and perceptual mode he represented became incorporated into the generalized modern perception of the crowd, in what came to be termed 'the society of mass consumption' (Buck-Morss 1986: 104). This presupposed an *absorption* in the panoramic gaze – a spatial and perceptual relation that emphasized mobility and the succession of sights; an expansiveness created by the display of goods in the open arrangement of counters and plate-glass windows in the department stores, the developing forms of entertainment such as theatre and music-hall 'spectacles', later to be condensed in images of a proliferation of commodities on the cinema screen.

Walter Benjamin's connection between the *flâneur* and the prostitute has come to identify an ambivalence inherent in the nineteenth-century urban experience and its connection to commerce (Benjamin 1983: 35–66). But in the increased scrutiny of the prostitute as a figure in nineteenth-century topographies, we can also see evidence of a concern over the new relations offered to women in the restructuring of city space. The prostitute came to represent:

> the potential of an intolerable and dangerous sexuality, a sexuality which is out of bounds precisely as a result of the woman's revised relation to space, her new ability to 'wander' (and hence to 'err') . . . the prostitute ostentatiously exhibited the commodification of the human body, the point where the body and exchange value coincided . . . the new status of the body as exchangeable and profitable image. (Doane 1991: 263)

The prostitute, generally understood to be barren, was seen as an 'unproductive commodity'; without value and eroding value. Programmes of hygienic regulation of prostitution following the 1860s were based on the assertion by Jean Baptiste Parent-Duchatelet that the characteristics ascribed to prostitutes were the outcomes of pathologies specific to commercial urban society, products of the city's vices (Laqueur 1989: 337). As the public body became the centre of a nineteenth-century discourse concerning the problematic nature of value, the potency of its invocation in this female image lay in its connection to the way the economy now situated the *male* body as object of exchange, through the new relations of salaried labour.[6] As the exchangeability of the body turned it into a commodity, its most powerful form of management was identified as the sexual. During a period when sexual continence was seen as the prerequisite for a contribution to cultural and economic life and hence a responsible designation of social being, concerns over the irregularities of male bodies in the circuit of economic exchange centred on their susceptibility to the 'strains' of business life (another of modernity's 'shocks'), which had the potential to induce neurasthenic disorders, to be treated by rest cures to be taken in the country (McQueen 1991). Sicknesses clustered around the businessman's body, as symptoms of 'moral drain' were linked to the observations that businessmen were particularly susceptible to the temptations of habitual masturbation (McQueen 1991: 12). These observations can be seen as symptoms of a concern with the potential waste of human vigour that commodity exchange, as the base of new politico-economic systems, represented, but they also show a new disposition to invest the commodity with the potential for embodying human value; it could function as the sign of a healthy social body or its opposite. '[T]he humane critics of political economy imagine the commodity, the bearer of value, as freighted with mortality, as a sign of spent vitality, in order to demand all the more strenuously that it have a vitality-replenishing potential' (Gallagher 1989: 351).

Similarly, as Thomas Laqueur shows, the connection between masturbation, prostitution and usury made in the language of this period lay in their lack of productivity (1989). Usury was identified as an economic equivalent to sexual waste, a form of profit made without adding any value to the object traded, another kind of 'excitation'. Its dangerously internalized system of exchange and regeneration was identified in a similar way to that of masturbation, seen as 'perfectly healthy desire channelled back into itself' rather than along appropriately socialised channels (p. 336). Just as prostitution offered sexual exchanges outside the marital and domestic context, so usury, as 'pure exchange', could only be sterile and unproductive, as its relation to the market offered no foundational connection to the productive household economy. Both usury and prostitution, through their lack of origination in the natural realm of family, are thereby regarded as 'unnatural'. They can both be understood as signs of the suspicion of money as an adequate marker of value in systems of exchange, and value's lack of foundation in productive labour. The relations of the market, comprising an 'unnatural . . . mode by which men gain from one another', corresponded to the sexualized body's involvement in practices without reproductive potential, hence removing from the sexual any clear designation of a social value (p. 339).

Following Laqueur's argument, prostitution can be seen to offer a definitional link between the waste at the heart of masturbation (asocial and unproductive) and the waste at the heart of commerce (a diminishing relation of pure exchange), undermining the safeguard for 'human solidarities' that the family provides against the disintegrative forces of the market. We may also see the alignment of human waste, prostitution and commerce taking corporeal form in Mayhew's use of 'types' of body to distinguish between social groups. In his writings on urban types, the prostitute becomes linked to other nomadic groups operating in the marketplace, such as costermongers, female street-sellers, whose vigorous bodies gain strength without producing anything; a feature which Mayhew uses to show their parasitic relation to the 'honest workers'' productive bodies, losing value through their labour (Gallagher 1987: 91). For, according to Malthusian models influential in Mayhew's writing,[7] while the labouring body is fixed in its capacity for productivity (both in its potential for expenditure of energy and its spatial location), the consuming body may not only move about, but also it may expand, or reproduce, and thereby bring degeneration to the social body by the pressure of an accelerating underclass.[8] The prostitute's parasitic and unproductive vigour derives from her operation in a newly commodified marketplace which offers her access to resources while detracting from the strength and value of those who are contracted by salaried labour. Such a group more visibly includes middle-class men in the second half of the nineteenth century, as a result of the proliferation of salaried occupations and professions in the new commercial centres of metropolitan cities.

The force of the connection between the prostitute and other public femininities can here be seen in Mayhew's condemnation of the costermonger's choice of street peddling over domestic service on the basis that it was a vice that a modest woman would struggle to avoid, and distasteful in its imposition of the competitive marketplace on the city dweller (Gallagher 1987: 101). An exchange between *selling* and consuming, rather than *producing* and consuming, one common to both prostitute and costermonger, shows how consumption impacts upon concepts of female sexuality; promiscuous and fickle, unfounded in either natural or rational laws, damaging to the autonomy of urban masculinity.

The correspondence of sex and commercial city life was produced through a concept of waste, then, whose inscription on the bodies of men was a story about the new relations of commerce in city life. As David Walker notes in his analysis of the damage to a project of developing a vigorous Australian national and metropolitan identity attributed to seminal waste:

> *If masturbation represented the unproductive expenditure of energy in the individual, likewise the city was commonly regarded as wasteful of human energies ... The cities ... exhausted and diminished their inhabitants. Exhaustion became the symbol of what was assumed to be a troubling imbalance between the high expenditure of energy and a low personal reward. (Walker 1985, cited in McQueen 1991: 21)*

The concept of expenditure as waste was one which infused commentary on sexual relations within mass culture. In the popular address to disordered femininity in debates over prostitution, an extension of women's 'passionlessness' allowed the female body to be situated as an object of consumption for men.[9] The prostitute therefore figures not as a *responsible agent* of pathology, but as *a problem of masculinity*, a problem that is reversed back onto the male body itself in a scenario of an inadequate mastery of corporeal drives and its consequent wasting – of the body and of moral character. The attention to the prostitute can here be allied to that given to the masturbator to the extent that it shows an inadequacy of social being for masculinity.[10]

Thus, as Walter Benjamin's comment that 'prostitution can claim to count as "work" at the moment work becomes prostitution' (Benjamin, cited in Buck-Morss 1986: 121) indicates, the figure of the prostitute represents more than 'just' woman; it designates a whole complex of sexual, social and economic relations that problematize the reorganization of social life in the city as a reflection of sexual differences and the maintenance of secure forms of masculine social identity.[11] The prostitute, whose meanings are formed in this period by a commodification that embodies the lack of authenticity attached to salaried labour, also points to the potential inadequacy of the body politic to sustain the human body's 'well-being'. The figure of a collapse between the boundaries of sex and work, public and private, in a woman 'gone awry', the prostitute offers an image of the loss of cultural authority for male subjects that urban life entails and, as Patrice Petro shows, she does this in a devouring and demonic image of 'seduction and cruelty' (1987: 116). The prostitute therefore becomes an exemplar of the fascinations and dangers of modern forms of urban life, its 'lures', and their interference with a regulation of the corporeal in the interest of cultural achievement and civilization.

That the meanings of the prostitute are also generalized to designate qualities specific to femininity itself is shown in Freud's development of the concept of female sexuality as a 'dark continent'. The term 'dark continent' initially invoked the unstable and uncivilized dangerous classes, the 'heathens', 'savages', 'barbarians', 'denizens' or 'wandering tribes' of the 'unknown country' of Europe's inner cities referred to in Mayhew, Chadwick, Charles Booth etc. Just as earlier in the century the prostitute was figured as the 'sewer', discharging the wastes of masculine disorder, the proletariat was associated with the 'fetid effluvia' and the miasma emanating from insanitary waste which characterized the geography of their inhabitation of the city. In the second part of the century, both prostitute and the proletarian poor became seen as a 'vast dungheap of ignorance and vice . . . the social pestilence' which threatened to pollute health and corrupt civilization in metropolitan centres. This inscribes Freud's use of the term 'dark continent' with a very particular notion of the feminine: a pathologized female sexuality to be found in the figure of the prostitute, signified by a diseased, open ('blackened') body haunting the dark recesses of the nineteenth-century city (see Chevalier 1973; Himmelfarb 1984: 312–70, Corbin 1987: 211; Armstrong 1990). The potential of the city to refashion public femininities also presents a challenge to the fixed zoning whereby civilization, subjectivity and sexuality are understood to be secured. Instead of stable cultural achievements, they are shown to be fragile, tenuous and incomplete. Subject to the unknown dangers contained by the unstable relations of a respatialized city life of promiscuous sociabilities, the threat that is posed is one of the incoherence of the terms organizing the social (Swanson 1993: 183).

The concept of a pathological femininity did not only designate the incompleteness of models of appropriate female sexuality, however, but also drew attention to its own incomplete formulation, for it was used in uneven and contradictory ways. The picture of modern life's ability to induce insanity has been well drawn; as a disease of affluence and over-ambition as much as a sign of excess and indulgence, it became indicative of advanced civilization and national achievement. One of the features that is less commonly noted is that while women were seen as physiologically more prone to manias and nervous disorders, defined under the category of intellectual insanity or irrationality, they were not associated *per se* with the importantly distinct state of moral insanity, or perversion. Interestingly, the increasing 'epidemic' of modern life was to overlook women as potential suicides; rather, it was understood to be 'axiomatic that, if traditional family life protected its members from suicide, those most subsumed in traditional roles – women – ought to demonstrate the greatest resistance to suicide' – and its pathologies. For ' "Although women were more exposed to mental illness than men", wrote Esquirol in 1821, "suicide is less frequent among them. Observers from all nations are in agreement on that issue" ' (Kushner 1993: 467).

While 'the excessive intensity of any passion' (Bourne-Taylor 1988: 47–8), could bring about a state of moral insanity, this became seen as a generalized 'function of modern urban life' and its loss of authority, requiring a form of medico-moral treatment which would find, in internal self-discipline, a substitute for the lack of external authority in modern civilizations (Gates 1988: 17–18; Kushner 1993: 463). The concept of moral insanity, the incapacity to conduct oneself with decency and propriety in the business of life, was developed in an attempt to define a state of mind which could account for the 'modern' epidemic of suicide (Gates 1988: 13). Women in general were considered to maintain an immunity to moral insanity, then, as a result of their domestic, familial nature. Instead, *certain forms* of femininity became indicative of the instabilities that placed men in danger of being claimed by this epidemic, as women's involvement in activities that took them away from traditional roles also weakened the influence of family and home on men's ability to withstand the pressures created by modern life.[12] Such movements overrode boundaries between the world of work and home, undermining the distinctive coherence of a private domain as the source of 'human solidarities' which offered a logic for appropriate forms of organizing the social.

The displacements available to women in the scenarios I have been outlining have a particular foundation in the new forms of engagement women formed with city life from the middle of the nineteenth century. These came into visibility between the 1860s and 1920s in the development of retailing industries and popular entertainments. The figure of the prostitute, in its foregrounding of the woman as seller and commodity, shows a very specific oversight – her role as consumer (Bowlby 1985: 11). The drawing of the prostitute in this way masks the range of women participating in public consumption, desocializing their relations in its foregrounding of sexual and intellectual instabilities of physiological origin. But in fact women's presences in the city had a very definite sociality. While not exhausting the involvements they claimed in this period, perhaps the most visible and noted forms of social presence women could take up were based on a connection to retailing industries and the development of the technologies of entertainment, such as cinema. Such activities were seen as signs of the denigration of modern life and its possibilities for authentic social exchange. The derogation of consumption as worthless and 'feminine' can thus be seen as linked to a resistance to the modernization of city culture and the changes in social relations attached to the new forms of presence and mobility women take up. The feminine thereby becomes deployed as a symptom of the loss of authoritative self-presence (Petro 1987: 139). What seems to be fearful about city spaces and consumption, two features of modern life viewed as engulfing and monstrous, is the reorganization of masculine and feminine distinctions that was brought about in this phase of urban expansion, one feature of which was the development of consumption industries.

CONSUMPTION AND THE REFORMING OF FEMININITY

When the New Women demanded entry into the professions and educational institutions from the nineteenth century, opponents of the New Freedom as a feature of modern city life presented the changes as damaging to social and sexual order, as they predicted 'the collapse of the family, of society and of civilisation itself if "natural sexual distinctions" were ignored' (Pumphrey 1987: 184). It was in the specific uses women made of commodities that a recasting of 'natural sexual distinctions' through fashionable appearance also helped to recast cultural attitudes and social definition.[13]

One important aspect to note is the spatial relations that provided the possibility for this recasting of public life and femininity to occur. Women entered the city just as it developed into a space of broad streets, busy traffic, and geometric city planning; for example, Haussmann's restructuring of Paris in a grid of wide boulevards flanked by imposing high terraces. These geographies are normally seen as problematic for less powerful groups, especially women in their supposed attachment to domestic, private, intimate space. While by some Haussmannism is seen as a more oppressive form of disciplinary landscape, presenting further opportunities for surveillance of proletarian neighbourhoods and crowd management, contemporary commentators also talked of the dehumanization of the modern urban metropolis, which threatened to overwhelm the individual and in whose huge and endless thoroughfares one ran the risk of bumping into new and unknown people. It is in the context of these urban stages that women began to occupy city space, as a more expansive landscape for women than the home or locality could ever provide. An endlessly receding horizon, unfamiliar spaces at every turn of the street, and huge edifices with a plethora of goods drawn from all over the world displayed to the shopper's gaze allowed for quite a different way for women to experience their relationship to the social. These spatial co-ordinates offered anonymity, mobility, unknown possibilities; they precisely reversed the features of domestic landscape, offering refashioned public femininities.

My argument is not that these processes occurred for the first time in the nineteenth century, but that their distinctiveness derives from their doing so in a way which was mapped on to the consolidation of sexual difference as the central definer of public identity. Such a consolidation occurred through the convergence of medical, psychological and proto-sociological forms of commentary and definition, concerning sexual roles and characters and their intersection with a conception of a social world organized in terms of separate and incommensurate spheres and functions. While this separation was not always physical, it was nevertheless evident in the 'mental compartmentalizations' which were felt in the organization of everyday life and self-determination (Tosh 1991: 49).[14]

There were specific tensions and difficulties associated with men and women occupying the separate spheres of public and private life, however, which arose from the connection between their difference and their mutual dependence. Public masculinity was underpinned by, as well as defined against, a domestic form of masculine affectivity; the ways men conducted themselves as husbands and fathers, exhibiting forms of care as much as authority. Yet this was to be moderate, and by 1871 Samuel Smiles was warning that 'too great an attachment to home might breed unmanly dependence' (Tosh 1991: 51). Public masculinity was also underpinned by masculinity's complementary relationship to domestic femininity. As such, then, the displacements of femininities disrupted not only the complementary nature of sexually differentiated roles and spheres, but also the complementary balance and separation of elements in the masculine persona.

That women are seen to 'enter' the city through the route of commerce and consumption, that this is understood in terms of the taking up of a public presence, is also a significant element in the distinctiveness of this period's construction of women's relation to the city. For it is not only a particular group of middle-class women who thereby come to represent 'women' in these debates, but also that the city – specifically as a place of inauthentic diversion and licence – comes to be constituted through the spaces of commerce. These together form the co-ordinates of the disruptions attributed to 'modern life'. Women's participation in other 'public' activities (such as the attendance of public functions, philanthropic work or their representation in local councils) is seen, by contrast, as an extension of their domestic role, bringing the principles of maternal influence into contact with those regulating the public sphere, to provide a balance to the government of civil life. Women's involvements in consumption and entertainments, on the other hand, are seen in terms of their displacements and the adoption of alternative channels of desire, taking up the offer of self-directed pleasures and forms of self-fashioning that contradict the concepts of duty and sacrifice and moral moderation which regulate domestic femininity. Doubtless the concern that is voiced over such recasting of feminine function is connected to the lessening of domestic responsibilities pressing directly on the middle-class wife which has been observed to occur from the 1860s (Tosh 1991: 53). But just as significant may be the recasting of masculinity. Masculine discipline in the home, and the split between masculine and feminine functions and attributes, seem to have become more pronounced and severe in the period from the mid- to the late nineteenth century, for example, leading to a 'severance between manliness and domesticity' by the end of the century (p. 68). The persuasiveness of the well-balanced masculine character, able to incorporate domesticity as part of manliness, a prerequisite of public status and esteem, is also under question in the concern over the appropriate forms for maintaining the separation between public and private life.

DRUNK WITH THE GLITTER

Towards the end of the nineteenth century, the sexual becomes used as a way of managing the instabilities of new social relations in the metropolis, giving rise to a theory of sexual management which, while addressing the body as a repository of energies, demands that it should be made into a site of responsible, civic action. Why might the sexual be seen to have this significance in the formation of new urban subjectivities?

Part of the answer lies in a general intensification of the management of individual action that results from a transition in economic theory. This occurred as a shift from the classical economics of eighteenth-century liberal political theory which centralized production – positing an infinitely self-generating social order around the hierarchy of estates – to neo-classical theories which centred consumption – understood as dispersed across individuals as originators of desires and the finite end points of economic processes. Towards the end of the nineteenth century, 'productivity' as a criterion of human activity became understood not so much as a capacity for the activity of production itself, but rather one concerning appropriate and modified forms of consumption. Thus modes of consumption were an important focus in debates over the extent and form of programmes of social management; they stood not only as an eventual *outcome* of production processes but also as the *evidence* of human productivity.

As a continually progressive and expanding system of production envisaged in classical economic theory gave way to the neo-classical emphasis on consumption, economic systems were shown to have a finite end point. As the value of products ceased to be defined by the transformations wrought on primary materials by labour, the commodity's value derived from its scarcity, hence its desirability for consumption (Birken 1988). Productive labour as a prerequisite of bourgeois masculine value and a sign of the achievement of human societies falls away in this new schema, as value is attached to individual taste and idiosyncratic desire. As it was now 'simply attached to objects by the subjective desire of consumers . . . value lost its social nature and took on a radical individual character' (Birken 1988: 32), and the satisfaction of idiosyncratic desire became the end of productivity. The focus on consumption could thus be seen to skew the relation between the economic and the social towards a privatized, hence more acutely femininized, individuality whose points of reference lay beyond the social and its mechanisms for self-regulation.

As the new relations of the city were read within this economic theory of consumption, they became associated with the feminine. Such a move can only be understood in the context of a culture whose own productivity had, in the dependence on consumption, expenditure – thus potentially *waste* – somehow become suspect. There is here not just a use of the feminine as a motif in the discourse of mass culture but an explicit address to a problematic feminine figure in the context of modernity, as a sign of the redefinitions of sexual difference that reorganized social relations and practices demanded. The ambivalence of the relation to mass culture is also the mark of its relation to the new presences that women are offered in the public spaces of consumption. Andreas Huyssens has shown the extent to which the feminine becomes inscribed onto mass culture as a sign of its inauthenticity; imitative and reproductive, corrupted by the success of its own degenerative allure, mass culture is understood in terms of a feminine threat to civilization (1986: 44–62).

That women's consumption in the context of technologies of mass culture elicited a particular and focused moral attention was shown in the way the figure of the kleptomaniac was developed as a pathological condition indicative of the 'deregulating effects of modernity' (Camhi 1993: 30), but positioned on a continuum with the behaviours of consuming women generally. News reports would contain comments that 'women . . . were unable to resist buying above their means . . . [t]hey may strain their allowance and curtail their children's wardrobe, but they must have a French loomed camel's hair shawl'

(Abelson 1989: 56). The pathological sexualization of kleptomania is shown, Leslie Camhi argues, through its association with a passive form of fetishism in psychiatric commentary – allowing silk to fall against the body, for example – hence designating women's susceptibility to the pleasures of what was argued to be the lowliest of the senses and which, as we will remember, has particular connotations of vice, that of touch (1993: 40–1). That the need to regulate the consumption of the leisured urban women was as urgent as the problem of masturbation for men can be seen in the identification of the conditions for kleptomania as the 'promiscuous mingling' of merchandises near the consumer's touch (Camhi 1993: 29), and even more especially in concerns over 'the perils of desire unleashed by the *vicious habit* of shopping' (Abelson 1989: 6, my emphasis).

Although Petro's analysis of the ambivalence over urban culture shows that the connections between modernity, urban life, mass production and woman that were made in order to identify its dangers had another side – the fascination, charm, enigma and mystery that positions this culture as feminine – the attachment to modern entertainments that these terms describe was nevertheless linked to a debased form of anti-knowledge. In contradistinction to the contemplative, reflective and intellectual distance cultivated for a culture of achievement, this attachment was seen as absorption, embodied in the female cinema audience and the figure of the 'shopgirl'. In the context of mass culture, the derogation of modern 'pastimes' served to replay the older association between woman and pleasure in terms which were now characterized by passivity and distraction (Petro 1986: 6). In Siegfried Kracauer's 1927 essay, 'The Little Shopgirls Go to the Movies' (referred to in Petro 1986), the irrational tendencies of mass taste are shown by the shopgirls' preference for sentiment 'because to cry is sometimes easier than to think'. The 'illusory' domain of cinematic pleasure forms a particular connection to women's susceptibility. As 'they gladly let themselves be led astray by that which enchants their souls', they become 'drunk with the glitter'.[15] Here, mass consumption is shown to have an explicit connection to a loss of self which is embodied in female figures lost to pleasure. The dominant motif which comes to be inscribed with these instabilities was that of the glittering commodity, as it represented the co-ordinates of the problems and fascinations of new forms of relation between the subject and the social in city space.

The transformed relation to the object that the commodity represented was embodied in the consuming individual, understood as the originator of an unpredictable realm of desire with multiple orientations. As the finite outcome of economic systems, the consumer always posed the problematic potential of waste, the unruly outlet of energies offered by undisciplined expenditure. Lawrence Birken shows how this refigured system of value posed a problem for the economic as a self-regulating system:

> To evaluate value as subjective evaluation arising from idiosyncratic and arbitrary taste was to root the economic in the psychological . . . the economic gradually ceased to understand itself as the autonomous centre of social life and instead constituted itself simply as a means (technique) of satisfying radically idiosyncratic psychologies . . . Neoclassical thought thus explicitly granted what psychology was implicitly claiming at the same time: the primacy of the idiosyncratic consumer. (Birken 1988: 32–3)

Birken's argument is that these psychological laws, which would come to explain the economic through the language of desire and tastes, link the economic to the sexological as sexology becomes 'the actual successor to the classical political economy of the eighteenth and nineteenth centuries . . . [f]or sexual science . . . explicitly claimed to have discovered a self-determined order' (p. 41). His point is that its impact on consumption was to mark it as outside the economic, originating in the realm of the private. Mine, however, is that this connection could only be made sense of in the context of the construction of a domain of the feminine, as both a principle of disorder and an object of management.

The connection between femininity as disorder and the management of the feminine, is shown in the use of psychology in marketing, as a way of scientifically organizing an address to the consumer and predicting her patterns of behaviour. The dependence of these ways of centring the feminine on the sexual as the irreducible origin of individual motivations and compulsions is shown in the writing surrounding the female shoplifter, which moved with the various psycho-sexual models developed from the 1870s to the mid-twentieth century. Kleptomania was first seen as a sign of women's 'natural' irrationality, either as a consequence of imbalances in nervous energies related to the periodic crises of her reproductive organs, or as a mania women succumbed to as a result of biological inferiority. Through the twentieth century a theory emerged that it was a 'palliative for individual psychological and sexual distress', an expression of the 'symbolic needs of sexual gratification' or the 'need to be caught to alleviate unconscious guilt' (Abelson 1989: 7–8, 198–201). Made sense of in ways relevant to forms of knowledge which, in each period, designated the sexual as a central term in the organization of personality and behaviour, these show both the malleability of definitions of gender and the persistence of a conception of feminine disorder requiring forms of management.

RECASTING CONSUMPTION

The point of looking to the figures which have populated our ways of imagining city spaces and their forms of sociability is to note the ways they have conceived of a set of categories around absolute differences in sexual but also in other social terms. The sexual has been used as a way of managing certain weak points set up by systems of consumption which posit individuals as the end points of productive systems, individuals who are self-willed, authoritative only to themselves. Yet as we have seen, the forms of management proposed can only work with dichotomized notions of sexual identity and sexual spheres. Concepts of sexual disorder, or consuming presences, and the drawing of distinctions between public and private, have defined the terms by which subjectivity and social presence can be formulated.

Transformations in nineteenth-century urban culture disorganized the relations of spaces and bodies demanded by the geographies of sexual difference. As the sexual crossed the public/private divide maintained by politico-economic and psycho-sexual theories of the subject, it provided a vehicle for addressing the public management of individuals as consumers. Its route through consumption constitutes a way in which women's occupation of public space became visible, providing a focus for the reformation – as well as the pathologization – of femininities. While we have seen the definitions of individuality, desire and sexual difference that contemporary models of consumption draw on and presuppose, we should also note how far these models overlook the tactical negotiations women have made with public life through the domain of consumption.

It is important to see the reorganizations afforded by cultures of consumption in terms that avoid co-ordinates that continue to pose female public presence in terms of either pathology and disorder or absolute desire and self-realization, for these rely upon and perpetuate the dichotomies outlined above. The propensity to read the activities of women according to dichotomies of sexual difference has led to them being seen in terms of an erosion of the terms of stable masculinity. The suspicion of the activity of consumption (and the realm of commodified entertainments) can also be seen as having an origin in a resistance to various kinds of reorganization; of the criteria of value, the location of the individual within economic systems, and the relation of sexual identity to social geography. Both the fixity of sexual categories and an inherently negative view of consumption need to be superseded so that the involvements of women in the city and the various forms of cultural consumption that form part of modern urban experience can be included as components of civic life.[16] A remodelling of the relations of consumption entails an engagement with the material forms that cultural life takes, the practical encounters afforded by consumption in the social and spatial arrangements of the city. It also entails focusing on the culturally specific forms of exchange between subjects; identifying them both locally and with a view to their historical formation.

These considerations point us to specific contexts and the dispositions that embodied and situated subjects bring with them in their engagement with the social. If we take note of these, we have to be less willing to see consumption and technologies of commodified entertainment as distractions which lure women from a more authentic form of self-realization. Equally there is no reason to take a populist view that sees these very activities as endorsed by the involvement of women; their visibility should not lead us to suppose that they occupy any privileged role above other, less tangible involvements, nor to see in them evidence of any necessary female predisposition. Instead I would argue that since these various engagements are part of the development of a modern feminine experience of the urban, and they have been used in this tactical way for the formation of sociabilities that are part of the texture of cultural life for women, they form part of a range of factors available for the making of contemporary female subjectivity. They can thus be used, equally tactically, to make visible, to develop and extend, the contours of women's citizenship.

A recognition of the histories forming the enactment of our social life and the performative capacities of the self can provide the basis of a conception of consumption that is not restricted by its negative characterization, or by solely commercial interests, or to the features ascribed to one particular group of women which in the nineteenth century comes to stand as indicative of women in general. This can usefully be developed according to models of ethical exchange. This would not be a project which aims to uncover an illusory set of common interests that is the basis of concepts of community or freedoms as they are conventionally used, but one which formulates social policy on the basis of a set of agreements, or perhaps rather a set of protocols, concerning the access to cultural resources whereby effective citizenships may be established within the spaces of public life.

This agenda demands a more contingent model and understanding of consumption, used as a basis for resourcing social and cultural life in the recognition that concepts of community or freedom are inappropriate as a basis for providing access to civic resources. We can rely neither on a unitary concept of a constituency formed in agreement[17] nor on one established as plural, diverse, but formed in mutual tolerance.[18] These variously reify similarity and difference as ways of organizing ethical relations in public life. In fact, the identification of a concept of consumption as a way of understanding civic associa-tion points to the inadequacy of a singular model of social identity and exchange, and hence of its ethical underpinning. The concept Drucilla Cornell uses is that of 'affinity', which acknowledges a relation of both similarity *and* difference.[19] If we pluralize her term, in the recognition of the diversity of those associations of difference and similarity that subjects combine, we see that to chart such relations, formed in changeable and practical ways, would allow us to identify the pattern of women's varied encounters with the city and can therefore provide the basis of protocols for resourcing. These urban encounters are formed by a mobile, temporary, contingent set of affinities that allow us to resist designating an absolute set of social groupings or identities and instead offer a remit for resourcing strategies that see the associations individuals form as lying beyond those formed only within an internalized community sharing similar and restricted interests. While precedents of affinity may be acknowledged for a group to become visible in resourcing protocols, they need not assume *either* that the group 'women' is defined as a static unity across all interests and activities *or* that women's patterns of civic engagement or resourcing will remain constant or be always – and in all ways – prioritized. Affinities, in other words, do not just exist between individuals designated by social grouping, assuming forms of identity or roles as the basis of a transcendent connection between social subjects; rather, they are circumstantial. This should direct us, then, towards an urban cultural agenda which escapes the pathologization or idealization of consumption and other activities associated with the feminine, to form an address to women deriving from a more diverse and contingent picture of city life and city spaces.

NOTES

1 See Elizabeth Wilson's chapter in this volume, especially her engagement with the arguments of Janet Wolff and Griselda Pollock.
2 Moira Gatens indicates that women threaten to transmit a '*political* hysteria' to the social body (Gatens 1988: 65).
3 The prostitute was understood as susceptible to the temptations of consumption from the mid-century. As her love of 'vanities' was seen as cause and sign of her fall by William Acton in 1857, Henry Mayhew saw 'showy dress' as an indicator of vice in the 1880s (Valverde 1989: 178–9).

4 Christine Stansell uses this term to characterize the way urban reformers addressed women's presence on the streets in their attempts to instil a domestic and privatized femininity as guarantor of civilized urban society in New York in the mid-nineteenth century. This term suggests the force of the connection between a public urban femininity and 'the evil of prostitution spreading through the streets' (Stansell 1982: 322–5).

5 See Benjamin's discussion of 'shocks' (Benjamin 1973: 157–202).

6 Catherine Gallagher indicates the relationship between exchange value and the human body as a pervasive pattern in mid-Victorian debates in political economy. As the labour theory of value gives classical economic theory a biological centre in the exertion of human energies, so its critics also assume a corporeal investment as they decry this theory's inadequate focus on valuing the commodity in terms of its ability to sustain life, satisfy biological need and cultivate bodily well-being (Gallagher 1989: 346–9). These debates give a sense of the instability of the concept of productivity in this period, in both social and corporeal terms.

7 The Malthusian model of the behavioural body, subject to environmental influences, is one which is eventually also adopted in frameworks used in the development of preventive medicine, especially active in Edwardian Britain, and seen in its influence on the development of the Town Planning Movement. It argues for the provision of urban conditions which eradicate disease and cultivate vigorous and happy citizens, a holistic approach to the body and the possibilities of guarding against the spread of degeneration to the social body (Porter 1991).

8 In her discussion of this argument, Gallagher indicates that although Mayhew cannot be seen as an economic thinker, he drew upon popularly held opinions concerning economic theory in his social commentary, indicating the currency of Malthusian models (Gallagher 1987: 98).

9 Mary Poovey indicates the way social commentators were able to draw on the 'passionlessness' of women to delineate the prostitute *in opposition to* a notion of sexual pathology or voraciousness in the 1840s or 1850s. As she shows, W.R. Greg asserts the prostitute is 'innately moral' in her self-sacrifice for the love of a man, aligning her with the virtuous, asexual, passive and domestic middle-class woman and thus laying the foundations for reforming movements active in the 1860s–1880s, which situated the prostitute as victim of men's natural promiscuity, fallen from virtue from the exploitation of her essentially maternal qualities and thus an object of philanthropic rescue (Poovey 1990).

10 This erosion of the cultural authority of masculinity becomes further evidenced in the debates over the homosexual propensities that are argued to render men inadequate to effective citizenship, or their role in public life, from this period to the middle of the twentieth century (Swanson 1994b). From the 1860s to 1920s a shift occurs in medicomoral writings on masturbation, as they come to see the source of danger in terms of its potential to lead to male homosexual activity rather than, as in the earlier part of this period, towards the temptations of prostitutes (Hall 1992: 374).

11 I have already made the arguments contained in this and the next paragraph (Swanson 1993: 181–3).

12 The forms of 'morbid perversion of feeling' developed by Henry Maudsley in 1879 embraced the 'mischievous, erotic, homicidal, or suicidal' (Gates 1988: 17), linking the sexual to the criminal and suicidal. As well as suicidal impulses, Maudsley's treatments

addressed hysteria (long understood as characterized by forms of female behaviour which deviated from conventions of domestic and sexual duty) and homosexuality, suggesting that if these pathologies identified something specific about the effect of the modern on relations between the sexes, they linked female displacements with a problematic connection between men as well as a susceptibility for suicide. Perhaps a cultural link between homosexuality and suicide finds its origin in this taxonomy of 'morbidity' (see Swanson 1994b).

13 See for example Rolley (1990).

14 I agree with Elizabeth Wilson's discussion of Mary Poovey's approach in this regard, in her chapter in this volume.

15 From Bruno Schonlank's poem, 'Kino', cited in Petro (1987: 119).

16 For a discussion of urban cultural policy implications of this argument, see Swanson (1994a).

17 Here I am thinking of some reservations I have about the model of community proposed by Seyla Benhabib (1992), whose focus on the exchange between a mobile and adaptive set of competences and principles of conduct formed in public *and* private life helps in many respects to rethink women's relationship to public life. One reservation is based on her privileging of relations formed in private over those more explicitly governed by institutions, based on an assumed commonness and reciprocity between subjects. The point I am focusing on, deriving from this, is her reliance on an assumption of the symmetry of the relationship to public life formed by members of this community. This is a feature identified in Cornell (1992: 39) and Young (1990: 231–2).

18 Iris Young's critique of Benhabib, on the lines outlined in note 13, allows her to develop a concept of 'differentiation without exclusion' (Young 1990: 238). While Paul Patton, in his chapter in this volume, argues against this being seen as utopian on material grounds on the basis that it is 'a widely shared positive experience of city life', I would see it as utopian, or perhaps romantic, in the assumption of the unitarily beneficial nature of this association as individuals form a transcendent affiliation that allows freedom to be experienced at the level of subjectivity.

19 Drucilla Cornell's concept of the ethical relation is one defined as both *phenomenologically symmetrical* (the other is always other in concrete and irreducible terms) and *asymmetrical in the specificity of its differences* (the particularity of its otherness gives it a being in practical terms (1992: 39, 171–2)).

REFERENCES

Abelson, E.S. 1989: *When Ladies Go A-Thieving: Middle-Class Shoplifters in the Victorian Department Store*, New York and Oxford: Oxford University Press.

Armstrong, N. 1990: 'The Occidental Alice', *Differences*, 2, 2: 3–40.

Benhabib, S. 1992: *Situating the Self: Gender, Community and Postmodernism in Contemporary Ethics*, Cambridge: Polity Press.

Benjamin, W. 1973: 'On Some Motifs in Baudelaire', in *Illuminations*, London: Fontana.

Benjamin, W. 1983: 'The *Flâneur*', in *Charles Baudelaire: A Lyric Poet in the Era of High Capitalism*, London and New York: Verso.

Birken, L. 1988: *Consuming Desire: Sexual Science and the Emergence of a Culture of Abundance, 1871–1914*, Ithaca and London: Cornell University Press.

Bourne-Taylor, J. 1988: *In the Secret Theatre of Home: Wilkie Collins, Sensational Narrative and Nineteenth-century Psychology*, London: Routledge.

Bowlby, R. 1985: *Just Looking: Consumer Culture in Dreiser, Gissing and Zola*, London and New York: Methuen.

Buck-Morss, S. 1986: 'The *Flâneur*, the Sandwichman and the Whore: The Politics of Loitering', *New German Critique*, 39: 99–104.

Camhi, L. 1993: 'Stealing Femininity: Department Store Kleptomania as Sexual Disorder', *Differences*, 5, 1: 26–50.

Chevalier, L. 1973: *The Labouring Classes and Dangerous Classes*, Princeton, NJ: Princeton University Press.

Corbin, A. 1987: 'Commercial Sexuality in Nineteenth-century France: A System of Images and Regulations', in C. Gallagher and T. Laqueur (eds), *The Making of the Modern Body: Sexuality and Society in the Nineteenth Century*, Berkeley, Los Angeles and London: University of California Press.

Cornell, D. 1992: *The Philosophy of the Limit*, New York and London: Routledge.

Doane, M.A. 1991: 'On Sublimation', in *Femmes Fatales*, London and New York: Routledge.

Douglas, A. 1977: *The Feminization of American Culture*, New York: Avon, cited in T. Modleski, 'Femininity as Masquerade', in C. MacCabe (ed.) (1986), *High Theory/Low Culture*, Manchester: Manchester University Press.

Gallagher, C. 1987: 'The Body Versus the Social Body in Malthus and Mayhew', in C. Gallagher and T. Laqueur (eds), *The Making of the Modern Body: Sexuality and Society in the Nineteenth Century*, Berkeley, Los Angeles and London: University of California Press.

Gallagher, C. 1989: 'The Bioeconomics of *Our Mutual Friend*', in Michel Feher with Ramona Naddaff and Nadia Tazi (eds), *Fragments for a History of the Human Body. Zone Part III*, New York: Urzone Inc.

Gatens, M. 1988: 'Towards a Feminist Philosophy of the Body', in B. Caine, E.A. Grosz and M. de Lepervanche (eds), *Crossing Boundaries: Feminisms and the Critique of Knowledges*, Sydney: Allen and Unwin.

Gates, B. 1988: *Victorian Suicide: Mad Crimes and Sad Histories*, Princeton, NJ: Princeton University Press.

Hall, L.A. 1992: 'Forbidden by God, Despised by Men: Masturbation, Medical Warnings, Moral Panic, and Manhood in Great Britain, 1850–1950', *Journal of the History of Sexuality*, 2, 3: 365–87.

Himmelfarb, G. 1984: *The Idea of Poverty: England in the Early Industrial Age*, London: Faber & Faber.

Huyssen, A. 1986: *After the Great Divide: Modernism, Mass Culture, Postmodernism*, Bloomington and Indianapolis: Indiana University Press.

Kaplan, C. 1986: 'Wild Nights: Pleasure/Sexuality/Feminism', in *Sea Changes*, London: Verso.

Kushner, H.I. 1993: 'Suicide, Gender, and the Fear of Modernity in Nineteenth-century Medical and Social Thought', *Journal of Social History*, 26, 3: 461–90.

Laqueur, T. 1987: 'Orgasm, Generation and the Politics of Reproductive Biology', in C. Gallagher and T. Laqueur (eds), *The Making of the Modern Body: Sexuality and Society in the Nineteenth Century*, Berkeley, Los Angeles and London: University of California Press.

Laqueur, T.W. 1989: 'The Social Evil, the Solitary Vice and Pouring Tea', in Michel Feher with Ramona Naddaff and Nadia Tazi (eds), *Fragments for a History of the Human Body. Zone Part III*, New York: Urzone Inc.

McQueen, R. 1991: 'Mortified and Punished: The Businessman and his Body in the Victorian Age', paper presented at the Tenth Annual Law in History Conference, (Melbourne).

Pateman, C. 1989: '"The Disorder of Women": Women, Love and the Sense of Justice', in *The Disorder of Women*, Cambridge: Polity Press and Blackwell.

Petro, P. 1986: 'Mass Culture and the Feminine: The 'Place' of Television in Film Studies', *Cinema Journal*, 25, 3: 5–21.

Petro, P. 1987: 'Modernity and Mass Culture in Weimar: Contours of a Discourse on Sexuality in Early Theories of Reception and Representation', *New German Critique*, 40: 115–46.

Poovey, M. 1990: 'Speaking of the Body: Mid-Victorian Constructions of Female Desire', in M. Jacobus, E. Fox, Keller and S. Shuttleworth (eds), *Body/Politics, Women and the Discourses of Science*, London and New York: Routledge.

Porter, D. 1991: '"Enemies of the Race": Biologism, Environmentalism, and Public Health in Edwardian England', *Victorian Studies*, 34, 2: 163–78.

Pumphrey, M. 1987: 'The Flapper, the Housewife and the Making of Modernity', *Cultural Studies*, 1, 2: 179–94

Rolley, K. 1990: 'Fashion, Femininity and the Fight for the Vote', *Art History*, 13, 1: 47–71.

Shivelbusch, W. 1979: *The Railway Journey: Trains and Travel in the 19th Century*, New York: Urizen Books.

Stansell, C. 1982: 'Women, Children and the Uses of the Streets: Class and Gender Conflict in New York City, 1850–1860', *Feminist Studies*, 8, 2: 309–35.

Swanson, G. 1993: 'Mary Ann Doane, *Femmes Fatales: Feminism, Film Theory, Psychoanalysis*, New York and London: Routledge, 1991; Jackie Byars, *All That Hollywood Allows: Re-reading Gender in 1950s Melodrama*, New York and London: Routledge; Christine Gledhill (ed.), *Stardom: Industry of Desire*, New York and London: Routledge, 1991', review essay, *Screen*, 34, 2: 179–89.

Swanson, G. 1994a: *Gone Shopping: Women, Consumption and the Resourcing of Civic Cultures*, Brisbane: Griffith University, Institute for Cultural Policy Studies.

Swanson, G. 1994b: 'Good-Time Girls, Men of Truth and a Thoroughly Filthy Fellow', *New Formations*, 24.

Tosh, J. 1991: 'Domesticity and Manliness in the Victorian Middle-class. The Family of Edward White Benson', in M. Roper and J. Tosh (eds), *Manful Assertions: Masculinities in Britain since 1800*, London and New York: Routledge.

Valverde, M. 1989: 'The Love of Finery: Fashion and the Fallen Woman in Nineteenth Century Social Discourse', *Victorian Studies*, Winter: 168–88.

Walker, D. 1985: 'Continence for a Nation: Seminal Loss and National Vigour', *Labour History*, 48: 1–14.

Wigley, P. 1992: 'Untitled: The Housing of Gender', in B. Colomina (ed.), *Sexuality and Space*, New York: Princeton Architectural Press.

Young, I. 1990: *Justice and the Politics of Difference*, Princeton, NJ: Princeton University Press.

Zemon Davies, N. 1987: *Society and Culture in Early Modern France*, Cambridge: Polity Press and Blackwell.

7. (Not) Belonging in Postmodern Space

John Lechte

[F]unctionalist organization, by privileging progress (i.e., time), causes the condition of [the city's] own possibility – space itself – to be forgotten; space thus becomes the blind spot in a scientific and political technology.

Michel de Certeau, 'Walking in the City'

POSTMODERN SCIENCE

To begin, and to set the scene for this chapter, I turn to that part of *The Postmodern Condition* which speaks directly about the postmodern paradigm of knowledge. This is the section of Lyotard's book which is central to his argument and at the same time the least read, so concerned have commentators been to demonstrate their adherence to, or their dissatisfaction with, the notion of the collapse of the grand narrative. The section in question distinguishes postmodern science from other forms of science. At one crucial point, Lyotard summarizes his discussion by saying that: 'Postmodern science – by concerning itself with such things as undecidables, the limits of precise control, conflict characterized by incomplete information, *'fracta,'* catastrophes, and pragmatic paradoxes – is theorizing its own evolution as discontinuous, catastrophic, nonrectifiable, and para-doxical. It is changing the meaning of the word *knowledge'* (Lyotard 1988: 60).[1]

First of all we note that in this passage Lyotard is talking about science. He is not talking about politics or philosophy – least of all literary theory. I think that this is important because by limiting (but is it a limit?) himself to science, Lyotard is remaining within an area where there is still a good deal of consensus about the nature and importance of developments, even if these are poorly understood. Few people, for instance, would want to argue that quantum theory, or the theory of relativity, is ideologically charged. Secondly, Lyotard, a philosopher, clearly links a fundamentally important dimension of knowledge to scientific knowledge. There is a postmodern science. Whatever we might think about this, science clearly figures extremely largely in Lyotard's book – and this one would never guess from the response to it. Finally, let us note that postmodern science is discontinuous with the science that preceded it. Figures like Gödel (undecidability), Heisenberg (uncertainty principle), Thom (catastrophe theory), and, to a lesser extent, Mandelbrot (theory of fractals) dominate postmodern science. Doubtless Lyotard is also concerned with the sociological context of science and with the issue of its legitimation. However, at a certain point, undecidability itself takes over so that the very nature of postmodern science feeds back into and affects the sociological context, at least as much as the latter affects the nature of science.

Why, then, this detour into *The Postmodern Condition* when our brief is to look at the so-called postmodern city? The writings of someone like Charles Jencks might have been thought to be a more pertinent point of departure given that architecture and the city are our concern. And we know that Jencks only reads Lyotard in order to classify him as a late-modernist, that is, as someone who is not a postmodernist at all (Jencks 1986: 38). My reply is that I refer to Lyotard because, whatever he might say, *The Postmodern Condition* has been for more than a decade crucial to discussions about the nature of postmodernity; I also refer to him here because I want to suggest that developments in science are fundamental for helping us to understand what has happened in the modern (or the postmodern) city, and in particular what has happened in its architecture, as witnessed, for example, in the work of Bernard Tschumi (I shall return to this).

Lyotard mentions undecidability in talking about Gödel's theorem, but he could also have referred to indetermination. Let us examine this notion in a little detail. To do so, I shall look first of all at Julia Kristeva's use of the notion of *chora* (taken up also by Elizabeth Grosz in this volume), inspired by Plato's *Timaeus*, before going on to discuss indetermination in the work of Michel Serres.

THE *CHORA*

The *chora*, according to Kristeva, 'is a nonexpressive totality formed', from a psycho-analytical perspective, 'by the drives and their stases in a motility that is as full of movement as it is regulated' (Kristeva 1984: 25). In particular, we see that the *chora* is fundamentally a space. But it is neither the space of 'phenomenological intuition' nor the space of Euclidean geometry, being closer to the deformations of topological space. Indeed, the *chora* is prior to the order and regulation such notions of space imply. It is an unordered space. Although Kristeva herself says that the *chora* 'precedes' nomination and figuration, this is not meant in any chronological sense. For the *chora* is also 'prior' to the ordering of chronological time. The *chora*, therefore, is not an origin, nor is it in any sense a cause which would produce predictable effects. Just the reverse: the *chora*, as indeterminacy, is a harbinger of pure chance. For, it 'can never be definitively posited: as a result, one can situate the *chora*, and, if necessary, lend it a topology, but one can never give it axiomatic form' (Kristeva 1984: 26). The *chora*, in sum, is an 'uncertain and indeterminate articulation' (Kristeva 1984: 25, Kristeva's italics). This is paradoxical. For if the *chora* has the status of indeterminacy, it also renders problematic the very possibility of articulation. Such, then, would be confirmation of the *chora*'s paradoxical status, a status linking it to the effects of uncertainty, paradox, and undecidability referred to in Lyotard's description of postmodern science.

Michel Serres has also taken up the notion of the *chora* in his writing on science and the arts. Of particular interest is the fact that Serres explains the *chora* within the context of the history of science, a context which is implicit in Kristeva's elaboration, and which must be understood if we are to grasp the significance of the *chora*'s paradoxical status. Like Kristeva, Serres also says that the *chora* is prior to nomination and to form (Serres 1977: 61). Importantly, though, Serres argues that the *chora* is an 'amorphous hyle' (indeterminate matter) which as such is 'transportable, communicable, applicable, importable and exportable'. Because the *chora* is detached from place, because it is context-less and indeterminate, it can be transported anywhere (Serres 1972: 121). It has the 'paradoxical characteristic of being independent and conservable, detachable and attachable or individualising' (Serres 1972: 121). From Serres, we see that nineteenth-century science (and literature – cf. Balzac) is still haunted by the spectre of Laplace. That is, its quest consists of ridding knowledge of uncertainty and indeterminacy. For the nine-teenth-century scientist, indeterminacy and chance are blots on the copybook of a science which sees chance as a most unfortunate, subjective limit to knowledge – as 'the mask of ignorance', in sum (Lestienne 1993: 35). The nineteenth-century scientist could only hope that, one day, these limits would be overcome – even if, at the time, this seemed to entail the fantastic notion of assuming the place of God. As Ian Hacking has also shown, chance was the great enemy to be tamed by nineteenth-century science (Hacking 1991: 151). This is the science of equilibrium and stasis. Within this Laplacian framework space is very much 'that of the Sun King, that of the jacobin monarchy: centred on the fixed point, the invariant of similitudes' (Serres 1980: 35).

As the Laplacian search for complete knowledge receded towards the end of the nineteenth and at the beginning of the twentieth century, and as thermodynamics opened the way to an interest in stochastics and random processes – processes which could not easily be channelled into the framework of probability, prediction, and thus determination – the idea of a system in space also took on a new significance. This was the beginning of the theory of an open system. An open system has an aspect of the *chora* in it: its 'normal' state is one of disequilibrium, transformation and change. It contains a fundamental element of indeterminacy – unlike the Laplacian closed system which would always be in equilibrium. Now, with the open system, aleatory effects become important: the effects of disorder, chance, and random distributions. Smoke, the light of the sun, ice, steam and clouds are examples of such random, unordered distributions. Turner, who painted these phenomena, has attracted Serres's attention. He sees Turner translating into painting the principles of thermodynamics as first postulated by Sadi Carnot. Serres writes that in Turner's paintings,

> the stochastic is essential . . . and, as boundaries dissolve, the way is set for a new time. The instant is not statically set or secured like a mast, but an unforeseen, hazardous state, suspended and drowned, melted in duration and then dissolved. The instant can never return regularly like the Indian Mail berthed in the Thames: for time itself is irreversible. (Serres 1982: 54)

And in Turner's paintings wherein exactly (if one can be exact) lies randomness and stochastic processes? In smoke (steam ships, locomotives, iron and steel foundries); in flames (burning wrecks); in ice (Chamonix, glaciers, a whaler entangled in an ice-field). Here, then, would be another exemplification of Kristeva's *chora*, only now, the drive-element of the semiotic gives way to the indeterminacy of topological space. Thus would the very emblems of the modern industrial city give way to the indeterminacy which, as I will try to show, makes for a different understanding of the city. Postmodernity, I shall suggest, is, in part, this new understanding.

To justify this claim we need to be aware of the extent to which the modern/postmodern city can be understood in terms of the *chora*. In effect, we want to know what kind of space is constitutive of the postmodern city. Joyce's writings open the way here. We pause a moment with *Ulysses* and the notion of indeterminacy before coming to consider the Great Arch on the outskirts of Paris, and Bernard Tschumi's design of the Parc de la Villette in Paris. Joyce – as well as Derrida – has been a fundamental influence on Tschumi, one of the major architects of postmodern space.

JOYCE

Let us turn, then, to Leopold Bloom's walk in Dublin in chapter 5 of *Ulysses*. Bloom, clearly, is walking in a city. Can we predict the trajectory of his walk – where he will go, whom and what he will see, who he will he talk to etc.? And if, in a moment of boldness, we were to answer 'yes' to this question because, as a piece of fiction which is narrated, the structure has to be predictable to some extent, can we say that each element of the narrative description is necessary to the novel? In fact, to answer in the affirmative to either question – but particularly the latter – is to misunderstand the nature of Joyce's project. Before elaborating on this point, let us read the first few sentences of chapter 5:

> By lorries along sir John Rogerson's quay Mr Bloom walked soberly, past Windmill lane, Leask's the linseed crusher, the postal telegraph office. Could have given that address too. And past the sailors' home. He turned from the morning noises of the quayside and walked through Lime street. By Brady's cottages a boy for the skins lolled, his bucket of offal linked, smoking a chewed fagbutt. A smaller girl with scars of eczema on her forehead eyed him, listlessly holding her battered caskhoop. Tell him if he smokes he won't grow. O let him! His life isn't a bed of roses. Waiting outside pubs to bring da home. (Joyce 1986: 58)

A short time later, Bloom 'crossed Townsend street' (Joyce 1986: 58), then he went 'past Nichols' the undertaker' (Joyce 1986: 58). A little further on, 'in Westland row he halted before the window of the Belfast and Oriental Tea Company' (Joyce 1986: 58). Still further on, Bloom 'turned away and sauntered across the road' (Joyce 1986: 59), and then, 'he darted a keen glance through the door of the postoffice'. Later, 'He strolled out of the postoffice and turned right' (Joyce 1986: 59), and so on. A subsequent chapter –

chapter 10, 'The Wandering of the Rocks' – is famously a much more complex and elaborate version, involving a number of walkers, of the kind of walk just cited.

THE *FLÂNEUR* – WRIT LARGE

Since Baudelaire, we know that walking in the city opened up a modernist paradigm. Walking in the city signified being away from home – read: being away from the familiar and being exposed to difference and the unfamiliar, to what Freud would call *unheimlichkeit* (unhomeliness) (Freud 1985: 335–76). Although much more sceptical as to the possibilities of encountering difference in modernist Paris, Walter Benjamin, too, saw in Baudelaire's *flâneur* the archetype of the one who is not at home: 'The *flâneur* is still on the threshold, of the city as of the bourgeois class. Neither has yet engulfed him; in neither is he at home. He seeks refuge in the crowd' (Benjamin 1986: 156). What Baudelaire actually says is that the *flâneur* is at home when he is not at home (in the crowd). The *flâneur*, indeed, is 'an ego athirst for the non-ego' (Baudelaire 1972: 400). The *flâneur* searches out the ephemeral, the transitory and the contingent. The *flâneur*'s trajectory leads nowhere and comes from nowhere. It is a trajectory without fixed spatial coordinates; there is, in short, no reference point from which to make predictions about the *flâneur*'s future. For the *flâneur* is an entity without past or future, without identity: an entity of contingency and indeterminacy.

A strictly modernist reading of Baudelaire would link the *flâneur*'s trajectory to the rise of the modern city and to the capitalist fetishism of commodities. The *flâneur* then turns into the walker in search of novelty, governed by fashion, and more or less powerless to resist the inexorable tide of consumerist culture as exemplified by the Parisian *grands magasins*. Such a view, however, loses touch with the chance effects emerging if the *flâneur*'s trajectory is understood as an indeterminate *chora* of contingency. No doubt Bloom's trajectory in *Ulysses* can be plotted on a map of Dublin, as has been done many times – as though anyone could subsequently imitate Joyce's hero's peregrinations. Bloom's walk is the walk of the *flâneur*. It is an event resulting from chance effects. Its emblem is also the steam, smoke and the fire often thought to be specific to the city produced by industrialization. In fact, as we have seen, the steam etc. are an index of randomness and chance effects. No one can predict the shape of steam; its shape is indeterminate – *chora*-like, let us add.

Lest it be objected that Bloom's, or the *flâneur*'s, walk is in fact determined because it is written down, we should perhaps remind ourselves of the problem the 'writing down' involves. It is nothing less than the writing of contingency. Strictly speaking, the contingent constitutes an impossible determination, and that is what Joyce is concerned to demonstrate. Detail piled upon detail, chance encounter upon chance encounter until it seems impossible to take any more. Or, as the text itself says:

> the coincidence of meeting, discussion, dance, row, old salt of the here today and gone tomorrow type, night loafers, the whole galaxy of events, all went to make up a miniature

cameo of the world we live in especially as the lives of the submerged tenth, viz. coalminers, divers, scavengers etc., were very much under the microscope lately. (Joyce 1986: 528)

To some extent, Joyce's project seems to verge on the impossible: to produce a text which has the contingency of the *flâneur's* trajectory. This would mean, paradoxically, that the text would lose contact with a referential outside. And indeed, *Finnegans Wake* is the exemplary instance of writing as indeterminate, of writing whose purpose is its very aleatory nature. *Finnegans Wake* problematizes the notions of beginning and end, inside and outside, and, most of all for our concerns here, cause and effect. In short, Joyce's last novel is *chora*-like. Walking is here transformed into writing for the most classical of reasons: being designated as secondary (in relation to speech and meaning), writing would have no intrinsic link with signification. In postmodern parlance, it has the status of allegory.

This allegorical element of writing has implications for the notion of space. Gregory Ulmer, one of the most astute and interesting commentators on Jacques Derrida's theory of grammatology, shows that Derrida thinks through the implications of writing as artificial memory, or 'hypomnesis' – the practice that Plato opposed so vigorously. Artificial memory can be a kind of personal code constructed for the sole purpose of recalling lived memory. It is supposedly supplementary, or secondary, to lived memory, and this is why it so disturbed Plato. He claimed that if people became dependent on artificial memory, lived memory would be diminished. For Plato, artificial memory was to lived memory much as, for Saussure, writing was to speech – a purely secondary, and thus inferior, phenomenon. Ulmer, however, relates that 'mnemo-technique' – the construction of signs to represent meanings: once known, the meaning will be remembered through the sign – is explained in a Roman textbook compiled in 86–82 BC. 'It contains', Ulmer points out, 'what became the stock definition of artificial memory, a procedure for relating places to images' (Ulmer 1985: 71). Ulmer then cites a passage explaining the way this mnemonics of place works:

A locus is a place easily grasped by the memory, such as a house, an inter-columnar space, a corner, an arch, or the like. Images are forms, marks or simulacra of what we wish to remember . . . The art of memory is like an inner writing. Those who know the letters of the alphabet can write down what is dictated to them and read out what they have written. Likewise those who have learned mnemonics can set in places what they have heard and deliver it from memory. 'For the places are very much like wax tablets or papyrus, the images like the script, and the delivery like the reading.' (Yates 1966: 6–7)

Ulmer also notes that memory was activated by an imaginary walk, with images (whether of words or things) to be remembered located at various sites along the way. The places were to be familiar to the individual; that is, they would have personal, autobiographical significance. But at the same time, they had to contain an 'active' and striking element – comic, grotesque, or 'disfigured' images (Ulmer 1985: 72) – otherwise the images might fade into an entirely banal and homely past. As Ulmer says, this memory is a kind of picture-puzzle, or rebus (Ulmer 1985: 73). Crucial to understanding the significance of a rebus is its status as a radically heterogeneous totality. As in Freud's work on dreams, each element – or image – can give rise to associations which are incommensurate with the whole. That is, the relationship between each element – or signifier – and what it signifies – or the signified – is, as structuralism showed, arbitrary. This is why there is no general code for interpreting dreams. For the dream itself contains its own code. It has the qualities of an idiolect. Writing as a rebus thus has a dream-like quality. It becomes an idiolect, especially when the walk of images has the task of remembering words, rather than things. An idiolect is indeterminate in as far as its 'grammar' comes from itself. The idiolect is simultaneously its own cause and effect. There is nothing else in terms of which it can be explained.

Michel de Certeau's essay, 'Walking in the City', evokes this link between walking (in the city) and an idiolect when he compares the geometrical space of urbanists and architects to the 'proper meaning' 'constructed by grammarians and linguists' (de Certeau 1988: 100). The proper meaning of urban space is the meaning based exclusively on causality and determination. Its inevitable accompaniment is a functionalist notion of space. The space of the idiolect, by contrast, is produced by an absolutely singular appropriation of space. Considered from the perpective of the collectivity of idiolects, the singular appropriation of space gives way to random distributions of all kinds, distributions which *are* people walking in the city. For de Certeau, although he does not say so directly, this is the aleatory, 'noise' dimension of the city ('noise' to be understood as difference and otherness, as Michel Serres has shown) – its life blood, in fact. Without noise in this sense the system of the city will die. In another essay entitled, precisely, 'Indeterminate', de Certeau summarizes part of what is at stake:

Thus to eliminate the unforeseen or expel it from calculation as an illegitimate accident and an obstacle to rationality is to interdict the possibility of a living and 'mythical' practice of the city. It is to leave its inhabitants only the scraps of a programming produced by the power of the other and altered by the event. Casual time is what is narrated in the actual discourse of the city: an indeterminate fable, better articulated on the metaphorical practices and stratified places than on the empire of the evident functionalist technocracy. (de Certeau 1988: 203)

Casual time is precisely the space-time of *Ulysses* when Bloom wanders around Dublin. Casual time is the time of idiolectic writing as it is the time – in its indeterminacy – of the *chora*. Indeterminacy, in particular as regards reference, characterizes this potentially allegorical activity: the writing of the city. This is, to repeat the now familiar litany, a writing that is heterogeneous, undecidable with regard to reference and meaning, the source – like *Finnegans Wake* – of multiple meanings, of layers of meaning in so far as such writing also has the features of a palimpsest: one level of meaning contains another – perhaps fainter, perhaps heterogeneous – one in the background. And what did Wittgenstein call language in his now celebrated statement? 'Our language can be seen as an ancient city: a maze of little streets and squares, of old and new houses, and of houses with additions from various periods; and this surrounded by a multitude of new boroughs with straight regular streets and uniform houses' (Wittgenstein 1978: 8). This is Wittgenstein's palimpsest image of language: various levels of language would show up 'beneath' the surface of the standard version. This palimpsest quality renders determination fragile. It opens language up to the pun-form manifest in *Finnegans Wake*, where the Kabbalistic tradition, Catholic theology, the philosophy of Duns Scotus, the old Irish Ogham (tree) writing, and much more all figure in the surface event of the wake for Tim Finnegan in Dublin. Meaning is rendered indeterminate here, becoming a 'babeling' of languages and of voices, 'misceginations on miscegenations' of a 'meanderthalltale' (Joyce 1971: 6, 18–19). Like walking in the city, meaning in *Finnegans Wake* goes in all directions. It does not follow the model of a message from a sender being passed to a receiver. The city of the *Wake* is indeed the city of the Tower of Babel. But in the light of the notion of the *chora* and of indeterminacy, in the light of Serres's reminder that the veritable symbols of the cities of industrialism are also random distributions, in the light, too, of de Certeau's notion of walking in the city, is it not the case that every truly modern city is in fact a Tower of Babel? Such would be the structure of modernism in the city that postmodern theory is concerned to elaborate.

The truly modern city, therefore, is a city of indetermination. It is a phenomenon of flows, of clouds of people and clouds of letters, of a multiplicity of writings and differences. What is the architecture of this city which can barely be described and named – which may only exist as a simulacrum?

Old European cities, we know, are the embodiment of symbols and meanings. Paris is no exception. At least central Paris is no exception. A walk soon reveals evidence of the Middle Ages, the Renaissance, the Enlightenment and, of course, the Revolution. But most of all, it is Haussmann who is in evidence. The most familiar street-scapes are in fact a product of the second half of the nineteenth century. Paris is, for the most part, a modern city. It had, and still has in many of its domains, a project to be realized: better housing, better systems of transport, more meaningful uses of space, better ways of preserving the patrimony for the benefit of future generations, more opportunities for innovative works of architecture etc. Paris is very much a layered city; a certain discourse about the city, however, almost invariably emphasizes the place of tradition in the evolution of Paris, often to the exclusion of all else. This tradition is couched in examples of political and religious symbolism: place de la Bastille and Notre Dame are perhaps cited most often. There is, too, the network of monuments which, from the air, give a stereotypically 'continental garden' aspect to the city: a neat, symmetrical grid of points and lines joins key edifices, like the Arc de Triomphe, Les Invalides and the Eiffel Tower. In this discourse of the city, buildings are deemed to have a story to tell even if, eventually, this becomes the story of the building's use. The Centre Georges Pompidou is perhaps the most striking instance of this meaning as 'use-value'. In effect, such a discourse is the discourse of determination and causality.

There are, however, two architectural pieces which perhaps cannot be understood in such unambiguously modernist terms. These are the Arch at La Défense on the north-western boundary of central Paris, and the Parc de la Villette on its north-eastern perimeter.

THE GREAT ARCH

La Grande Arche – the Great Arch – at La Défense soars above an often wind-swept pedestrian space (the *parvis*, or concourse) before it. Surrounding this open space overlooked by the Great Arch are buildings of international-style modernism: glass or shiny façades seem to follow the on-looker at every turn. At first appearance, the arch itself appears to be nothing more than a purer version of this very same international style: a huge three-sided figure with a space in the middle. Some have likened it to a late-twentieth-century version of the Arc de Triomphe, while others, like Marguerite Duras, have said that it is the symbol of God in our secular age – the void is God's Place (Duras 1990: 33). To look at the arch from the pedestrian concourse is to look through it and above it as though it were transparent, as though it were there simply to encircle the void while at the same time disappearing in the void as though disappearing into part of itself; a kind of giant Klein bottle, perhaps, where the distinction between inside and outside becomes problematic. The point is that there are no stories to be told on this surface (as with the Arc de Triomphe). There is no event marked – as with the Obelisk covered with Egyptian hieroglyphics in place de la Concorde. On the contrary, the arch is more like Mallarmé's white page waiting to receive an inscription. On the other hand, the shape of the arch is unambiguous: a three-sided parallelogram enclosing a void; a geometrical figure imposing a definite shape on space; a specific place from which one can view central Paris and the network of major monuments – if one is game enough to take the lift which runs up and down one of the arch's columns. This figure is determined. It is as though it were a symbol of the cause-and-effect logic of the nineteenth-century science which valorized determination above all else. This figure, clearly, is not cloud-like.

WALKING IN THE ARCH

At three o'clock in the afternoon of 1 March 1993, I make the metro journey from Gare St Lazare in central Paris to the Great Arch at La Défense. A sharp wind makes conditions bitterly cold on the pedestrian concourse. I walk underneath the huge edifice, ready to photograph it from below. With my camera I (naively?) try to photograph the quasi-sacred void of the arch. At one side of the rise upon which the arch is built, there is a cemetery. I put death and the void together. But am I right? On the other side of the concourse, not far from the merry-go-round, is a nineteenth-century memorial to the Paris Commune of 1871 set incongruously against a back-drop of reflective glass and steel. Reminders of death thus take up space at either extremity of the arch's surrounds. Death haunts the arch.

At the base of the arch I am only at the end of the Paris metro line, and yet central Paris is out of sight. It could well be a thousand miles away. I am alone – we, who are at the arch, are alone in its void. This void extends for the whole of the concourse.

Nothing signifies; the arch least of all. Its architectural purpose – which would provide something to go on – is mysteriously concealed. As a result, people do not communicate. The mysterious and the mystical are, at one level, an absence of communication. People are not in touch with each other. They are separated, alienated from each other. Central Paris, I remind myself, is, by contrast, the city of meaning and unity – almost to a fault. There, exclusion of the non-conformist can at times be brutal. I am here in the void unable to speak. I stand with my camera at the ready. What can I photograph? How can I photograph a void?

There is another dimension of which I am a part, however: chance. On the concourse, skate-boarders rush past in quick succession, people walk, talk, jog. Japanese tourists in dark amorphous shapes meander on the concourse. How wonderful to see patterns forming and reforming in a show of unpredictable human presence. Everything is in flux. I photograph the scene a number of times: each photograph is simultaneously the same and different: different configurations of the same scene. No photograph is, strictly speaking, representative of what I am experiencing; no single photograph can depict the movement – that is, the difference of the scene. 'Scene' – the word rings in my head for a moment, and I turn to look at the arch. At such close quarters, it is impossible to take in all of its extremities. From a distance of several hundred metres my thought is confirmed. I focus intently on the edges of the arch: they are recessed like a picture frame. The transversal beam of the arch reflects the perspective of the steps leading up to it. The idea grows on me more forcefully the more I look at the structure in front of me on this, the most wintry of Parisian days.

As a frame, the arch becomes almost surreal. It is enormous in its mass: perfectly opaque. At the same time, as a frame, it presides over the pedestrian concourse on one side, and the cemetery on the other. As a frame, the arch is simultaneously there and not there – present and absent; it belongs and does not belong to the space it inhabits. This means, too, that it is both determined and not determined. Thus when, from a distance of a hundred metres, the huge structure disappears in the mists of winter rain, and when in the summer sun the arch shines forth, clearly, with presence, as it does in every postcard, these chance processes do nothing less than confirm the arch's entirely ambiguous status as a frame. Finally, as a frame the arch could be erected – if not anywhere – at least in a variety of sites. Its very abstract, geometrical quality detaches it from its surroundings; it could, as Derrida has said of speech-acts, be re-iterated. By contrast, the buildings surrounding St Mark's Square in Venice, or the Sydney Opera House in relation to its forecourt and Sydney Harbour, are wedded to their sites. The Opera House 'sails' in particular seem to be irrevocably linked to the sails on the harbour.

CHANCE AND TSCHUMI'S FOLLY

The arch presides over chance and indeterminacy. The walk in the city is here on the concourse for all to see. As the French writer Maurice Blanchot says, in speaking of surrealism – and in particular in speaking of André Breton's novel about a chance encounter in Paris, *Nadja*:

> Game, die *[l'aléa]*, encounter. *These words designate, without defining it, a new space – space as the vertigo of spacing: dis-tance, dis-location, dis-course – from which, whether in life through desire, in knowledge through the expression not at all controlled of an absence of knowledge, in time through the affirmation of intermittence, in the whole of the Universe through refusing the Unique and through the expectation of a relation without unity, in the work [oeuvre], finally, through a liberation of the absence of a work, the* unknown *announces itself and, outside the game, enters into the game. Space which is only ever the proximity of another space, the closeness of the faraway, the beyond, but without transcendence as without immanence. (Blanchot 1967: 307–8)*

In this passage, chance turns space into an unrepresentable – because indeterminable and unpredictable – otherness. Space ceases to be homely and becomes uncanny.

In the light of Blanchot, we note that the American architect Bernard Tschumi has allowed chance to figure prominently in his design for Parc de la Villette in Paris. Chance arises in the space of buildings, alley-ways, lawns (surfaces) – and in the red tower-like structures which go to make up the *folies*. Most of all, Tschumi has tried to avoid creating a unified, harmonious architectural work. He claims to go against the Cartesian impulse in modern architecture in doing so. Is it possible to have an architectural work that is not simply the product of identity, homogeneity and synthesis? Such would be the question at Tschumi's point of departure. As Tschumi explains it, his key terms are 'superimposition', 'dissociation' and 'dispersion', rather than unity and harmony. Influenced by Derrida and Joyce, as well as by Calvino, Bataille, Kafka and Poe, Tschumi aimed, in the *folies* project, to emphasize the heterogeneous non-relation between elements. Through programmatic disjunctions at the planning stage, Tschumi breaks up the surface of the space to be built into fragments. He then reassembles these fragments according to a principle selected at random. Often, fragments are superimposed upon each other with neither element entirely in dominance.

To talk about Tschumi's 'plan' is misleading. Rather, this deconstructive artist treats as problematic the relationship of plan to work. Although cognizant of tradition, Tschumi does not accept that an architect's plan is the origin of the work. In effect, he bypasses the principle enunciated by Marx, amongst others, to the effect that what distinguishes the worst of architects from the best of bees is that the architect first of all forms an image of the work in the imagination before it is realized. This is a version of cause-and-effect logic. For Tschumi, on the other hand, the Parc de la Villette project 'directed an attack against cause-and-effect relationships' (Tschumi 1988: 38). Again, Tschumi says that the design for the Parc 'eliminated the presumption of a pre-established causality between programme, architecture and signification' (Tschumi 1988: 38).

Chance has its place in Tschumi's three-structures approach, beyond the intended outcome. (Let us recall here Cournot's definition of chance as the intersection of two or more chains of causality.) These consist of three 'autonomous systems of points, lines and surfaces'. In its own right, each system is, or aims to be, entirely logical and coherent. The interaction of the three is what encourages 'conflict over synthesis' (Tschumi 1988: 38). For Tschumi, the Parc subverts the very notion of borders upon which 'context depends'.

At a less abstract level, the vistor to the Parc finds three notable constellations of buildings: the main hall of the science museum, the spherical Géode, and the series of red *folies* – built masses distributed throughout the park in the form of a grid. Surfaces of lawn and alley-ways surround the *folies*. The main hall – composed of rectangles, triangles and squares, all distributed to form two sections which mirror each other – confronts the Géode: a 36-metre sphere with 6,433 convex triangles made of 'mirrored' stainless steel. What cannot be known from the exterior is that the sphere contains a revolutionary, 'state-of-the-art' cinema. The form of the Géode thus has no necessary relationship to its ostensible function. The changing nature of topological space is comprehended in the Géode's mirrored surface. Beyond it, there is the space of the red *folies*. Two things in particular are surprising about the park. The first is that it is indeed difficult to tell where its boundary actually is, so much does it open out onto the adjoining spaces – echoing Blanchot's notion that space is the proximity of another space. The second thing is that while the main hall seems to be cut off from the spaces of the *folies*, the Géode's mirrored surface forms a mediating link between the main hall and the remainder of the park. The Géode partially mediates between the main hall and the red *folies*. *Folie*: an extravagant and useless structure, something that did not need to be built and is often left unfinished. Taken together, Tschumi's *folies* are an adventure in non-determination and undecidability. They upset any attempt at an overriding and hierarchical equilibrium in the park. Parc de la Villette is perhaps emblematic of the city today: the borderless city of chance configurations and an absence of meaning.

AS A CONCLUSION: NON-KNOWLEDGE

Let me conclude by returning to postmodern science. If postmodern science takes us to the limits of knowledge and the beginning of chance, if it discovers that non-knowledge (as the undecidable, as uncertainty, as indeterminacy) is structurally inescapable, what it also discovers – if this essay has been successful – is that through space, writing is tied to science; for writing is also indeterminate. Who would have thought that grammatology might have such scientific connections? The political implications of this are perhaps still to be recognized.

NOTES

1 When I say that this is the 'least read' part of *The Postmodern Condition*, I do not mean that it has never mentioned in commentaries, but that the implications have rarely been drawn out or reflected upon.

REFERENCES

Bajomée, D. 1990: 'Veiller sur le sens absent', *Le Magazine littéraire*, 278, 33.

Baudelaire, C. 1972: 'The Painter and Modern Life', in *Selected Writings on Art and Artists*, trans. P.E. Charvet, Harmondsworth: Penguin.

Benjamin, W. 1986: 'Paris, Capital of the Nineteenth Century', in *Reflections: Essays, Aphorisms, Autobiographical Writings*, trans. Edmund Jephcott, New York: Schocken Books.

Blanchot, M. 1967: 'Le demain joueur', *La Nouvelle Revue Française*, April: 283–308.

de Certeau, M. 1988: *The Practice of Everyday Life*, trans. Steven Rendall, Berkeley: University of California Press.

Duras, M. 1990: 'Interview with Marianne Alphant', *Libération*, 11 January.

Freud, S. 1985: 'The Uncanny' ('Das Unheimliche'), *The Pelican Freud Library*, vol. 14, Harmondsworth: Penguin.

Hacking, I. 1991: *The Taming of Chance*, Cambridge: Cambridge University Press.

Jencks, C. 1986: *What is Post-modernism?*, London: Academy.

Joyce, J. 1971: *Finnegans Wake*, second edition, London: Faber and Faber. Original publication 1939.

Joyce, J. 1986: *Ulysses*, the Corrected Text, London: Bodley Head

Kristeva, J. 1984: *Revolution in Poetic Language*, trans. Margaret Waller, New York: Columbia University Press.

Lestienne, R. 1993: *Le Hasard créateur*, Paris: Editions de la Découverte.

Lyotard, J.-F. 1988: *The Postmodern Condition: A Report on Knowledge*, trans. G. Bennington and B. Massumi, Minneapolis: University of Minnesota Press. Original publication 1984.

Serres, M. 1972: *Hermès II. L'Interférence*, Paris: Editions de Minuit.

Serres, M. 1977: *Hermès IV. La Distribution*, Paris: Editions de Minuit.

Serres, M. 1980: *Hermès V. Le Passage du nord-ouest*, Paris: Editions de Minuit.

Serres, M. 1982: 'Turner Translates Carnot', trans. M. Shortland, *Block*, 6, 54: 46–55.

Tschumi, B. 1988: 'Parc de la Villette', *Architectural Design* (Deconstruction in Architecture), 58, 3/4: 32–9.

Ulmer, G. 1985: *Applied Grammatology: Post(e)-Pedagogy from Jacques Derrida to Joseph Beuys*, Baltimore and London: Johns Hopkins.

Wittgenstein, L. 1978: *Philosophical Investigations*, trans. G.E.M. Anscombe, Oxford: Blackwell, third edition, reprinted 1978.

Yates, F.A. 1966: *The Art of Memory*, London: Routledge and Kegan Paul.

8. Imaginary Cities: Images of Postmodernity

Paul Patton

Images of the city play a crucial role in accounts of the postmodern condition. As a matter of course, these accounts include as one of their essential moments a description of the experience of contemporary urban life. Thus, Fredric Jameson's 1984 essay 'Postmodernism, or the Cultural Logic of Late Capitalism' concludes with a section devoted to the analysis of 'a full-blown postmodern building', the Bonaventure Hotel in Los Angeles. David Harvey's *The Condition of Postmodernity* (1990) opens with a commentary upon the picture of urban life presented in Jonathan Raban's *Soft City* (1974). In what follows I shall examine both of these influential accounts of the postmodern experience of cities, and compare them, firstly, with Raban's account, and secondly, with the account of city life given by Iris Marion Young in *Justice and the Politics of Difference* (1990b). In all cases, I propose that we are dealing with imaginary cities. These are not simply the products of memory or desire, like many of Calvino's invisible cities, but rather complex objects which include both realities and their description: cities confused with the words used to describe them (Calvino 1979: 51). To call these imaginary cities is not to suggest that these are not real in their way, or that they do not have effects. Nor is it to suggest that they are all imaginary in the same sense: one of the aims of this chapter will be to separate out some of the different senses in which these postmodern cities are 'imaginary'.

In aligning in this manner the distinctive character of (post)modern life, its art, politics and predominant sense of self, with the experience of urban existence, the theorists of postmodernity are continuing a literary and philosophical tradition which dates from at least the end of the eighteenth century. Marshall Berman's *All That is Solid Melts into Air* (1982) shows that there is a characteristic experience of modernity, repeated in its variant recorded forms throughout the nineteenth and early twentieth century. The tenor of much postmodern discourse on the city remains surprisingly consistent with the city-experience of modernity. In most cases, we find a general mistrust of the artificial or ephemeral character of city life, a sense that it encourages moral and other kinds of confusion, often juxtaposed with a reluctant admission that there is none the less something appealing or even exciting about the space of possibilities that it unfolds. Elements of this city-imaginary have in turn affected the development of real cities. To the extent that the designs of architects and urban planners have been affected by this widespread nervousness about the moral consequences of city living, a kind of feedback loop has operated between the recorded experience of city life and changes to its material space. According to Harvey, and consistent with his argument that postmodernity itself is an effect of the compression of space and time under late capitalism, this feedback has recently become even more direct. He argues that postmodernism existed as a representation of the experience of urban life before it was explicitly taken up by architects and planners to produce the kinds of multifunctional space which Jameson takes to be emblematic of the postmodern condition itself: 'Postmodern built environments typically seek out and deliberately replicate themes that Raban so strongly emphasized in *Soft City*: [these include] an emporium of styles, an encyclopaedia, a "maniacal scrap-book filled with colourful entries"' (Harvey 1990: 83).

I take this to be a tacit admission that all such accounts of the postmodern condition of urban life present us with imaginary cities, as well as an example of the manner in which these can nevertheless have real effects. While it would be interesting to pursue the question of relations between these imaginary cities and the real cities we inhabit, I propose instead to examine the imaginary cities themselves, as a way of questioning the philosophical and political diagnoses of postmodernity in which they occur. In the end, it may be that Calvino is right to suggest that we only ever inhabit a city of signs: 'However the city may really be, beneath this thick coating of signs, whatever it may contain or conceal, you leave Tamara without having discovered it' (Calvino 1979: 15–16). The problem then would not be to interpret or decode these signs, where that would mean attaining a reality beyond signs, but to 'read' them (which means to produce further signs) in ways which might enhance our capacities to live in proximity with strangers. In Iris Marion Young's work we find some indication as to how this task might be pursued.

Jameson concludes his influential account of the postmodern condition with an analysis of the Bonaventure Hotel in LA's city centre. The point of this analysis is to amplify and render explicit the terms of his preceding account of postmodernity, and in doing so to exemplify the consequence that he draws:

> I am proposing the notion that we are here in the presence of something like a mutation in built space itself. My implication is that we ourselves, the human subjects who happen into this new space, have not kept pace with that evolution; there has been a mutation in the object unaccompanied as yet by any equivalent mutation in the subject. We do not yet possess the perceptual equipment to match this new hyperspace, as I will call it, in part because our perceptual habits were formed in that older kind of space I have called the space of high modernism. (Jameson 1991: 39)

Jameson's description then traces some of the more confusing aspects of this 'new hyperspace': the profusion of 'curiously unmarked' entrances to the building, all 'lateral and rather backdoor affairs'; the combination of functions which suggest that 'the Bonaventure aspires to being a total space, a complete world, a kind of miniature city'; the reflective exterior which 'achieves a peculiar and placeless dissociation of the Bonaventure from its neighbourhood'; and the central space of the hotel lobby which brings the bewildered reader back once more to Jameson's conclusion: 'that this latest mutation in space – postmodern hyperspace – has finally succeeded in transcending the capacities of the human body to locate itself, to organise its immediate surroundings perceptually, and cognitively to map its position in a mappable external world' (Jameson 1991: 45).

It is tempting to ridicule this analysis.[1] First, because the passage of time and the diffusion of the design features of this building have now made it a familiar environment. In my neighbourhood, the Ramada Hotel at Bondi has many of the features of this 'full-blown postmodern building': the multi-level back and side entrances, the incorporation of shopping arcade space, the central atrium with open lifts. Second, because Jameson's analysis always seemed a somewhat overblown response to a novel architectural design (this is someone who gets lost in large department stores). Jameson's postmodern space is an imaginary space in the most banal sense of the term: a made-up image of reality, the invention of an overheated theoretical imagination.

The attempt to connect the confusion provoked by an unfamiliar space with the socio-historical condition of postmodernity is unconvincing. Postmodern space is aligned with certain theoretical and artistic treatments of difference, in which, he suggests, the very materials of the text 'tend to fall apart into random and inert passivity' (Jameson 1991: 31). Clearly, for Jameson, the experience of postmodern space is disorienting and disabling. Yet he seeks to assimilate the loss of the capacity for orientation and 'cognitive mapping' brought about by postmodern space to the breakdown of normal linguistic and temporal unities which characterizes schizophrenic experience, and both of these to the dominant aesthetic of postmodernism:

> If, indeed, the subject has lost its capacity actively to extend its pro-tensions and re-tensions across the temporal manifold and to organise its past and future into coherent experience, it becomes difficult to see how the cultural productions of such a subject could result in anything but 'heaps of fragments' and in a practice of the randomly heterogeneous and fragmentary and the aleatory. These are, however, very precisely some of the privileged terms in which postmodernist cultural production has been analyzed. (Jameson 1991: 25)

Jameson's own account seeks to problematize these terms by locating them as effects of late capitalism, and to counter them by calling for a new aesthetic of cognitive mapping. His analysis of the experience of postmodern space is ultimately no more than a tactical manoeuvre in this attempted discursive capture of postmodernity.

David Harvey's diagnosis of postmodernity is also based upon a representation of urban experience. In this case, however, the representation is not simply his own, but taken from Jonathan Raban's account of urban life in *Soft City*. It is a more broadly based representation since the book recounts the author's experience of the city as a social, commercial and cultural as well as a built environment. Raban describes his urban experience around the early 1970s in terms of the extreme variety and flexibility of individual life in cities, its magical and illusory quality and the manner in which the city appears to offer an endless array of possibilities for social being and action. As such, Harvey comments, the city is a theatrical space, 'a series of stages upon which individuals could work their own distinctive magic while performing a multiplicity of roles' (Harvey 1990: 5). But the very success of the city in these terms only contributes to its failings at the level of rational social order. The city is a place where individuals can assume different identities with comparative' ease, but where they run the risk of losing themselves in the process, or being harmed by the violence of others.

Harvey presents *Soft City* as 'a vital affirmation that the postmodernist moment has arrived' (Harvey 1990: 6). In Raban's account, Harvey finds evidence of an eclecticism in city life that parallels the design features so confusing to Jameson. These include a positive attitude towards the attention to image which is part of city living: the sense in which the city offers an 'emporium of styles' from which the individual might choose an identity. Along with this allusion to consumerism as a style of life, Harvey identifies an appeal to 'notions of subjective individualism' at the heart of Raban's response. In fact, it is misleading to suggest that *Soft City* is simply an affirmation of the experience of city life as a space of unrivalled freedom and open-ended possibility. Raban draws our attention repeatedly to the dangers and risks of such a space in which 'nothing is fixed, [and] the possibilities of personal change and renewal are endless and open' (Raban 1974: 245). Harvey recognizes that Raban does point to dangers as well as possibilities inherent in city living: the city may well be a theatre in Raban's eyes, but that means there are opportunities for villains and fools to strut the stage as well. Nevertheless, Harvey's account of the postmodern experience of the city tends to flatten such nuances, as he relies upon Raban primarily to set the scene for his own analysis of the postmodern condition as the effect of a new stage in the compression of social time and space under the conditions of production, exchange and circulation of late capitalism.

Harvey's analysis adds detail to Jameson's assertion of economic determinism. The acceleration in the turnover time of capital in production brought about by the new strategies of flexible accumulation require parallel accelerations in exchange and consumption. Technological changes in transportation and communication allow much more rapid circulation of people, commodities and money. As such, they constitute a relative compression of spatial borders. Harvey points to two developments in consumption which meet the demand for increased speed: the increased importance of fashion across a whole range of life-style activities, and the tendency towards consumption of services and recreational events. In this way, he proposes to deduce the ethics and aesthetics of postmodernism from fundamental changes in the process of capital accumulation. For example, the growth of an 'image industry' can be seen on the one hand to respond to the underlying exigencies of capital accumulation, on the other to give rise to the proliferation of simulacra and the importance widely attached to appearances. Similarly, the annihilation of space through rapid transportation changes the mix of commodities available in local markets and thereby contributes to the experience of the city as an 'emporium of styles', in Raban's phrase (Harvey 1990: 299).

Given this type of analysis, it should come as no surprise that Harvey offers a generally unfavourable diagnosis of the postmodern condition. It is presented as a superficial phenomenon, albeit one that threatens our capacity to understand and to control social processes. As a new *phase* of space-time compression, Harvey suggests that it repeats to some degree the conditions of an earlier phase around the beginning of this century. He points to similarities between aspects of turn-of-the-century modernism and the present, such as the concern with forms of local cultural identity in the midst of a general celebration of universalism, and worries that the present tendency to 'aestheticize' social and political thought may lead to a repetition of fascism. There are many levels at which one might object to such an analysis. The one on which I wish to insist here is the representation of city life on which it all hangs. While there is no doubt that many of the phenomena to which Harvey draws attention are significant features of present-day urban life, it is not clear that they are the most important features of the experience which Raban describes. Harvey's postmodern city is in effect the habitat of the consumer, who in turn is a puppet manipulated by more powerful forces. The theatricality of postmodern urban life is a distant effect of the increase in the turnover time of capital, manifest in social life by means of the industries and technologies of the image. The city itself is ultimately a distorted image of the material possibilities for human community. Harvey's city is imaginary in a structural sense of the term: a realm of appearance which is undoubtedly real but nevertheless dependent upon a deeper reality; an epiphenomenon in the sense that, for Marx, the entire sphere of exchange and consumption is dependent upon relations of production.

Raban's hypothesis is in many respects richer than Harvey's. It is not simply that urban life has become more superficial, more image- and consumption-based under the conditions of late capitalism, but rather that the city in itself is an imaginary space. The important difference from Harvey's account is that Raban refuses to draw a distinction between the imaginary city and its real conditions of existence. The city itself is 'soft', in the sense that it is a type of reality for which the boundary between imagination and fact is not absolute (Raban 1974: 70). In a passage near the beginning of the book and cited by Harvey, Raban writes

> *Cities, unlike villages and small towns, are plastic by nature. We mould them in our images: they, in their turn, shape us by the resistance they offer when we try to impose a personal form on them. In this sense, it seems to me that living in a city is an art, and we need the vocabulary of art, of style, to describe the particular relation between man and material that exists in the continual creative play of urban living. The city as we might imagine it, the soft city of illusion, myth, aspiration, nightmare, is as real, maybe more real, than the hard city one can locate in maps and statistics, in monographs on urban sociology and demography and architecture. (Raban 1974: 10)*

Raban's reasons for this view are instructive. He argues from the premise that the fundamental condition of city life, the source of its most basic dynamic, is not the fact of greater abundance of commodities and services, nor the fact of greater speed in their delivery and consumption, but the fact that in cities we live in constant and close proximity to strangers: 'to live in a city is to live in a community of people who are strangers to one another' (Raban 1974: 15). The point is not that we are all condemned to isolation, anomie or loneliness, even though those are a feature of urban life for many, but rather that for the most part our daily encounters with others are encounters with people we do not know, or know only a little. Yet our contacts may involve the most 'personal' parts of their lives or our own: our bodies touch on buses or in queues; we overhear snatches of conversation in restaurants or on the street; if we live in apartments we are exposed to the sounds and occasional sights of others going about their daily lives. What we see are fragmentary glimpses, snapshots of the lives of others, and on the basis of these fragments we extrapolate, identify and make judgements about them. Hitchcock's *Rear Window* is based entirely upon this dimension of urban living. It shows both the attraction, or compulsion, to observe the lives of others and the dangers of doing so in the fragmentary way that this kind of life allows. Raban draws attention to another consequence: we rely of necessity upon stereotypes or cues to determine the manner of person we are dealing with, the cut of their clothes or of their hair, an accent or a manner of speaking. In cities, people identify other people on the basis of their appearance, their social role or other singular characteristics. In turn, this mode of relating to others reacts back upon their own sense of self and they experience themselves as actors. It is this phenomenon, rather than the dynamics of consumption, which is the basis of the 'intrinsic theatricality' of city life which Raban describes: 'In cities, people are given to acting, putting on a show of themselves' (Raban 1974: 37).

This dynamic whereby, once a human being becomes aware that he or she is acting, he or she becomes an actor has always been part of the experience of cities. Plato worried about theatre on these grounds, and Nietzsche devoted several passages in *The Gay Science* to 'the problem of the actor'. However, what sets the present experience of city life apart from that of earlier periods is simply the extent to which this dynamic has affected our sense of ourselves and our lives: to a greater degree than ever before, the self is collapsed into its manner of presentation. This is at once the source of both the sense of freedom and endless possibility in relation to personal identity, and the fear of becoming a 'stranger to oneself' (Raban 1974: 250). The ironic detachment from the forms of meaningful activity in which one is nevertheless engaged might be seen as an effect of this sense of freedom. Some theorists have argued that such irony is precisely what characterizes postmodernity understood as a mood or structure of feeling (Jencks 1992; Rorty 1989; Kolb 1990). Raban's account suggests that the origins of this mood might be found in the ironic sense of self to which city life gives rise. By contrast, the widespread concern with identity and self-definition in present city life might be seen as a response to this fear of losing oneself in the play of representations: 'we need to hold on tight to avoid going completely soft in a soft city' (Raban 1974: 250). To the extent that the inhabitant of the (post)modern city is no longer a subject apart from his or her performances, the border between self and city has become fluid. Raban's city is thus imaginary in a deconstructive sense of the term: it is the city as experienced by a subject which is itself the product of urban existence, a decentred subject which can neither fully identify with nor fully dissociate from the signs which constitute the city.

Raban is not a deconstructive theorist nor even a theorist of postmodernity, but in describing the dynamic inherent in the experience of cities he touches upon many of the issues central to accounts of the postmodern condition: the nature of personal identity, the locus of responsibility and the grounds of judgement to name a few. The richness of his account lies in the degree to which it intersects with this field of problems. On the one hand, he argues that we belong in cities to the extent that we have developed special skills for living in them: living in cities is an art and it requires a kind of creative competence. On the other hand, he worries that we live in cities badly. It is hard to live among strangers and still think of oneself as a citizen, he argues: 'it is hard to learn to live as generously as real citizenship demands' (Raban 1974: 245). Raban's inability to do more than pose this question of how to live as citizens in cities appears to be a consequence of his understanding citizenship only in terms of the social conditions found in smaller and less urban communities. In villages and towns, he argues, one knows what it means to belong to a community just as, or indeed because, one knows one's neighbours.

By contrast, Iris Marion Young employs an image of the city precisely to contradict the ideal of community predominant within feminist and anti-capitalist political theory. Her objections to this ideal are couched in deconstructive terms: the ideal of community privileges unity over difference, thereby denying the reality and value of irreducible differences between individuals and between types of people. It threatens to reinstate the structures of exclusion which operate in ethnic and other forms of chauvinism. The ideal of community is therefore undesirable as well as implausible. It is founded upon a unitary ideal of subjectivity which misrepresents the play of unconscious forces, desires and language in terms of which individual identity is achieved. It presupposes an ideal of direct, unmediated social interaction between persons which denies the mediation through language, voice and gesture which operates even in face-to-face encounters. The fact of communication by means of language implies difference and distance in both temporal and spatial senses: it therefore implies the possibility of misunderstanding, of distorted or failed communication. But it also implies the possibility of concealment, creativity and play. Moreover, the desire to communicate across differences of culture, language, race and age might be seen to imply a recognition and a respect for others. There is a pleasure 'in being drawn out of oneself' through the realization that there are other ways of thinking and acting (Young 1990b: 240).

Young points out that social relations predicated upon difference and mediation are instantiated in city life. Cities are places in which different kinds of people live in relative proximity to one another, sharing services as well as spaces, but not always belonging to a single community. The ideal of community thus flies in the face of the economic and political realities of (post)modern urban life. Impersonal networks of communication, transportation and distribution of goods and services structure the material conditions of urban existence. Because these are unlikely to be readily disassembled, Young argues, 'urbanity is the condition of the modern, not to mention the postmodern, condition' (Young 1990b: 237). Further, because this horizon does not lack attractions, the ideal of community also sets itself against the pleasures of city life. Young sketches an account of the experience of living in cities that draws attention to the benefits of its spatial, temporal, ethnic and cultural diversity. For example, the city allows differences of religious, cultural or sexual orientation to flourish in ways not possible in smaller and more homogenous communities. There is an erotic dimension to city life that flows from the concentration and variety of people. Much of city life takes place in public, much of it in motion: the possibilities for encounter with others are endless. By relating this eroticism to the 'social and spatial inexhaustibility' of the city, and both of these to its social, architectural and cultural diversity, Young touches upon themes familiar within accounts of city life. However, as Berman shows, the recurrent experience of modernity and urbanity was always ambivalent, alternating between the sense of endless possibility and the sense of loss, between exhilaration and despair. Whereas earlier theorists of postmodernity such as Jameson and Harvey tended to emphasize the negative aspect of this experience, emphasizing the potential for disorientation and loss of self, Young's account emphasizes the positive. In its open embrace of decentred subjectivity, its affirmation of difference and the attendant possibilities for new forms of social being, hers is a *postmodern* representation of city life in the sense that Lyotard gives to this term: not that which comes after the modern but that in the modern which seeks to refashion the self, the conditions of life and the means of representation (Lyotard 1986).

The moral and political interest of this image of the city derives from the sense in which it embodies 'a kind of relationship' which people may have to one another (Young 1990a: 318). Building upon the positive aspects of the experience of cities, Young proposes an ideal of the city as a metaphor for a politics of difference. At its best, city life embodies an ideal form of social relations between strangers, a form of coexistence that Young calls 'openness to unassimilated otherness' (Young 1990b: 227). Such openness is not always found in urban social relations: there are hierarchies of wealth and power within cities that create asymmetrical and impenetrable barriers between segments of the population. However, this does not detract from the interest of the normative ideal of city life as an alternative to both liberal individualism and communitarianism. Against the ideal of community, Young argues that 'politics must be conceived as a relationship of strangers who do not understand one another in a subjective and immediate sense' (Young 1990b: 234). Against liberal individualism, she insists upon the value of the kinds of coexistence and interdependence which occur in cities. Like Raban, Young insists that city life is primarily a 'being together of strangers' (Young 1990b: 237). Public spaces are both a primary means by which social relationships are enacted and a metaphor for the relationships of city life. Unlike Raban, however, she takes public spaces to embody the kind of free access and freedom to speak which are necessary conditions of democratic citizenship. The result is a spatialized ideal of political life, a return of politics to the *polis*.[2]

Finally, this is an imaginary city in yet another sense of this term. By virtue of its positive emphasis upon difference, the erotic and aesthetic variety of city life, Young's imaginary city is recognizably postmodern. By virtue of its normative character and its pragmatic political intent, it is a thoroughly modern image. While not simply utopian, since it is grounded in a widely shared positive experience of city life, it is none the less a normative ideal, intended to serve as a basis and an orientation for a politics of difference. While not simply heterotopic, since it refers as much to unrealized possibilities within city life as it does to any existing aspects or institutions, this imaginary city is nevertheless a differential space in which politics is possible and conflict unavoidable. Neither fully real nor entirely imaginary, but partly both, the unoppressive city is a postmodern object *par excellence*: undecidably modern and postmodern, visible and invisible, it is both a dimension of the experience of city life and a metaphor of politics.[3]

NOTES

1 Jean Baudrillard appears to have succumbed to this temptation: see his account of the revolving cocktail bar at the top of the Bonaventure Hotel (Baudrillard 1988: 59–60). A detailed comparison of Jameson's description of the Bonaventure Hotel and Baudrillard's essay on the Pompidou Centre is provided in Gane (1991: 143–56). See also the remarks in Soja (1990: 16–20).
2 See the remarks on politics and spatiality in Soja (1990: 34).
3 This conception of the city as simultaneously real and metaphorical, and the possibilities for social and political theory opened up by such a conception, are discussed with reference to the writings of Walter Benjamin and Salman Rushdie (1993: 9, 21).

REFERENCES

Baudrillard, J. 1988: *America*, trans. Chris Turner, London and New York: Verso.
Benjamin, W. and Rushdie, S. 1993: 'The Politics of Place', in M. Keith and S. Pile (eds), *Place and the Politics of Identity*, London: Routledge.
Berman, M. 1982: *All That is Solid Melts into Air*, New York: Simon and Schuster.
Calvino, I. 1979: *Invisible Cities*, London: Pan Books.
Gane, M. 1991: *Baudrillard's Bestiary: Baudrillard and Culture*, London and New York: Routledge.
Harvey, D. 1990: *The Condition of Postmodernity*, Oxford: Blackwell.
Keith, M. and Pile, S. (eds) 1993: *Place and the Politics of Identity*, London: Routledge.
Jameson, F. 1984: 'Postmodernism, or the Cultural Logic of Late Capitalism', *New Left Review*, 146: 53–92.
Jameson, F. 1988: 'Cognitive Mapping', in C. Nelson and L. Grossberg (eds), *Marxism and the Interpretation of Culture*, London: Macmillan Education.
Jameson, F. 1991: *Postmodernism, or the Cultural Logic of Late Capitalism*, Durham: Duke University Press.
Jencks, C. 1992: 'The Post-Modern Agenda', in C. Jencks (ed.), *The Post-modern Reader*, London: Academy Editions.

Kolb, D. 1990: *Postmodern Sophistications: Philosophy, Architecture and Tradition*, Chicago and London: University of Chicago Press.

Lyotard, J.-F. 1986: 'An Answer to the Question "What is Postmodernism?"', appendix to *The Postmodern Condition: A Report on Knowledge*, trans. G. Bennington and B. Massumi, Manchester: Manchester University Press.

Raban, J. 1974: *Soft City*, London: Hamish Hamilton.

Rorty, R. 1989: *Contingency, Irony and Solidarity*, Cambridge and New York: Cambridge University Press.

Soja, E.W. 1990: 'Heteropologies: A Remembrance of Other Spaces in Citadel-LA', *Strategies: A Journal of Theory, Culture and Politics*, 3: 6–39.

Young, I.M. 1990a: 'The Ideal of Community and the Politics of Difference', in L.J. Nicholson (ed.), *Feminism/Postmodernism*, New York and London: Routledge.

Young, I.M. 1990b: *Justice and the Politics of Difference*, Princeton, NJ: Princeton University Press.

Part II

POSTMODERN CITIES

9. Postmodern Urbanization: The Six Restructurings of Los Angeles

Edward W. Soja

Katherine Gibson and Sophie Watson in their introduction refer to the notion of postmodernity as both 'epoch' and 'condition', terms which have focused the debates on postmodernity around questions of periodization (for example, how great is the break between the modern and postmodern eras, or indeed whether there is a significant break at all); and what can be described as 'newness' (what are the distinctive attributes, if any, of the postmodern contemporary). Rather than stimulating still another round of contentiousness over these questions, the editors chose a more challenging strategy of 'assuming postmodernity' and inviting contributors to explore freely how this assumption might provide new insights into contemporary urban studies.

Based on this assumption of postmodernity, and hence of the existence of postmodern spaces, cities and politics – assumptions which have been guiding my own work over the past decade – a *postmodern urbanization process* can be defined as a summative depiction of the major changes that have been taking place in cities during the last quarter of the twentieth century. Using Los Angeles as my empirical case, I will present here an overview of six intertwined postmodern urbanization processes and try to explain how each departs sufficiently from previous, modern urbanization trends to deserve the affixation of a postmodern label.

Implicit in this presentation and embedded in virtually every chapter in *Postmodern Cities and Spaces* are several epistemological questions which extend the debate beyond mere effective empirical description. If there is indeed a very different urbanization process operating in the last decades of the twentieth century, how amenable is it to being understood, both practically and theoretically, from the presently established perspectives of modern urban studies? Must urban studies, following the empirical restructuring of its urban 'texts', undergo a similar deconstruction and reconstruction, to use the terminology so closely associated with postmodern critical theory? Has a new postmodern epistemology of urban studies already begun to take shape in response to the new urbanization processes, and if so what are its major features? These questions are not answered directly in *Postmodern Cities and Spaces*, but some of the directions the answers might take are effectively explored.

Before turning to the six restructurings of Los Angeles, both the concepts of the postmodern city and the postmodern urbanization process need some further clarification. As with the appropriate use of the term 'restructuring' (almost as much abused and misused as the term 'postmodern'), postmodern urbanization refers to something less than a total transformation, a complete urban revolution, an unequivocal break with the past; but also to something more than continuous piecemeal reform without significant redirection. As such, there is not only change but continuity as well, a persistence of past trends and established forms of (modern) urbanism amidst an increasing intrusion of postmodernization. In the postmodern city the modern city has not disappeared. Its presence may be diminished, but it continues to articulate with both older and newer forms of urbanization and to maintain its own dynamic of change, making the normal adjustments and reformations of the modern city and the distinctive processes of postmodern restructuring difficult to disentangle.

But again, if there is a postmodern urbanization process going on, then it is becoming increasingly clear that the modern city is no longer what it used to be. Postmodernity makes a difference, not only in producing its own distinctive conditions, but also in its particular articulations with pre-existing urban forms, fabrics, and ways of life. Extending this argument further, it can be said that today every city in the world is to some degree a postmodern city. It is not only in Los Angeles that one can see the effects of postmodern urbanization, but also in Huddersfield, Wollongong, Kingston, and Kuala Lumpur. Furthermore, like every social process we can think of, postmodern urbanization is socially produced (and therefore socially transformable), and also geographically unevenly developed; that is, it varies in intensity from place to place, city to city. At the same time, there is no purely postmodern city, no place which can be entirely studied and understood from a postmodern critical or interpretive perspective.

These observations magnify the value of the editors' introductory challenge to set aside the divisive battles between modernists and postmodernists so that we can more effectively explore postmodern cities from a wide range of perspectives. Modernism should not involve the rejection of postmodernism, nor should postmodernism inherently imply the complete disappearance of modernism and the uselessness of modernist modes of urban analysis. Each is contained within the other rather than being rigidly set in categorical opposition. There is, however, an argument to be made in favor of emphasizing more explicitly postmodern perspectives and epistemologies in making practical sense of the contemporary world and, in particular, the contemporary city. At the core of this argument is the political and theoretical significance attached to 'newness'.

All forms of modernism (including postmodernism) are strategic responses to three leading questions: What is new in the contemporary world? Is what is new of such significance that we must change our theoretical and/or political practices? And in response to these questions, what is to be done, here and now? These are the questions that have shaped the development of modernity since the Enlightenment. At present, postmodernism represents a decision to seek new and different practices based on the belief that even the most resilient and productive of established modern forms of thinking and acting are becoming increasingly ineffective in the contemporary world. Translated into urban studies, this involves a deconstructive critique of all prevailing urban epistemologies, from positivist social science to marxist scientific socialism, and an attempt to reconstitute a more flexible, eclectic, and appropriate urban epistemology to guide our practical, political, and/or theoretical projects: our new answers to that old question, 'What is to be done?'

The particular expressions of this postmodern deconstruction and reconstruction of modernism are by now familiar: the critique of totalizing discourses, master narratives, essentialism; the exposure of critical silences in modernist texts and practices; the reconceptualization and reassertion of difference and otherness, especially in the criss-crossing contexts of gender, race, and class; the crisis of representation and the dissolution of the expected relationship between signifier and signified; the growing interest in hyperreality, hyperspace, simulations, simulacra in shaping everyday life; the rise of a new cultural politics of identity and radical subjectivity, etc. As these critiques enter into contemporary urban studies, they contend most directly with the very best of late modernist approaches, in particular with that mixture of neo-marxian urban sociology, urban political economy, and urban geography that has come to define the core of critical urban studies over the past thirty years.

This late modernist version of critical urban studies, perhaps most effectively represented in the still evolving work of Manuel Castells and David Harvey, was built on insightful critical interpretations of post–World War II urbanization processes, of what Castells alternatively called Monopolville or the Wild City and what is currently being increasingly described as the Fordist and/or Keynesian, state-managed metropolis. The deep contradictions implicit in the Fordist city were unravelled in studies of collective consumption, urban planning and politics, the regressive redistribution of real income built into the normal workings of the urban system, and the rise of new urban social movements as vanguards for radical social change.

By the mid-1970s, this version of critical urban analysis had become the leading edge of modern urban studies and it has continued to be a powerful influence up to the present. What has been happening to the capitalist city since the early 1970s, however, has created a new trajectory of urbanization that has become increasingly inaccessible to the interpretive gaze of late modernism. Both Harvey and Castells have tried to adjust to these new urbanization processes in major recent works which contribute a great deal to our understanding of the contemporary capitalist city, but the scope of their insights has become increasingly narrowed as new streams of thought have entered into urban studies, especially from the broad realm of what is currently being called critical cultural studies and, in particular, from explicitly postmodern versions of feminism, black studies, film and literary criticism, the 'postcolonial' debates, and other post-prefixed approaches (poststructuralism, postmarxism, postfordism).[1]

In many years, late modernist critical urban studies had progressively despecified the urban, shifting attention away from what was particular to cities to larger social processes of capitalist accumulation and class struggle. As the capitalist world economy was booming its way to another round of crisis formation, a marxian critique provided an incisive foundation for interpreting events and conditions at every geographical scale, from the local to the global. After the urban uprisings of the late 1960s and the global recession and related crisis of the early 1970s (all rather easily predictable from a marxist perspective), the capitalist world economy entered a reactive phase of restructuring, increasingly cognizant that business as usual was no longer as reliable as it had been throughout the Fordist–Keynesian era and that new pathways to accumulation and social control needed to be found.

This crisis-generated restructuring was, as it had always been in the past, less easily susceptible to rigorous marxian analysis. I do not mean to say that marxism became irrelevant to understanding urban, regional, national, and international restructuring processes, but rather that it was no longer as diagnostically powerful as it once was. Stated in the terms used earlier to define the key questions associated with urban modernism and postmodernism, the new urbanization recontextualized critical urban studies and triggered the development of new approaches to 'What is to be done?' that differed significantly from the late modernist position, even as it has been so resiliently reformed by such figures as Harvey and Castells. In the wake of these developments, a postmodern critical urban studies has been taking shape which is much more pluralistic in its perspectives, much more open to alternative viewpoints, and, with some irony, much more attentive to the specificities of the urban, to the particular qualities of what can now, without qualification, be called postmodern cities. With this as a backdrop, I turn now to an exploration of the specificities of postmodern urbanization in Los Angeles.

Los Angeles has been a particularly vivid context from which to explore postmodern urbanization in virtually all its dimensions. I have called it the quintessential postmodern metropolis not because I see it as a 'model' for all other cities to follow or as a doomsday scenario to warn the rest of the world. If there is anything which places Los Angeles in a special position with respect to an understanding of postmodern urbanization processes, it is that comprehensive vividness I referred to, the particular clarity these restructuring processes have taken in this region of Southern California. In part, this is due to the relative absence of residual landscapes derived from preindustrial, mercantile, and nineteenth-century industrial urbanizations. Although founded in 1781, Los Angeles is pre-eminently a twentieth-century metropolis. Since 1900, the population of the Los Angeles region has grown by more than 14 million, more than almost any other city in the world.

What makes Los Angeles even more exemplary or symptomatic of the new urbanization is the magnitude and the scope of urban change that has taken place since 1965, the date of the Watts uprising, one of the earliest shocks in the breakdown of the postwar capitalist boom. Few major urban regions have experienced the extraordinary intensity of urban restructuring that has transformed Los Angeles over the past thirty years. From the vantage point of the present, the manifestations of postmodern urbanization are easier to see (and more difficult to avoid seeing) in Los Angeles than in most other places. It is no wonder then that there has developed a sizeable body of urban research on Los Angeles that examines both the particular local expressions of urban restructuring as well as the more general patterning of postmodern urbanization elsewhere in the world.

I will briefly summarize some of the major findings of this new literature on the restructuring of Los Angeles around six 'geographies'. Each has become the focus for a cluster of researchers giving their particular restructuring process and its spatial manifestations privileged attention. To comprehend the scope of Los Angeles as a postmodern city, all six of these geographies of restructuring must be considered together as an intertwined set of processes and relationships producing a composite postmodern urban geography. In a crude division, the first three restructurings can be seen as major causes of urban change, the second three as consequences, although too much should not be made of this partitioning of cause and effect. The postmodern city is never so easily delineated.

The *first geography* arises from the restructuring of the economic base of urbanization, from fundamental changes in the organization and technology of industrial production and the attendant urban social and spatial division of labor. In the simplest terms, this represents a shift from Fordist to postfordist urbanization, from the tight organization of mass production and mass consumption around large industrial complexes to more flexible production systems, vertically disintegrated but geographically clustered in 'new industrial spaces'. Another way of describing this first geography is as the metropolitan expression of such large-scale (and related) changes as the Rustbelt-to-Sunbelt shift in the regional economy of the US; or the rise of the NICs, the newly industrialized countries, such as Korea and Taiwan, within a changing international division of labor.

This first restructuring can also be described as a combined process of deindustrialization and reindustrialization, or in postmodern terminology a deconstruction of the Fordist city and the beginnings of a reconstruction of a new regime of urban industrial development that can be variably called flexible production, flexible accumulation, postfordism, or simply not-Fordism as it once was. Debates still rage over naming, interpreting, and deriving implications from this industrial shift in theory and practice, but that there has been a dramatic change in the foundations of the urban economy and that this change has had a significant effect on urban social and economic geographies is increasingly difficult to deny, especially in Los Angeles.

There are three components to the new industrial geography of Los Angeles. The first and best studied are the new 'technopoles' that have developed outside the old industrial zone in what were once dormitory suburbs or agricultural land. The best known of these transactions-rich clusterings of high technology aerospace and electronics firms, office buildings, and industrial parks are in Orange County. Others exist in the San Fernando Valley and in the zone extending from LAX (LA International Airport) to the giant ports of Los Angeles–Long Beach. More concentrated in and around downtown Los Angeles, but increasingly dispersing throughout the urban landscape, are low-skill, labor-intensive, and design- or fashion-sensitive growth industries such as apparel, furniture, and jewelry; and close by are the major centers for a vast entertainment industry keyed to the production of films, television programs, and popular music, another of the large craft-based industries that have been primarily responsible for the continued growth of Los Angeles over the past thirty years. Closely tied to all these industries is a growing FIRE sector – finance, insurance, real estate – providing business services to both domestic and foreign capital.

Postfordist industrial expansion, typically dominated by small and middle-sized firms, has covered over the rapid decline of what was once the largest Fordist industrial complex west of the Mississippi and propelled Los Angeles into its present position as the leading industrial metropolis in North America. It has not only led to an urbanization of suburbia (leading some Orange County analysts to describe these outer cities as 'postsuburbia') but has also contributed to the rapid growth of downtown Los Angeles, not only as an employment nucleus but as a command and control center for the regional, California, and Pacific Basin economies.

The rise of the postfordist metropolis has been an integral part of the development of the postmodern city. The balance between deindustrialization and reindustrialization differs from place to place, but whether one looks at Los Angeles or Detroit (perhaps the extreme cases in the US), the implications are clear: industrial restructuring has had a dramatic impact on the urban economy and the residential as well as employment geography of the city. The impact on urban research, theory, and planning is also important to note, for the attention focused on industrial production and related business services is in marked contrast to the concentration on collective consumption and consumption-oriented social movements that was at the center of late-modern critical urban studies. Perhaps more than at any other time in this century, the dynamics of industrial production have become a central issue in the study of urbanization and city building. One result of this shift has been a growing dissatisfaction with the simplified concept of 'postindustrial' society as a way of describing and interpreting global economic change in the latter half of the twentieth century.

The *second geography* of restructuring arises from the now familiar processes of internationalization, the expansion of globalized capital, and the formation of a global system of 'world cities'. This has involved both an expansion in the outreach of cities, making almost every corner of the world part of the hinterland of such world cities as Los Angeles, New York, Tokyo, Hong Kong, London, Paris, Sydney, and São Paulo; and an extraordinary 'inreach', bringing into the global city pools of capital and labor from nearly every world culture. Here again Los Angeles has been an especially vivid exemplar of world city formation, adding to its growing importance as a global financial and trade center what today may be the most culturally heterogeneous population ever agglomerated in any city in history.

More than one-third of the nine million residents of Los Angeles County are foreign-born, and within the urbanized region are the largest enclaves outside their home countries of an extraordinary array of cultures: Mexican, Salvadoran (around 400,000, or 10 per cent of the entire population of El Salvador), Guatemalan, Filipino, Japanese, Korean, Vietnamese, Cambodian, Hmong, Armenian, Iranian, Samoan. If one adds to this the African American urban population, the third largest in the country, Los Angeles is now a 'majority minority' city. This demographic transformation of a metropolis that was around 80 per cent 'Anglo', or non-hispanic white, in 1960 is continuing at a rapid rate, with nearly 100,000 immigrants receiving permanent legal resident status in Los Angeles County in 1992 alone.

The impact of this globalization of Los Angeles has triggered many different frameworks for interpretation. For many, the emphasis is on the creative as well as destructive dynamics of urban multiculturalism; others see Los Angeles as a Third World city filled both with squalid favelas and bidonvilles and successful, upwardly mobile ethnic entrepreneurs; still others focus on the influx of foreign capital and the globalization of local economy. To these I will add another; the creation of a new kind of 'dual city' consisting of a growing global bourgeoisie and global proletariat that are reconstituting the class structure of the industrial capitalist city. Along with massive federal spending for military defense (itself not unconnected with globalization), foreign capital investment and the availability of cheap, weakly organized, and easily manipulable foreign labor have probably been the most significant factors sustaining the continued economic growth of Los Angeles over the past thirty years.

However one interprets this globalization process, its impact on the urban fabric and on urban life has been enormous and is likely to continue to be so in the future. Many cities were world cities before the 1960s, but since then, if you will excuse the turn of phrase, the globalization of the city has itself become increasingly globalized. Every contemporary city is to some significant degree also a world city in much the same way as it is postmodern. Everywhere the local is becoming globalized and the global is becoming localized, giving birth to another of those neologisms that attempt to describe the distinctive results of contemporary restructuring processes, the concept of 'glocalization'.

new form of speech

The *third geography* has generated perhaps the greatest flurry of neologisms to describe its newness. A short list would include such terms as megacities, outer cities, edge cities, metroplex, technoburbs, postsuburbia, technopolis, heteropolis, exopolis. What is being described in these terms is a radical restructuring of urban form and of the conventional language we have been using to describe cities. Following on the odd combinations of opposing tendencies that have been used to describe the first two geographies of restructuring – deindustrialization and reindustrialization, globalizing the local and localizing the global – the third restructuring can be described as a combination of decentralization and recentralization, the peripheralization of the center and the centralization of the periphery, the city simultaneously being turned inside out and outside in.

Whatever terms you may use to describe it, the urban form or spatial organization of the postmodern city is becoming significantly different from that of the early modern city, exemplified in the neat concentricities and specialized sectors of the Chicago School models; or the late modern city, the more disjointed metropolis revolving around a dominant central business district, an inner city of the poor and blue-collar workers, and a sprawl of largely middle-class dormitory suburbs stretching to exurbia. Much of this modernist patterning of the city remains, but postmodern urbanization is shuffling it about and introducing new and different forms into the urban built environment. Perhaps the most obvious of the changes taking place is the urbanization of suburbia, but changes are also taking place in the older central cities, ranging from significant reductions in density in such places as New York City and Chicago (usually accompanied by gentrification in former working-class neighborhoods) to the development of newly skyscrapered downtowns and the infilling of surrounding areas by poor as well as wealthy immigrants, as has occurred in Los Angeles.

One outgrowth of postmodern urbanization has been the emergence of megacities such as Mexico City and São Paulo, far surpassing the population size one might have thought any city could grow to thirty years ago. On a smaller scale but closely related to the restructuring of urban form has been the renewed growth of large metropolitan regions. After many years of studying what was called 'the great non-metropolitan turnaround', the growth of smaller cities outside the metropolises and their suburbs, many urbanists were surprised to discover that the 1990 US census showed that for the first time in US history the majority of Americans lived in cities of greater than one million inhabitants. The turnaround had turned around again.

Another, more direct, result of the restructuring of urban form has been a breaking down of the neat, tent-like density gradients stretching outward from the central city to the suburbs that feature so prominently in urban geography textbooks. Old suburban-like densities of jobs and residents now appear occasionally almost next to the central business district, while new cities sprout fifty miles away amidst the urban sprawl. Some urbanists might contend that this is just an extension of older models of urban decentralization, and to some extent they are correct. But I suspect that much will be missed if this restructuring of urban form is viewed simply as more of the same rather than as something significantly different and characteristically postmodern.

The geography arising from this third restructuring has been shaped by a very complex redistribution of jobs, affordable housing, and access to mass transit, and modified significantly by income, racial, and ethnic differentiation. While these factors have always played a role in urban change, they seem to have become more chaotic and less susceptible to being explained by conventional urban theory and analysis. Two examples illustrate my point. The city of Gardena, with a population of 50,000, is fast approaching the ultimate in racial diversity, a composite of cultural groupings that has never before been achieved in any other city: an even quartering of the population, with Asians, Latinos, African Americans, and Anglos each making up about 25 percent of the total. The ethnicities do not necessarily mix together in Gardena, but the multicultural context of urban life is unlike anything seen before.

A second example is provided by the city of Moreno Valley, the fastest growing city in the US – over 100,000 according to the 1990 census. Sprouting near the city of Riverside in what is called the Inland Empire, Moreno Valley has fast become a sort of postmodern suburban slum, caught cruelly in the mismatch between the growth of affordable housing and the locations of employment opportunities. Fed by the dream of becoming part of a new Orange County, tens of thousands of families poured into the tract housing and 'planned communities' of Moreno Valley, only to find that the promised jobs did not come. The result has been overcrowded schools, poor social services, gridlocked freeways, and journeys to work that are frequently greater than two hours each way.

The *fourth geography* of restructuring picks up again from the examples of Gardena and Moreno Valley and condenses many of the effects described for the first three restructuring processes. Here we are dealing with the changing social structure of urbanism, especially the development of new patterns of social fragmentation, segregation, and polarization. Postmodern urbanization in Los Angeles and elsewhere has been associated with marked increases in social, economic, and cultural inequalities that are difficult to explain and understand from the traditional viewpoints of urban sociology. Not only has the social mosaic of the postmodern city become more kaleidoscopic, with rapidly shifting patterns of urban differentiation reversing older arrangements and then reversing them again, but new forms of inequality and geographically uneven development seem to be emerging in unexpected ways.

Neologisms have proliferated here too in an attempt to describe the urban social geography of postmodernity. At the core of this flurry of linguistic creativity is the reshaping of the urban labor market, described variably as increasingly taking on the form of a dumbbell or a bowling pin, pinched at the waist with a small bulge above and an even larger one below. The pinching at the waist reflects the squeezed middle class and the impact of Fordist deindustrialization on highly unionized blue-collar employment. Rising above the waist is an expanding managerial technocracy of yuppies, dinks (double income no kids households), entertainment superstars, electronics wizards, junk bond dealers, ethnic entrepreneurs, etc.; while below is a much swollen base comprising the homeless (as many as 80,000 people are homeless on any given night in the Los Angeles region), the new orphans (children as well as the elderly), the new slaves (illegally imported house servants kept privately by their 'owners'), the unemployed and welfare dependant, the products of what is called the feminization and latinization of poverty, and more generally the composite group that has received the greatest attention from contemporary urban sociologists, the permanent urban underclass.

The aggregate result of these changes has been a widening income gap and the multiplication on the urban landscape of blatant contrasts between wealth and poverty. Much more so than in the early or late modern city, differences in income, in culture and language, in lifestyles, are starkly visible in the everyday life of the postmodern city. On the one hand, this has fostered some creative mixing and intercultural and cross-class solidarities in the arts, in business, and in politics, which many in Los Angeles feel offers great hope for the future. On the other hand, it has generated new landscapes of despair, interethnic conflict, crime, and violence. Perhaps the greatest challenge facing the postmodern city is how to build on the former while keeping the latter under control.

The *fifth geography* arises in (often armed) response to the preceding four. The postmodern city, with all its kaleidoscopic complexities, has become increasingly ungovernable, at least within the confines of its traditional local government structures. As a result, it has become an increasingly 'carceral' city, with walled-in estates protected by armed guards, bold signs threatening that 'trespassers will be shot', panopticon-like shopping centers made safe through the most advanced forms of spatial surveillance, smart office buildings impenetrable to outsiders, neighborhood watches backed by gun-toting home owners, a proliferation of gangs equally obsessed with guarding their turf, and a police force armed with the latest advances in military technology.

The carceral landscape of Los Angeles is brilliantly explored in Mike Davis's *City of Quartz* (1990). The book's cover is an eerily beautiful night photograph of the new Federal Detention Center, the crown jewel in an urban prison system that incarcerates more people than any other in the country. Filled to overflowing, the explicit prisons of Los Angeles are forced to dismiss all but the most dangerous criminals for lack of space. Davis moves on to explore the implicit imprisoning of Los Angeles that has become part of the postmodern built environment: bunkered-in buildings and fortress-like 'stealth-houses'; sadistic street environments with razor-wire-protected trash bins, spiked park benches, and overhead sprinkler systems operating at night to guard against the homeless; the destruction of public space in monumental architecture; and the transformation of public housing projects into strategic hamlets.

The new topography of race, class, gender, age, income, and ethnicity has produced an incendiary urban geography in Los Angeles, a landscape filled with violent edges, colliding turfs, unstable boundaries, peculiarly juxtaposed lifespaces, and enclaves of outrageous wealth and despair. That there may be a positive side to this splintered labyrinth of postmodern Los Angeles requires some stretch of the imagination, but it is worthwhile imagining nonetheless. In a peculiar way, the restructuring of Los Angeles has had the side effect of refocusing political attention on to what Michel Foucault (who originated the term 'carceral city') once called 'the little tactics of the habitat' or what contemporary urban scholars call 'the politics of place'. Perhaps never before have the people of Los Angeles been so politically involved in their immediate neighborhoods and localities – and so open to coalition building across ethnic and class lines. Similarly, there has also been a significant increase in regional consciousness, an awareness that the problems of Southern California require some form of regional planning and coordination that cannot be provided by present-day structures of city, county, and state government. Whether these two levels of renewed spatial consciousness, the locality and the region, can develop together to take greater control over the postmodern urbanization process is another of the great questions facing the postmodern city of Los Angeles.

The *sixth geography* is both a summary and new dimension. It also, in more subtle ways, can be seen as part of the emerging system of social control – what the industrial geographers call a mode of regulation – that has developed in response to the incendiary qualities of the postmodern city. It flows from a deeper behavioral, cultural, and ideological restructuring and is accordingly more difficult to capture in quick descriptions. What it represents is the product of a radical change in the 'urban imaginary', in the ways we relate our images of what is real to empirical reality itself. It is thus at its roots the product of an epistemological restructuring that affects urbanism as a way of life, how we act and make choices as city dwellers, how we make practical sense of the urban world around us.

In many ways, this is the most postmodern of the geographies of restructuring, the most reflective of the core issues of the postmodern critique of modernism. I can take only one aspect of this sixth restructuring to discuss here, but it is a particularly important one in understanding postmodern urbanization. It involves the intrusion and growing power of an urban hyperreality, of simulations and simulacra (defined as exact copies of originals that do not exist), into the material reality and ideological imaginary of urban life. In short, it can be described as the development of an alternative Simcity, a hypersimulation that confounds and reorders the traditional ways we have been able to distinguish between what is real and what is imagined.

The postmodern city, and Los Angeles perhaps more so than any other, is filled with 'factories' of hyperreality, places which produce what Umberto Eco once called 'real fakes', fantasy worlds that are experienced as if they were real. This is not a new development. 'Simulacrum' is a biblical term referring to the belief, for example, that church statues were actual and faithful personifications of, say, the Virgin Mary. World fairs were veritable fountains of hyperreality offered as both education and entertainment, while the visual arts, from cave paintings to the cinema, offered their own versions of hyperreality designed to capture the real world. In Hollywood and Disneyland, Los Angeles cornered the market on the modernist production of hyperreality as entertainment and diversion. But what has been happening in the postmodern city is the diffusion of hyperreality from its specialized factories into everyday life in households, neighborhoods, workplaces, shopping malls, voting booths, virtually everywhere in the city. Today, you do not just choose to visit the hyperreal; it visits you wherever you choose to be.

The neologisms associated with the sixth restructuring are increasingly abundant: sound bites and spin doctors, virtual reality, cyberspace, cyberpunk. Think also of the pop-language of today's youth and television programming: get real, really groty, rilly?, reality-based TV, re-enacted reality, neo-reality fiction. Elsewhere I have explored the hyperreality of everyday life in Orange County in terms of the creation of a new 'scamscape' in which the difference between truth and fiction, the real and the imagined, fact and lie has been slowly disappearing (Soja 1992). Orange County has become the fraud capital of the US, ranging from its disastrous leadership in the massive savings and loan scandals currently costing the country hundreds of billions of dollars, to various types of consumer, insurance, and government agency fraud, including the production of thousand-dollar screwdrivers and simulated testing of nuclear firing devices for the Department of Defense (the latter confidently excused by the deep belief in the quality of the product produced). In one of the dozens of 'boiler rooms' (telemarketing centers for attracting speculative investments in often nonexistent enterprises) in Orange County, a sign is proudly placed to summarize the new ideologic: 'We cheat the other guy and pass the savings on to you!'

This brief picture of the sixth restructuring does not close the discussion on postmodern urbanization and postmodern cities. Instead, it opens it up again to further rounds of analysis, interpretation, and debate in Los Angeles and in every other city in the world. Before closing, however, and in keeping with earlier efforts to find a more positive and progressive side to postmodern urbanization processes that have predominantly served neoconservative and anti-progressive interests, I must comment on the events of late April and early May 1992 in Los Angeles, for they too are an integral part of the analysis of postmodern urbanization and perhaps also provide another opportunity to learn from the Los Angeles experience.

In 1965 and then again in 1992, Los Angeles was the site of the two most violent episodes of urban social unrest in twentieth-century America. Both were immediately sparked by unique local events and conditions, but were also generalized and generalizable events that have or have had much more global repercussions. As I have noted earlier, the Watts rebellion in 1965 was one of the first explosive indications that the long postwar, Fordist-led boom had peaked and that business as usual, for corporations, governments, and unions, could no longer be depended upon to sustain continued economic expansion in the same ways it had in the past. In retrospect, what ensued from these shocks to the system, and especially the deep world recession of the early 1970s, was a crisis-generated process of restructuring that searched after new means of stimulating increased productivity in an increasingly competitive global economy while also seeking improved ways to restore and maintain social order at home.

The six geographies of restructuring I have outlined here represent what I consider to have been the main lines taken since 1965 in response to the crises of the 1960s and 1970s. Together they define not only what I have chosen to call a postmodern urbanization process but a much more general patterning of change at every geographical scale, from the local to global, that I believe is best understood as part of the transition from modernity to postmodernity, or at least to something very significantly different from what existed thirty years ago. In terms of responding to crisis and sustaining a continued if not accelerated economic expansion, Los Angeles was one of the great success stories of the last three decades. For this reason alone, it provides a particularly interesting laboratory for making practical sense of the contemporary world.

From this perspective, the events of 1992 in Los Angeles can also be seen as a harbinger of the end of one era and the beginning of another. If 1965 was the start of a period of crisis-generated restructuring, then 1992 may be the first shock in what can be described as a *restructuring-generated crisis*, a crisis of and in postmodernity. That both urban upheavals and turning points occurred in Los Angeles and were sparked in large part by the African American community is not surprising, for Los Angeles was an exemplary economic success story in both the postwar boom and the postmodern restructuring periods; while in both periods African Americans were not only the segment of the population most obviously oppressed by the changes taking place, they were also at the leading edge of radical resistance to the dominant political forces of the time, in Los Angeles and in the country at large.

Today in Los Angeles, the restructuring-led boom is over. What worked for most of the past three decades along the lines of the six geographies of restructuring I have discussed has begun to unravel in new kinds of crisis. The end of the Cold War has taken the federally injected steam out of the economy, the real-estate market has passed its peak, and even the bustling outer cities are feeling the economic pinch. Interethnic violence and hate crimes are on the rise, the LAPD is demoralized (if not repentant), the shortage of prison space continues, and the cosmopolis of world cultures seems closer than ever to the ominous *Blade Runner* scenario. Homelessness is widening its scope, unemployment is rising, and the profound housing and environmental crises exacerbated by restructuring appear to be getting worse in both the inner and outer cities.

But as usual, crisis is filled with both dangers and opportunities, and much can be said of the more positive side of the crisis of postmodernity. I have alluded to some of these before and will not repeat them here, except to state again that postmodern urbanization has significantly raised popular consciousness in Los Angeles at the local and regional level over the very nature of the urbanization process itself, over who controls and benefits from the social production – and restructuring – of urban space. The hope for a more progressive future in Los Angeles and other postmodern cities will rest largely on what comes from this growing and creatively postmodern spatial consciousness.

NOTES

Adapted from the transcripts of a plenary lecture presented at the Postmodern Cities Conference, Department of Urban and Regional Planning, the University of Sydney, April 1993. For a fuller development of some of the same themes, see Soja (1994).
1 See, for example, Edward W. Soja and Barbara Hooper (1993).

REFERENCES

Davis, M. 1990: *City of Quartz: Excavating the Future in Los Angeles*, London: Verso.

Soja, E.W. 1992: 'Inside Exopolis: Scenes from Orange County', in M. Sorkin (ed.), *Variations on a Theme Park: The New American City and the End of Public Space*, New York: Noonday Press.

Soja, E.W. 1994: 'Los Angeles 1965–1992: The Six Geographies of Urban Restructuring', in A. Scott, E.W. Soja and R. Weinstein (eds), *Los Angeles: Geographical Essays*, Los Angeles and Berkeley: University of California Press.

Soja, E.W. and Hooper, B. 1993: 'The Spaces that Difference Makes: Some Notes on the Geographical Margins of the New Cultural Politics', in M. Keith and S. Pile (eds), *Place and Politics of Identity*, London: Routledge.

10. Under the Volcano: Postmodern Space in Hong Kong

Alexander Cuthbert

As a major world city, Hong Kong's race into postmodernism is both manic and vertiginous. Here we witness a fully fledged capitalist state being slowly absorbed into socialism against all the rules of contemporary world history, where the reverse is the norm. Many of the accepted characteristics of postindustrialism and postmodernity appear exaggerated rather than diminished: space-time compression, ideological discourse, deconstruction, internationalization and other existential truths are central to the lives of Hong Kong people. Symbolically, the city lives *under the volcano* in several dimensions: in its relation to China, to international trade, to emigration and other factors. Hong Kong's industrial paradigm has demonstrated to the world a seminal model of capitalism in action. Today it offers laboratory conditions to examine the central features of postindustrialism and postmodern space.

HONG KONG: HISTORICAL ANTECEDENTS

Historically, Britain was the first country to establish bourgeois rule, and an increasing number of industrial capitalists built up vast fortunes which demanded new markets for investment. By 1860 Britain had colonized 2.5 million square miles of foreign territory, and Hong Kong was therefore a consequence of Britain leading the world into the industrial revolution (Lenin 1982). From the middle of the eighteenth century, Britain dominated trade in the Far East through the monopoly of the East Asia Trading company. But it was not until this monopoly was abolished in 1834 that British capitalists began to focus in earnest on the China Trade (Rodzinski 1981).

Fifty years previously the British had begun the systematic production of opium in India to trade for China's tea and silk. By 1838 the export of opium exceeded six million pounds weight per annum, requiring an additional 20 million ounces of silver per annum in payment. Intentionally or otherwise, the British succeeded in destabilizing China's feudal system, which had endured for 3,000 years (Epstein 1980). As the price of silver rose sharply in China, grain prices fell, and tax collectors took a larger portion of crops to maintain their incomes at previous levels. Peasant uprisings took place, forcing the Manchu government to seize the opium stock. In reprisal, the British invaded China and the first opium war began. China suffered a massive defeat. As a result of the Treaty of Nanking in 1842, Britain extracted the much-sought-after trade agreements, opening up treaty ports along the mainland and establishing the British Crown Colony of Hong Kong (Waley 1958).

Paradoxically, between 1840 and 1860, the most vibrant period of premonopoly capitalism, bourgeois politicians lobbied against colonization. Lenin quotes Disraeli as saying 'The colonies are millstones round our necks.' Hong Kong was never intended to become a colony in the usual sense, 'but a *factory* similar to the establishments of the East India Company' (Endacott 1964).

THE EVOLUTION OF A WORLD CITY

Hong Kong did not grow on the basis of massive cash injections from the metropole; quite the opposite. Up until the beginning of World War II, the export of British capital in the Far East went mainly to Shanghai, not to Hong Kong. Immediately after the Japanese invasion, Hong Kong was described as 'a run down, war damaged, pre-industrial society with no very evident future' (Youngson 1982). The merchant mentality still prevailed after the war, and it was not until 1955 that a fully fledged capitalist system became operational. At that time Hong Kong was forced into a public housing pro-gramme and elementary social provisions, and the government made a conscious deci-sion to involve itself in the extended reproduction of labour power at floorspace ratios of 2.2 square metres per person (Castells 1990). The intervening 40 years have seen phenomenal economic growth. In the twenty years from 1960 to 1980 alone, GDP averaged close to 10 per cent per annum, dropping to some 6 per cent today. The last 25 years have seen an incredible 540 per cent increase in GDP. Currently, the well-being of Hong Kong's six million population remains inextricably linked with the state of the international economy, a relationship supposedly driven by the ideology of *laissez faire* (Rabushka 1979), more recently referred to in Hong Kong as 'positive non-interven-tionism'. But in fact, 'market forces rest on an infrastructural support system of non-market regulation of economic activities, administration of key prices, subsidisation of *the social wage*, interference in and distortion of all factor markets, and ownership of one of the two factors of production that are subject to such property arrangements' (Schiffer 1991).

Transparently, the government massively intervenes in the operation of all factory markets through its regulatory policies. It owns all the land, and subsidizes wages to industrialists by housing half the population in state-subsidized public housing. In addition, China supplies between 50 per cent and 80 per cent of Hong Kong's water, food, and clothing at subsidized prices, fuelling Hong Kong's industrial and service sectors with labour released from agricultural production (Schiffer 1983). Being hyper-sensitive to changes in the international economy through its status as an entrepôt, Hong Kong has gradually experienced a radical transformation of economy and society since 1973, when the Arab countries set in place an oil embargo against the West. That event marked the beginning of an entirely new regime of accumulation, a new international division of labour, and a period in history which has been called 'postmodernism' (Berman 1983).

THE ECONOMIC IMPERATIVE

Over the last two decades, a sea-change has taken place in capitalist urbanization, where the organization of production at a global scale has finally come into being. This has coincided with a revolution in human relations where the production of *the material world* has given way to the production of *symbols*, sometimes called the information revolution (Poster 1990). Indeed, Toffler (1990: 69) argues that the 'world exports of services and intellectual property are now equal to that of electronics and autos combined, or of the combined exports in food and fuels'.

In this new era, electronic information replaces money as the new medium of exchange within symbolic economies. The application of the new electronic infrastruc-ture to managerial and production systems simultaneously creates new social and spatial arrangements, new styles and patterns of consumption and the deepening of commodity culture to a point where the commodity becomes the universal category of society as a whole (Lukacs 1971). This idea was updated recently by performance artist Barbara Kruger to 'I shop, therefore I am.' While the literature on postmodernism is by now extensive, I find it useful to distinguish between the rapid change from *industrialism* to *postindustrialism*, or from *organized* to *disorganized* capitalism as qualitative changes in the capitalist economic system, and *postmodernism*, which maps changes in social relations, culture, creativity and consciousness (Lash and Urry 1987. See table 10.1.)

While many theorists are convinced that a new social order is being established, David Harvey considers 'that when these changes are set against the basic rules of capitalistic accumulation, they appear more as shifts in surface appearance rather than as signs of some entirely new postcapitalist or even postindustrial society' (Harvey 1989: 7), and I will examine the implications of this in the following analysis of Hong Kong. In order to do this I have chosen to look at three of the important characteristics of postindustrial production, namely flexibility, deregulation and dispersal. In tandem with these, I will also look at some of the changes in Hong Kong's emergent postmodern society – a culture where discourses are in collision, given Hong Kong's recombination with China in four years' time (Cuthbert 1993: table 1).

POSTINDUSTRIAL PRODUCTION

In a nutshell, most of these conditions currently apply to Hong Kong. The concepts of flexible production and demassification which have gained so much recent attention

Table 10.1 Properties of industrial and cultural forms and practices

Characteristic	Industrial		Cultural	
	Industrialism	Post-industrialism	Modernism	Post-modernism
Qualities	Regulation	Deregulation	Order	Anarchy
	Rigidity	Flexibility	Control	Chance
	Fusion	Diffusion	Direction	Indeterminacy
	Standardization	Diversification	Need	Desire
	Material base	Information base	Product	Process
	Hierarchies	Grids and	History	Destiny
	Legitimation	networks	Function	Signification
		Discretion		
Properties	State power	Corporate power	Construction	Deconstruction
	Class politics	New class politics	Society	Ethnicity
	Mass production	In time production	Community	Locality
	Strategic	Contextual	Monoculturalism	Pluralism
	planning	planning	Class culture	Commodity
	Development	Adaptation	Permanence	culture
	Nationalism	Ethnic fission	Similarity	Transience
	Economy of	Economy of scale		Diversity
	scope	Individual		
	Welfare statism	accountability		
	Specialization	Labour synergy		
	Unionization	Industrial		
		bargaining		
Philosophical	Scientific	Neo-Darwinism	Structuralism	Poststructuralism
attributes	rational	Functionalism	Realism	Hyperreality
	Keynesianism	Flexible specialism	Romanticism	Mysticism
	Taylorism	Diversification	Formalism	Imagery
	Fordism		Narrative	Discursive
			Contiguity	Difference
Spatial effects	Massification	Demassification	Urban functions	Urban landsape
and	Concentration	Diffusion	State symbols	Corporate
implications	Centralization	Dispersal	Architectural	symbolism
	Community	Locality	'styles'	Architectural
	Zoning	Integration	Paradigmatic	rhetoric
	Suburban focus	Urban focus	Syntactic	Eclectic
			Design	Metaphoric
				Codification

(Harvey 1989: 147) have been an essential part of Hong Kong's success for decades, relying as it has done on small, highly skilled production units which can be assembled almost overnight in response to changing markets and products (Davies and Roberts 1990). Major changes can be seen both within and between economic sectors. By 1990, finance and related services contributed more than manufacturing to the local economy

(20.6 per cent as against 16.7 per cent of GDP: see table 10.2) and the tertiary sector as a whole now contributes some 70 per cent of GDP.

Moreover, the numbers of persons employed in each has been shrinking in proportion. In addition, even the size of manufacturing establishments has been decreasing since 1950, a situation which is hard to believe, given the incredible versatility and demassification of Hong Kong's industrial base in the first place (table 10.3).

Hong Kong as a colonial state maintains the ideology of *laissez faire* or 'positive non-interventionism', as it is now called, suggesting a pre-existing structure of deregulation in the economy as a whole. This is massively oversimplified. In fact at least three main distinctions can be made here between areas of the economy which are regulated, monopolized by corporations, or deregulated (Cuthbert 1991).

Firstly, the state is involved in the regulation and manipulation of land prices and in the provision of public housing to half of the population (therefore it indirectly intervenes in labour supply through housing location). It also regulates the price of the staple food – namely rice. The state has regulated the banking system since the crisis of 1965, and it also had to intervene in the operation of the local stock market from 1989. Secondly, the creation of monopolies is still rife, particularly in the area of public utilities (gas, electricity, communications), transportation (buses, light rail system, mini buses, rapid transit, airline, ferries, shipping) and a near monopoly in the private housing market and the movie industry. Mega-millionaires are household names – Lee Ka Shing, Stanley Ho, Gordon Wu, Dickson Poon, Henry Fok, Run Run Shaw, Y.K. Pau etc.

Deregulation is therefore limited to two key areas: namely the manufacturing and service sectors of the economy. In other words, state-led economic development predominates in spite of the official ideological smokescreen, with one significant exception. Government has recently launched a programme to deregulate its own control over social reproduction by privatizing state housing provision. In contrast to the last forty years of state-led economic development fuelled by public housing provision, the local economy has recently moved into a phase of infrastructure-led development. It is also important to recognize the place of organized crime in Hong Kong as an unofficial regulatory

Table 10.2 Contribution to GDP at factory cost by finance and manufacturing sectors in Hong Kong

Economic sector	1970	1975	1980	1985	1990
Finance, insurance real estate, business	2,855 (14.9)	6,283 (17.0)	29,292 (22.8)	39,589 (16.3)	109,135 (20.6)
Manufacture	5,913 (30.9)	9,954 (26.9)	30,549 (23.8)	53,071 (21.9)	88,825 (16.7)

Value in Hong Kong $million. Brackets denote respective percentage share of the column total.
Source: Hong Kong government.

mechanism in tandem with state control, but over the entire economy. Triad control over the film and construction industries, over commercial enterprises and the sale of private housing, over public transportation, food markets, the hotel and other industries, as well as the family businesses of prostitution, gambling, drug dealing and smuggling, is endemic and all encompassing. It is interesting to note that in Hong Kong $1 billion or 8 per cent of government revenues come from horse racing alone.

Dispersal, decentralization and deindustrialization simultaneously refer to capital flight as well as geographic restructuring of production processes in order to access the shifting source of cheap and skilled labour, frequently reinforced by tax advantages, wage subsidies and land prices unavailable elsewhere. In Hong Kong's case these two processes occur in several dimensions: firstly, as a consequence of the economic and political implications of reinstating China's sovereignty in Hong Kong in 1997; secondly through massive investment in China; thirdly, and in severe contrast to other localities, in China's investment in Hong Kong.

Firstly, the 1997 issue combined with high inflation and land prices in Hong Kong has seen enormous capital and population flight, both of which are on the increase. Major multinationals such as Jardine Mathieson have transferred their entire financial operation offshore. Cathay Pacific, another multinational, is rearranging its entire operation, returning pilots to their home base, ticketing to Guandong province and data processing to Sydney. Emigration has risen from 30,000 per annum in 1987 to 60,000 in 1992. Since a high percentage of these persons are in the business and professional categories, we can suggest a virtual elimination of the entire middle class by 1997. This could be massively accelerated since China has not yet pronounced what category of person will be considered to be Chinese after that date.

Secondly, as part of good business practice, as well as in the purchase of favours, enormous amounts of capital from Hong Kong are being invested in China by decanting its manufacturing sector (and many of its polluting industries) but also through investment into infrastructure, land development, tourism and other areas. One third of all Hong Kong-listed companies now have investments in China, and Hong Kong-invested enterprises now employ over three million persons in Guandong province alone. But Hong Kong money is also being invested elsewhere, for example in Vietnam (the number

Table 10.3 Number of establishments and persons engaged in manufacturing 1950–91

Year	No. of establishments	Total no. of persons employed	Average no. of persons engaged per establishment
1950	1,478	81,718	55
1960	5,346	218,405	41
1970	16,507	549,178	33
1980	45,409	892,140	20
1991	46,376	654,662	14

1 investor) and in Thailand (US$3 billion in rapid transit by a single Hong Kong company).

Thirdly, while Hong Kong manufacturing industries are moving en masse to China, Hong Kong's role has now changed to a re-exporting zone for China's US$80 billion re-export trade, now growing at 10.6 per cent per annum. Along with this, China had invested US$10 billion in Hong Kong by 1990.

So far I have examined some of the conditions surrounding Hong Kong's postindustrial development, and I now move to examine the conditions of postmodern life and culture. But the relationship between these is no easy one to draw. While I do not have the space for an extended discussion here, none the less a few brief observations will help to contextualize some of the key relationships locally. For the very nature of postmodern theory discourages the reduction of society and economy to essential or immutable structural properties, or even to artificial distinctions such as Giddens's 'structure' and 'agency'. In a philosophy of deconstruction, the grand narratives of the past can be unpacked to expose hidden meanings. Metaphor emerges as the means of exchange, and the text becomes the accepted vehicle of representation. Culture is then revealed not as an ideological superstructure but as an archaeology of practices, philosophies, beliefs and material conditions which deny any fixed agenda or easy description.

In Marxist theorizing there has always been a reluctance to recognize culture as a separate sphere of production, which is relatively unaffected by material production as a whole. Marcuse reformed the Marxist idea of culture by denying both the independence of culture and its existence as a mere reflection of the economic base. Marcuse, along with Adorno and Horkheimer, focused on the relation between culture and the commodity principle. Here it was suggested that the higher culture represented by artistic endeavour was collapsing into the degraded material culture of commodity production. This idea has been carried to its final form where the term 'spectacle' is used to describe the moment 'when the commodity has attained the total occupation of social life' (Debord 1983: 38).

While Hong Kong has not yet attained this status, the idea has singular relevance in the local context, in terms of both the commodification of social life and the built environment (Cuthbert 1987). Without making too fine a point, Hong Kong's origins as an entrepôt and its entire history have been linked to commodity production. In the process it has created 'a fetishism of material wealth' characterized by 'a rampant and rapacious desire for material advancement' (Lau 1984: 69). In a society where even social class is perceived in cash terms, commodity fetishism rules. This overall condition is deepening due to several key phenomena. Most important among these are the transition of Hong Kong's economy as a whole from commodity production to commodity circulation as its entire manufacturing base becomes transferred to China. Secondly, as 1997 approaches, Hong Kong remains, for many local people, a place simply to be mined for material wealth. Thirdly, after 1997, Hong Kong's position as a global supermarket will in all probability accelerate with China's rapid economic expansion, currently running at 14 per cent per annum. The impact of these developments is discussed in greater detail below.

DISCOURSES IN COLLISION

Hong Kong has been profoundly affected in its history by two major discursive systems: traditional Chinese culture on the one hand and British imperialism on the other. Within these, the most significant influences have been Confucianism–Taoism and English law. Now a third discourse has entered the arena, that of the Constitution of the People's Republic of China, dominated by Marxist-Leninist, Mao Tse-tung thought. Without my wishing to appear too dramatic, Hong Kong is crossing an ideological tightrope from the discourse of capitalism to that of socialism. At any point in the process the rope could snap for one of many reasons – trade wars, civil unrest, ideological conflict, the death of Deng, or even Lee Pang's recent posturing over minimalist improvements to Hong Kong's democratic process. All of these would profoundly affect Hong Kong's entire existence, and the flight of population, knowledge and capital would be instantaneous.

Two discourses are of paramount importance; one which deals with legitimation, the other with space. These are the *Basic Law*, and the *Comprehensive Review of the Town Planning Ordinance* currently under consideration. The first documents the agreement between Britain and China after 1997 and to date does not include a bill of rights. The second involves the Town Planning Ordinance of 1939, unchanged for fifty years and written on three pages of paper. The debates surrounding both of these are legion. The *Basic Law* is a semiotic nightmare, with each party to its signing interpreting every word according to its own political and cultural bias. On the other hand the comprehensive review of a non-ordinance makes a mockery of the democratic process, and has developers screaming about slowing down the velocity of capital accumulation from land development. A modern system of town and environmental controls in the territory has been studiously avoided for two main reasons, firstly in order to allow unfettered commodity production as a whole, and secondly to allow the rampant commodification of land. Now that most of the seriously polluting industries have been relocated to Guandong province, the Hong Kong Government will be able to announce 'the success' of its new environmental legislation.

Hong Kong has an architecture of four ecologies, which have eroded into each other over time (Banham 1971). These correspond to three phases of capitalist development, namely merchant, industrial and finance capital. Because of Hong Kong's rapacious economy, little remains of the architecture of merchant capital beyond its most powerful symbols – the bank, the law court, the church, and the university (Cuthbert 1991). Industrial capital was responsible for reproducing the conditions of the working class in England in a subtropical colonial setting, in the form of high-rise industrial development, and frequently in 'new towns' such as Tuen Wan and Tuen Mun, which are probably more toxic than Chernobyl. This industrial period was also responsible from 1955 until today for creating one of the most efficient public housing systems anywhere, with the possible exception of Singapore.

The last ten years have seen the reification of finance capital in the physical form of the city through the redevelopment of many central area sites, and the sale of 'symbolic capital' to the private sector by the architectural profession. Here the *space of experience* becomes finally deconstructed into *commodity space* or what we may call the *antisocietal space of postmodernism*. Since Hong Kong's land market retains much of its original strategy in the commodification of land into 'parcels' to be sold to the highest bidder, commodity space is conflated to social space. In this context, the citizen's rights to space only exist in the sphere of personal or luxury consumption, increasingly carried out under the gaze of electronic systems of surveillance.

While modern architects focused on meaning as the expression of function, postmodern architecture generates meaning through allusion, illusion, fiction and metaphor; properties, in other words, which could also be applied to the commodity as a social relation (Jencks 1984). Recently, nascent postmodern space in Hong Kong was forced out of the closet by an interesting phenomenon involving Hong Kong's imported domestic labour. Every Sunday a large part of the city's 80,000 Filipinas take over most of the central city in order to meet friends and to create a familiar environment of their own. During the week they underwrite the production of the entire middle and upper class by releasing educated local women into the workforce. Part of the street system is pedestrianized in order to accommodate the crowds, who dance, play music, sing, eat food, gamble, trade and generally have a good time. Alternatively stated, they began to undermine the prevailing value systems of large corporations who saw the city centre in the terms described above, and to a certain extent those of local people, but for different reasons. In September 1982, a major corporation decided it had tolerated normal behaviour long enough, and cordoned off a significant amount of open space surrounding its building. There was a large measure of public support for others doing the same, and the conflict had a considerable racial dimension to it. What should have been asked is 'Whose space is it anyway?'

Hong Kong is so densely developed that if all corporate headquarters did the same, people could not leave their homes. Because of the government's unwillingness to provide open space in the central city, a policy of giving plot ratio benefits to developers, and added advantages if they provide large internal 'open spaces' in developments has been pursued. Having been given a public benefit, developers still retain the space in private control and surveillance. This is leading to the gradual, and I think inexorable, elimination of social space, and a corresponding domination of commodity space in central areas. These are spaces of total surveillance and control. They set the scene for the future, where the commodification of urban land is now matched by the progressive commodification of urban form, and therefore the totalization of postmodern space in the city in accordance with these principles. In the process, 'normal' social activities are rendered deviant.

CONCLUSION

Although Hong Kong shares many of the features associated with postindustrialism and postmodernism, the form that these take is in many respects altogether different from that in other world cities. First, the dynamic underlying the export of industry from Hong Kong to China is not the same as that which has seen industry being exported, for example, from the United States to Jamaica. Hong Kong and China will soon become a unified economic and political entity. Second, there is evidence that Hong Kong is creating a new class from its professional-technocratic elite, whereas class politics in other areas are embracing the green agenda as a general reaction to the inertia of traditional politics in dealing with the environment. Third, as Hong Kong and China struggle to develop a new nationalism where both can survive, ethnicity and supranationalism appear to take political precedence elsewhere. Rather than creating a multicultural Hong Kong, building strength from difference, the prevailing ideology is that of 'localization', a euphemism for racialization as Britain finally loses its grip on the colony. My feeling is that this tendency will soon be expanded by the mainland Chinese to include the Hong Kong Chinese themselves, replacing local Chinese in key sectors of the economy with people from the People's Republic of China. Fourth, the emancipation of women in Hong Kong is progressing via the exploitation of other women from the Third World, not through adjustments in traditional role relationships. With Hong Kong's increasing nationalism, this may soon change as China makes demands on the expenditure of foreign reserves which these women represent, and insists on replacing imported domestic labour with mainland Chinese women. Importation of male labour on the other hand is primarily through illegal immigration from China.

In terms of the geography of postmodern space, we can see other differences. First, in Hong Kong the entire socio-spatial structure emerges from a state monopoly over urban land, where all land is leased from the government with minimal planning controls. Elsewhere, an open land market prevails, controlled by a highly developed system of urban planning legislation. This has led to a situation where the gross population density in the urban areas averages 27,000 persons per square kilometre (Cuthbert 1991). Then we also have to look at the fact that Hong Kong is now infrastructure-led, whereas science and technology is the central agenda in most other countries. In this respect Hong Kong is some ten years behind its competitors (Singapore, Taiwan etc). Next, urban space in Hong Kong is largely an artificial construct, and is in the main provided by reclamation adjacent to the urban area, which has been going on since 1843. In contrast, massive urban redevelopment projects are the order of the day in the United States, Britain, Germany and other countries. Given the extent of the problem, urban redevelopment in Hong Kong is almost non-existent (Cuthbert and Dimitriou 1992). Finally, the pedestrian in the city is increasingly viewed as a servo-mechanism of commerce and business, and the movement of individuals is increasingly constrained, controlled, channelled and limited by architectural form. This is particularly evident as the pedestrian becomes elevated two and three floors above the ground.

In the context of Hong Kong it would appear that David Harvey is correct in suggesting that postindustrialism does not create a different social order; it merely impacts on and deepens the pre-existing relations of the capitalist system. However, in Hong Kong, there do appear to be significant departures from some of the more expected patterns and outcomes.

NOTES

The main title of this essay is taken from Malcolm Lowry's book of the same name.

REFERENCES

Banham, R. 1971: *The Architecture of Four Ecologies*, London: Allen Lane.

Berman, M. 1983: *All That is Solid Melts into Air*, London: Simon and Schuster.

Castells, M. 1990: *The Informational City*, Oxford: Blackwell.

Cuthbert, A. 1987: 'Hong Kong 1997: The Transition to Socialism – Ideology, Discourse and Urban Spatial Structure', *Environment and Planning D: Society and Space*, 5: 123–50.

Cuthbert, A. 1991: 'For a Few Dollars More: Urban Planning and the Legitimation Process in Hong Kong', *The International Journal of Urban and Regional Research*, 15, 4: 575–93.

Cuthbert, A. 1993: 'Flexible Production: Flexible Education: An Agenda for Planning Education into the Nineties', unpublished paper, School of Town Planning, University of New South Wales.

Cuthbert, A. and Dimitriou, H. 1992: 'Redeveloping the Fifth Quarter: A Case Study of Redevelopment in Hong Kong', *Cities*, 9, 3: 186–204.

Davies, S. and Roberts, E. 1990: *A Political Dictionary for Hong Kong*, Hong Kong: Macmillan.

Debord, G. 1983: *The Society of the Spectacle*, Detroit: Black and Red Press.

Derrida, J. 1978: *Writing and Difference*, London: Routledge and Kegan Paul.

Endacott, G. 1964: *A History of Hong Kong*, Hong Kong: Oxford.

Epstein, I. 1980: *From Opium War to Liberation*, Hong Kong: Joint Publishing Co.

Harvey, D. 1989: *The Condition of Post Modernity*, Oxford: Blackwell.

Jencks, C. 1984: *The Language of Post Modern Architecture*, New York: Rizzoli.

Lash, S. and Urry, J. 1987: *The End of Organised Capitalism*, Oxford: Blackwell.

Lau, S.K. 1984: *Society and Politics in Hong Kong*, Hong Kong: Chinese University Press.

Lenin, V. 1982: *Imperialism*, Moscow: Progress.

Lowry, M. 1962: *Under the Volcano*, Middlesex: Penguin.

Lukacs, G. 1971: *History and Class Consciousness*, London: Academy.

Poster, M. 1990: *The Mode of Information*, Cambridge: Polity Press.

Rabushka, A. 1978: *Hong Kong: A Study in Economic Freedom*, Chicago: University of Chicago Press.

Rabushka, A. 1979: *Hong Kong: A Study of Economic Freedom*, Chicago: University of Chicago Press.

Rodzinski, W. 1981: *The Walled Kingdom*, London: Fontana.

Schiffer, J. 1983: 'Urban Enterprise Zones: A Comment on the Hong Kong Model', *The International Journal of Urban and Regional Research*, 7, 3: 429–38.

Schiffer, J. 1991: 'State Policy and Economic Growth: A Comment on the Hong Kong Model', *The International Journal of Urban and Regional Research*, 15, 2: 188–209.

Toffler, A. 1990: *The Third Wave*, London: Bantam.

Waley, A. 1958: *The Opium War through Chinese Eyes*, London: Oxford University Press.

Youngson, A.J. 1982: *Hong Kong Economic Growth and Policy*, Hong Kong: Oxford University Press.

11. Gay Nights and Kingston Town: Representations of Kingston, Jamaica

Diane J. Austin-Broos

The societies in which our cities exist are, and have been for centuries, hierarchical; the inequalities among their residents are reflected in inequalities in the space they occupy.

Peter Marcuse, 'The Partitioned City'

[W]e are in the epoch of juxtaposition, the epoch of the near and the far, of the side-by-side, of the dispersed.

Michel Foucault, 'Of Other Spaces'

INTRODUCTION

In a more recent reincarnation, Kingston and Jamaica have been tourist destinations for a larger metropolitan world. The island and its capital emerged as a site for tourism in the early twentieth century, following in the wake of the banana boom. Kingston remained as a sight-seeing destination until the early 1960s. Today, with a population of over 600,000 in a society of 2.3 million people, Kingston is a city for its indigenes. It is rather seldom on the tourists' itineraries, many of which are confined to the north-coast beaches. Though seldom stated in print, the message is that Kingston is a dangerous place to be. Lord Olivier, a former governor of the island, described Kingston in 1936 as 'the sink of all the unthrifty indigence of the Island' (Olivier 1936: 34). More than one tourist operator would mouth that view today. Dirty, untidy, sprawling, dangerous, Kingston is a blight on the tourist map. And yet, even Kingston had its day as a tropical locale for the weary retreating from modernity.

That period of romantic representation began at the turn of the century. Especially from England, but also from New England, Jamaica was 'away', tropical, pleasingly exotic. Yet, unlike Africa or even India, it was also properly tempered by more than two hundred years of British civilization. One could land in Kingston to see a busy African market, luxurious bougainvillea and hibiscus everywhere, and then proceed to the eminently proper Myrtle Bank Hotel, past Up-Park-Camp and the garrison of the city, and on to the cool hill station of Newcastle. Noel Coward loved it, and so did Errol Flynn; just two among the many notaries who made a home in Jamaica and would have been familiar with 'Kingston Town'. The construction of romantic, tropical 'awayness' is a small and yet important part of twentieth-century modernity. As clean lines and concrete overtook the cities of Europe and the European New World, so there also developed the resort to another place in which to be fleetingly non-modern, 'on vacation'. And, as this process emerged in Jamaica, so too there developed a genre of tourist writing, laced with just a little anthropology, to give the intrepid modern the proper sense of adventure in foreign and fetchingly backward lands. Herbert deLisser published his popular Jamaican survey in 1913, aimed at the American market and its curious east coasters. He was preceded by a battery of writers around the turn of the century all playing a part in exoticizing Jamaica: Banbury (1894) with his *Jamaica Superstitions or the Obeah Book*; Cundall (1900) with his contribution to the British Empire Series; and Walter Jekyll (1966), dilettante folklorist and patron of the arts, with his account of *Jamaican Song and Story*, especially of the spider-trickster type.[1] Jamaica, which was for over a hundred and fifty years Britain's most famous and wealthiest slave colony, and Kingston, the colony's unglamorous trading centre, site of major slave sales and drunkenness, became exoticized as havens from the modern world. Kingston was a space at once juxtaposed and also dispersed from the metropolitan centres it had always served. It was rendered both of and not of metropolitan life; a haven not only from a modern Europe, but also from its own hellish history of slavery.

Yet this image of Kingston as a haven was shortlived and always precarious. The height of Kingston's exoticization probably occurred in the 1950s when Harry Belafonte's two calypsoes, 'Kingston Town' and the 'Banana Boat Song', hit the pop charts around the world. As a schoolgirl I was enticed by the place that was 'down the way' and 'where the nights are gay', and rocked into complacency by the 'Day-O!' of a sanitized banana loader. But the raw edge of the banana loader's life rapidly broke through this representation. Kingston's exoticization quickly faded, not only due to Jamaica's past, but also due to its present and likely future. The trading town that watched slaves 'in' and sugar, rum and molasses 'out' became, after a sojourn as a banana port, the principal site of Jamaica's urbanization; a town ringed with slums and shanty towns by the 1950s, but pronounced a sprawling ghetto by the 1980s. And with this massive urban expansion came, first, the effort to modernize Kingston and make of it a mini-metropolis, and then the rapid retreat of Kingston's wealthy to the hills as 'downtown' became an uncontrollable morass of violent creativity and also negativity that the middle class despaired of ever retrieving. In the period from the 1950s to the late 1970s, Kingston moved through three modernist moments: colonial haven from the metropolitan world; metropolis aspiring to modernity itself; and finally, in the 1980s and 1990s, to a city with slums that parry modernity and press back the effort to mask Jamaica's more disturbing side. The discussion below will focus on these three representations of Kingston: as haven and ostensible obverse of the modern; as modernity itself and hope for the poor; and as 'postmodern' trangression in the form of a downtown life that refuses to mask Jamaica's history.

Given the title of this collection, it behoves me, however, also to address 'postmodernity'. Notwithstanding the debates on whether the term should be taken to denote a style, a moment, or perhaps a period (see for instance Huyssen 1988; Jameson 1988; Kellner 1989; Harvey 1989; Norris 1990; Giddens 1991), I think that I can use it in a sense that is real for the people with whom I have worked in Kingston. I want to call them a 'postmodern' people because of their scepticism concerning modernity. They are sceptical not only of Jamaica's romanticization, of an indolent image that means little to them, but also of the purported hope of the modern to bring new and more prosperous ways of life. As a Jamaican friend once put it to me, this hope proposes a situation 'of no working class, just middle and upper'; a situation, he remarked with somber glee, that would take 'a very long time to get in working order'. Kingston and its slums shaped this droll observation.

The Kingston poor are a product of late modernity that allows them islands of affluence in a larger sea of want. Gaining a well-paid job for six months, or having a Chicago or London relative feel lonely, can mean that a Kingston dweller flies to America or England for a visit. When that person returns it will not be alone, but with cardboard drums of clothes, shoes, washing powder, appliances and a range of other wondrous things brought from the metropolis. Whether or not they are paired with a traveller, the cardboard drums will arrive in any case, as well-meaning relatives in England or America stock and restock their families at home. Jamaicans, and not least the poor among them, are, like numerous other Third World peoples, extremely urbane. Movement, travel, other places, itinerancy are part of the daily cut and thrust of life. An inclination forged in the midst of labour migration continues now as a studied style as well as a pragmatic search for income. This style for the poor has joined with the desire of the post-colonial middle classes to engage the metropolitan world in debates defined by their own experience and designed to disarm the 'foreign expert'. Knowing about 'foreign' is an integral part of Jamaica, and learning about 'foreign' is part of being Jamaican. As a consequence, many residents of Kingston's slums know that Kingston does not and probably cannot offer very much of the life linked with modernity. They know that adequate housing and education for children will be in fact extremely hard to obtain; that good quality clothes and electrical appliances that are up to date will generally just outstrip their reach; that the shoes from Florida, 'better than Jamaican ones', will be earnestly sought but infrequently acquired. They will also know that a working sojourn in the metropolitan world will bring a large proportion of these goods, but with it the destruction of a local way of life infused with kinship and parish affiliations that Jamaicans value enormously.[2] They will therefore aspire to leave Jamaica, but always only for a while. The Jamaicans I know among Kingston's poor only half believe the myths of modernity proposed for Jamaica and the metropolitan world. They may want the commodities of a modern world but not the individuation that strips them of kin or the rootlessness that leaves them un-Jamaican. They have seen too much to be simply 'true believers'. And it is from this lengthy transnational experience that there springs the creativity that is found in their music. Ska and reggae, not to mention calypso, speak of Caribbean joy and trial in a world that, notwithstanding its modernity, is still not metropolitan.

Jamaicans are postmodern and transgressors in this sense. They are sceptics with regard to modernity. They can be this way, and with a certain panache, just because they partake of late modernity: of a radical hierarchy in urban space that defines downtowners as poor and powerless; and also of a communications network that hurtles information around the world and provides them with a critical distance from their local and the metropolitan world. Below I trace this distance as it has emerged through the three moments of Kingston Town, but also as it is represented in Kingston's music (cf. Waters 1986). The stimulus to imagination that comes with Jamaica's transnational milieu does not dissolve Kingston's hierarchy. It does, however, offer a space for popular critique and hope that is evident on the streets of Kingston and especially in its popular music, which has become itself a transnational phenomenon in the last forty years.

KINGSTON AS HAVEN: THE THEN, AND NOW

Kingston was from its very beginnings a city which harboured the vast majority of whites and people of colour living within Jamaica. Always a city that was majority black both in the days of slavery and freedom, it remained, nevertheless, the home of Jamaica's commercial and professional wealthy. When the site of the capital was moved to Kingston from Spanish Town in 1872, this move confirmed that Kingston would accommodate a small society within a society; the commercial and professional elite as well as the governor's circle (C. Clarke 1975: 29ff).[3] These people focused their activities in Kingston on a small area of residential sites lying on the open savannah just north of Kingston's harbourside and at the foot of the mountains that encircle the city. Owing to the earthquakes and perennial fires that destroyed most of the early wooden structures, this elite housed themselves in relatively new and sumptuous surroundings often built at the turn of the century, or in the 1910s and 1920s. They focused their social activity between these large and airy homes, the governor's residence in the same locale, and Kingston's leading hotels. From this arena the men sallied daily to commercial and professional concerns in King Street, Harbour Street, Laws Street, and Duke Street, only to return in the mid-afternoon by buggy and, later, chauffeur-driven vehicle. The social round, structured by the governor's activities and those of his wife, was announced with suitable aplomb each week in the pages of the *Daily Gleaner*, Jamaica's extraordinary journal of record extant since the slavery days. This flowering of a colonial gentility, lived through a series of turn-of-the-century buildings, rested on prosperity from banana planting and a shortlived revival of sugar. It was fuelled in any case by Kingston's commercialism, which carried staples in and out of the island. And in the 1910s it was momentarily protected, as we shall see, from cataclysmic changes elsewhere in Jamaica. Still oblivious to the impact these changes would bring, deLisser could see Kingston's tourist potential. His optimism tumbled forth in an extraordinary set of images. Speaking of Kingston, deLisser observed in 1913,

> *The city possesses hotels of course, and these in the months when tourists come to the island are filled to overflowing. The chief hotels in Kingston are the Myrtle Bank and the South Camp Road Hotels; the first is built by the sea, and the second is situated in the city's finest residential quarter, and both have the benefit of the breeze that comes from the sea in the*

day-time and of the delightful winds that steal down from the mountains at night. It is these breezes that . . . make the heat of a tropical city like Kingston so different from what one has to endure in New York, Boston, or the eastern cities of Canada. . . . To return to the hotels, it may be said that they serve a double function: the first, naturally, is to cater for guests and this they do in a manner creditable to them; the other function is the organising of public dances, and in this they also succeed admirably. Balls are frequently given by them, and at some of these you will find hundreds of handsomely dressed people – Jamaica's best – and will get some idea of what a social function in the West Indies is like. On the whole, there is nothing quite so lively in the way of public entertainment as the dances arranged by these hotels, and their foreign guests seem to enjoy them thoroughly. . . .

But I think I have said enough of Kingston . . . there is something about it, something about the life of it, which one cannot tell of on paper, but which gives to it an individuality of its own and constitutes its main source of interest. It is not beautiful; except in the winter months it is not cool; it is not in the slightest degree impressive; it is not charming like Havana; it is not even historic. And yet it is interesting, and the more familiar you are with it the more interesting it grows. One loves to watch its people walking, sauntering along its streets, standing at the street corners, greeting one another with audible cordiality, obviously taking life as it comes, and not troubling about the morrow. . . . Life does not vary much in this city; change, unless caused by accident or catastrophe, comes imperceptibly; old age creeps upon one unawares. The cables bring daily the news of the outer world, of battles, murders, great speeches, epidemics, and epoch-making discoveries, and the people take them all as a matter of course. It is not ignorance, it is not lack of interest, this. It is habit mainly, the habit of going through the day calmly, through the long days of resplendent sunlight, only varied now and then by the darkness which the thunder-clouds cast, a darkness which resolves itself into a torrential shower that washes the atmosphere to a crystaline purity, through which one looks at the soft-shining snow-clouds drifting and floating above in a concave ocean of azure and gold. (deLisser 1913: 79–80)

The evocation of backwardness beyond modernity, which can accommodate the traveller nevertheless, is here displayed with all its power turned to America's busy eastern seaboard. DeLisser entices the residents of New York, Boston and Montreal to visit what he describes as 'one of the three most beautiful islands in the world' to gaze on a sky of 'azure and gold'.[4] The creation of space and experienced distance from the milieu of the American modern is also, however, a creation of distance and space in relation to another Jamaica. At the very time that deLisser was writing, Jamaica was involved in momentous change. This was the period of the second great migration of Jamaican male labour to the Panama Canal construction site, now managed by the United States, which had succeeded the French in 1904 (Newton 1984: 94). There was also massive labour migration to Costa Rica, Cuba and the United States itself (Eisner 1961: 149–51; Roberts 1957: 139). These migrations were a symptom of the fact that scarcity of good land in Jamaica meant that farming alone could never occupy the descendants of those emancipated from slavery. The first great moments of this realization were manifest in labour migrations, as

Jamaicans chose to go overseas rather than return to plantations where their wages remained appallingly low (Olivier 1910, 1936). These migrations, however, came to an end during the course of the 1920s. With the advent of the Great Depression this labour was forced back into Jamaica and onto the farms that in the interim had been tended and managed by Jamaican women. The women, in turn, from the 1920s on, began the internal migrations to Kingston looking for all forms of service employment as incomes from farming were increasingly depleted (Roberts 1957: 152–8). These women were followed by their men as emigration opportunities declined; and the process unleashed on Kingston Town culminated in 1938 with the labour rebellion island-wide that hurried the British out of Jamaica. DeLisser wrote in the pause of the 1910s, just before these events began to unfold.

Between 1921 and 1943 the population of the Kingston corporate area doubled, and confirmed the modern shape of Kingston with its middle-class suburbs towards the mountains and its creeping slums by the southern seaboard. By the early 1950s the West Kingston slums called 'Back-O-Wall' and 'Dungle' were, with shanty towns, firmly established. The northern tourist towns of Port Antonio, Ocho Rios and Montego Bay were also beginning to expand. But in this period of New World prosperity, especially for white America, it was Kingston still that had the name. The calypsonian who 'left a little girl' in Kingston Town also extolled Jamaica's 'gay nights' of fêtes or parties beginning around ten or eleven in the evening and pulsing through to three or four in the morning. These cool nights of feast and frivolity merged with the sun 'on the mountain tops' to create a languid and eudemonic air which would leave the traveller soulfully depressed as his sailing ship moved away again and, ultimately, out of tropical climes. The song 'Kingston Town' was not inappropiate for one real space in the city of Kingston. Even today in Kingston Town the space of the haven still exists; a space which evokes an indeterminate past but one always helped by anonymous hands to make the wealthy's pace of life a little premodern.

As a fieldworker in Kingston's slums I happened to meet an unusual woman married to a fairskinned man. She herself was brown-skinned, darker than he, and told me she came from an unprivileged past. She was beautiful and commmercially astute. She had helped her husband in his business to become a more than usually wealthy man. Her house was located on the savannah, a locale that she preferred to maintain even when others in the middle class had moved further up the hills. Noting my residence in a Kingston 'yard', she proposed that I should come to her every Friday evening, stay overnight, and return to my yard on the Saturday morning. She was not the first middle-class Kingstonian to be shocked by the circumstances in which I lived. I took the opportunity, rationalizing to myself that this was an excellent way to observe the (upper) middle class who did not actually constitute a part of my study. Friday afternoons and nights with my friend were not, in fact, especially spectacular. In the evening – this was the early 1970s – we would go downtown and sometimes to the fledgling development of New Kingston, to window shop in furniture and luxury goods stores. Her house, entirely carpeted, air-conditioned, furnished with antiques and priceless pieces of crockery and crystal, seemed fairly to burst at the seams with European symbols of affluence strung together in a Jamaican code. Always with an eye to a new acquisition, however, she passed restlessly between these stores enquiring about new shipments and checking on items ordered from England. Later in the night, having sent her housemaid home, we would sit in her bedroom with its quiet tropical courtyard, eating small delights brought by the parlour maid. Before long we would lie about on cushions and pillows heaped up for us by the very same maid who slept in a small apartment alongside her mistress's room. I would retire to my allotted bed, having gossiped half the night away, to arise in the morning to the West Indian breakfast. The master of the house would join us then to survey the extensive meal coming forth on silver servers laid on starched linen cloths: tropical fruits and juice, at least three types of cooked meat, breadfruit in season, fried Johnny cakes and bacon, and callaloo (a certain kind of spinach), washed down with hot chocolate, coffee or tea. The indolence of this Kingston style evoked for me the note-taking of Lady Nugent, the governor's wife, in the first four years of the nineteenth century when the slave regime was at its height. Lady Nugent wrote in her diary,

> It is extraordinary to witness the immediate effect that the climate and habit of living in this country have upon the minds and manners of Europeans... In the upper ranks they become indolent and inactive, regardless of every thing but eating, drinking, and indulging themselves . . .

> The Creole language is not confined to the negroes. Many of the ladies, who have not been educated in England, speak a sort of broken English, with an indolent drawling out of their words . . . I stood next to a lady one night, . . . and by way of saying something, remarked that the air was much cooler than usual; to which she answered, Yes, ma'am, him rail-ly too fra-ish. (Wright 1966: 98)

Lady Nugent's account of a breakfast went like this:

> we breakfasted in the Creole style. – [Cassava] cakes, chocolate, coffee tea, fruits of all sorts, pigeon pies, hams, tongues, rounds of beef, etc. I only wonder there was no turtle. Mr. M.'s delight is to stuff his guests, and I should think it would be quite a triumph to him, to hear of a fever or apoplexy, in consequence of his good cheer. He is immensely rich [and] his house is truly Creole. (Wright 1966: 55)

Conspicuous consumption in the early nineteenth century, along with conspicuous revelry, were the practices on which a tourist trade could draw in painting Kingston and Jamaica as exotic haven to the metropolitan world. The haven that was beyond the modern, even as modernity created it; the haven as distant from its own people's space as it was from a North American metropolis. If Kingston today has dropped off the tourist map, it still has the power to create that space for the foreign expert and the business adventurer, not to mention the intrepid anthropologist. As that space cajoles and beckons it also bends the will to accommodate modernity. In the words of the anthropologist Sidney Mintz, it is the sugar that sweetens the taste of power. No one knows this better than Kingstonians who remain below Half-Way Tree or Torrington Bridge, the moving and various spatial markers that are used by the middle class to delimit the slum from the savannah.

KINGSTON AS METROPOLIS AND HOPE OF THE POOR

In the early 1970s when I began my research, the slums were still not called a 'ghetto'. In fact, when I first went to Kingston there was still a great deal of hope among the poor. To the question on the neighbourhood survey that asked respondents to compare the present with the past of twenty years ago, everyone replied that the present was better, and often, because life was more 'modern'. People talked of country huts with banana thatch roofs, and beds made of burlap stretched across wooden frames. They talked of dirt floors and no piped water, and of children with no shoes to wear at all. Town was different and life was better. 'Country people' were looked down upon. The driving force of this urbanization, and also of the 1950s migrations to Britain, was the expansion of Jamaica's bauxite mines and the prosperity that initially flowed from that concern (Austin 1975, 1984: 3–12; Foner 1979). In the 1950s North America was stockpiling aluminium, engaged in a Korean war, and still mindful of the Eastern bloc and the conflagration of World War II. Jamaica's red soil was full of bauxite. Many peasant farmers sold their land and had the means to migrate to England. They were still, at that stage, British citizens. The less moneyed or courageous came to Kingston. Downtown Kingston was a booming service centre, and the new commercial and banking section, New Kingston, was itself growing apace. In 1972, a general election brought Michael Manley's party to power, promising a new national pride for Jamaica. He, along with his parliamentarians, strode through the centre of Kingston heralding a second 'New Day'.[5] Service stations had sprung up everywhere; American drugstores were all the go; open-air cinemas multiplied and showed American movies grades B down to Z; tourism had a new, popular face; and education was being expanded. African nationalism was blossoming forth; the middle-class youth was critical and confident. Perky 'rude boys' strode the lanes of the slums and produced their own strains of reggae music blasted out in venues called 'Blue Mist' and 'Stud Farm,' the forerunners of today's dancehalls. Michael Manley had come to power on the very end of the bauxite boom. As he pursued social programmes for the poor, and assumed a non-aligned position which meant support for Cuba in Angola and at home, rapidly things began to change (see Manley 1987).

The violence that erupted in downtown Kingston and eventually spread from the western sections to the east, curving around to the Wareika Hills and encapsulating slums becoming a 'ghetto', laid waste the booming service centre and the employment it had provided. Some of this violence was simply crime. Much of it came from neighbourhood gangs armed through the 'ganja' trade[6] and turning their weapons to the service of various politicians. As party politics became embittered, in a climate of economic scarcity in part created by international relations, frustration erupted as neighbourhood warfare.

More than 40,000 people were displaced from the slums, and in the worst period of violence over 500 were killed (cf. Eyre 1986). The dream of modernity faltered and stumbled. As the worst of the violence subsided in the later 1980s, the dream was resurrected again through attempts to reinvigorate the harbourside. A new hotel, some banks and an international seaboard authority could not, however, accomplish the task. New Kingston, safely away from the violence, expanded relentlessly onto the savannah, gobbling up residential sites that relocated themselves in the hills. The charm and price of bauxite slipped away, just as they had for bananas and sugar. The wave of optimism of 1972 already had its base hollowed out. Lower Kingston was increasingly described as 'a ghetto' and the commercial classes cut their losses and relocated in the 'New' Kingston. With so many Jamaicans now abroad, money still circulated in the economy. If the cost of living went up and up, there were still jobs, of a sort, to be had. And as transnational travel proceeded apace, the youth of the poor looked even more to America, and to its form of ghetto style – exaggerated jewellery and crazy hair – along with Jamaica's own 'dub' music, and the increasing smell of cash from cocaine.

The media event that foreshadowed all this was Jimmy Cliff's film and recording, *The Harder they Come*, both released in 1972, the year that I started my research in the slums. I began my neighbourhood survey on a Sunday that also happened to be my birthday. That night I went to an open-air cinema to watch Jimmy Cliff in *The Harder they Come*. The story of the film will be familiar to many: a young country lad comes to Kingston Town full of aspirations for a better future and hoping to become a reggae star. After various adventures and misadventures he finally manages to cut a successful recording, only to be cheated by the studio. He turns to a new set of friends, some rude boys and some Rastafarians, and begins to make a living selling ganja in Kingston. He learns very soon that the police are involved, rebels, and finds himself in a shoot-out. On the run, he is comforted by his woman, and is eventually pressed to escape to Cuba, the alternative vision of modernist salvation. Bleeding and weak from his fiery encounter, he waits on a lonely stretch of beach for the ship to pass that is sailing to Cuba. He swims to grasp the ladder thrown for him by the Jamaican seamen travelling on board. Too weak, however, he misses his chance and crawls back to shore to await his fate.

The songs in the film move with the story and begin with the optimistic announcement, 'You can get it if you really want . . . But you must try, try and try, try and try.' 'Rome', the song says, was never built 'in a day' and so for the youth growing up in Jamica the battle to suceed is inevitable, but the victory all the sweeter because of it. As Ivan, the character in the film, learns about urban life, love, and the power of the pastors to control womenfolk, he also senses complexity. The poignant 'Many Rivers to Cross' announces a condition in which 'it's only my will that keeps me alive' and 'I merely survive because of my pride.' The initial despair is cast aside, however, in a new wave of hope and steely determination that produces the title song of the film. 'The Harder they Come' is an extraordinary song within the context of Jamaican culture because it rejects the transcendentalism of Jamaica's long revival tradition. In that tradition successive waves of Afro-Christianity have taught the young and reassured the old that in the next world their redemptive victory will come. Cliff's title song, on the other hand, embraces the inevitability of conflict – the harder they come, the harder they fall – but on the way to a redemption in the present. Playing on common figures of speech, the singer observes that he wants 'now' the 'pie in the sky' promised to Jamaican Christians when they die. The most telling lines from a Jamaican point of view come closer to the end of the song, however, when the singer observes that it is better to be 'a freeman in [a] grave' than to live life as 'a puppet or a slave'. The hard edge of modernity and youth that leads Ivan into conflict with the law expresses itself in the message of the song that, irrespective of the consequences, a man should get his 'share now, what's mine'.

The songs 'Johnny Too Bad', 'Shanty Town', and 'Pressure Drop' record Ivan's passage into Kingston's underworld. Finally, as he waits for his ship to Cuba, comes the song that confirms disillusion with modernity; the song that speaks of man as 'a bird without a song', and of victims 'waiting for the dice to roll'. Having missed the boat that will take him to Cuba and a second vision of modernity, Ivan is sitting 'in limbo' now, confused about the nature of his life and barely daring to contemplate the future. 'Sitting in Limbo' describes an experience which Jimmy Cliff avoided by becoming a star. He constructed this experience as his product, his commodity, and thereby traded himself out of the slums. For those less fortunate, this final song suggests, faith is after all the only resort. The very production of the film also called *The Harder they Come* is itself modernity in all its aspects. Yet as image and representation it does not entirely capture the Kingston downtown slums.

KINGSTON AS POSTMODERN TRANSGRESSION

The streets of downtown Kingston are busy through the day and a good part of the night. Women sit by little trays selling cigarettes and sweets. Men push carts around with a variety of wares and refuse. The betting shops are open for most of the day and streetside vendors compete with the occasional supermarket and tiny corner shops. Environment affects bodies in different ways. For older men in work it is a matter of gnarled hands and weathered faces, for women the distinctive drop of the arms and ponderous stride that comes from constant bending and carrying or scouring in vending, domestic or factory work. Men learn to walk slowly with very long strides and hood their eyes against the sun and gritty wind. Women fat and thin become pot-bellied young in life from too many children and a diet of sugar and starch. For those who are involved in manual work the sun produces skins that are distinctively black even in a 'black' society. For others, bodies are moulded by an environment less intrusively material, by a certain languid pace of life that makes walk a play upon dance and speech a perpetual performance pursuing the completed account of life (cf. Abrahams 1983). If the people of downtown Kingston lived in a homogeneous society without Jamaica's hierarchy of colour shade, they would still be recognized and certainly distinguished by an environmental and historically conferred cultural milieu. Indeed, feedback from the United States and Britain, where the position of these people is represented in song, elaborates and maintains the cultural impact of a ghetto style at once local, transnational and also international (S. Clarke 1980; Hebdige 1987; cf. Gilroy 1987). Ghetto blacks in Kingston are readily recognized. The ease of their identification comes from an environment that works on phenotype and imprints a history of exclusion and confrontation onto each and every body that remains in the slum. Culture, class and race do not merely coincide. They merge as phenotype is rendered through culture; inheritance made potent through environment and experienced inscriptions on the body.

Affluent residents of Kingston avoid downtown. For many, it is a fearful environment. The services it offers are duplicated elsewhere. Except en route to an industrial location, many in the middle class would only enter the area possibly to consult a Revival healer or a motor mechanic.[7] This avoidance has about it a touch of shame as well as fear. In a society that has experienced concurrently social mobility and rapid and violent ghettoization on a much larger scale, there is a sense that the poor have failed their society (cf. Gordon 1987). For the mobile it is often difficult to explain why their confrères remain unprivileged, and these frontline members of the middle class are generally quite vehement in discounting race. Most of these new middle-class are black and they maintain that the major principles of differentiation in Jamaica are education and wealth: they are distinguished by education from their fellows, while they are distinguished from the more powerful in turn merely by wealth (Austin 1983, 1984; Douglass 1992). It is this milieu that explains downtown in terms of historical and environmental legacies that reach back to the days of slavery. These genealogies of social milieux begin from the disorganization of culture that both a ghetto and slavery are presumed to represent. The fear of this disorganization is magnified by an appreciation among the middle-class that the tourist industry is crucial to Jamaica. Letters to the press complaining about shabby people, unruly vendors and the insane on the streets are commonly couched in terms of what 'visitors' must think of these transgressions of 'civilized' behaviour. Downtown confronts modernity and its notions of haven and encultured order. These notions find their roots, in turn, in the Jamaican elite and the metropolitan world.

The downtown black is identified not only by a phenotype interpreted through culture, but also by various motifs of disorder that identify supposedly ghetto practices. The principal among these are those of the Rastafarians, with their wild hair and exaggerated walk, commonly associated with the madmen themselves. These men who wander the streets of Kingston are generally barefoot, unshaven and unkempt. They talk to themselves, expose themselves, beg, and in a multitude of ways violate the codes of a modern society. Women higglers and religious fundamentalists, dogged and aggressive in their pursuits, become an embarrassment to the more controlled. The popularity of Pentecostalism in Kingston with its orgasmic forms of spirit possession remains a source of constant annoyance to the more conventionally religious. The higgler-entrepreneurs who arrive at the Miami airport with cartons stacked high to be flown down to Kingston are a particular and perpetual concern to the transient middle class for their untidiness, loudness and relentless bargaining in the presence of the more ordered metropolis. The desire to contain downtown disorder is also manifest in the sometimes indignant response of drivers to the army of boys who come out of the ghetto to stand at intersections and clean car windows. Drivers wind up their windows and wave in frustration for the boys to go away. Some in the middle class see these boys as the product of a 'promiscuous' Afro-lower class that has remained illegitimate since slavery. The ultimate disorder is of course gang warfare, the violence that joins politics and crime in a fashion that questions the order of the state. The sordid stories of associations between eminent politicians and ghetto thugs challenge the legitimacy of the nation and its claim to embody modernity.[8]

The new recording star, Shabba Ranks, with his own version of Jamaican dub that confronts the senses, and shocks with its references to sex and violence, is an integral part of this downtown scene. And yet downtown has also produced musical images of a more enduring type. These were captured by Bob Marley in the 1970s and 1980s as he sought to reveal the hope of the slum in the intimacy of its daily life. Not for Marley the modernist urge to build Rome in a day. He evoked a gentler side of life; that of kin, romance and religious engagement, which persists in Kingston's yards and lanes even as Shabba assaults a taken-for-granted aesthetic. In a fashion similar to those of Jimmy Cliff, many of Marley's songs speak of travel and movement; of thresholds never entirely crossed. That extraordinary Jamaican sense of being uprooted so long ago, perhaps to be in transit forever, is there in the singing of 'Exodus' as it was in Cliff's 'Many Rivers to Cross'. But along with this inevitable movement comes the conjoining of place and sentiment in relations of kinship, romance and worship; Jamaica's three major moments of transcendence. These moments have echoed around the world, but can be 'known', I think, only in Kingston.

In his song 'No Woman No Cry' Marley evokes the ghetto environment when he sings of life in a 'government yard in Trench Town'. Trench Town is one of the more famous of the west Kingston slum neighbourhoods, and also the site of extensive patronage by one of the major political parties in power. Cheap housing in the form of government tenement yards and a large range of community services have been provided for the area and often stimulated the envy of others, resulting in eruptions of gang warfare. The area remains extremely poor and life there always modest and sometimes cruel. Marley sings, however, of the joys of the milieu: of 'good friends' who would mingle in the lanes and tenement yards; of preachers singing and people talking in the yards as 'logwood [lay] burning through the night'. He reminds his listeners, and especially the women, that notwithstanding their hopes for the future in this milieu 'you can't forget your past.' And this past and present are evoked by a reference to cornmeal cooked as a porridge and used as a staple for the poor. Cornmeal is identified as an African food, and as a food for the contemporary poor one notch down in desperation from rice porridge, the preferred form of the gruel. Cornmeal porridge is often fed to dogs, even in the ghetto milieu. In the midst of this scene the theme of travel re-emerges as Marley observes that though his feet are his 'only carriage' he must nevertheless move on his way. Despite the fact that domestic intimacy is shattered by itinerancy, he proclaims that everything will 'be all right' so that 'woman n'cry,/No woman no cry'. This song to a lover could also be to a mother; to the women with children who stayed at home while men became itinerants. Women today, however, are as mobile as men; both seeking employment in the metropolitan world.

Marley strikes a happier note when he sings of 'friending' or the 'visiting' relationships that young men and women share together before they settle in stable concubinage or, less commonly, in marriage. This life is called the 'sweetheart life' and creates its own realm of freeness. In a song that begins 'I want to love . . . you every day and every night', Marley once again evokes an intimate domesticity of two young people sharing shelter and a single bed. They rely on 'Ja' on God to provide their 'bread' and feel grateful for their modest security. 'Is this Love?' is a joyous song that celebrates the art of Jamaican courtship and makes the most of a culture in which dalliance is the major form of amusement. Moreover, this is a form that can quite appropriately proceed in a one-roomed 'zinc' or corrugated iron structure delicately described in Kingston as an 'apartment'. The 'shelter' of the singer's bed is the shelter of the intimacy created by poverty, which here becomes a charming, even tantalizing, warmth.

In his celebrated 'Redemption Song', Marley evokes a local environment entirely lost in a transnational imagery. The title of the song is also the title of Jamaica's favourite Pentecostal hymnal, a small red book very cheap in price that is owned by most Pentecostal women, who fill the ranks of the ghetto's religious. Singing as a Rastafarian affiliate and critical of 'white' religion, Marley plays on the ambiguity of redemption constrained and redemption unleashed to freedom. Building on Christianity's traditional gift of healing, again a gift conferred by a mother, he foreshadows a forward movement that passes from the past to an imaginary future. He calls for an emancipation from the 'mental slavery' bequeathed to Jamaica by a lengthy colonialism and manifest strikingly, he might propose, in the minds of the more religious. Marley remarks, however, on the rising tide of optimism and progress which the passage from mental slavery can achieve for a people. They know, as is written in their textbook-Bible, that prophets of the people will inevitably fall. Yet, rather than simply 'stand aside and look', Marley calls for his listeners to sing the freedom songs; the only songs they every had – redemption songs. With these songs Marley ends on the same ambiguous note as the musical comment of Jimmy Cliff, which seeks to go beyond Jamaica's redemptive culture, with its roots in a slave and Afro-Christian past, and yet finds in that very culture images of strength for a life to come.

Marley's future is not a future of material progress, but rather a transcendental imaginary which has been shaped within Jamaican culture by generations of revivalists bringing their New World African stamp to old forms of metropolitan Christianity. It is from this tradition that Rastafarianism rose to confront Jamaica's moral order and contest the logic of the nation-state. In these types of reggae image the ghetto dwellers move beyond a conception of themselves as modern into an imaginary space that figures utopias not yet present. These utopias combine a transcendental urge with the intimacy of immediate social space that attaches sentiment to place even in the midst of downtown life. The everyday milieu of this imaginary space, by its dirt, disorder, violence and grief, transgresses the progressive image of the modern and makes of it its own disorder. The imaginary space of reggae music also transforms this slum milieu by presenting a transcendental image, embodied in Rastafarian thought, as the only appropriate comment on the modern.

CONCLUSION

Kingston is one of those wonderful cities at once displaced from metropolitan life and yet so much a part of that world that we really understand what 'the modern' is: a system that creates hierarchical space even as it links the 'near' and 'far away'. This is so for the different quarters of Kingston: for the suburbs of the hills; for the savannah's New Kingston; and for the ghetto milieu downtown. Each space is defined through a sense of hierarchy and through avid communication. If this is true for Kingston's parts, it is also true for Kingston Town in its relations with the metropolitan world. Whether as haven, metropolis or ghetto, Kingston takes its identity both from its sense of peripheral position, and from expanding transnational experience. It is the power of the imagery of the ghetto, exemplified in the music it has produced, that demands that Kingston be seen as positioned in and yet as confronting modernity. I like to think of my Kingston friends, some of them more travelled than I, as a really postmodern people; as born sceptics of a gleeful type; as a people who transgress the modern. They transgress it through their intimacy, through their hope, and through their musical imagination.

NOTES

1 'Obeah' is the Jamaican word for witchcraft or magic. The trickster tales mainly concern Anancy, the spider trickster who came originally from the Ashanti in West Africa. See Rattray (1926).
2 Raymond Smith (1988) has written extensively on the importance of kin associations in Caribbean, including in Jamaican, life. The sentimental attachment to a parish of origin is less remarked upon, although Jean Besson (1992) touches on these issues in her discussion of family land. Almost all residents of Kingston also claim affiliation with a parish that is sometimes Kingston or St Andrew itself, but often a rural parish of origin.
3 Colin Clarke's *Kingston, Jamaica* (1975) is undoubtedly the major historical work on Kingston. Austin (1984) portrays the forms of class and racialized culture that different areas of the city harbour today. Douglass (1992) gives a further overview. Cross (1979) gives a useful overview of urbanization in the Caribbean.
4 In deLissers's view the two most beautiful islands in the world other than Jamaica are Bali and Java (deLisser 1913: 81).
5 The first 'New Day' was 1938, heralded in his novel of the same name by Victor Stafford Reid.
6 'Ganja' is the Jamaican term for marihuana, which is used by Rastafarians for ritual purposes. It has long been used by Jamaica's small farmers as a medicine and mild hallucinogen. See Dreher (1982).
7 Lisa Douglass (1992: 25–88) gives an excellent account of 'spaces' as 'practiced place' in Kingston (see deCerteau 1984: 117). She observes that 'to note the importance of these distinctions [between uptown and downtown] is not to ignore [that] . . . the two are part of a single tradition and history' (Douglass 1992: 88). Marx and many others would not have denied this. *Contra* Douglass's suggestions, however, 'a single tradition and history' does not mean shared values throughout the society (see Douglass 1992: 268–74).

8 There is evidence that this period of Jamaican politics is now coming to an end, at least for a while. The 1993 return of the People's National Party to power with an increased majority suggests that gang politics is on the wane.

REFERENCES

Abrahams, R.D. 1983: *The Man-of-Words in the West Indies: Performance and the Emergence of Creole Culture*, Baltimore and London: Johns Hopkins.

Austin, D.J. 1975: 'Jamaican Bauxite: A Case Study in Multi-national Investment', *Australian and New Zealand Journal of Sociology*, 11: 53–9.

Austin, D.J. 1983: 'Culture and Ideology in the English-speaking Caribbean: A View from Jamaica', *American Ethnologist*, 10: 223–40.

Austin, D.J. 1984: *Urban Life in Kingston, Jamaica: The Culture and Class Ideology of Two Neighbourhoods*, Caribbean Studies Series, vol. 3, New York and London: Gordon and Breach.

Banbury, R.T. 1894: *Jamaican Superstitions or the Obeah Book*, Kingston: DeSouza.

Besson, J. 1992: 'Freedom and Community: The British West Indies', in F. McGlynn and S. Drescher (eds), *The Meaning of Freedom: Economics, Politics, and Culture after Slavery*, Pittsburgh and London: Pittsburgh University Press.

deCerteau, M. 1984: *The Practice of Everyday Life*, trans. S. Rendall, Berkeley, Los Angeles and London: University of California Press.

Clarke, C. 1975: *Kingston, Jamaica: Urban Growth and Social Change 1692–1962*, Berkeley: University of California Press.

Clarke, S. 1980: *Jah Music: The Evolution of Popular Jamaican Song*, London: Heinemann.

Cross, M. 1979: *Urbanization and Urban Growth in the Caribbean*, Urbanization in Developing Countries Series, vol. 3, Cambridge and London: Cambridge University Press.

Cundall, F. 1900: 'Jamaica', in *British America*, British Empire Series, vol. III, London: Kegan Paul, Trench, Trubner.

Douglass, L. 1992: *The Power of Sentiment: Love, Hierarchy and the Jamaican Family Elite*, Boulder, San Francisco and Oxford: Westview Press.

Dreher, M. 1982: *Working Men and Ganja: Marihuana Use in Rural Jamaica*, Philadelphia: Institute for the Study of Human Issues.

Eisner, G. 1961: *Jamaica 1830–1930: A Study of Economic Growth*, Manchester: Manchester University Press.

Eyre, L. A. 1986: 'The effects of political terrorism on the location of the poor in Kingston', *Urban Geography*, 7: 227–42.

Foner, N. 1979: *Jamaica Farewell: Jamaican Migrants in London*, London and Henley: Routledge and Kegan Paul.

Foucault, M. 1986: 'Of Other Spaces', *Diacritics*, 16: 22-7.

Giddens, A. 1991: *Modernity and Self-Identity: Self and Society in the Late Modern Age*, Cambridge and Oxford: Polity Press.

Gilroy, P. 1987: *There Ain't no Black in the Union Jack*, London: Hutchinson.

Gordon, D. 1987: *Class, Status and Social Mobility in Jamaica*, Mona: Institute of Social and Economic Research.

Harvey D. 1989: *The Condition of Postmodernity*, Oxford: Blackwell.

Hebdige, D. 1987: *Cut'N'Mix: Culture, Identity and Caribbean Music*, London: Routledge.

Huyssen, A. 1988: *After the Great Divide: Modernism, Mass Culture and Postmodernism*, London: Macmillan.

Jameson, F. 1988: 'Postmodernism and Consumer Society', in E.A. Kaplan (ed.), *Postmodernism and its Discontents*, London and New York: Verso.

Jekyll, W. 1966: *Jamaican Song and Story*, Publications of the Folklore Society 55, New York: Dover. Original publication 1907.

Kellner, D. (ed.) 1989: *Postmodernism/Jameson/Critique*, Washington, DC: Maisonneuve Press.

deLisser, H.G. 1913: *Twentieth Century Jamaica*, Kingston: The Jamaica Times Ltd.

Manley, M. 1987: *Up the Down Escalator: Development and the International Economy, a Jamaican Case Study*, London: Andre Deutsch.

Marcuse, P. 1993: 'The Partitioned City', in *Postmodern Cities Conference Proceedings*, Sydney: University of Sydney, Department of Urban and Regional Planning.

Newton, V. 1984: *The Silver Men: West Indian labour migration to Panama*, Mona: Institute of Social and Economic Research.

Norris, C. 1990: *What's Wrong with Postmodernism: Critical Theory and the Ends of Philosophy*, New York and London: Harvester Wheatsheaf.

Olivier, S. 1910: *White Capital and Coloured Labour*, London: Independent Labour Party.

Olivier, S. 1936: *Jamaica, the Blessed Land*, London: Faber and Faber.

Rattray, R.S. 1926: *Akan–Ashanti Folk-tales*, Oxford: Clarendon Press.

Reid, V.S. 1973: *New Day*, London and Kingston: Heinemann.

Roberts, G. 1957: *The Population of Jamaica*, Cambridge: Cambridge University Press.

Smith, R.T. 1988: *Kinship and Class in the West Indies: A Genealogical Study of Jamaica and Guyana*, Cambridge: Cambridge University Press.

Waters, A.M. 1986: *Race, Class and Political Symbols: Rastafari and Reggae in Jamaican Politics*, New Brunswick and Oxford: Transaction Books.

Wright, P. 1966: *Lady Nugent's Journal of her Residence in Jamaica from 1801 to 1805*, Kingston: Institute of Jamaica.

12. Distant Places, Other Cities? Urban Life in Contemporary Papua New Guinea

John Connell and John Lea

In no part of the world is urbanization so recent as in the South Pacific and above all in the predominantly Melanesian state of Papua New Guinea (PNG), which achieved independence in 1975. In 1971 the urban component of the population numbered some 282,000, or less than 10 per cent of the national total, and by 1990 it had almost doubled to 500,000 out of a national total of 2,600,000. Much of the urban population is in Port Moresby, the capital, where more than 200,000 live and where conditions of urban life have been best documented. Cities and towns are small (both in size and as a proportion of the total population) and are first and foremost colonial impositions – centres of trade, administration or resource extraction. There was no Melanesian urbanization, despite early domestication of agriculture and extensive, long-distance trade; even the smallest central places were absent. There were no pre-modern cities in these traditional worlds that might be added to, replaced, or challenged by colonial order and discipline. Urbanization was a product of the colonial encounter. This chapter seeks threads of unity and diversity in the post-colonial towns and cities; in doing so it outlines the lack of cohesion, disarray and divisions distinguishing places in which most residents are still closely tied to rural and often distant origins.

COLONIAL BEGINNINGS

The towns and cities of Melanesia are a product of foreign intervention and necessarily took on colonial form. Residential areas were modelled on those of Australia, itself a colony at the time when Melanesian urbanization first began. The houses too were the same; in the nineteenth-century Papuan mining boom they were even dismantled in Cooktown, Queensland, and rebuilt in Papua. As cars were imported, cities sprawled over considerable distances; there was no notion of urban consolidation, pedestrian or bicycle transport. Europeans – bureaucrats, traders and even missionaries – did not walk. The towns were small-scale and peripheral colonial endeavours at the ends of empire, seedy and dusty outliers of largely uninterested colonial powers. In the 1920s Port Moresby resembled 'a superior mining town' or 'a collection of hot tin roofs'. Indeed, 'it was hard to persuade the residents of Port Moresby to take enough interest in the town to beautify it: nor did the government consider that building beautiful colonial towns in the German manner was the Australian way' (Inglis 1974: 35). These were not expressive colonial places and representations of order and discipline.

Melanesians were not part of the urban world. Until after World War II they were permitted in towns only under employment contracts, and these were of limited duration; urban residence had a wholly economic rationale. In the 1920s Port Moresby residents of Melanesian origin were regulated by curfews; whistles or bells demarcated periods when they were allowed in town (Connell and Curtain 1982: 462–5). Workers were almost always housed by their employers; domestic workers were accommodated in the *boi haus* that still survives in the grounds of many large houses. Surveillance was thorough. Otherwise from early days the Melanesian and European areas were segregated and, where there were Chinese traders, these areas were also separate. In Port Moresby Melanesians and Europeans had their own hospitals, and the swimming pool was reserved for European use. In rural areas migrants, whether in town or plantation, were recorded by patrol officers (*kiaps*) in the village book as 'absentees'; their true place was in the village where 'the social, the racial and the spatial were embodied in explicit linguistic and conceptual form' (King 1990: 9). Until secondary and tertiary education arrived belatedly in the post-war years, only rare hospitalization led to urban visits beyond the economic sphere, and hospitals were assuredly places in which to die.

Distinctiveness was regulated; assimilation, sexual relations and marriage between different groups were discouraged, and multiculturalism was wholly implausible. Thus, though civilized Europeans covered their bodies and Papuans were forced to wear loincloths in towns, covering the upper part of the body was expressly forbidden for Melanesian men and women. The 'other' remained exotic. The government anthropologist, F.E. Williams, wrote in 1932: 'You can never be quite the same as the white man; and you will only look silly if you try to be. When we see a native in European clothes we usually laugh at him' (quoted in Inglis 1974: 6). Gambling and alcohol consumption were also forbidden. Attitudes to houses paralleled those to clothes; when Motu and Koita villagers on the fringes of Port Moresby built houses with iron roofs, Williams wrote 'We like to see the Motu and Koita houses. If you build one like a European copra shed it will not look very pretty' (quoted in Inglis 1974: 7), even if some European houses were little more than small copra sheds. In Mitchell's (1988: 164) words, 'Both economically and in a larger sense the colonial order depended upon at once creating and excluding its own opposite.' In Port Moresby Papuans who had become Christians, earned wages and had some education were feared and resented as a threat to European supremacy in a way that was impossible in rural areas. This was emphasized by the fear, even paranoia, of black attacks on white women that led to the passing in 1926 of the

White Women's Protection Ordinance. But there were few white women and even fewer Melanesian women in towns. Distinctiveness was emphasized by the social and political context of gender. As the colonial era continued through the post-war years, urban separation of all kinds was a characteristic legacy.

Divisions and attendant discrimination have contributed to the small contemporary Melanesian urban population. Cities, though now largely Melanesian in ethnic structure, retain their colonial layouts, housing estates, supermarkets; and have acquired airports, TV stations and multi-lane highways rather than pavements or bicycle tracks. The informal sector is largely absent, a victim of retained colonial legislation (for example, against food vendors who provide competition to established interests), lack of skills, small markets and the often more than comparable earnings in the rural sector. The hustle and bustle of Asian and African cities is absent, especially on Sundays, because Christianity and trading legislation combine to impose peace. There are few urban festivals, political rallies or strikes where crowds gather. Urban life is more of a personal phenomenon. Although there are third or even fourth generation urban residents today, impermanence is still inherent in some aspects of urban life. Built into the contracts of many workers, including the prestigious occupations of mineworkers and bureaucrats, are annual return fares to village 'homes'. In such a context even long-established urban residents have a rural home.

CITIES OF PARTS

As early as 1875 Port Moresby had been described as 'a regular metropolis and a complete babel' (quoted in Inglis 1974: 46). Over the subsequent century it, and other Melanesian cities, have become both more metropolitan and more cosmopolitan. PNG has more than 750 languages, and a greater number of cultural groups (or tribes). In the urban areas there are residents from most of these cultural groups, forming an unparalleled cultural diversity. Most urban residents are migrants born outside the city and speak their 'home' language, some Pidgin English, English or Motu, but are more confident in their vernacular, which possesses a cultural resonance and complexity that imported and recently constructed languages lack. Most live with fellow migrants, identify with their social concerns, and experience city life via a world of kinship contacts. As long as employment is primarily a male phenomenon – enabling males to cut across social ties in their workplace – and migration of women is mainly passive, social life in the city remains a gendered world.

In many spheres access to employment is gained through kinship or *wantok* associations. Even elements of the 'modern' sector, such as the hundreds of buses that ply the roads of Port Moresby, are owned and operated by kin groups mainly from the Highlands. Few organizations cut across such social phenomena. Unions are few, rarely militant, and primarily associated with the upper echelons of employment; in Melanesian cities class consciousness remains weaker than ethnic affiliation and is largely something studied by outsiders: a procrustean bed of external intellectual endeavour (Stevenson

1986). Other organizations – churches, sports clubs and so on – subsume social groups rather than cut across them. Few Melanesians are active or prominent members of church or sports groups; most such organizations have an ethnic base, even amongst tiny migrant groups (Strathern 1975: 164, 364ff; Battaglia 1986: 9). The urban gang is 'one of the few structures in which tribal lines are blurred in favour of larger social groupings' (Harris 1988: 47; Nibbrig 1992). Urban residents can live the bulk of their lives as members of their own cultural group and most choose to do so. Ties with 'home' and kin are vastly more important than links to neighbours from other cultural groups, though these may be mobilized for special reasons (Strathern 1975: 256–73). Even for those in formal sector employment, urban life is rarely intended to be permanent; for most migrants urban residence is a 'rural-oriented' strategy, designed to generate income and prestige for a successful return to the security of rural life where land rights exist. The intention to return reinforces group affiliation in town.

In the largest cities encounters with those others who are not kin and *wantoks* are transient, being characterized by standardized workplace and market interactions, and myriads of temporary commercial transactions, but always in the context of difference: especially ethnic variations (most striking between coastal and highland Papua New Guineans) and the opaqueness of linguistic variation. Encounters with those who are socially peripheral – Melanesians from other cultural groups – are fraught with uncertainty, and thus 'charged with excitement, stemming from a sense of freedom, potentiality and adventure' (Gewertz and Errington 1991: 104), but adventure may trigger conflict and disputes, which can often evolve into extended tribal fights within town, though these may merely replicate rural divisions. Numerically small urban cultural groups, such as the Trobrianders, feel vulnerable, explicitly try to ensure that competition is intra-ethnic, and express concern that others might misinterpret their self-esteem as defiance and give them trouble on the streets or football pitches (Battaglia 1986: 20–1). Insecurity inevitably reinforces identity. At the same time connections with others are generally considered to be an advantage and prestigious, but difficult to obtain, retain and place trust in. In the smaller towns the formalities of culture contact are more apparent, less anonymous and thus less fraught with tension (for example, Gewertz and Errington 1991: 103). The external world is most likely to be perceived geographically, but that geography is contingent on ethnicity, and highly flexible, alongside the terminology and use of *wantoks*.

Encounters between Melanesians and Europeans (and other migrant groups) are almost entirely generated in the context of employment and commerce. Other elements of social life demonstrate the fragility of such contacts; at rugby league matches (the dominant male sport in PNG), for example, crowd and players are Melanesian but referee and touch judges often European. So rare and tangential are such inter-racial contacts that most analysts of Melanesian life ignore their occurrence and significance. Asian groups are recent arrivals, intendedly transient and largely introspective. For some Europeans, many of whom prefer the anonymity of supermarkets to the necessary contact and dialogue of markets, the 'other' is visible only through windows or from afar. In 1920 an angry resident wrote to the *Papuan Courier*, 'Although we are in a native country, we have not the desire to be amongst native-inhabited buildings along the foreshore or within the town limits, and desire less to be continually annoyed by coloured folk permitted within the town vicinity' (quoted in Inglis 1974: 48–9). In some respects little has changed; there is continuity rather than disjuncture.

Housing the growing Melanesian urban population has proved difficult, and policies have largely failed (Connell and Lea 1993), hence informal squatter settlements increasingly characterize city life. Over time migrant cultural groups in towns may have therefore become more rather than less concentrated, though for any single group such as the Trobrianders there is considerable dispersion (Strathern 1975; Battaglia 1986) as there is for even small groups in formal housing (Connell 1988). Over time the urban squatter settlements have come to resemble rural villages. As kinship ties in towns become more elaborate, residential patterns replicate village life, trees and gardens reach fruition, rituals are enacted in an urban setting, incomes are turned to social objectives, urban leaders emerge and 'village' courts provide social control. Enacting such rituals provides a moral dimension in opposition to the dissoluteness of urban life (Battaglia 1986). The Trobrianders, like so many others in town, combine nostalgia, ideology and alienation into the retention (and modification) of custom, and the reassertion of identity.

More permanent urban residence, far from paradoxically, allows, even ensures, such efflorescence of culture and identity. Beyond cultural cohesion the actual physical enactment of rituals – often with music and dance – usually generates a crowd, or at least a widespread recognition that a particular cultural group retains its traditions in some form, thus emphasizing the identities and distinctiveness of others. Identity is reinforced by the differences readily apparent in urban life and is dependent on what it excludes. Culture and ethnicity are the most essential components of personal identity, most obvious in the difficulties that are posed in marriages across cultural boundaries (Strathern 1975; Connell 1988). In the cities therefore social and economic relationships are largely based on a local place (a 'settlement'), or kinship relations, that link urban and rural places (rather than on personal relationships of friendship or workplace ties). Urban Melanesians, like the Trobrianders in Port Moresby, define themselves through their cultural identity in the self-esteem and pride that follows the appropriate and successful attention to tradition (however this may have been reconstructed in town).

In Port Moresby, at least, growing security concerns have provided a contrary differentiation of the city. Europeans and other expatriates have increasingly withdrawn to the confines of Tuaguba Hill and barricaded themselves behind high walls and fences, with guard dogs and elaborate security systems Many have moved into the increasingly common tower blocks with their shared security. Far fewer Melanesians have adopted such procedures. Altitudinal differentiation, in diverse ways, has never been so apparent. The neo-colonial city has thus reverted to something akin to the more segregated colonial city:

> *The identity of the modern city is created by what it keeps out. The modernity is contingent upon the exclusion of its own opposite. In order to determine itself as the place of order, reason, propriety, cleanliness, civilisation and power, it must represent outside itself what is irrational, disordered, dirty, libidinous, barbarian and cowed. (Mitchell 1988: 165)*

The 'other' in Melanesian cities may not be cowed, but such representations explain the elite distaste for the 'disorder' of squatter settlements (and therefore opposition to them), in terms of the reluctance to condone their presence or provide them with services (see below). In quite different ways security and tradition enable the replication of the old order.

Life in Melanesian cities may be more exciting than a rural existence but may also be hard and difficult. Most urban residents, above all those in the squatter settlements, come from the more economically marginal areas where income-earning opportunities are few and social services like education are inadequate; migrants are, therefore, poorly equipped to gain employment and cope with urban life. City incomes are often barely adequate to support the migrants, let alone provide for remittances to rural kin. Not only is urban life thus hard and difficult, it may also be dangerous. Crime is more common in urban areas, as are street gangs, and there is a widespread perception that urban life is violent and rural life relatively harmonious with the added benefit of plenty of food. This rhetorical view remains strong even amongst those with little or no experience of it (Ryan 1989: 22).

Such ideology, and hence ethnic identity, is powerfully reinforced for those – particularly the children born in town – who have had no personal and direct experience of 'home' areas in their everyday life. Children are often sent to board with grandparents, especially when their linguistic skills are weak. For example, a Sepik woman, whose eight-year-old son asked *what* her home village was, removed the child from school in mid-term and sent him back to her village, to remain there 'until he knew where everything was and what everything looked like' (Gewertz and Errington 1991: 116). None the less, many without substantial incomes choose to remain in town, despite the pervasive nostalgia for rural life. In the case of long-term migrants from Chambri (part of rural East Sepik province) in Wewak (the small provincial capital), they chose 'freedom', escape from 'big-men' (and their perceived arbitrary social control) and from sorcerers. Yet, despite this urban preference, which was a function of the life-cycle, being most appropriate to young men and women without husbands, none rejected his or her Chambri identity. In fifteen years Gewertz and Errington 'met only one adult Chambri who said he rejected his identity as a Chambri, including those claims other Chambri might make on him' (Gewertz and Errington 1991: 116–17). Even this unique rejection was contextual; his redefinition of self was also partial and caused him disquiet. Though there are 'incipient townsmen' (Strathern 1975: 411), townsfolk are more often temporary, even if they seek permanence (Connell 1988); none can discount or ignore his or her cultural identity (Ryan 1989) or is able, or allowed, to choose to do so.

There are urban Melanesians who have sought to disavow rural life, ethnic identity and cultural commitment and have adopted urban lifestyles. Such people, and households, are those who perceive rural commitment as irksome and unnecessary in an era of modernization. They stress that rural folk should work hard, be self-reliant and not wait for the government or kin to help them. They are invariably those who have succeeded in a career.

Yet their relatives and other urban *wantoks* visit them, speak in *tokples* (home language) and address rural affairs. Only a degree of distance from village and rural ideology is possible in the first generation, and most Melanesian urban residents belong to this group. Gang members in Port Moresby, however, are part of another group, being mainly those who were born and raised in the city and thus said to be 'largely alienated from their "home" areas and customs. Thus, while they may maintain the ethnic sensibility which characterises Papua New Guinea society in general, they share a transcendent urban lifestyle and world view, which . . . overrides the divisions which commonly exist between ethnic groups' (Goddard 1992: 23). None the less, beyond the gang members, some Melanesians are now retiring and choosing to stay in the city; a few are even being buried there.

For all their inability to differentiate themselves fully from the rural sector, some urban Melanesians have nevertheless established a very different lifestyle to that of their parents and many of their peers. They have kin, friends and colleagues. This 'apartness' is clearly recognized in the villages, where people see such lifestyles as attempts to put themselves above rural folk, a distinction symbolized in the pidgin term *susokman*, rather than the thong-wearing or barefooted villagers. Urban Hageners assumed that those wearing shoes, socks and sunglasses must have ready cash (Strathern 1975: 233). An elite choose to distance themselves behind darkened windscreens, in air conditioned cars, sure targets for the gang *rascals*, envious and unimpressed with such alienation. In political and bureaucratic circles, a male elite are now adding neckties to their ensemble (in the face of calls by one politician for a national dress). In dress, lifestyle and language (the elite refuse to speak Pidgin, recent migrants may not yet have learned it) – reflections of the economic sphere – there are vast differences within Melanesian cities.

The notion that there should be a 'national dress' is symptomatic of attempts to create a national identity. In the past, efforts to agree upon a national flag, language, anthem or even the name of a country proved extraordinarily difficult, while agreement on a national language has never been reached. The problem of symbols reflects the problems of nation-building – to date an exercise which has largely been unsuccessful. In a country of considerable physical, but above all ethnic and cultural, diversity, where contact, development and decolonization have all come late, the task of creating a nation and a national identity is enormous. Even the circumstances of early urban life slowed nationalism; for Melanesians 'the texture of their urban existence must surely be one of the most important reasons for the slow development of nationalism among a people who were never allowed to mix freely together away from home, and to meet people from far-distant places' (Wolfers 1975: 50), other than on some plantations. More recently the design of such national symbols as the parliament houses has proved difficult because of its importance in contexts where Melanesian cities (especially outside the capitals) lack corporate municipal institutions. Thus the designs of parliament houses were crucial for the democratic theme of unity in diversity; the PNG design was strongly challenged on the grounds that its style represented just one region (Rosi 1991). The symbols of national identity have been difficult to achieve.

PNG gained independence without struggle and with some internal resistance to what was perceived as an inappropriate and precipitous rush. Nationalism acquires its greatest legitimacy when ethnic boundaries do not cut across political ones (Gellner 1983), but in Melanesia 'the great extent to which people's sense of self remains bound up in the gross actualities of blood, race, language, locality, religion or tradition' (Geertz 1973: 258) limits the extent to which individuals might identify with a wider entity. At best the partial mixing of cultures and the rise of a lingua franca have created the possibility of families of culture (A. Smith 1990: 188), though, in Melanesia, these have tended to take a sub-national form, most obviously in Bougainville, where the greater ethnic consciousness that followed more diverse contact with other parts of PNG stimulated secessionism in defence of identity (for example, Nash and Ogan 1990). Moreover, to enact and seek to restore elements of tradition and custom, essential components of the search for nationalism, is at once to follow the rules of everyday life and to assert political autonomy (Keesing 1982). Despite the familiar term 'nation-state', there can be no presumption that where there is a state there is necessarily a nation. Few if any nations are more imagined than Papua New Guinea.

PNG is typified by the extent of social differentiation across small areas and by such late contact with global economy and society that these distinctions retain extraordinary vitality. The speed of development is well summarized in the subtitle of the former Minister of Foreign Affairs, the late Sir Maori Kiki's, autobiography, *Ten Thousand Years in a Lifetime* (1968). Travel documentaries conflict with this view and emphasize another Melanesia, a distinctive region characterized by labels such as 'stone age society', 'unchanged over time', and so on. A largely absent tourism has as yet barely exploited these themes in 'the land of the unexpected' (cf. Errington and Gewertz 1989). Such inauthenticity – the Melanesian world as exhibition – engenders curiosity, degradation and spectacle: the realm of the 'other', rendered in perpetuity on film and video (Kulick and Willson 1992). It also emphasizes the supposed timelessness of Melanesia, as one personal history documents: *Long Ago is Far Away* (Hope 1979). Nibbrig's (1992) unreflexive reference to 'Paradise' is merely one recent example. Despite the occasional barbaric elements (such as cannibalism), the sorts of self-contained, pre-capitalist totality that inevitably follow have acquired the awful handicap of having to satisfy a yearning for a lost age of innocence and order (Derrida 1976: 114–15; Taussig 1980). Early ethnographies, such as those of Malinowski, despite his views of 'savages', had a similar impact on the construction of utopias (Trouillot 1991). Not only have these always been absent, but the kind of autonomy sought by most Melanesians is quite different and is not based on ideas of remoteness and pristine splendour, most apparent when the remote Hagahai, barely known to their neighbours, sought to 'enter the world' in search of medicine for the malaria that had been transmitted to them (Jenkins 1987). Rather than escape from historical process, people wish to engage more fully with it and become prime negotiators. Since this cannot occur, as often as there is incorporation there is disengagement (Townsend 1980), in a constant process of conservation and dissolution. 'Every longing for change carries with it apprehension, the ambivalence of wishing to adopt and reap new rewards yet also wanting to hold past certainties. Acceptance and hostility are two sides of the one coin' (Hempenstall and Rutherford 1984: 126). Disengagement and the visible effects of disruption have assisted in the romanticization and generation of utopias in the historic Pacific by insiders and outsiders.

In almost every context tribal and regional affiliations are more important than national identity. Hirsch (1990) has argued that the spread of betel-nut consumption (and its emergence as a commodity sufficiently important to be part of the Consumer Price Index) is part of a potential, but still incipient, national process towards the establishment of a formative national culture, where a system of ideas and practices has a roughly uniform significance in many different places. Betel-nut has emerged as a central object of consumption because of its associations with authority, politics and 'civilized' behaviour, themes that are also associated with Port Moresby, where its use is considerable and where many are introduced to its delights. Similar statements might be made about rice consumption, much more pervasive than betel-nut (and around which there are national obsessions with self-reliance), attendance at church, or the dominance of rugby league. As much as anything else the culture of popular music both has contributed to some measure of national identity and is very much an urban phenomenon. In March 1993 the PNG national Top Twenty contained 'Heal Our Nation' (Higher Vision), 'Swit Bougainville' (Trouble Zone Band), 'Peace in PNG' (Telek and Friends), alongside several *tokples* songs and reggae derivatives (*Times of Papua New Guinea*, 1 April 1993). In this relatively novel form of mass culture, the almost everyday practices of ordinary people are transforming global culture into local/national culture, constantly modifying and reinventing new modes of urban culture and providing 'shreds of content' (Jameson 1979: 44) for the articulation of nationalism. The cultural significance of these and other practices in town is none the less generally marginal rather than central, and their role in stimulating national identity is superficial. It is still evident people labelled as Papua New Guineans are found outside and not within the country.

Though the lone Chambri and others may have distanced themselves from their cultural identity, the anomie and loneliness that they experience is partly a result of the impossibility of gaining a new identity, let alone a national identity. They cannot be anything other than Chambri, Hageners etc., and in subsequent generations there may even be some reassertion and revival of a symbolic ethnic identity (Gans 1979). Cultural diversity – without multiculturalism – ensures that ethnic identity triumphs over class, meaning over employment; tension, conflict and the search for order foster exclusion and tradition in a variety of forms.

CITIES APART?

If Melanesian cities are intricately subdivided, with ethnicity and cultural identity prevailing over class divisions, they are assuredly part of a post-colonial world that has contributed to urbanization and, as yet, to hesitant and undefined movements towards the formation of national and regional cultures and identities. They are part nevertheless of the world system; the economy of PNG, and especially the cities – the entrepôts and administrative centres – depends on fluctuations in the world capitalist system. Notwithstanding the continued significance of subsistence economies throughout the country, the trade systems and price fluctuations (that cannot be influenced by PNG's marginal presence), whose terms of trade disadvantage commodity producers, have embedded towns, cities and villages in a global economy, cultural and political system (Jameson 1986: xiv), though there is endless debate both on the extent of globalization of culture and, especially, on politics.

The nature of world economy and society and whether such notions exist, make sense, or are envisaged in similar ways in different places are highly problematic questions. Is the modernity that emerged in Europe around the seventeenth century (and subsequently evolved in space and time) the same modernity that belatedly reached much of PNG in the mid-twentieth century? Has PNG adopted modernity, let alone moved on to embrace an era suggested by terms such as 'information society' and 'consumer society', or to the era of 'postmodernity', 'post-industrial', 'post-capitalist' or 'post-Fordist' that suggests the period of modernization is over (Giddens 1992: 1–2)? Given that most such phrases cover a proliferation of meanings, there are few grounds for optimism that the diversity of PNG can easily be incorporated into this global discourse. In a cultural world of such variety, where contemporary actions and events are often poorly understood, and can only with difficulty be grounded in local epistemologies, cities and societies appear to be as much part of a pre-modern world as they are of a post-modern one.

PNG and its cities are part – though very much a peripheral part – of the world capitalist economy. Indeed, despite the recency of modern economic development, the dominance and significance of the world economy are most apparent because of the limited importance of the state, itself a function of newly won independence (and lack of nationalism), but also of shortages of bureaucratic and political skills, and the clamour for foreign investment. PNG is peripheral both in the sense that foreign investment is concentrated in resource-based activities like mining and forestry, and because this investment generates most exports. Manufactured exports are conspicuous by their absence. There is no internal economic hegemony to speak of and only rare attempts to flex national if not local muscles against multinational corporations. All of these characteristics are particularly striking in countries where most live without the benefits of modern technology (other than the radio that provides a powerful link with the 'global village').

Throughout the region modernity has resulted in a disjuncture between space and place. In premodern times space and place largely coincided, since the spatial dimensions of social life were for most dominated by localized activities. External links were tenuous and often highly dangerous, epitomized by the 'barter markets' where 'traders laid down their goods and withdrew to a safe distance while the exchange was made' (Gewertz 1978). Modernity disrupted the relationship between space and place, and migration led to crucial relationships developing with 'absent' kin, the Melanesians whose 'dual dependency' ensured that they migrate for cash but return for security. Subsequently, economic relationships, notably commodity pricing in one form or another, have influenced local life in almost every society.

The introduction into villages – far beyond the towns – of the money acquired elsewhere frequently generated an efflorescence of the village-based gift economy (Carrier and Carrier 1989), as people amplified and made sense of their relations with capitalism. More directly the village trade stores have become the final points of distribution in the world system; their goods, with their distant origins, are the symbols and substance of the diverse structure of incorporation and accommodation (McInnes and Connell 1988). In a sense place has become 'increasingly phantasmagoric' (Giddens 1992: 19) as localities are thoroughly penetrated and influenced by very distinct social, political and economic influences, whose genesis and local ramifications are often beyond comprehension.

Changes inevitably produce contrasts between modernity and tradition; indeed tradition can only be comprehended in relation to modernity, hence the ubiquity of the pidgin term *pasin* (custom). In modernized Melanesian society, tradition continues to play a role. In most circumstances it is more likely to be rendered as *pasin bilong mipela* (the way we do things); it has not always been reinvented or codified. Moreover the binary division between 'tradition' as variable inheritance, history and a lived past, and 'tradition' as invariant, invented, rhetorical and self-conscious contemporary practice, is clearly a false one (Jolly 1992). Equally, 'difference is encountered in the adjoining neighbourhoods, the familiar turns up at the ends of the earth' (Clifford 1988: 13). The shift from 'tradition' to 'modernity' is enormously complex – in time and space – and, in any case, no one in PNG lives, or has lived, without some awareness of cultural (and more recently, economic) alternatives.

As this process of change 'moves both ways, it preserves, while at the same time amputating the principles which used to underpin the thoughts and workings of a society in order to withstand the march of history' (Godelier 1986: 206). History is not a linear progression. Knowledge and technologies are selectively incorporated, transformed and transcended, reinterpreted and imbued with a particular significance for local social practice. Culture and identity are not direct products of new, increasingly global economic (and perhaps political) arrangements – and their socio-spatial impact on the material form and social structure of cities (M.P. Smith 1992) – but are shaped by the everyday practices of ordinary people, and their feelings and understanding of their conditions of existence.

In a sense 'globalisation – which is a process of uneven development that fragments as it coordinates – introduces new forms of world interdependence, in which, once again, there are no "others"' (Giddens 1992: 175). Yet, as Schieffelin and Crittenden (1991) make clear, the globalization of social and economic life is far from complete; many people are very distant both in space and impact from the institutional transformations of modernity. Much more important, there are reactions against, and responses to, modernity. The processes of development have mapped out a contested landscape of environmental, economic and cultural change, dramatically apparent around the Bougainville copper mine, but all Melanesian cultures are products of a history of appropriation, resistance and accommodation. Local struggles of resistance are more important than either regional, class or gender issues, as the battle for an ethnic identity demonstrates.

Global culture, economy and society have come to PNG. Satellite dishes bring Indonesian and Australian television channels; rugby league (sponsored by Winfield cigarettes) is the male national sport, and a new lingua franca enables accommodation to overcome elements of incomprehension. Nevertheless intermittent 'cargo cults', whose very terminology (and practice) mark the extent of dissonance with the received world, demonstrate the differences that remain. However, 'contemporary communications have collapsed the "usual space and time boundaries" and produced both a new internationalism and internal differentiations within cities and societies based on place, function and social interest' (Harvey 1989: 75), but such 'usual' space and time boundaries were never immutable. (Sweet potato, introduced in the seventeenth century, proved to be a critical factor in some of the most striking changes of all in pre-colonial Melanesia.) Social relationships were invariably highly flexible to accommodate shifting allegiances, opportunities and domestic events, including natural disasters: 'polyphonic patterns of accommodation and resistance to domination' (M.P. Smith 1992: 496). While it may be extraordinarily difficult to represent adequately difference in the larger and more impersonal global context, demanding a focus on reflexivity (for example, Strathern 1992), despite various forms of resistance and accommodation, towns and cities – and the rural hinterlands beyond – are very much part of, and not apart from, world systems.

CITIES IN DISARRAY

An important outcome after the changeover from colony to independent state in PNG in 1975 was a rapid weakening in the inherited control mechanisms which govern urban development. Western urban planning systems are both prescriptive and proscriptive and depend ultimately on popular acceptance of government intervention in everyday life. Such interference is tolerated because local government is usually reasonably responsive to local wishes and its powers are clearly defined. Urban management is one facet of a complete system of local governance and alterations to some of its parts must affect the whole. Rarely have municipal governments in the primate cities of small developing countries enjoyed the preconditions necessary for them to operate effectively. They are commonly subjugated by national government located in the same city and make do with scant resources. In PNG the change in municipal affairs was soon seen primarily in the declining control over regulations, with reduced attention paid to land-use zoning and building by-laws, but also in the failure to maintain and provide for the major urban infrastructure of roads, water supplies and sewage treatment. This was not due entirely to either changed priorities or even a shortage of funds for urban investment, or to adopting new principles, but was rather the outcome of ignoring rules created to manage urban affairs in a different political context.

The effective removal of a range of factors inhibiting urbanization mainly after independence (Connell and Lea 1993: 53–4) has contributed towards the substantial increase in the proportion of the population living in town. This has made the tasks of urban management and planning more difficult. As elsewhere, breakdowns in basic urban services and deterioration in infrastructure provision and maintenance characterize urban society. In PNG urban heritage is being made on the run. A distinctive form of urbanization has appeared, based overwhelmingly on the rights or non-rights of urban residents to customary land. Cities are characterized by rapidly growing uncontrolled fringes of peri-urban customary land and pockets of traditional villages engulfed in the expanding modern town. Modern offices, new tourist establishments and the expensive dwellings of the elite (still largely expatriate in most of the region) co-exist with the low-income Melanesian suburbs and place huge demands on the poorly developed network of infrastructure services. This complex and highly differentiated urban mosaic is rarely under the jurisdiction of a single municipal authority and is the chief theatre of operations for a host of national government agencies, NGOs and landowning groups, all with contestatory claims.

A growing extent of social disorganization and crime is a function of substantial inequalities in access to land, housing and other services in the largest cities, but there is a paradox: 'Everyone blames the squatters for the sudden increase in crime. Some have petitioned the government to get rid of these settlements, yet politicians visit these same places at election time with money, beer and rice bags to win their vote' (*Times of Papua New Guinea*, 25 October 1984). Media reports regularly plead for firm government action, oblivious to the effects of a permissive political environment in post-colonial times. Squatters are part of an entrenched constituency in post-colonial PNG which cannot be sorted out by attempts at social engineering of a kind which might have been possible in former times. Despite official concern to manage urbanization, alongside an expressed focus on rural development, there have been few real attempts to constrain urban development. Urbanization has been limited primarily because of reasonable income-earning opportunities in many rural areas.

Town planning broadly follows historic British principles of land-use zoning but without coordination among the various branches of government responsible for urban development. Management difficulties lie deeper than a lack of coordination and include the questionable capabilities of local governance itself. Elected municipal local governments have been weak; the result is domination by central government and its consequent and inappropriate involvement in municipal affairs. The future of urban management in Melanesia is very much bound up with the ability of urban authorities to become more self-sufficient, but taxes and fees are hard to collect and grants difficult to obtain. Solutions materialize in expensive responses to crises; urban management thus becomes crisis management, rather than the good housekeeping that might avert problems, and emphasizes grandiose 'solutions' rather than planned development.

There are widespread problems of access to housing, and both social and physical variations in character within towns are in part determined by and in part reflected in the availability and provision of housing. There are enormous differences in residential standards. In Port Moresby, for example, there are the extremely expensive homes and multi-storey luxury flats of Tuaguba Hill, as well as low-cost National Housing Commission (NHC) buildings, and the flimsy plywood and other constructions of shantytowns (Lea 1983), which represent the most rapidly growing proportion of the urban housing stock. Such 'marginal' housing reflects status: illegal or barely tolerated and hence somewhat insecure. Yet even between settlements there are enormous differences; the provision of finance for housing is a political issue, funds are scarce and some settlements are populated by groups who are believed to be 'trouble makers' and criminals, hence their claims on finance for residential improvement are less likely to be met. Scarcity of finance and therefore of housing (and related services) reflects and often entrenches urban inequalities. At best, recent policies towards settlements can be described as benign neglect. Although existing strategies could be much more positive and cost-effective, it is not the policies that are the problem but an institutional paralysis which prevents action. The same situation is true with reference to the provision of other basic needs such as water and sanitation (Connell and Lea 1993: 134–53). It is a testimony to the poor in the cities of Melanesia that they have found ways of housing themselves which are appropriate, flexible and of a higher standard than in some other parts of the world. In this process the colonial orderliness has not survived.

In the post-independence years the disjuncture between economic and physical planning has substantially increased and become formalized. Current policies are largely aimed at economic growth, rather than more broadly based economic development, and are unlikely to reduce problems associated with equity and the distribution of urban (and other) services. Even in small towns urban service provision is fragmented between numerous activities. Fragmentation, and tension between landowners and migrants in the face of land shortages, growing urban unemployment, bureaucratic ineptitude and political corruption – hastening privatization – have all contributed to disarray and division. Most aspects of infrastructure provision can only be addressed with the support of the urban population at large. In Melanesia history, geography and the gulf between 'traditional' and 'modern' has made the creation of this 'community of interest', or any approximation to it, very difficult indeed.

CITY LIFE

Ethnic and cultural fragmentation and modernist homogenization are not two arguments, two opposing views of what is happening in the world today, but two constitutive trends of global reality.

J. Friedman, 'Being in the World'

The 'last' parts of rural Melanesia were probably not 'contacted' (an imprecise term) until the 1970s – in the final flurry of world exploration – yet throughout the region there are T-shirts (even Gucci and Benetton look-alikes), Toyotas, Coca-Cola, sunglasses and digital watches; Madonna – though banned from PNG television – emanates from the same 'walkmans': universal images, sounds and brand names. In this universalization Melanesia has gone from pre-literacy to post-literacy, with only a rudimentary intervening stage. There is the juxtaposition of corporate monoliths and plywood shacks, and of air-conditioned vehicles and bare feet – a juxtaposition not postmodernist but universal and, in different formats, long-established between rich and poor. It is the era of late modernity, in impoverished states of the Third World periphery, that emphasizes such phenomena through the increasing visibility of global reach. On a different scale, for a different audience, images of 'tradition' are transmitted globally – through tourism, travelogue and the splendours of tropical nature – whilst global culture in diverse forms flows through the satellite dishes of the cities. 'Tradition' moves out as 'modernity' moves in.

Consumption demarcates incipient class divisions, yet ethnicity and also gender complicate and minimize emergent boundaries within ethnic groups. Women, more confined – especially as urban crime increases – are more conscious of identity. That elite Melanesians may be differentiated by their pattern of food consumption emphasizes that eating is a social act and an act of self-identification; in a social rather than biological sense 'you are what you eat' (Friedman 1990: 314) but not what you wear. It is men who dine out. Yet, as elsewhere, 'There is relatively little consideration of how people define themselves, how identities are cobbled together to act in the new spaces of a post-fordist economy. Amidst the shards of modernist fragmentation and disengagement, how can identity be constructed at all?' (Watts 1992: 123). In states that are not nations, where tribes are also recent inventions – local and national constructs – and urbanization has preceded industrialization the task becomes more difficult. Yet, as with the Chambri, few question who they are. In this, and in the acquisition of cars and clothes, 'The practice of identity is the acquisition of otherness' (Friedman 1990: 324), but such 'otherness' as is acquired results in no radical break with the past. The linguistic and philosophical identity, even of such long-established urban residents as the Toaripi (Ryan 1989), memories (Strathern 1992: 12) or land tenure, where land is owned by the ancestors and held in trust by the living for those as yet unborn, are vastly more important than the recent trappings of modernity.

Consumption – and modern culture – are influenced, even engendered, by the establishment of a global economy. But the 'strong globalizing influence arising from the emptying of social space and its filling-up by large bureaucratic organizations, based on systems of concentrated reflexive monitoring, the multinational corporations, state apparatus, financial systems and the like' (Thrift 1993: 117) is weak in Melanesia. Such influences may dominate the lives of the urban elite; they are weakly transmitted to remote rural areas, where materialism takes on different forms. Similarly whilst 'a Congolese can identify everyone's social rank in a crowd by their outward appearance' (Friedman 1990: 315), this would be an impossible task in Melanesia, even though there, as elsewhere (Manning 1991), T-shirts provide subtle but changing markers of identity. Modernization and homogeneity have far from overwhelmed identity and difference.

Elite Melanesians, especially those who have married 'outside' their *tokples* (cultural group), have tended to become a more permanent urban population. This is particularly true of bureaucrats – with long employment tenure – who, if not already in capital cities, seek to migrate there (Allen 1983). Similarly most university students seek to, and do, remain in the capital (Weinand and Ward 1979). Yet wealthy urbanites are more easily able to keep in touch with rural areas, invest there and often plan to retire there. Other facets of their behaviour may change. After barely half a century of any kind of 'modern' government, and a decade after independence, 'Chambri expected that those in government, including Chambri, would frequently fail to deliver on promises and would intercept government funds for personal use' (Gewertz and Errington 1991: 123). More generally these are also the regional and national politicians who 'raised in urban settings and educated overseas proclaim the virtues of a *kastom* [custom] they have never known' (Keesing 1982: 299). There are distinct attractions to urban life for some and though these attractions provide personal gains they do not challenge the ideological construction of ethnic identity.

To retain urban privileges, urban resources must be diverted from the poor, hence policies that favour equity in service distribution have faded from view (or are merely not implemented) whilst there is strong opposition to the growth of poor, migrant urban populations. Typical of recent attempts to remove squatters from PNG towns are those of mid-1991 in Lae and Rabaul. In Lae the provincial premier stated, 'My plan to eject settlers is a genuine one for the sake of my people who want a trouble-free environment for their children . . . As for Papua New Guinea which has a large area of land, I do not see why people should move from province to province. I am sure there are better things to do in their own villages or towns' (*Times of Papua New Guinea*, 6 June 1991). Not surprisingly, such was not the settlers' perception. In Rabaul the provincial premier stressed, 'We want to help the settlers so they can have dignity and that they can grow their own cash crops in their respective villages. Villages are still the best and least expensive places to live in. Furthermore we want settlers to understand that they were not born to be slaves in towns. However they are making themselves slaves' (*Times of Papua New Guinea*, 29 August 1991). The rural ideology has held very firm in the minds of long-established urban residents, especially where their urban privileges have been at stake. Urbanization has contributed to the undermining of authority, hierarchy and dignity; distinctions of rank were challenged and patriarchal authority undermined (Wilson 1992: 91), yet only to be recreated in other forms. Women, especially those who are unskilled and unmarried, have invariably been discouraged from, and disadvantaged in, Melanesian city life. Most apparent in the opposition to urbanization and especially squatter settlements is the manner in which historic European colonial perceptions have become replicated in contemporary Melanesian perceptions. In a sense the colonial order had penetrated and colonized local discourse (cf. Mitchell 1988), though this colonizing process has never fully succeeded. The elite of the post-colonial era have adopted some of the mores of the colonialists, thus reinforcing old divisions within the cities.

Melanesian urbanism emphasizes the role of historical specificity, plurality and difference; there are few universals in a region where culture (and emotion and desire) are of pervasive importance. Local Melanesian languages and the (usually geographically limited) circuits of communication in which they are involved are resources as well as limits, partly acting as shields against 'global' influences (M.P. Smith 1992: 496–7; Seers 1983: 69–76), however these may be defined in a world where 'local' and 'global' are imprecise. PNG contains an astonishing variety of languages, cultures and ecologies; consequently – since long before colonialism – identities (necessary fictions, in which rhetoric and invention are integral elements) are always in the process of becoming, formed and reformed, devalued and revalued, invented and discarded. Context and conflict have produced complex cities and nations; in Maori Kiki's world, contexts are fluid (for example, gold bonanzas at Mount Kare, secessionist struggles in Bougainville). Political practices constantly challenge identities. Contemporary urban politicians and gang-leaders have adapted rural leadership skills in urban contexts, resulting in the efflores-cence of the gift economy and involving social relations typical of 'pre-capitalist' Melanesian societies (for example, Goddard 1992; Warry 1987), hence notions of ethics, rationality, and justice are diverse. Political practice barely puts identities at risk as yet, hence the tasks of urban planning and management have proved unusually difficult. They scarcely take account of, or provide a voice for, the different groups which have not formed into communities but also live in the cities. Notions of ethnicity and identity are crucial to power relations, hence barely formed political practice – the art of the possible – is vital to the future of Melanesian cities and societies. Where land retains its crucial role, urban life will continue to display extraordinary diversity and incoherence.

REFERENCES

Allen, B.J. 1983: 'Paradise Lost? Rural Development in an Export Led Economy: The Case of Papua New Guinea', in D.A.M. Lea and D.P. Chaudhri (eds), *Rural Development and the State: Contradictions and Dilemmas in Developing Countries*, London: Methuen.

Battaglia, D. 1986: *Bringing Home to Moresby. Urban Gardening and Ethnic Pride among Trobriand Islanders in the National Capital*, Port Moresby: Institute of Applied Social and Economic Research, Special Publication 11.

Carrier, J. and Carrier, A. 1989: *Wage, Trade and Exchange in Melanesia*, Berkeley: University of California Press.

Clifford, J. 1988: *The Predicament of Culture*, Cambridge, MA: Harvard University Press.

Connell, J. 1988: 'Temporary Townsfolk? Siwai Migrants in Urban Papua New Guinea', *Pacific Studies*, 11: 77–100.

Connell, J. and Curtain, R. 1982: 'Urbanisation and Inequality in Melanesia', in R.J. May and H. Nelson (eds), *Melanesia: Beyond Diversity*, Canberra: Australian National University Press.

Connell, J. and Lea, J.P. 1993: *Planning the Future. Melanesian Cities in 2010*, Canberra: National Centre for Development Studies, Pacific Policy Paper 11.

Derrida, J. 1976: *Of Grammatology*, Baltimore: Johns Hopkins.

Errington, F. and Gewertz, D. 1989: 'Tourism and Anthropology in a Post-modern World', *Oceania*, 60: 37–54.

Friedman, J. 1990: 'Being in the World: Globalization and Localization', *Theory, Culture and Society*, 7: 311–28.

Gans, H.J. 1979: 'Symbolic Ethnicity: The Future of Ethnic Groups and Cultures in America', *Ethnic and Racial Studies*, 2: 1–20.

Geertz, C. 1973: *The Interpretation of Cultures*, New York: Hutchinson.

Gellner, E. 1983: *Nations and Nationalism*, Oxford: Blackwell.

Gewertz, D. 1978: 'Tit for Tat. Barter Markets in the Middle Sepik', *Anthropological Quarterly*, 51: 37–44.

Gewertz, D. and Errington, F. 1991: *Twisted Histories, Altered Contexts: Representing the Chambri in a World System*, Cambridge: Cambridge University Press.

Giddens, A. 1992: *The Consequences of Modernity*, Cambridge: Polity Press.

Goddard, M. 1992: 'Big Men, Thief. The Social Organization of Groups in Port Moresby', *Canberra Anthropology*, 15: 20–34.

Godelier, M. 1986: *The Making of Great Men. Male Domination and Power among the New Guinea Baruya*, Cambridge: Cambridge University Press.

Harris, B. 1988: *The Rise of Rascalism: Action and Reaction in the Evolution of Rascal Gangs*, Port Moresby: IASER Discussion Paper 24.

Harvey, D. 1989: *The Condition of Postmodernity*, Oxford: Blackwell.

Hempenstall, P. and Rutherford, N. 1984: *Protest and Dissent in the Colonial Pacific*, Suva: Institute of Pacific Studies.

Hirsch, E. 1990: 'From Bones to Betelnuts: Processes of Ritual Transformation and the Development of "National Culture" in Papua New Guinea', *Man*, 25: 18–34.

Hope, P. 1979: *Long Ago is Far Away*, Canberra: Australian National University Press.

Inglis, A. 1974: *Not a White Woman Safe. Sexual Anxiety and Politics in Port Moresby, 1920–1934*, Canberra: Australian National University Press.

Jameson, F. 1979: 'Reification and Utopia in Mass Culture', *Social Text*, 1: 134–46.

Jameson, F. 1986: 'Foreword', in J.-F. Lyotard (ed.), *Postmodern Condition*, Manchester: Manchester University Press.

Jenkins, C. 1987: 'Medical Anthropology in the Western Schrader Range, Papua New Guinea', *National Geographic Research*, 3: 412–30.

Jolly, M. 1992: 'Specters of Inauthenticity', *The Contemporary Pacific*, 4: 49–72.

Keesing, R. 1982: '*Kastom* in Melanesia: An Overview', *Mankind*, 13: 297–301.

Kiki, A.M. 1968: *Kiki. Ten Thousand Years in a Lifetime*, Melbourne: Cheshire.

King, A.D. 1990: *Urbanism, Colonialism and the World-Economy*, London: Routledge.

Kulick, D. and Willson, M.E. 1992: 'Echoing Images: The Construction of Savagery among Papua New Guinean Villagers', *Visual Anthropology*, 5: 143–52.

Lea, J.P. 1983: 'Customary Land Tenure and Urban Housing Land: Partnership and Participation in Developing Societies', in S. Angel, R.W. Archer, S. Tanphiphet and E.A. Wegelin (eds), *Land for Housing the Poor*, Singapore: Select Books.

Manning, P.K. 1991: 'Semiotic Ethnographic Research', *American Journal of Semiotics*, 8: 27–45.

Marcus, G.E. and Fischer, M. 1986: *Anthropology as Cultural Critique*, Chicago: University of Chicago Press.

McInnes, L. and Connell, J. 1988: 'The World System in a Fijian Store', *South Pacific Forum*, 4: 116–21.

Mitchell, T. 1988: *Colonizing Egypt*, Cambridge: Cambridge University Press.

Nash, J. and Ogan, E. 1990: 'The Red and the Black: Bougainvillean Perceptions of other Papua New Guineans', *Pacific Studies*, 13: 1–17.

Nibbrig, N. 1992: 'Rascals in Paradise: Urban Gangs in Papua New Guinea', *Pacific Studies*, 15: 115–34.

Rogers, A. 1992: 'The Boundaries of Reason: The World, the Homeland and Edward Said', *Environment and Planning D: Society and Space*, 10: 511–26.

Rosi, P. 1991: 'Papua New Guinea's Parliament House: A Contested National Symbol', *The Contemporary Pacific*, 3: 289–324.

Ryan, D. 1989: 'Home Ties in Town: Toaripi in Port Moresby', *Canberra Anthropology*, 12: 19–27.

Schieffelin, E.L. and Crittenden, R. 1991: *Like People You See in a Dream*, Stanford: Stanford University Press.

Seers, D. 1983: *The Political Economy of Nationalism*, Oxford: Oxford University Press.

Slater, D. 1992: 'Theories of Development and Politics of the Postmodern – Exploring a Border Zone', *Development and Change*, 23: 283–319.

Smith, A. 1990: 'Towards a Global Culture?', *Theory, Culture and Society*, 7: 171–91.

Smith, M.P. 1992: 'Postmodernism, Urban Ethnography and the New Social Space of Ethnic Identity', *Theory and Society*, 21: 493 531.

Stevenson, M. 1986: *Wokmani: Work, Money and Discontent in Melanesia*, Sydney: Oceania Ethnographies 1.

Strathern, M. 1975: *No Money on our Skins. Hagen Migrants in Port Moresby*, Canberra and Port Moresby: New Guinea Research Bulletin 61.

Strathern, M. 1992: 'Writing Societies, Writing Persons', *History of the Human Sciences*, 5: 5–16.

Taussig, M. 1980: *The Devil and Commodity Fetishism in South America*, Chapel Iill: University of North Carolina Press.

Thrift, N. 1993: 'The Art of the Living, the Beauty of the Dead', *Progress in Human Geography*, 17: 111–22.

Townsend, D. 1980: 'Disengagement and Incorporation: The Post-colonial Reaction in Rural Villages of Papua New Guinea', *Pacific Viewpoint*, 21: 1–25.

Trouillot, M.-R. 1991: 'Anthropology as Metaphor. The Savage's Legacy and the Postmodern World', *Review*, 14: 29–54.

Warry, W. 1987: *Chuave Politics. Changing Patterns of Leadership in the Papua New Guinea Highlands*, Canberra: ANU Department of Political and Social Change Monograph 4.

Watts, M.J. 1992: 'Space for Everything', *Cultural Anthropology*, 7: 115–29.

Weinand, H. and Ward, R.G. 1979: 'Area Preferences in Papua New Guinea', *Australian Geographical Studies*, 17: 64–75.

Wilson, E. 1992: 'The Invisible *Flâneur*', *New Left Review*, 191: 90–110. [Adapted as ch. 5 in this volume.]

Wolfers, 1975: *Race Relations and Colonial Rule in Papua New Guinea*, Sydney: Australian and New Zealand Book Company.

Part III

POSTMODERN POLITICS

13. On the Problems and Prospects of Overcoming Segregation and Fragmentation in Southern Africa's Cities in the Postmodern Era

Alan Mabin

Times change. So do people's collective projects, priorities, paradigms. But the same is true for the broader processes and structures that determine shifting patterns of hegemony and incorporation, and for the search for autonomy and a decent existence they invariably engender. As patterns of domination reshape themselves in the wake of changing priorities and justifications, so do the foci and strategies of emancipatory movements or indeed all social action seeking to define liberation, equality, social justice.

M. Doornbos, 'Foreword'

On the brow of a hill overlooking the original central business area of Johannesburg, after a century still the financial heart of southern Africa,[1] stands a forbidding modernist citadel designed to dwarf the approaching pedestrian. This grey edifice is the 'civic centre', headquarters of the largest local authority in the region and workplace for many of its 23,000 employees. The complex has also become the symbolic central target of the partially successful popular challenge to the ways in which urban space has been constructed and managed over the long decades of colonialism and apartheid.

On any work day, in the panelled committee rooms which bear the traditions of long-established white, male, settler authority, multiple meetings may be found taking place between apparently unlikely associates.[2] Typically – if such a term be allowed – a small group of mostly casually dressed, mainly earnest and most often male young people (of varied colour) at one end of a table faces a much larger and apparently less differentiated crew of uniformly besuited, generally older, and overwhelmingly white men (admitting of a few exceptions – usually some assertive, tremendously well dressed and obviously highly competent women). The latter grouping will consist of local authority officials from a variety of levels, working mostly for Johannesburg but also for some surrounding and higher level authorities; in each meeting they will be drawn from particular sections of the bureaucracy – now treasury, here public health, there general administration, and of course planners. They find their opposites in the small core of organizers and workers, whose corps can be numbered on the hands, who staff the community-based organizations (CBOs) (what South Africans call 'civics')[3] ultimately responsible for bringing local authority (and some would add, South Africa) to its metaphorical knees during the late 1980s – and therefore, both responsible for the very process of negotiation represented in these multiple meetings and seemingly vital to the resolution of the crisis which (the 'official' side fears) threatens to engulf urban South Africa. Those CBO staff sit together with their 'advisers', usually able NGO staff (and sometimes volunteers) who often dominate proceedings with their creativity, political acumen and super-confidence in their own greater grasp of the stakes as well as the moral bankruptcy of their opposites.

An occasional air of confrontation between the two predominant groupings will usually be softened to some extent by the presence and active participation of some who fall, in quite literal senses, between the two 'sides'. These will be closer in age to the suits-and-ties, in dress somewhere between the groups, and in speech closer to the CBO/NGO team. They will be drawn from NGOs not quite so close to the civics, from potential funding organizations and from professional consultancies which have somehow secured a toe-hold in the process. Occasionally they will include academics. Their contributions may eagerly be seized upon by the CBO/NGO team, and not purely because of some degree of sympathy between this middle minority and the more powerful representatives of the disenfranchised. More significantly, the latter group will be desperately short of capacity to engage successfully in the process which they have helped to unleash.

What the civic movement confronts in the enormous numbers of meetings which they must, despite thin numbers of available and able representatives in this context, attend is a phalanx of expertise and time capacity which it is impossible to match. Yet the course of discussions and decisions, not only at the lowest committee levels but through the meetings which bring together the most senior officials and, finally, the political leaders from the various parties, remains substantially determined by the civics. The worrying point, from the civic side, is that there is a perceptible decline in the extent to which the civics determine the agenda. When negotiations began in 1989, in the context of a state of emergency, massive boycotts of rents on public housing and service charges generally in the townships, and a mounting debt on the part of the authorities responsible for service provision in those townships, all the creative thinking seemed to come from the civic side. Indeed, in the extension and broadening of negotiation from issues related to ending the boycotts to the nature, structure and operation of local government, the incumbent white minority authorities seemed to be bowled over by the force of civic argument. It seemed that this emancipatory movement, which sought to represent the township masses, stood at the point of taking power at the local level from existing authorities.

But, as Nederveen Pieterse (1992: 5) reflects, modern emancipatory movements have been best at saying no to oppression, while not terribly well prepared to handle the intricacies and problems of development. Faced with those complexities, movements have been known to fade in strength in reasonably dramatic ways. On occasion it might be electoral defeat after a triumph in the early stages of (restored) democracy, as with the Parti do Trabaladores (PT) in São Paulo, Brazil. In Johannesburg, where the relationship between existing authority not yet out of power and the popular challengers is now primarily shaped in the repetitive rounds of meetings in the Central Witwatersrand Metropolitan Chamber (CWMC), as the negotiating forum is called,[4] the unpreparedness and lack of expertise of the popular movement – in this case the civics – begins to show.

As Nederveen Pieterse (1992: 31ff) suggests, there is also a problem of unpreparedness among emancipatory movements related to the shift from modern to postmodern, connected to the difficulties of democratization of the 'total ideologies which seek to define and master the foundations of the social' (Laclau 1992: 169) so often associated – and certainly so in South Africa – with emancipatory movements with their roots in the fifties and sixties.

In this chapter I wish to draw attention to the particular difficulties associated with the emerging empowerment of a long-subjugated set of social movements in South Africa, an emergence which brings movements whose goals and methods were formulated firmly in the modernist period into sharp difficulties associated with the alterations which postfordism and postmodernism have wrought in the cities. A secondary objective is to suggest that the case in question is not merely of idiosyncratic and exceptionalist interest, but that there are aspects of the difficulties of emancipation in that context which speak to experience in other parts of the world.

SOUTHERN AFRICAN URBAN CONTEXTS

Maputo, Harare, Windhoek, Johannesburg, Pretoria, Cape Town, Durban, Port Elizabeth – cities founded by colonialism, developed under apartheid or colonial variations on a theme. There has been, and is, in all of these cities, a *political drive for change* – a political drive which developed during the modern era – which is now attempting to find expression in another period.

What is this period? What is obvious is that emancipation is coming at, at least, a postfordist time. What are the features of the postmodern in southern Africa and especially its cities?

The first point is that the period is hardly confined to southern Africa. Its overarching characteristic would seem to be its global nature. Conditions have shifted greatly in the international context. The fates of socialist government, even of straight-up militarism, provide pointers to the shifts in the global political and ideological environment, in particular the environment in which political opposition to conservatism, capitalism, racism functions or is practised.

The period is also one in which the broader material context has altered quite fundamentally. IMF-dictated structural readjustment programmes (witness Mozambique, Zimbabwe), the impact of World Bank lending policies and even intellectual pronouncements, international recession, old industrial models facing collapse, new forms of production, new information-based spheres, electronic controls over (and means of) production, etc. – the list is familiar elsewhere and has its own impact in cities such as Johannesburg. The main material difficulty appears to be one of finding ways of increasing production, and of altering divisions of labour in ways which do not simply expel and exclude still greater numbers and proportions of the populace. The shallowness of ascribing developmental failure to 'a kind of all-encompassing logic of imperialism' (Storper 1990: 441) – Lipietz's (1986) 'beast of the apocalypse' – are obvious enough, and some argue that 'it is now, to a large degree, necessary to approach problems of development in a way that is both post-fordist and postimperialist' (Storper 1990: 441). Thus the present period demands new approaches if the material conditions of large sections of the populace are to see improvement: one reason for the widespread adoption of IMF-type programmes is precisely the lack of powerful alternatives, in a situation where emancipatory movements continue to base their policy proposals on concepts developed in earlier periods.

Political drives for change in the cities of southern Africa base their concepts on political demands shaped in an era of industrial growth, best encapsulated in the famous Freedom Charter drawn up by the ANC and its allies in 1955. Yet the movements which carry these political drives find themselves living in the postmodern results of modern wars of liberation. Southern Africa is not Vietnam, where (admittedly from a distance) we might visualize modern results of a modern war. Instead by the time liberation, emancipation came (comes?) to southern Africa's cities, wars were no longer modern but postmodern, and the division, fragmentation and disruption which the wars of liberation produced in a postmodern era left many of its victims as basket cases. If Zimbabwe and Namibia squeaked in as modern victors, Mozambique and Angola most assuredly have not. Potentially South Africa lost its chance for a modern emancipation as the era moved to postmodern and as the thoroughly modern movement which bore the standard of that liberation found itself struggling with the conditions of postmodernity.

So the political drive for change is now a complex creature, fraught with internal difficulties and locked into quite different material and ideological circumstances, at local, national, regional and global scales, from those which until extremely recently seemed to be relevant to certain and relatively uncomplicated victory. No longer do the ringing tones of the Freedom Charter's demands for nationalization of the commanding heights of the economy pour forth from spokespersons for the ANC. 'ANC PLEDGES FISCAL DISCIPLINE . . . an ANC government would not significantly raise taxes . . . would phase out existing stringent exchange controls . . . and . . . a priority would be to eliminate waste and corruption in the civil service', the largest daily circulation newspaper in the country breathlessly reported during 1993.[5]

Looking backward, the demands of the Freedom Charter were very much the demands of those seeking to make new divisions of labour work successfully to the benefit of a wider (and different) range of the population than apartheid was doing. 'The failure to complement mass production methods with compatible income structures and growth dynamics' (Storper 1990: 441) might have been alleviated by successful class struggle on the part of a massively growing labour movement. But by the time those gains came, in the 1970s and 1980s, the conditions had changed: now the higher wages, job security and social benefits which had propelled some industrializing countries along moderately successful modernist paths (Australia?) became stumbling blocks to flexible accumulation. All these new problems confronted, however, not simply the old political masters: the emancipatory movements forged in the modernist era found themselves able to move towards (some) power precisely because the old patterns of accumulation had cracked and even crumbled. The implications of this shift for southern African cities must now be examined.

FOR THE CITIES, WHAT DOES THIS CHANGE?

South Africa's cities, and those of the rest of southern Africa, have been shaped in large and small ways by very modernist conceptions of planning – the achievement of structures which would support the society and economy of apartheid (cf. Robinson 1992). Such an application of planning may be recognized as one designed, like that Yiftachel describes in this section, to promote social control and economic retardation – though its origins may be rather different (Mabin 1991). The opposition to apartheid planning based itself, of course, on an alternative but very much a modernist conception of planning – planning intended to redistribute power and comfort in a comprehensive and rationalist way, predicated on the notion of continued change in what seemed to be the relatively unilinear processes of economic development of the period. Thus conflict over the shape of the cities was essentially a conflict, heightened in the late 1970s and early 1980s, between two rationalist movements and planning approaches, despite their basis in conflicting inationalisms'. King (1992: 146) notes that in 'developing countries', 'it was thought that modernism would save cities from Europe's industrial-capitalist urban chaos.' Both the rationalist views of urban South Africa sought to do just that, one through planned oppression, the other through planned emancipation.

Confusion and uncertainty about urban management necessarily follow in a period in which the ground has shifted so profoundly. Unfortunately scholars of southern African cities have not yet begun to examine the meanings and implications of the postmodern shifts, at least not in the light of the findings of research and the speculations published elsewhere.[6] For example, while some feminists are exploring postmodernism and postmodern changes, no substantial work has yet appeared which connects those investigations to space, to urban form, to the cities, along lines provocatively suggested by Bondi and Domosh (1992). While the lack of engagement with the great range of postmodernist interpretations means an absence of divided and acrimonious debate on the meaning and especially the political meaning of the postmodern era, it does tend to impoverish our understanding of the complexity of the situation. The following remarks on some of the shifts affecting the cities are thus a very preliminary outline.

• The broad apartheid rationality imposed in the 1950s and 1960s (illustrated, for example, by the destruction of the small, older 'locations' and the laying out of well-separated, huge wedges of peripheral land for the new public housing, segregated black townships of, say, the 'East Rand') created a shift from something which served an early, small-scale industrial development to one which 'worked' for fordist, mass-production industrial development in the period.

- The shifts in industrial products, processes, costs, profits and competitiveness usually associated with the period beginning sometime around 1970 have produced profound problems for the protected industrial economy of South Africa, with declines of up to half of the industrial workforce in some subregions and an absolute decline in industrial production and employment throughout the region.

- At the same time the 'freeway shift', involving massive public investment in infrastructure, has transformed metropolitan areas in the direction of suburbanization of various economic activities. Whether new production opportunities have been opened up by these shifts is debatable, but some would certainly hold that there are indeed new high-technology suburban locations, and certainly some information-based spheres of activity have developed rapidly in new subcores, concomitant with some measure of decline – sometimes very severe (for example, the old Germiston town centre) in older cores, a selective abandonment of the now relatively smaller central cities leaving established urban cores with a mix including a bloated irregular marginal economy comprised of the poorest segments of the population – a description which could be fitted to Johannesburg without too much alteration.

- There has been a built environment shift: no longer are there the massive public housing construction programmes yielding 100,000 houses in Johannesburg in 10 years as between 1955 and 1965, or tens of thousands of high-rise private rental units, but instead 'greater investment in office buildings, luxury housing and waterfront development, and less in manufacturing plant, affordable housing and public open space' (Beauregard 1991: 90).

- Classes have polarized – wealth, poverty, the rise of homelessness, abandoned ghettos and luxury enclaves (Peter Marcuse, cited in Silver 1992: 652). Extreme examples can be found in the Bertrams area of Johannesburg, in which older single-family dwellings have been tenemented to a degree unimaginable among the homeless of western Europe or north America – up to 100 people occupying what were previously five or six quite ordinary rooms and up to 16 shacks in backyards: something which you would find in the *cortiços* of São Paulo (Mabin 1991). A new form of fragmentation and segregation of space emerges.

- There has been an urbanward shift, complicated not only by increasing migration from far-flung regions such as Zaire to relatively wealthy areas like Johannesburg, but also by the persistence of circular migration patterns – rural-urban links, if you will – which have profound consequences for the aspirations and abilities of residents of urban areas, not infrequently helping to generate conflict, including violent conflict, in conditions in which, in any event, large proportions of excluded populations must accept irregular and usually illegal activity as the basis of their material survival (Royston 1991).

- There has been a shift to multiple land uses despite the continuation of increasingly irrelevant zoning schemes – like Roodepoort Road in Soweto, or the breakdown of regulation of zoning for small business in the suburbs of Cape Town (Watson 1993).

- In these circumstances the negotiations shift – the CWMC described above being an example one could generalize in various specific ways to many other urban areas of South Africa – reflects the fact that neither existing authorities nor emancipatory movements believe that they possess the sole franchise on urban management any longer. Thus emerges a new form of politics, which takes shape in new political spaces.
- There has been a violence shift – as noted by Young (1990) and Harvey (1992b), it is indeed impossible to contemplate urban futures 'without confronting the problem of burgeoning levels of physical violence' (Harvey 1992b: 599). It is necessary to record that levels of violence in some areas of South African cities are, for what any statistics are worth, as high as any in the world: Bogota and some Brazilian cities come to mind as parallels. This is perhaps the essence of the postmodern city seen from the ugly underbelly up, and that is not to confuse the reality of violence with the middle-class dinner-party fears expressed behind the high walls of the northern suburbs of Johannesburg (or many similar zones).[7] Here violence follows from the inclusion of middle-class people into malls and atria, as Harvey puts it, and the exclusion of the poor, not only into homelessness (really shack areas) and joblessness. Unsurprisingly the worst excesses of violence are perpetrated within the poorest communities, sometimes surrounded by razor wire – that ugliest of walls.
- There has been a diversity shift – cultural and linguistic; not that South African cities have ever been short on cultural and linguistic diversity (slaves from Malaya and Angola, free blacks from Sierra Leone and the West Indies, immigrants from the Philippines, Friesland and the Shetlands in Cape Town in the nineteenth century). But such diversity is now increasing at a rapid pace – especially in Johannesburg, with poor Zaireans and Malawians as well as Ugandans and West Africans contributing to increasing amounts of French in street markets, Portuguese in shack areas and other languages in all sorts of space, with uneven linkages to the urbanward shift taking place.

In short, 'The replacement of the technological-institutional model of mass production by [the] as yet emergent regime of production flexibility introduces a new set of realities to which policies for industrialisation, urbanisation and regional economic development must be addressed' (Storper 1990: 441). It is partly the attempt to address these shifts which leads to the abandonment of former rhetoric on the part of emancipatory leaders in southern Africa. The specifically urban spatial questions which arise are being addressed in negotiations, as the case of the 'interim strategic framework' in the CWMC shows.

NEW APPROACHES TO PLANNING

If there is an emerging orthodoxy concerning the necessities of shaping South African cities to match the necessities of the postmodern, postfordist phase, it is the idea of the compact city. Thus in the CWMC, whose committees and whose difficulties have been alluded to earlier in this essay, the key proposals for overcoming fragmentation and segregation in our urban environments are for the compacting of the cities: what I think is called urban consolidation in Australia and goes by other terms elsewhere. Compactness has a particular twist in cities whose spatial form bears the profound impress of official segregation and widely separated residential areas. The prescription of Krier, in which the disabilities of the modern city, such as overconcentration of single uses in single zones and massive concentration of resources on circulation of people between zones, would be overcome by 'the good city' in which 'the totality of urban functions' would exist within 'compatible and pleasant walking distances' (Krier 1987), comes to mind, and is elaborated in the South African context by authors such as Dewar (1992). In local negotiations, thus, definitely postmodernist conceptions begin unconsciously to inform the shaping of how to move forward. The process is driven no longer by the creativity of the civic movement, but by a global philosophy of 'the good city' which has roots as suspect as any of the problems generated by the disabilities of the modernist city in southern Africa.

The vision propounded by those who wish to compact South African cities – and it is difficult to fault the general image – begins to break down as it is moved into practice. The integrating vision at the metropolitan scale is apparently based on a (postmodernist) critique of the fragmented city; but the necessary integrating power is less and less likely to be available as a simultaneous tide rises of deregulation and dependence on the zoning power of land rent (cf. Harvey 1989: 77). The means to overcome the problem is not yet to hand, though the elaboration of what is necessary to achieve worthwhile compactness proceeds apace (Central Witwatersrand Metropolitan Chamber 1992b).

In other contexts, a variety of problems have been raised with respect to the compact city notion. For example,

> *If urban consolidation is not to turn out to be a passing fad and an exercise in sophisticated niche marketing, then the conditions have got to be right. Australians are not going to give up their traditional ways merely because some of their leaders have a yen for what they believe to be a European life-style. They are far too shrewd. (Kirwan 1992: 19)*

In the CWMC, the civics have pushed for an 'interim strategic framework' (ISF) based essentially on an approach to compacting the apartheid city form. The objective is to integrate what has been fragmented – to bring home and (potentially) work together, to overcome wide spatial divides, to reduce segregation in racial and perhaps other social-spatial senses. But the evidence of new and powerful forces of fragmentation, represented by the suburbanization of forms of economic activity, poses a real challenge to the ISF–compacting approach. A key question, not yet at all examined let alone determined, is the relative strengths of varied integrative versus fragmenting forces. In extremely vague terms, if some of the new integrating forces of the period can be found and maximized, the planning framework can be expected to work towards overcoming the fragmentation of colonialism and apartheid. If not, a much more profound problem of limited integration and new and extended fragmentation producing new disabilities for oppressed groups in the city can be anticipated.

If we try to measure emerging planning approaches within local negotiations in South Africa against Harvey's (1992b) propositions on the construction of just planning and policy practices, it will emerge that some of these propositions demand practices which go far beyond the possible in the circumstances described above. For example, to confront the exploitation of labour power at work and at home in the face of radical industrial decline and rampant free market ideological victories becomes increasingly difficult. On the other hand, in cities like Johannesburg, Bogota or São Paulo, the collection of huge groups of people whom 'the system of labour cannot or will not use' (Harvey 1992b: 598) is not a marginal phenomenon: it is central to the politics of the future. Approaches to non-paternalistic incorporation of the excluded are painful and take enormous amounts of resources, especially time, to develop. Yet the building of participation on even so broad a subject as the reshaping of the metropolitan area of Johannesburg has some successes to show, mainly through the building of the painstaking process of workshopping ideas from the smallest units of communities on the ground through gradually increasing efforts to bring mandated representatives of some of the poorest communities together to examine their collective agreements and disagreements (cf. Central Witwatersrand Metropolitan Chamber 1992a).

Inclusionary and mediatory forms of social control are beginning to emerge as ways to resolve problems of violence, though in some project circumstances misapprehension of the depth and complexity of social divisions has led to deepening violence rather than conflict resolution (as at Phola Park, a shack area of several thousand residents some 20 km from central Johannesburg).[8] And there are cases where urban areas are being, however slowly at present, reshaped by careful inclusive negotiation, as at the land invasion/upgrading project at Tamboville, an area of the eastern Witwatersrand some 35 km from Johannesburg's centre.[9]

CONCLUSION

[T]he most satisfying story about postmodern urban forms is a story about real people and power.
S. Zukin, 'The Postmodern Invasion'

So new planning practices appropriate to the specific postmodern circumstances of Johannesburg and its surroundings are beginning to emerge. The question which hangs over them lies in the degree to which the civic movement can sustain development of these practices, in a period in which the forces of fragmentation can be expected to multiply and weaken what is in any event an uneven and loosely developed social movement. When local government has legitimacy, in contrast to the past, the civic movement may no longer be able to sustain the powerful but modernist move to urban reform which the pressures of the present threaten to defeat, despite the progress which has been made in the past two or three years (cf. Seekings 1992: 235–6). But riotous and disorganized political behaviour may threaten this project every bit as much as it did the older planning now being reformed in new political spaces.

The narrative of contemporary change in Johannesburg and other southern African cities is partly about the problems of finding a means to handle, politically, waking up in a postmodern era while equipped only with the politics and planning practices of a modernist past. The preliminary explorations reported here indicate merely how substantial some of the difficulties are, how some intersect with the experiences recounted from other parts of the world, and how some of the approaches to change which emancipatory movements find themselves adopting are full of difficulties and dangerous limitations. The attempts to confront some of the disabilities of the modernist forms under distinctly postmodern circumstances are surely relevant to a wider frame.

The politics of urban emancipation in a society marked by massive unemployment, historically substantial but very incomplete proletarianization, disaffection and industrial decline as well as particularly deeply etched patterns of social and spatial fragmentation are not matters of merely idiosyncratic interest. They certainly bear comparison with other societies in the South, and much greater sharing and testing of experiences across the global South can be anticipated.

NOTES

This chapter is drawn in part from work completed under the auspices of the National Local Government and Planning Policy Research Project (LOGOPOP) based at the University of the Western Cape and funded by IDRC-Canada. Research on a project on the history of urban planning in South Africa funded by the HSRC-South Africa has also contributed.

1 Readers will discern a tension in the use of 'southern Africa' in this essay. It has no political intent, but does seek to capture the point that – as in west Africa – 'regional economic solutions might be on the horizon sooner than we might expect' (Lubeck 1992: 22), and that to treat the past, present or future of South Africa's cities in isolation from those of others in the broader region makes little or no sense.

2 The following paragraphs are based on participant observation in the processes described between August 1991 and April 1993.

3 For an excellent summary of the history, structures and difficulties of the civic movement in the black townships, see Seekings (1992).

4 A more or less continuously built-up area extends for considerable distances to all points of the compass around Johannesburg. While northern and southwestern extensions have recently become major lines of growth, the older east–west axis associated with gold mining, coal mining and manufacturing could be considered as a unit and is generally known as the Witwatersrand, stretching 40 km west and 50 east from the centre of Johannesburg. Together with newer eastern and western mining extensions, and with the major cores situated 60 km to north and south, the whole metropolitan region is called the PWV – the Pretoria–Witwatersrand–Vereeniging area. This region of over 100 local authorities covers about 10,000 square km, of which perhaps half are built up, albeit often to densities familiar in California and Australia rather than in New York, Paris or Cairo. The population of the whole area was about 8 million in 1991; of which the central Witwatersrand portion contained over 2 million.

5 *The Star* (Johannesburg), 29 March 1993, quoting Trevor Manuel, head of the ANC's Department of Economics and Planning.

6 There are beginning to be some partial exceptions, such as the work of Jenny Robinson at the University of Natal, Durban; cf. Robinson (1992).

7 The walling of these many fragments of middle-class space does reach particular heights in Johannesburg, realizing an extreme of the circumstances which Marcuse describes for other cities in chapter 16.

8 For a graphic illustration of the unpredictable and yet reasonably successful approach being taken to reduction of violence in some areas of South Africa, under the watchful eyes of European Community and United Nations observers, see the first programme in the series 'Ordinary People' (Weekly Mail TV/SATV 1), *Sharpeville Day 1993*, first broadcast 28 March 1993. The episode deals with conflict avoidance strategy on Sharpeville Day in Katlehong and Vosloorus townships in the Witwatersrand area.

9 For graphic coverage, see 'Tamboville: One City from Below', a video produced for Planact and the Wattville Concerned Residents Committee, 1991.

REFERENCES

Beauregard, R.A. 1991: 'Capital Restructuring and the New Built Environment of Global Cities: New York and Los Angeles', *International Journal of Urban and Regional Research*, 15, 1: 90–106.

Bondi, L. and Domosh, M. 1992: 'On Feminism, Postmodernism and Geography', *Environment and Planning D: Society and Space*, 10, 2: 199–213.

Central Witwatersrand Metropolitan Chamber 1992a: *Land Availability Study: Report B: Community Participation*, Johannesburg: CWMC.

Central Witwatersrand Metropolitan Chamber 1992b: *Physical Development Working Group: Interim Strategic Framework: Policy Approaches*, Johannesburg: CWMC.

Davis, M. 1990: *City of Quartz: Excavating the Future in Los Angeles*, London: Verso.

Dewar, D. 1992: 'South African Cities: A Framework for Intervention', *Architecture SA*, 5, 6: 16–9.

Doornbos, M. 1992: 'Foreword' (to issue on Emancipations, modern and postmodern), *Development and Change*, 23, 3: 1–4.

Harvey, D. 1989: *The Condition of Postmodernity*, Oxford: Blackwell.

Harvey, D. 1992a: 'Postmodern Morality Plays', *Antipode*, 24, 4: 300–26.

Harvey, D. 1992b: 'Social Justice, Postmodernism and the City', *International Journal of Urban and Regional Research*, 16, 4: 594–601.

Holston, J. 1989: *The Modernist City: An Anthropological Critique of Brasilia*, Chicago: University of Chicago Press.

Horvath, R. 1992: 'Between Political Economy and Postmodernism', *Antipode*, 24, 2: 157–62.

King, A. 1992: 'Review of Holston: *The Modernist City*', *International Journal of Urban and Regional Research*, 16, 1: 146–7.

Kirwan, R. 1992: 'Urban Consolidation: The Economic Potential', *Australian Planner*, 30, 1: 13–9.

Krier, R. 1987: *Tradition-Modernity-Modernism: Some Necessary Explanations*, Architectural Design Profile, 65, London: Academy.

Laclau, E. 1992: *New Reflections on the Revolution of Our Time*, London: Verso.

Lipietz, A. 1986: 'New Tendencies in the International Division of Labour: Regimes of Accumulation and Modes of Regulation', in A.J. Scott and M. Storper (eds), *Production Work Territory: The Geographical Anatomy of Industrial Capitalism*, London: Allen and Unwin.

Lubeck, P. M. 1992: 'Restructuring Nigeria's Urban-industrial Sector within the West African Region: The Interplay of Crisis, Linkages and Popular Resistance', *International Journal of Urban and Regional Research*, 16, 1: 6–23.

Mabin, A. 1991: 'Origins of Segregatory Urban Planning in South Africa', *Planning History*, 13, 3: 8–16.

Mabin, A. 1992: 'Learning from Sao Paulo', *Urban Forum*, 2, 2: 81–9.

Nederveen Pieterse, J. 1992: 'Emancipations, Modern and Postmodern', *Development and Change*, 23, 3: 5–42.

Robinson, J. 1992: 'Power, Space and the City: Historical Reflections on Apartheid and Post-apartheid Urban Orders', in D.M. Smith (ed.), *The Apartheid City and Beyond: Urbanisation and Social Change in South Africa*, London: Routledge.

Royston, L. 1991: 'Persistent Circular Migration: Theory, Approaches and Planning Response', unpublished MScDP dissertation, University of the Witwatersrand, Johannesburg.

Seekings, J. 1992: 'Civic Organisations in South African Townships', in G. Moss and I. Obery (eds), *South African Review, 6*, Johannesburg: Ravan.

Sidaway, J.D. 1992: 'In Other Worlds: On the Politics of Research by "First World" Geographers in the Third World,' *Area*, 24, 4: 403–8.

Silver, H. 1992: 'A New Urban and Regional Hierarchy? Impacts of Modernisation, Restructuring and the End of Bipolarity: Conference, Los Angeles, April 1992', *International Journal of Urban and Regional Research*, 16, 4: 651–3.

Slater, D. 1992: 'On the Borders of Social Theory: Learning from Other Regions', *Environment and Planning D: Society and Space*, 10, 3: 307–27.

Storper, M. 1990: 'Industrialisation and the Regional Question in the Third World: Lessons of Postimperialism; Prospects of Post-Fordism', *International Journal of Urban and Regional Research*, 15, 3: 423–45.

Watson, V. 1993: 'Home Businesses: Patterns, Opinions and Management', Project Report, Urban Problems Research Unit, University of Cape Town.

Young, I.M. 1990: *Justice and the Politics of Difference*, Princeton, NJ: Princeton University Press.

Zukin, S. 1992: 'The Postmodern Invasion', *International Journal of Urban and Regional Research*, 16, 3: 488–95.

14. Postmodern Bombay: Fractured Discourses

Jim Masselos

I

The riots that broke out in Bombay in January 1993 were the worst the city had experienced since the virtual civil war that surrounded independence in 1947 and the partitioning of India and Pakistan. Over the eight days of severe and ten further days of less severe rioting in 1993 more than 550 people were killed and Rs4,000 crores of property destroyed ($A2 billion). Trading losses in business were estimated at Rs1,000 crores ($A500m); the loss of gross value of output of goods and services at Rs1,250 crores; the loss of exports Rs2,000 crores, and the loss of tax revenue Rs150 crores (Tata Services Limited 1993).[1]

It was not merely the loss of property or revenue that was traumatic but rather the extended duration of the riots and the fact that they spread over the entire city area affecting all localities and hence all classes and groups within the population. In turn the riots questioned clichés and axioms about what the city represented and how it functioned and, by implication, they threw into prominence the fact that Bombay had changed as a city. Over the preceding decades Bombay had become a different kind of place and the riots in their dramatic way pointed out how it was different – populous, fragmented, economically developed, antagonistic, and shorn of an encompassing consensus. It is these changes I want to explore here by using the riots as a way into the different kind of place that Bombay was becoming in the 1990s. Before I do so, it will be useful to look briefly at the riots as a series of specific events which I can use as texts on which to base my analysis.

II

Conjoined within the January riots were a number of disparate forces both internal and external to the city. Muslims were still angry over the destruction a month earlier, on 6

December 1992, of the Babri Masjid, an ancient mosque built by Emperor Babar in 1562 at Ayodhya. There had been an immediate reaction then which took the form of rioting throughout the country. Among the most intense and savage were outbreaks in Bombay. They lasted about a week during which time over 227 people died (Padgaonkar 1993): the majority were Muslims killed in police firings in a manner which suggested police bias in favour of Hindus and against Muslims. The December riots highlighted and were the result of a polarization of attitudes along communal lines. Groups of people were being defined by religious affiliation as Hindu and Muslim, although at issue were not differing religious beliefs or fundamentalist ideas but rather the creation of exterior categories, inclusions and exclusions, Indians as Hindus, and Indianness as Hinduness or Hindutva. Muslims were categorized as outsiders, as other, by the India-wide Bharatiya Janata Party (the BJP) and by the regional Bombay-based party, the Shiv Sena. Their attempts to swing the national rhetoric away from the socially consensual secularism of the dominant political national force, the Indian National Congress,[2] was part of their battle to establish their own political hegemony and attain political control. By construing Hindus as Indian and Muslims as outsiders they managed to create a highly charged, intensely emotional atmosphere of antagonism among large sections of the city's Hindu population – and support for the BJP platform. Driving both parties was a determination to build and maintain political power bases. In the Lok Sabha, the nation's parliament at the centre, the BJP had become after the 1991 general elections the largest opposition political party and since then had been trying to ensure it would win the next elections whenever they were called and form a government.

Both the BJP and the Shiv Sena had been active in Bombay for some time previously, a fact which partly explains the intensity of the first round of riots in December 1992. The social divide in popular mentality was largely already in place even before the destruction of the Masjid: the outbreaks that followed it confirmed and reinforced the sense of division among those already influenced by BJP/Shiv Sena activism. The divisiveness had long been promoted in Bombay by the Shiv Sena, which was under the command of Bal Thackeray, the former newspaper cartoonist who had founded the Sena in 1966. The Sena was created to champion the cause of Marathis or Maharashtrians who saw themselves being displaced in their own capital city by migrants from parts of the country other than Maharashtra. Initially the Sena's activities had been directed against south Indians but from the 1980s the organization had focused its attention increasingly on the city's Muslims, many of whom were in fact Marathis. A chauvinistic regional party, the Sena appealed to Bombay's lower- and middle-class Marathis as well as to its workers and proletariat, and it did so through the use of regional symbols and of the historical past of Maharashtra, as well as through a tight-knit organization of party cells located in strategic positions in the dominant Marathi areas of the city, in its residential lower-middle-class areas as well as in the city's shanty settlements and slums. It had cadres of young men who were willing and able to support its message and the directives of its leaders.

Late in December 1992 Thackeray, building on the sense of triumph left to the Hindu political party groups after the destruction of the Masjid, focused on the Friday *namaz* (prayers). When Muslims congregated together for their noon Friday prayers in Bombay, they spilled out from the mosques and on to the streets, since the mosques were too small to fit all devotees inside them. Thackeray directed that Hindus should perform a *maha aarti* or religious worship each night outside a specified temple; by doing so they would block traffic just as the Muslims did during the Friday *namaz*. The protest was against the favourable discrimination allowed Muslims in undertaking their worship, but of course it had other connotations and intentions. It provided rallying points for the continuation of the anti-Muslim stance of the Sena and promoted its message – and it brought sizeable numbers of people on to the streets able and willing to move into action if required to do so. The *maha aartis* added to an atmosphere that had still not settled after the Babri Masjid destruction and the December riots: they continued and heightened an atmosphere dominated by the sense of triumph of Sena activists and by the sense of anger of Muslims insulted by the demolition of the mosque and intensified by the apparent police discrimination during the riots.

In the first days of January 1993, disconnected incidents set rumours rolling around the city.[3] In the dock areas, newspapers reported, two *mathadi* workers (headload labourers and carters) were killed during the night while they were sleeping. A number of people living in a shanty settlement in Jogeshwari in north Bombay were reported to have been forced into a hut and burnt to death. Their number was initially said to be eight, then eleven, then eighteen, then twenty-one, and they were rumoured to be Hindus burnt at the hands of a vengeful Muslim crowd. In another slum, in Dharavi, a Hindu youth was said to have been abducted by Muslims. Men from *maha aarti* congregations, after singing and dancing for a couple of hours in the evening, went out to attack Muslims and other dwellers in the shanty areas of the city. Elsewhere, in the more central areas of the city where Muslim and Hindu areas were adjacent, there were attacks into the rival territory as well as on people of the opposite religion who happened to be passing by, as well as attacks on taxis and other forms of transport. Shiv Sena bands of young men, acting in an apparently concerted and directed manner, went around the city claiming they were paying back the Muslims for what had happened to the *mathadi* workers and the Jogeshwari slum dwellers. The huts of Muslims in the slum areas were marked and over the next few days were looted and burnt and their inhabitants beaten and killed unless they managed to escape from the attacking crowds. In the later days of the riots, crowds marched to middle-class high-rise apartments, demanding that the Muslim families be identified so that their apartments could be ransacked and their inhabitants attacked. Muslim shops throughout the city were looted and burnt as were Muslim factories, timber depots, workshops, film studios, cinemas, hawkers' stalls, offices and storage places (godowns). There were also attacks on places of religious worship in a campaign that quickly spread throughout virtually all the city and certainly throughout all its range of localities, from elite suburbs to working-class areas to shanty settlements.

While the Shiv Sena drive provided a core to the ongoing direction of the riots, there were other elements involved in what became an especially diffuse and dispersed series of events. In the slum areas whole sections of hutments were set alight in a manner that did not distinguish between Muslim or Hindu. Either slum landlords were setting off the fires in order to regain the land and to rent it out again for higher key money, or the original owners of the land were making use of the state of anarchy to clear their land so they could build on it, something they could not do while the shanties were on it. In some cases, perhaps, branches of various political parties in the slums were paying off party rivals and in others there was probably a clear involvement of rival gangs using the situation to settle scores with opponents and to gain control of the slums and the various activities that went on in them.[4]

There was also more diffuse violence: clusters of attacks on individuals targeted sometimes by their religious affiliations but not necessarily or invariably so. In some areas there was a kind of territorial warfare waged between shanty quarters located on either side of main highways. Reporters covering the riots were also targets as they moved around in jeeps and other vehicles. A prominent Muslim journalist had his house torched and lost everything in it despite his access to city leaders, influential politicians and government agencies of control.[5] There were numerous other attacks against individuals whether living in middle-class housing or in shanty hutments.

The spread of rumours involved everyone in the city (Mathias and Pereira 1993: 3). On the Sunday after the riots began, there were rumours that the milk supply had been poisoned as had the bread that was still being baked and distributed. Virtually every family and every habitation became aware of the rumours, through word of mouth from one dwelling to another as well as by telephone. Not untypical was one household in Juhu which received six such calls before 7.30 in the morning from friends warning of the supposed poisoning. The rumour about milk benefited the private suppliers as distinct from government distribution agencies while the bread rumour was directed against Muslims since they owned most of the city's bakeries. Bakeries on that Sunday were the target of attack, most being burned and destroyed. Other rumours involved specific localities: in Dadar the rumour was that the suburb would be attacked by a convoy of armed fishing boats. So over the next couple of nights young Hindu males from the suburb camped out on the beach during the night waiting to repel the invasion.

In most suburbs, and especially the middle-class ones, whole compounds and blocks of buildings were converted into armed fortresses: the men patrolled the perimeters during the night or watched from the tops of buildings to guard against attack and to defend the compound or the building come what may. Specific localities established their defences as best they could: watching and waiting. In the daytime the watchfulness was less belligerent but nevertheless present: men sat around playing card games, talking, smoking, drinking tea and watching streets eerily empty of cars and movement until an attacking crowd descended on the area. Then the groups moved into action as best they could. The uncertainty enveloped everyone in the city, in all its areas and localities; there was no part unaffected and there was no part at all sure of what was happening or might happen. And in all this, the city diminished to its smallest constituent elements, and even among them it was clear that no one could be trusted and that there was no guarantee of security. In one incident reported in the early stages of the riots, a crowd invaded a hospital where doctors were treating three riot victims, and again attacked the victims

(Padgaonkar 1993: 67). There were of course many cases where individuals and families protected possible victims but there were many others where neighbours attacked other neighbours; people suddenly found themselves being attacked by people who had been their friends for a number of years: 'Our children used to play together. We used to visit them during their pujas and they would come over for Id.'[6]

Nothing was clear or certain and the norms on which the city had functioned seemed to dissolve during the days of the riots. Some places, however, seemed safe: the railway terminuses which became the holding ground for riot refugees, those whose huts, rooms or apartments had been destroyed or had been warned by friendly neighbours to leave and escape from the city. There they waited, trying to return to where they had come from. They left as soon as the railway authorities could schedule special trains or add carriages to those already timetabled. In all, some reports put the number of those who left Bombay during and immediately after the riots as high as a quarter of a million people.

Behind all these events was a loss of will and the disappearance of a willingness to control the situation. The police did not fire on the crowds as they had done the previous month. In many cases they stood back and let the crowds attack property, buildings and people. Nazira Khatoon's account of what happened to her was not untypical: '[The mob] took all my property and killed my son in front of me. The police just stood there watching' (quoted in Gargan 1993: 1). The reports indicate a significant police bias against Muslims and in favour of Hindus, reports supported by the publication of tapes of police radio messages sent during the riots.[7] One incident is probably typical of what was happening: a Muslim running desperately from a crowd that wanted to attack him was arrested by the watching police for inciting the crowd. And there were many other such incidents of the police standing by and watching crowds destroy and attack. At its best, police inactivity suggests inability to control what was happening; at its worst it suggests police collusion. The leader of the Congress government in power in Maharashtra, Sudhakarrao Naik, was equally ineffectual in taking decisive action and not until the appearance of Sharad Pawar, his political rival and defence minister in the central government, did government agencies begin to take determined action, but even then it was limited. Considered to be equally potent in influencing what was happening was Bal Thackeray, the leader of the Shiv Sena, to whom people appealed to stop the carnage. In press and TV interviews he claimed that Sena members were teaching Muslims a lesson, a claim reiterated by other members of his party.[8] They did eventually stop doing so and the city gradually began to return to its daily business.

In many ways the communal situation and the polarization of attitudes that went with it go a long way towards explaining what had happened in the January riots. But they do not provide an adequate explanation for the fractures in the norms of city life, and the abnormality of these riots. The city was accustomed to rioting and disturbances of various kinds and over the years had developed ways of handling and coping with them. They usually lasted only a handful of days and were limited to one or two areas. During such rioting most people outside the specific localities in which it occurred went on with their business unaffected. Those who were affected knew from past experience that the riots would soon be over and they could resume living much as before. The city had over the years developed mental and administrative mechanisms which handled with the minimum of dislocation all those occasions when street disputes and street violence broke out. But the January 1993 riots were different in kind, in their range and their extent. They suggest that something very different needs to be read from the event, something about the way that Bombay had grown and changed in recent years.

III

The range and depth of the disturbances were unprecedented in the city as was the disappearance of public law and order. What the riots revealed as particularly fragile were all those tacit assumptions, those accepted and unarticulated norms about the nature of urban living, which enable a city to function. The idea of a city as a site for social interaction, for joint habitation and shared space for work, living and relaxation was challenged by the continuity, extensiveness and ferocity of the riots. The axioms under-pinning city life no longer applied; their validity was no longer apparent. The urban consensus, the unstated assumptions about massive numbers of people living together and sharing the same space in tolerable amity, did not operate during the riots and left doubt as to whether a city-wide consensus could be re-established thereafter. Though there had been earlier riots in Bombay, the way in which the January 1993 riots took over the city as a whole was unprecedented and threw starkly into question the nature of how an urban population could live and work together in the future. Class tensions which also existed in the city were not the explanation for what had happened: in the past class polarization had certainly been apparent and had manifested itself in the form of organized demonstrations, strikes, 'stop work' meetings, marches and so on. But the kind of raging anarchy and the descent into mass violence and destruction that Bombay witnessed in January 1993 represented something very different from class tensions and antagonisms.

An enquiry into the nature of urban discourses was evident in articulated and unarticulated forms during and immediately after the riots and at all levels of the city's social structure. At one level the issue was posed by the mass exodus from Bombay of the victims of these events. Many riot victims who had lost their property and housing in shanty settlements fled to one of the two main railway terminuses for refuge and then squeezed on to whatever train was heading out of Bombay. Others who left did so not because they had lost everything they had in the riots but because they no longer felt safe. Some were family units but there were also clusters of women and children whose menfolk remained in town to try and protect their property and continue working. Press interviews among those encamped at Victoria Terminus waiting to get away highlight the uncertainties of the refugees. Typically, the interviews emphasized the refugees' state of shock, but they also brought out a sense of loss — feelings about the disappearance of what the city had promised as a place to find work and a place of relative equality and safety. These had disappeared with the riots. Selvan, who had fled with his family from Dharavi to wait for a train to Coimbatore, put the mood directly and immediately:

I have lived here for the last 30 years and never before have I felt that the life of my family is in danger. . . . We narrowly escaped being killed when mobs threw petrol bombs and acid bulbs inside our basti. *Even if things settle down, I don't think I will come back. I can't live here knowing that Bombay is capable of so much violence.*[9]

Part of the same equation of being under attack was being excluded: Bombay was no longer an open and jointly shared city; it was the preserve of some and not others. It excluded rather than incorporated. Thus was the explanation given to a Bombay reporter by Naseem Bano and Durgavati from Gonda in Uttar Pradesh (UP) as to why they decided to leave. The critical point was when the mob came for them, with hoodlums yelling, '*Bombai hamari hai, bhago bhago*' (Swaroop 1993: 4). What the crowd was saying was: Bombay is ours: destroy, destroy (them and their property). The crowd was excluding and the victims were excluded. For both, the result of the exclusion was the destroying of an idea of the city which had attracted the migrants to Bombay and which had retained those who lived in it or and were born there. Even those who were fleeing but thought they might come back considered at the end of January they would do so in a different way. Thus Naseem Bano and Durgavati noted '*Izzi aabroo ka sawaal hai, sirf mard lautenge*' (only menfolk will return) (Swaroop 1993: 4).

Bombay was no longer to be the place of primary allegiance but only somewhere to work and earn a living. The family location was to be away from and outside Bombay. Behind this change was the collapse of an idea about the city, an idea that had once applied as much to workers and the city's underclasses as it did to the more articulate. Structurally there is a surprising degree of congruence between ideas about the city inherent in what was being voiced by such riot victims, workers, labourers and the like, and the views about Bombay articulated by middle-class commentators, by its intelligentsia and its city worthies. However different the vocabulary and sophistication of the expression, there was a coinciding of what was being said.

Typical of such views of Bombay was that put forward in a leading weekly journal: 'For several decades, Bombay has been a symbol of all that India wants to become. It is prosperous, it is relatively efficiently run. It is full of success stories of the rags-to-riches variety and it has a cosmopolitan ethos in which it is what you do that matters, not where you come from' (*Sunday*, 24–30 January 1993: 29). And, it might have been added, not what religion you were. Again, as another paper noted, Bombay's image before had been a place 'which welcomed outsiders warmly into its ever-expanding fold' (Suri 1993: 2).

Bombay's growth into a major trading, industrial, administrative, cultural and educational nexus had been reflected in the expression of similar sentiments in the nineteenth century by its city politicians, its intelligentsia and even its British administrators. Such perceptions continued to be expressed after India became free and as the city grew even larger. The idea of a well-run, prosperous and open city – cosmopolitan, egalitarian and full of opportunity – was one that underlay post-independent Bombay's growth and was part of the clichéd city rhetoric trotted out over the years by city politicians and city intellectuals alike and accepted as axiomatic by its middle class as well as by immigrant workers (Masselos forthcoming).

But the January riots suggest that views which had held unquestioned acceptance for decades and represented the predominant discourse about the city need serious questioning. The riots threw into doubt the underlying assumptions on which such rhetoric was based. The assumptions were based on ideas of ordering of the city and placement within it. Bombay was an ordered city: it was well run administratively and its municipal functions worked adequately. It was an ordered city in that people were perceived as living in well-known sectors: mill hands in certain areas, the middle class in others, traders elsewhere and so on; certain linguistic groups in some parts and others in different sections; peoples of one religion in certain quarters and of other religions in other quarters. The city was socially ordered in that people knew their places and did not transgress them. The cells joined together in an organic totality; they did not attack the whole structure although there was from time to time jostling between particular cells. Mentally bound within a work and profit ethic, people in Bombay lived there and migrated there because they could enjoy the benefits that came from participating in what Bombay could offer. It was a mental ordering along social, economic and other criteria in which the dividing lines were not transgressed in any aggressive sense. Hence those who spoke for the city could purvey it as pluralist and progressive without making its representation appear contradictory. The idea of the cosmopolitan, open city depended upon the stability of a mental and social order, and it was this idea that the riots showed to be false. The reading of a stable city order may never have been accurate and there were certainly tensions and conflicts in earlier years that suggest any such reading was chimerical, but what 1993 did was to show that it clearly did not apply. The mapping of an urban ordering, the sense of an urban order, was dissipated. Instead it was replaced by another set of ordering, another set of ideas about what the city was about.

Essentially the riots showed the breakdown of the social consensus on which the city had been based. They also showed a breakdown in the discourse about that consensus, whatever its applicability to the city at any time in its past. It was the rioters who put forward a different idea about what the city represented and what the discourse about it should be and it was the riots that carried forth the message about distinction and difference. And it was a message that was understood painfully clearly by its recipients, its victims. The middle-class elite who, during the later stages of the riots and immediately after it, went on hunger strikes, protested to the government and took their concerns even to Thackeray were in fact trying to restore the earlier consensual discourse and operating within its constraints and within the privilege that position gave them. In these senses, then, the riots were not only about communal polarization, though it was communal polarization that created the situation in which the riots occurred. Rather the riots were about the fragmentation of urban life and the forces and the power that operated within that collection of buildings and structures, the power of landlords and criminal groups, the varied power of groupings, ethnic and otherwise, and most important of all perhaps the aggressiveness that derived from the variabilities within the city, the very variability on which the city laid its boasts of cosmopolitanism. While some observers talked of the riots in terms of the rising of the city's underclass, what was significant was that the city had many underclasses and many groups and many of these came out as aggressors or victims in the January events. Bombay had become fragmented – and it had become fragmented because the city itself had changed dramatically in the years since independence. Over those years Bombay had become a megalopolis and was subject to the same kinds of tension and benefit which characterize similar urban conglomerates elsewhere in the world. It is on these I now want to focus in order to understand some of the rhetoric of the riots as well as some of its characteristic violence and fury.

IV

Behind the pluralist and progressivist view of Bombay lay a perception of the way in which Bombay had become central within the Indian nation – in that it dominated and controlled the nation's commerce and its economic structures of power. It has, for instance, achieved a central position in almost all areas of production and finance. Perhaps as much as 75 per cent of the nation's stock exchange business is conducted through Bombay, but it also has: a 25.8 per cent share of net state domestic product; a 38.8 per cent share of total value of manufacturing (registered plus unregistered sectors) of output; 31.9 per cent of tertiary (or service) sector income; 44 per cent of total income generated from the banking and insurance industry; 36.4 per cent of total working factories; 39.9 per cent of average daily factory employment; approximately 300 major industrial enterprises; 18.6 per cent of total business enterprises; 18 per cent of total deposits; 21 per cent of total bank credit and 27.4 per cent of total cheque clearances in India (Tata Services Limited 1993: 1–2).

Bombay's role in the Indian economy structurally gives it the same kind of position within India as is possessed by other global cities in their own countries. It has been more than dominant, it is pre-eminent within India. Like other global cities, Bombay also has many of the features associated with a postmodern city.

It has the country's largest urban population, currently hovering around the 12 million mark, and it is a population that has expanded rapidly over the past four decades.[10] Its traditional industries, cotton mills for instance, have gone into decline and are being replaced either by small cottage-style production centres extensively spread throughout the city's slums or, as is the pattern elsewhere, by high-tech and service industries. As is the case with other global cities, the new industries are located on the peripheries of the city, since available land in the city heart is still occupied by the old and unprofitable industries. The effect has been partly to turn Bombay into a hub into which the new industries feed and from which they draw supplies, manpower and services. The new high-tech industries cluster along the transport arteries – roads and railways – that go outside what were the former city boundaries. The increasing spread of the city has occurred in areas where planning controls are less stringent than in the central city areas so that the dispersion and decentralization have been relatively free of development controls. Underpinning the changes has been the rapid growth of an immigrant population and the presence of labour not linked into trade unions or bound by labour controls – whatever the rhetoric spouted at government and political levels.

These are the kinds of feature associated with the global postmodern city elsewhere. But there are significant differences in appearance between Bombay and others such as Los Angeles. Although Bombay has spread outwards in an orgy of growth, it has not done so to anything like the extent of Los Angeles. Nor does it have the miles of freeways linking the various parts together in the intricate networks common in the US. It has a limited arterial road system and a limited local railway network, but the railways still manage daily to carry enormous numbers of people to an extent unimaginable in LA.

Bombay also has a distinctive city centre, located by historical accident at the far southern tip of the city. There have been attempts at establishing alternate foci – New Bombay on the other side of the harbour was designed to house 2 million people as well as to be the site for a relocated industrial, business and manufacturing centre. But New Bombay has not significantly affected the force of the city centre magnet. Similarly, other and smaller business centres in suburban locations have had little impact on the centre, though a limited degree of decentralization has occurred.

V

That Bombay has not spread out in the unlimited way of the Los Angeles model and that it has not quite acquired the formlessness of other urban megalopolis prototypes raises issues of definition and model. Is the LA pattern the product of specific local circumstances – earthquake controls and the easy availability of untrammelled and fairly useless nearby flat land – rather than being indicative of the necessary form of a global and postmodern city? Even though the LA model has assumed the status of prototype in urban studies literature it might well be that it represents the aberrant – the exceptional – rather than the typical.

What happens when the geographic environment enforces dense settlement, and promotes not a spatially flat development but high-rise structures? Put differently, what happens when the population packs in and goes up as well as spreads outwards, rather than only extending outwards and sideways? The mental map of the city then becomes something different: it is not the two-dimensional grid of population and housing categorized according to whatever criteria meet immediate analytical needs but assumes a three-dimensional shape – with populations in the air as well as on the ground. For my purposes it does not matter whether the air-living populations inhabit structures that are five storeys high rather than twenty-five or fifty-five. Of course if there are no significant differences in categorization between the ground and air dwellers then for all intents and purposes the two-dimensional grid retains its analytical relevance – but if there is significant difference then the issues of separateness and density expressed in height terms become relevant, as do the constructions of physical separateness and of mental separation.

The old parts of Bombay were based on ideas of akin concentrations of population and activities, localities or ghettoes determined by class, ethnicity, religion, language and occupation. They co-existed side by side and might mentally be conceived of as a flat, two-dimensional grid. The rich lived in particular areas, factory workers in others, Muslims elsewhere, Gujaratis also and so on. Though the match was never total, the idea of a locality as being the preserve of a particular kind of group rather than another, the concentrations of various kinds of group in different localities, were sufficient to be noticed and commented upon by both the city's inhabitants and outside observers – and became part of urban folklore – even when over time concentrations changed, groups moved away and new groups moved in, and the pattern altered (Masselos 1991).

Present-day Bombay inherits in part the old pattern of akin living areas which have survived from the days when the city was under British rule. Even now in the older parts of the city much of the form and appearance of the city remain unchanged because of the dead hand of tenancy laws and rent controls dating back to World War II. Tenants then and their children and children's children continue now to inhabit the same structures and to pay the same rents, unadjusted to inflation or to changing land values. As a result, buildings have deteriorated since landlords no longer receive a rent that even pays for municipal rates and taxes. This pattern applies particularly to rented accommodation in middle- and working-class areas. The ground plan of the city has in these parts remained largely unchanged.

There have been significant changes where buildings were occupied by owner-occupiers. Title and vacant possession being easily obtained, redevelopment has been easier. In such areas, largely areas that were already affluent, new enclaves of the wealthy have emerged in the form of massive high-rise apartments, creating localities of the ultra-wealthy and the upper middle classes. Notable among these are Malabar Hill, Cumballa Hill, Worli, and in the suburbs Bandra, Pali Hill, Juhu, and so on. In some areas where land has been reclaimed, such as at Cuffe Parade, similar construction has catered to the wealthy while on the outer fringes of the expanding city new areas have been opened up for the middle and lower middle classes. The effect has been to establish high-rise enclaves of great affluence, structures patrolled by security guards, and presenting images of a high-rise metropolis based upon the new wealth that Bombay has generated over the past few decades. Such areas also reinforce the idea of a spatial two-dimensional grid in which akin concentrations of population are gathered together even though they are air dwellers.

A similar trend has taken place in terms of the financial and commercial centres. Older areas have become more densely packed with offices and commercial establishments as the result of a process of division and subdivision of space. In such old centres the occasional building has collapsed under the weight of a century and more of neglect or during the monsoons, and has been replaced by new high-rise buildings poking above the level of the surrounding older buildings, through and above the commercial centres. In some cases the odd building has even been pulled down and new structures erected. But on reclaimed land, such as that at Cuffe Parade and Veer Nariman Point, new clusters of commercial structures have been erected, high-rise office blocks which form distinctive and highly visible commercial enclaves. Again, the commercial areas, along with the affluent residential areas, would seem to reinforce the image of a two-dimensional grid locating different areas according to function and usage. The twin city project on the other side of the harbour, that which established a New Bombay with a population of 2 million people, and with a tight ground plan of offices, industries, factories, and housing, also seems to satisfy the same perception of a two-dimensional grid urban demographic model, as does the city's creep into what was recently its hinterland – into village and farming land.

There are, however, other factors that need to be considered before a two-dimensional grid model can be accepted. Obviously in the past century there has been a significant increase in building to handle the growing population, but most of it has gone to serve the middle and upper classes and part to serve the elite workers, those who work in factories. Building has in no way managed to keep up with the rapid growth in population. The city has grown from 1 million to 12 million people over this century and along with it has been a massive increase in population density in the old parts of the city, as well as in expansion of the city area northwards. Density estimates during the 1980s put the figure at about 17,676 per square km and for a slum like Dharavi at around 187,500 per square km (Pestonji 1993: 11). But most of the city's population has not been absorbed into proper housing. The new arrivals to the city have had to survive by living on the city's pavements or else in shanties on whatever unbuilt land was available. Between 52 and 54 per cent of the city's population live in shanties or on the pavements – around 6.5 million people in all.[11] Bombay has been totally unable to handle the influx of population in terms of housing and does not seem likely to be able to do so in the near future (Lalit and Sudha Deshpande 1991).

When immigrants first arrive they usually settle down on whatever space they can find, a pavement or a secluded street corner or cranny. Later they move into any available unused space and gradually begin erecting temporary structures out of whatever cast-off materials they can find. The shelters become increasingly permanent, as the immigrants gather wide sheets of recycled, boiled-down plastic sold in the markets, or bits of wood, sticks and even bricks to add to their structures. Parts of pavements are colonized and become their property. An environment that mimics the pukka housing of their wealthier neighbours eventually emerges. Slum landlords, on the basis of gangster strength, develop control of the shanties and charge rents. Politicians, aware of the shanty settlements' importance as vote banks, milk municipal resources to provide some sort of street lighting and communal taps, and even manage to get pathways between the hutments bitumenized. The effect in the more established slums is to create value for the shanty – in some areas the asking price for key money for a hut, should a slum dweller want to leave it, can be as high as a lakh (hundred thousand) of rupees ($A20,000).

In established slums such as that in Dharavi, one of the oldest in the city and one that Bombay people half proudly claim as the largest slum in Asia, an informal economy has developed. It is not merely a place for shelter; it is a place where production occurs. In what must be one of the most efficient waste recycling structures anywhere, pickers sift through the city's garbage on site and then bring bits of plastic, paper, glass, and metal for sorting and recycling in Dharavi. There the plastic is boiled down and recycled as is the paper and the city's other cast-offs (cf. D'Monte 1992). Dharavi also has leather tanneries and leather processing units. Food is processed for sale, cloth is woven and clothing is manufactured, alcohol is distilled, drugs are smuggled as are other goods. One garment maker in Dharavi in 1993 was producing Rs3 crores of clothing ($A1.5m) for the export market and another manufactured and sold Rs1.75 crores' worth of catgut, surgical thread. Dharavi with its 600,000 population on 432 acres of land has a daily turnover of Rs75 lakhs ($A375,000) per day and two-thirds of its inhabitants work in the slum itself (*India Today*, 15 March 1993: 48–9; Nandgaonkar 1993: 2). Not all the enterprises in Dharavi are of course as large and there are numerous small, household-size production units as well as the larger-scale ones. In addition, some of the inhabitants are engaged in less easily quantifiable and less open non-productive enterprises as members of smuggling and *goonda* (criminal) gangs, though their extent and size are less clear.

In slums such as these the two-dimensional grid is repeated, with Muslims (40 per cent) and Hindus living in separate parts of the slum, as do Tamils, Gujaratis, people from UP, and so on. The slum is divided into localities, each with its own characteristics and its own name – Nawabnagar, Koliwada, Chamdabazaar and so on. But there are slum dwellers everywhere in the city, so many that they constitute an 'edge city' of their own, on the margins of all that a city has to offer (Panjwani 1993: 4). When a high-rise building is constructed, it is built by people who set up their shanties on the perimeters of the land on which they are building. They stay there until the building is completed, when some move on to other jobs, but many refuse to do so and stay in their shanties beside the high-rise buildings they built. The result is that the area acquires not only an upper-class high-rise enclave but also a shanty settlement at its base. Between them are walls and security guards but they inhabit the same locality, the one on the ground and the other in the air. There is virtually no high-rise enclave that does not have its surrounding *zopadpatti* (shanty settlement), and virtually no area in the city where there are not shanties, the exception being some of the most densely built-up parts of the old city where there is just not space for even a shanty. Bombay has a striking skyline of clusters of high towers spread throughout the city, but at their bases are equally distinctive shanty settlements. In some cases compounds containing a number of high-rise buildings have been constructed around or immediately abutting on to villages that had been there long before Bombay was itself founded or since its earliest days under British rule. The two-dimensional flat grid conceptually is unable to handle the demographic disjunction between the two kinds of settlement. Instead a three-dimensional representation of the city grid is required to take into account the diversity within even the most affluent areas. It was the existence of the three-dimensional grid that explains, for example, the eruption of shanty dwellers upon the elite housing colonies during the January riots, such as the attacks on the Cumballa Hill luxury apartments. The proximity of dwellings broke down the locality cellular division which had provided the dominant discourse of urban order and placement.

VI

When commentators talk of global cities and the global village, there is another way in which the term may be applied. A global city like Bombay is in fact predominantly a village, a series of villages represented in the shanty structures that permeate the city. They are omnipresent, and should not and cannot be ignored. They are in a symbiotic relationship with the city in which they are located. The economy of the city needs them – and employs the slum dwellers. A 1994 estimate of Bombay's unemployment put it at about the same level as Sydney's – around 11.4 per cent.[12] Where do these people go for work? The shanties supply servants for the high-rise buildings. The men are labourers and taxi drivers and the like. They work in the unorganized sectors of the city's economy, sectors which, in matters like cloth production, produce on handlooms in huts more cloth and at cheaper prices than the traditional industrial-revolution-style factories. As shanty settlements get older and a degree of social mobility occurs among the dwellers, some inhabitants may move into lower-middle-class jobs as clerks and so on but are unable to afford middle-class housing in 'proper' buildings.

Much of all that I have said meets the kind of definition which apply to a postmodern city: lack of centralization and diffusiveness, separation and interconnectedness, linkages to a global economy, and even the universalization of culture. Most Bombay slums have their own satellite dishes which receive world television, CNN and Star Television, and each slum has its own small locality cable network supplying a number of different channels, apart from whatever video theatres exist in a neighbourhood. The direction of this universalization of culture is, however, much more specific and creates a mass audience based on very specific elements of exclusion as well as inclusion, a point which requires discussion in another essay.

In many ways the archetypal postmodern architectural experience may not at all be the plunge into the Escher-like structures of the Westin Bonaventure in Los Angeles, but an excursion into the shanty slum. Shanty structures derive from village prototypes in rural India but are modified by the requirements of space and the availability of materials – plastic, tin, bits of cloth, wood and bricks, which draw on past and present materials. There are the tight packing together of structures, the unplanned pathways that wend their way through the massed huts, the pathways out into spaces that lead nowhere (though sometimes to spaces that serve as latrines), the dead ends, the hidden and clear exits, the makeshift entries through holes in fences and walls, and the juxtapositions of satellite saucers, make-do machines, trailing electric wires, bits and pieces of past and present crafts and technologies. All of these are, if anything, more consistently decentral-ized and diffuse in their experiental quality, more drawing on the pasts as needed, than anything the Westin can produce with its ordered pathways and hidden exits. All are the subject of an overall if confused planning process designed to appeal to a limited and selective stratum of society. The shanty settlement represents the other side of the enclave and a similar gathering of pasts and presents, but it creates something that is qualitatively different from any of the pasts and presents from which it draws.

VII

It is perhaps time to return to the starting point of the essay and bring together the threads of the discussion. I have argued that Bombay's growth has led to expansion but also to increased density as population has packed together within a limited area. To understand this density, and the constituent elements within it, I have argued it is necessary to develop a mental map that is not based on a simple, two-dimensional grid of localities, ghettoes, or enclaves, but one that is three-dimensional, allowing for the differences between those who live on the ground and in relationship to it and those separated in pukka buildings and in various forms of high-rise structures. In Bombay, the two kinds of map co-exist with, increasingly, the three-dimensional map being more valid as the city population continues to grow and as its economy acts as a kind of black hole drawing more and more energy from the surrounding countryside into it.

A three-dimensional grid and a sense of that grid is essential in understanding the form of the riots that occurred in Bombay in January – a form not quite like any that have occurred in the city's history until now. Perhaps they might be classed as the first postmodern riots in the city's history, whereas past riots occurred in and between different localities, and were expressions of matters of particular emotional import of the day: Hindu–Muslim antagonism, anti-plague emotionalism, regional cultural tensions (such as that between the Marathis and Gujaratis), and the like. All such outbreaks took the form of a fight for territory and control of the peripheries of the locality (Masselos, 1991, 1993: 181–8). The January riots were different; they were diffused through the city and not limited to one or two areas. People in the slums burnt each other's shanties and killed one another. Slum dwellers went out and attacked middle-class dwellings, middle-class people defended themselves and attacked others, slum dwellers attacked high-rise apartments and demanded that Muslims be produced for killing, middle-class Hindus went out on a pogrom against Muslims, burning shops and houses, killing and injuring. Behind all of these events were a number of elements that had created the emotional situation in which such things could happen – the politicization of religion, events elsewhere in India, the communalization of politics, slum gangs fighting for control of slums and control of hutments that represented real monetary value, criminal gangs fighting for dominance between themselves, and landlords trying to regain control of their land. In the process modern values of co-existence and cosmopolitanism went by the board, and communal harmony and economic prosperity were equally questioned. The lack of central control was demonstrated by the inability of the police or their unwillingness to control what was going on, and an equal inability or unwillingness on the part of the state government to quell the situation.

A sense of interconnectedness between the differing sections of the city's population as a whole was replaced by a sense of interconnectedness with certain parts only of the population, not all of it. The sense of separateness as represented in the communal antagonisms was what emerged as uppermost in the riots. Similarly, diffusiveness and lack of central and government control was equally demonstrated during the riots and to telling effect in terms of the cost to lives and property. The consequences of the disorder are such as to lead to a questioning of the nature of the global city, the postmodern urban phenomenon. The flipside of such developments, the underbelly of postmodernism, is disorder, separateness, antagonism, destructive rampages against property, and lethal vengeance and killing of people perceived as other, apart and different. And as these riots showed, there was not one but many axes by which difference and otherness was determined, not one but many agendas and likewise many messages conveyed in the lootings, burnings, violence and killings of the January events.

NOTES

1 As the estimates note, the figures regarding property destruction may be overestimates. One crore equals ten million.

2 For a brief discussion of the Congress creation of a national rhetoric see Masselos (1987: 2–3).

3 The following account on the January riots is based heavily on my impressions of what was happening while I was in Bombay during January. In addition I have drawn on discussions with a range of friends in Bombay during this period as well as on contemporary newspaper accounts and on a summary of the *Times of India* reports recently published under the editorship of Dileep Padgaonkar (1993).

4 At the time of writing this chapter, a government enquiry into the riots is in progress. It will presumably provide more information as to the involvement of such elements in the riots. A number of Bombay newspaper reports in January pointed to the involvement of landlords and criminal gangs as well to the presence of political infighting as factors in the riots. See, for example, Vernekar (1993: 1) and Najmi (1993: 3).

5 He was Haroun Rashid, editor of the Urdu *Blitz*, but other Muslim journalists also had their homes attacked. Hindu as well as Muslim journalists were attacked while on the streets when they were covering the riots. See Padgaonkar (1993: 62 and passim).

6 Interview with Salma and Roshan by Bharati Sadashivam (1993: 10).

7 Some of the contents of the tapes were first published in the *New York Times* (4 February 1993: 1 and A8).

8 *Time* (Australia, 25 January 1993: 37) reprinted Anita Pratap's interview with Thackeray in which he said: 'I want to teach Muslims a lesson. Our fortitude has gone too far.' See also 'We Did It, Claims Sena', *The Economic Times, Bombay* (15 January 1993); 'Shiv Sena Admits to Role in Bombay Riots', *The Times of India* (15 January 1993: 1).

9 Interview as published in *Indian Express Sunday Magazine* (Bombay edition, 17 January 1993: 2).

10 Bombay's population in 1951 was 2,994,000 and 8,243,000 in 1981 (Deshpande and Deshpande 1991: 19).

11 Personal communication from Professors Lalit and Sudha Deshpande, Dept. of Economics, the University of Bombay.

12 The daily unemployment for males over 15 is 7.56 and per cent, and for females 15.14 per cent (Deshpande and Deshpande 1991: 42).

REFERENCES

Deshpande, S. and Deshpande, L. 1991: *Problems of Urbanisation and Growth of Large Cities in Developing Countries. A Case Study of Bombay*, World Employment Programme Research Working Papers, Population and Labour Policies Programme, Working Paper No. 177, Geneva: International Labour Office.

Gargan, E.A. 1993: 'Trust is Torn: Police Role in Bombay Riots', *New York Times*, 4 February: 1.

Masselos, J. 1987: 'Comity and Commonality: The Forging of a Congress Identity', in J. Masselos (ed.), *Struggling and Ruling: The Indian National Congress 1885–1985*, Asian Studies Association of Australia, South Asian Publications Series 2, Delhi: Sterling.

Masselos, J. 1991: 'Appropriating Urban Space: Social Constructs of Bombay in the Time of the Raj', *South Asia*, N. S., XIV, 1, June: 33–64.

Masselos, J. 1992: 'Changing Definitions of Bombay: City State to Capital City', in Indu Banga (ed.), *Ports and their Hinterlands in India (1700–1950)*, Urban History Association of India, Nehru Memorial Museum and Library, and Indian Institute of Advanced Studies series, New Delhi: Manohar Books.

Masselos, J. forthcoming: 'Migration and Urban Identity: Bombay's Famine Refugees in the 19th Century', in S. Patel and A. Thorner (eds), *Bombay: Outer Influences, Inner Consciousness* Bombay: Oxford University Press.

Masselos, J. 1993: 'The City as Represented in Crowd Action: Bombay, 1893', *Economic and Political Weekly*, XXVIII, 5, 30 January: 182–8.

Mathias, L. and Pereira, C. 1993: 'That Dreaded Whisper in the Time of a Communal Riot', *Independent* (Bombay), 14 January: 3.

D'Monte, D. 1992: 'Lessons of Bombay's Riots. Not only Homes but Jobs', *Times of India* (Bombay), 31 December: 12.

Najmi, Q. 1993: 'Private Builders Razed Bakery Lands', *Indian Express* (Bombay), 19 January: 3.

Nandgaonkar, S. 1993: 'Dharavi Factories, a Shadow of Former Self', *Independent* (Bombay), 4 February: 2.

Padgaonkar, D. (ed.) 1993: *When Bombay Burned*, New Delhi: UBSPD.

Panjwani, N. 1993: 'An Ungovernable Metropolis', *Independent on Saturday* (Bombay), 16–17 January: 4.

Pestonji, M. 1993: 'Something Like a War', *Illustrated Weekly of India*, 16–22 January: 11.

Sadashivam, B. 1993: 'We Can Never Go Back', *Sunday Times of India* (Bombay), 17 January: 10.

Suri, R. 1993: 'Burning Bombay', *Indian Express Sunday Magazine*, Bombay edition, 17 January: 2.

Swaroop, S. 1993: 'Mass Exodus Alters Male–Female Ratio', *Metropolis on Saturday*, Bombay edition, 6–7 February: 4.

Tata Services Limited 1993: 'Quick Estimates of the Total Cost of Bombay's Riots, January 29, 1993', Dept of Economics and Statistics xerox: 4.

Vernekar, R. 1993: 'Arrests Reveal Dawood's Role in Riots', *Sunday Observer* (Bombay), 31 January–6 February: 1.

15. The Dark Side of Modernism: Planning as Control of an Ethnic Minority

Oren Yiftachel

INTRODUCTION

Urban and regional planning as an organized field of human endeavour came into being as an integral part of what is often termed 'the modernist project' (Dear 1986; Hall 1988). Consequently, it has been conceived, by planners and public alike, as a rational, professional activity, aimed at producing a 'public good' of one kind or another. Research into the theory and practice of urban and regional planning has therefore tended to concentrate on its capacity to contribute to the attainment of well-established societal (modernist) goals, such as residential amenity, economic efficiency, social equity, or environmental sustainability. Far less attention has been devoted to the ability of planning to promote goals of an opposite nature, such as social repression, economic retardation or environmental degradation. In particular, the links between planning policy, the problems of ethnic minorities and the political impact of modernist concepts in developing societies are yet to be explored fully.

In this chapter, I will attempt to focus on these under-researched issues, by (1) exploring some theoretical aspects of the link between modernist planning concepts and the control of ethnic minorities in developing deeply divided societies; and (2) examining in detail the practice of 'planning as control' in Majd el Krum – an urbanizing Arab village in Israel's Galilee region – where the government has continuously attempted to contain, segregate and dominate the process of Arab development. The chapter therefore provides a critique of widely established concepts and practices of modern urban and regional planning.[1]

'Planning' is defined here as the formulation, content and implementation of spatial policies. 'Reform' implies 'making things better', affecting amendment or improvement in the affairs of subject groups. 'Control' means the regulations of development enforced from above, with the aim of maintaining existing patterns of social, political and economic domination. 'Ethnicity' is defined as a set of group characteristics, based on belief in a common history and place, and usually including language, culture, race and/ or religion. The term 'Israel' refers to the country within its pre-1967 borders. 'Palestine' is the pre-1948 geographical unit between the Jordan River and the Mediterranean Sea.

PLANNING AND THE CONTROL OF MINORITIES: SOME THEORETICAL OBSERVATIONS

Planning: Reform or Control?

Urban and regional planning emerged out of the unacceptable and inhumane living conditions prevalent in the rapidly expanding industrial cities of the eighteenth and nineteenth centuries. The emergence of planning was intimately linked to a broader reform movement, which sought to redress the ills of unconstrained capitalism, through changes to the politics, economy and geography of cities (Cherry 1988; Hall 1988; Schaffer 1988). While early planning thinkers (like later ones) were clearly divided along ideological lines, a discernable consensus underlaid the development of planning thought and the emergence of the planning profession: planning should, first and foremost, act to improve people's (mainly physical) living conditions. This basic assumption formed the foundation for theories and tools which were later developed to guide public intervention in the development process and the land market. Most of the theories and concepts developed in planning during subsequent decades focused on two key questions: what is a good city? What is good planning? (see Cherry 1988; Hall 1988; Schaffer 1988; Yiftachel 1989).

Recent studies on the performance of planning systems clearly attest to the pervasive understanding of 'planning as reform'. Pearce (1992) and Healey (1992), for example, examine the historical performance of the British planning system by using as yardsticks the progressive concepts of amenity, order, efficiency, distributive justice and environmental protection. The recent evaluative works of Burgess (1993), Cherry (1988), Carmon (1990) and Schaffer (1988) also predominantly assess planning according to its ability to deliver improvement in the lives of subject populations. Even the thoroughly reflective work of Friedmann (1987) delineates four main perspectives which have dominated the development of planning theories and concepts: social reform, policy analysis, social learning and social mobilization. These are characterized, to varying degrees, by a view that planning has the capacity to reform and improve cities, regions and society. I argue here that this view of planning is narrow, too idealistic and often *unrealistic*. Furthermore, because planning has been widely interpreted as reform, relatively little research has focused on the instances when it acts as a regressive agent of change, particularly in the context of ethnic relations.

To be sure, the reformist–benevolent interpretation of planning is not universal. Contrasting accounts exist, particularly from Marxist, feminist and racial perspectives (see, for example: Dear and Scott 1981; Harvey 1992; Huxley 1993; Jackson 1986, 1987; Sandercock 1990; S. Smith 1989). However, even those explaining planning as assisting the domination of powerful interests observe that planners and politicians have shared a belief in its contribution to a 'better society', through development which would – if properly planned – maximize benefits for the largest number of people (for this popular utilitarian view, see Huxley 1994). The main argument of such critics has focused on planning's *unintentional* (or implicit) regressive consequences. Thus, planning has been widely perceived as part and parcel of the *modernization* of society, a process requiring the preparation of urban and regional plans (Cherry 1988; Hall 1988).

Planning in Deeply Divided Societies

Urban and regional planning in the form known today in the West first emerged in the Anglo-Saxon world, particularly in Great Britain. Subsequently, the debate over the goals, achievements and effectiveness of planning has been mainly confined to the institutional and political settings usually defined as 'liberal democracy'. This setting is characterized by a capitalist economy, a subsequent dominance of the market in politics (Lindblom 1977), a promotion of individualism, and a two-party political system with little minority representation (Lijphart 1984).

A fundamental difference exists between these liberal democracies and other, more collectively segmented societies. This difference can be highlighted by differentiating between two main types of multiethnic society: *pluralistic* and *deeply divided* (or plural). Pluralistic societies are typically composed of immigrant groups which tend to assimilate over time, and are usually governed by a liberal-democratic regime. In such societies, one's ethnic affiliation is a private matter, and ethnic movements mainly focus on the attainment of civil and economic equality. Ethnic affairs are often interwoven with *class issues*, which are the most dominant social cleavage in such societies.

On the other hand, deeply divided societies are composed of non-assimilating ethnic groups which occupy their historical (real or mythical) homeland. Hence, ethnic movements in such societies tend to promote goals of cultural and regional autonomy, recognition of national minority status for sizeable ethnic groups, and at times ethnic separatism. In deeply divided societies, ethnic conflicts are potentially more explosive, often threatening the very structure or unity of the state (Connor 1987). For that reason, government policies in such societies often attempt to *control* ethnic minorities, hoping to prevent serious challenge to the character or the territorial integrity of the state. Control policies typically attempt to retard the minority's economic development, contain its territorial expression, and exclude it from the state's centres of power and influence.

Notably, the Western countries where planning has flourished, as either an organized profession or a field of active research (Britain, Australia or New Zealand, the USA and Canada), are all pluralistic societies governed by liberal-democratic regimes. However, following British colonialism and the global spread of Western influence and capitalism, the ideas, concepts, methods and institutions of urban and regional planning have spread to many developing countries. Western planning ideas thus found their way to many deeply divided societies, where ethnic groups have often had a long history of struggles over land control, and where local political systems were far from the Western version of liberal democracy. The introduction of Anglo-Saxon planning ideas to these fundamentally different societies has created a set of problems and contradictions.

One of the most obvious problems has been the conversion of planning from a progressive tool of reform to an instrument of control and repression. This became possible because, in most post-colonial societies, one ethnic group came to dominate the state, using its apparatus (including planning) to maintain and strengthen this domination (Demaine 1984; Smooha 1990). While such ethnic domination may occur in Western pluralistic societies, it is usually more subtle, and is often constrained in such societies by the dominance of markets in politics (Lindblom 1977), and by legal mechanisms which protect civil rights. In many deeply divided societies – even those with formal democratic systems – these constraints to majority dominance are either weak or lacking all together (Esman 1985). In addition, the substance matter of planning – the use of land – is a vital issue in deeply divided societies, due to the historical attachment of ethnic groups to their homeland, which assumes extreme political importance, particularly in the current 'ethnic revival' age (A. Smith 1981).

As mentioned, the use of planning to control segments of the population has not been confined to deeply divided societies. It has undoubtedly occurred in Western (pluralistic) democratic societies, although this has usually transpired in relatively subtle ways, mainly through market mechanisms (see, for example: Harvey 1973; Huxley 1994; McLoughlin 1992) or male domination (Fincher 1990; Sandercock and Forsythe 1992; Little 1993). In such societies, the consequences of 'control through planning' have been usually manifested through class and gender relations, which are less tangible or visible than the primordial ethnicity characteristic of deeply divided societies. Even ethnic and racial discrimination has largely been expressed in Western-liberal societies through (usually distorted) market outcomes, rather than explicit ethnically based legislation and policies (S. Smith 1989; Thomas 1988). In contrast, the structural importance of ethnicity in deeply divided societies has meant that the use of planning as control has in many cases become quite explicit and blatant.

The very same planning tools usually introduced to assist social reform and improvement in people's quality of life can be used as a means of controlling and repressing minority groups. This explicitly regressive face of planning has yet to be widely studied or theorized. Studies of the impact of public policy on ethnic and racial relations abound, although they mostly address ethnic issues in pluralistic (not deeply divided) societies, and few specifically address the influence of land use (or spatial) planning policies (see Eyles 1990; Jackson 1986; S. Smith 1989; Thomas 1988; Williams 1985). The approach of many planners to the problem is typically summarized by Thomas and Krishnarayan (1993: 17), who claim that 'a positive approach to racial and ethnic equality in planning follows from taking principles and good professional practice seriously.'

The issue goes beyond the ethical and professional aspects of planning and planners, especially in deeply divided societies. It is directly linked to a *structural* understanding of the relations between the state, society and space. Constant use of planning as a tool for control is likely to exacerbate social tensions. This, in turn, can lead to increasing levels of intergroup conflict and violence, thereby undermining the entire 'modernist project'. This is particularly the case in deeply divided democracies, where ethnic (and not class) cleavages dominate, and where changes to the balance of ethnic relations may have an explosive potential. The sections below attempt to begin the task of defining and theorizing the control aspect of planning, by positing that function against the original ideas of reform and progress. Later in the essay, the concepts and framework developed here will be applied to the specific case study of Arab villages in Israel's Galilee region.

The Three Dimensions of Planning Control

The use of urban and regional planning as a means of control can be usefully studied by examining three key dimensions of planning policy: *territorial*, *procedural* and *socioeconomic*. These dimensions embody the most critical aspects of planning as an organized field of policy and professional practice: its spatial content (the territorial dimension); its power relations and decision-making processes (the procedural dimension); and its long-term consequences (the socioeconomic dimension).

The territorial dimension is defined as the spatial and land use content of plans and policies. This may include the location of settlements, neighbourhoods, industries, communal and social facilities, infrastructure services, and employment centres. It also includes the demarcation of administrative boundaries, according to which land use, development, and the provision of facilities and services are usually determined. Territorial policies can be used as a most powerful tool of control over minorities, particularly in deeply divided societies, where ethnic groups often reside in 'their own' regions. Planning policies can be used in such regional contexts to *contain* the territorial expression of such minorities, typically by imposing restrictions on minority land ownership, restricting the expansion of minority settlements, and settling members of the majority group within the minority region for control and *surveillance* (Marcuse, this volume). This is believed to impede the emergence of a powerful, regionally based, counter-culture, which may challenge the social and political order espoused by the central (majority controlled) state (Mikessel and Murphy 1991; Williams 1985; Yiftachel 1992b). On an urban scale, too, majority-controlled authorities can exercise (more subtle) forms of planning control, through land-use and housing policies, with the effect of creating *segregation* between social groups, usually according to class, race and/or ethnicity (Eyles 1990; S. Smith 1989). This process is elsewhere described as the recreation of walled cities, in which patterns of domination are expressed by physical division and spatial fragmentation (Marcuse, this volume). This, in turn, may further increase intergroup inequalities, as powerful groups would generally occupy the most desirable locations nearly exclusively, denying other groups the full share of the city's benefits and opportunities (Badcock 1984). The imposition of complex, inconsistent and unstable administrative boundaries can also function as a powerful tool of control, as ordinary citizens may encounter difficulties in dealing with such systems, which are usually more familiar to the wealthy and the powerful.

The procedural dimension covers the formulation and implementation processes of plans and policies. Here planning can directly affect power relations in society by controlling access to decision-making processes (Forester 1989). The procedural dimension includes statutory aspects which formally determine the relationship between various authorities and the public, and less formal aspects such as the rate of public participation, consultation and negotiation in policy making, and the on-going relations between authorities and communities. Planning processes can be used for the *exclusion* of various segments and groups from meaningful participation in decision making, thereby contributing to their *marginalization* and repression. This form of control can be explicit, as in the case of decisions imposed 'from above', or implicit, through sophisticated methods of information distortion and meaningless forms of public consultations (Forester and Krumbholtz 1990; Friedmann 1992; Hillier 1993).

The socioeconomic dimension is expressed as the long-term impact of planning on social and economic relations in society (as distinct from the immediate spatial impact). Bound up with the concept of 'planning externalities', land-use changes result in (usually indirect) positive or negative impact on neighbouring people or communities. That impact, which may include consequences such as improved accessibility, or proximity to environmental nuisance, forms an integral part of people's real income, whether it can or cannot be directly expressed in monetary terms. In that way, resources may shift between societal groups in what Harvey (1973: 100) termed 'the quiet distributive mechanism of land use planning'. Therefore, planning can be used as a tool of socioeconomic control and domination by helping to maintain and even widen socioeconomic gaps through the location of development costs and benefits in accordance with the interests of dominant groups (McLoughlin 1992). The systematic *deprivation* of subordinate groups by spatial policies often results in a growing level of *dependence* by weaker groups on dominant interests. This dependence, in turn, forms another powerful tool of socioeconomic control (Friedmann 1992; Harvey 1992).

The fact that ethnicity is the most pronounced cleavage in deeply divided societies does not reduce the importance of the socioeconomic consequences of planning. In such societies, the 'spin-offs' of negative externalities often add a class dimension to what was previously defined as a cultural-ethnic conflict (Mabin, this volume; Yiftachel 1992b). In general, and contrary to conventional wisdom, urban and regional planning is not just an arm of government which may or may not contribute to societal (modernist) reform, but also a public policy area with a potential for controlling subordinate groups, particularly in deeply divided societies (see also Mabin, this volume). This control can be exercised through the three dimensions of planning: territorial (affecting containment, surveillance and segregation), procedural (exclusion and marginalization), and socioeconomic (deprivation and dependence). Planning can therefore facilitate domination and control of three key societal resources: space, power and wealth, as will be detailed in the case study that follows.

PLANNING AS CONTROL IN PRACTICE: THE CASE OF AN URBANIZING ARAB VILLAGE IN ISRAEL

I examine here the planning of Majd el Krum – a large urbanizing Arab village in the Galilee – in order to illustrate the use of planning as a mechanism of controlling the development of an ethnic minority. The case study also illustrates how these control policies have spawned local mobilization and resistance, drawing on examples from the village's planning history, rather than a comprehensive account (for fuller details, see Yiftachel 1993). The selection of Majd el Krum as a case study was based on several characteristics typical to the majority of Arab villages in the country: it is Muslim, average in size and rapidly growing, located in a relatively remote region, and close to several new Jewish settlements. Majd el Krum can therefore be regarded as a representative example of an Arab village in Israel

Background

The Palestinian-Arabs in Israel

Some 820,000 Palestinian-Arabs reside in Israel, constituting 16 per cent of the country's population within its pre-1967 borders. The Arabs have lived in the country for centuries, and are currently concentrated in three main regions: the Galilee, the 'Triangle' and the Negev (figure 15.1). Forty-seven per cent of them live in the Galilee region, where they constitute 75 per cent of the population (CBS 1992). Arabs and Jews in Israel are non-assimilating groups, divided along national, religious, linguistic, cultural and social lines. The Arabs in Israel are full citizens of the state and are entitled to the formal legal and political rights given to Jews, under Israel's formal democratic system. They have enjoyed a range of positive consequences of living in Israel, such as rapid modernization and increasing living and educational standards (al Haj, 1988), but have also been subject to a range of discriminatory public policies (Benziman and Mansur 1992; Lustick 1980; Zureik 1993). As a result, the Arabs have recently increased their struggle for civil equality in Israel, led by the National Committee of Heads of Arab Local Councils (the National Committee) and several other voluntary movements, parties and organizations (al Haj and Rosenfeld 1990).

Israel's planning system

The Israeli planning system is highly centralized and powerful. Its authorities are endowed with wide powers of regulation, implementation and development (Alterman and Hill 1986). The system has two principal arms: developmental and regulatory (Gertel and Law Yone 1991). Developmental planning authorities are mainly public bodies with a mandate to develop land across the country, and include the Ministry of Housing, the Jewish Agency (JA) and the Jewish National Fund (JNF). Regulatory planning authorities are charged with approving urban and regional development. They operate mainly under the auspices of Israel's Ministry of the Interior and according to Israel's Planning

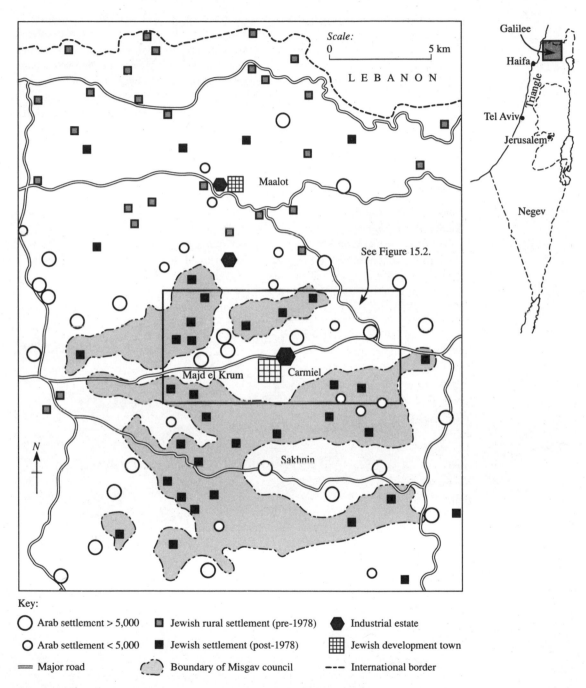

Scale:
0   5 km

L E B A N O N

See Figure 15.2.

Maalot

Majd el Krum   Carmiel

Sakhnin

N

Galilee

Haifa

Tel Aviv

Jerusalem

Triangle

Negev

Key:

○ Arab settlement > 5,000   ■ Jewish rural settlement (pre-1978)   ⬡ Industrial estate

○ Arab settlement < 5,000   ■ Jewish settlement (post-1978)   ▦ Jewish development town

══ Major road   ⌇ Boundary of Misgav council   --- International border

Figure 15.1 Arab and Jewish settlements in the Galilee, 1993

and Building Law (1965). The statutory system is composed of three hierarchical tiers: a national planning board, six district committees, and 121 local planning committees. Local and district committees are responsible for the preparation of statutory outline (land-use) plans for all settlements. Development in settlements without approved outline plans is illegal without the consent of the district planning committee. Quite often, when local communities do not prepare plans of their own accord, the government-appointed local committees initiate and control the formulation of statutory plans for individual settlements. This has been the case in most Arab villages.

Local historical context

Majd el Krum lies in the heart of Israel's northern region – the Galilee. The village is positioned near a famous spring at the north-western end of the fertile Bet Hakerem (or Shagur) valley (figures 15.1, 15.2), and was founded centuries ago by Muslim Arabs. Land surrounding the village has traditionally been cultivated for olives, grapes, figs, tobacco and cereal crops. In 1948, Majd el Krum reached a population of 1,400. Like most Arab villages in what is now Israel, it experienced tremendous upheavals during the 1948–9 war, when about half the village's population fled to Lebanon, while some 300 refugees from other (destroyed) Arab villages settled in the village.

The village received municipal status in 1963. Since then, a local council has been

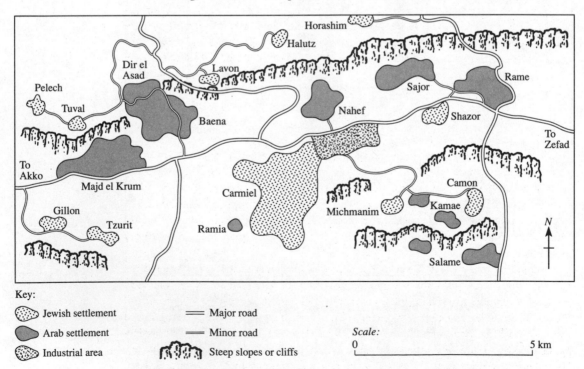

Key:

🌐 Jewish settlement   ══ Major road

⬛ Arab settlement   ══ Minor road

🌐 Industrial area   ⛰ Steep slopes or cliffs

Scale:
0 ——————————————— 5 km

Figure 15.2 Bet Hakerem (Shagur) Valley and surrounding hills

elected in regular elections and has taken control over basic municipal services, such as public health, water supply and education. However, local planning has remained the responsibility of a local planning committee appointed by the central government. During recent decades, the village has experienced many marked changes, which include: rapid spatial expansion and urbanization, sectoral shift in employment from agriculture to manual and self-employed labour, a marked rise in educational and health standards, and a steady (if slow) rise in average household incomes (see Haidar 1990). At the end of 1992, the village had a population of 8,200, and a built-up area which was eight times larger than its 1948 size. Although Majd el Krum can be classified as a town, most of Majd el Krum's residents still refer to it as a 'village'.

Local planning context

Planning in and around Majd el Krum began soon after Israel gained its independence in 1948. It was manifested in a range of governmental spatial policies, programmes and activities, including the enaction of new land statutes, the building of Jewish settlements, the expansion of Jewish agriculture, the development of infrastructure, and the establishment of regional industrial centres.

Israel's land and settlement policies in the area are documented in detail elsewhere (see Carmon et al. 1991; Falah 1989; Yiftachel 1992b). In brief, the area around the village has been affected by the following policy efforts (see figures 15.1, 15.2): (1) large-scale expropriation of private Arab land, mainly during the 1950s; (2) establishment of four new Jewish settlements or 'development towns' during the 1950s and 1960s (one outside the area shown in the figures); (3) establishment of 60 small 'rurban' (rural with urban features) Jewish settlements during the late 1970s and early 1980s; (4) development of four regional industrial estates or areas during the 1970s and 1980s (one outside the area shown in the figures); and (5) continuing development of regional infrastructure, particularly roads.

The regulatory process began in Majd el Krum during 1964, when the Northern District Planning Committee assigned a 'blue line' around the village, which denoted the permitted building zone. In 1978, the local planning and building committee appointed a Haifa-based (Jewish) planner to prepare an outline plan for the village. The plan-approval process, as detailed below, was replete with delays, conflicts and problems. As a result, the plan for the village did not receive preliminary approval ('deposit') until January 1986, and was not gazetted until July 1991 – some 21 years after the statutory process had began!

It should be stressed that due to the structure of the Israeli planning system, and the fact that the outline plan for the village was initiated and formulated by the local planning committee (that is, an Israeli government authority), the elected village council of Majd el Krum has had a very limited amount of formal influence over planning in and around the village. The planning of Majd el Krum has been carried out nearly entirely by the Israeli government (in the guise of its various provincial authorities and branches). Hence, in many respects, the case below represents a classic example of 'planning from above'.

TERRITORIAL CONTROL: CONTAINMENT, SURVEILLANCE AND SEGREGATION

Throughout the history of planning in and around Majd el Krum, the territorial dimension of planning implemented by government authorities has been characterized by strong elements of control over the village residents, exercised through land-ownership policies, and through the location of new settlements and municipal boundaries.

Land Ownership

Land seizure by the state

The first and most blatant instrument of territorial control has been the expropriation of village land by the state, mainly during the first three decades of Israel's independence. Majd el Krum has lost 13,865 of the 20,065 *dunams* owned by village residents prior to 1948 (1 *dunam* equals 1,000 square metres). This represents a loss of 69 per cent of village land, which had been transferred to the state due to a range of rules and regulations described elsewhere as affecting a 'de-Arabation' process of land in Israel (Benziman and Mansur 1992; Kimmerling 1983; see also Lustick 1980).

Most land loss was due to the state seizing ownership of land belonging to refugees who fled from the village during the 1948 war. This land was officially transferred to a state organ named the Development Authority, which is controlled by the Israeli Land Authority (see figure 15.3). Other land losses were due to the state confiscating land for 'public purposes', or assuming ownership of land for which no formal title existed (mainly those lands which were classified as 'communal village land' under the previous Ottoman land tenure system – see Hilali 1983). During the 1960s and 1970s, Majd el Krum lost most land due to expropriation of land (some 5,100 *dunams* in total) to enable the Israeli government to build and expand the town of Carmiel (figure 15.1).

This considerable loss of land occurred both in the areas surrounding the village and within the village itself (figure 15.3). It resulted in a marked decline of the reserves of both agricultural and potential building land. In addition, the widespread existence of state land within the village boundaries (a consequence of the seizure of refugee land) resulted in a high degree of land fragmentation, which in itself became an effective mechanism of control. This occurred because many developments of building and infrastructure needed to occupy state land, thereby requiring the consent of its authorities. State land would also be quite often leased back to village residents, resulting in another obvious dimension of state control over land uses and associated activities.

Land exchange

A more subtle form of territorial control has been the practice of land exchange. Under the control of the Israeli Land Authority (ILA), which manages all state land in the country, land expropriated from refugees who fled the village in 1948–9 has often been offered back to families who needed land for residential purposes (the 'Development

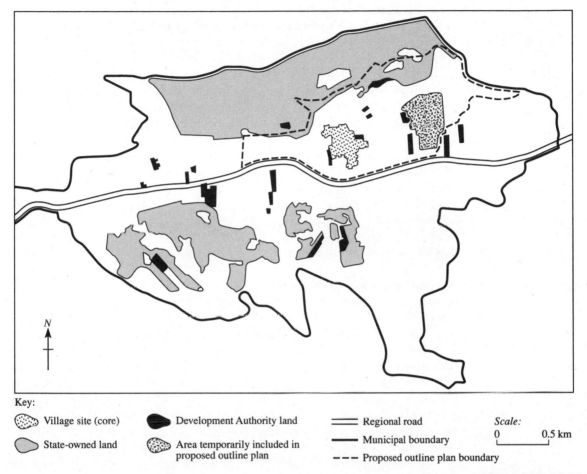

Key:

⬤ Village site (core)

⬤ State-owned land

⬤ Development Authority land

⬤ Area temporarily included in proposed outline plan

═══ Regional road

━━━ Municipal boundary

─ ─ ─ Proposed outline plan boundary

Scale:

0   0.5 km

Figure 15.3 Majd el Krum: outline plans and state land
Source: Majd el Krum Council and the Israeli Land Authority

Authority land' in figure 15.3). However, because Israel's Land Act (1960) prohibits the sale of state land, the only way for an Arab household to acquire a building lot within a permitted residential zone is to exchange land with the ILA. Because many Arab households own land in areas classified as 'agricultural' (usually rocky, uncultivated hills around the village where the construction of housing is prohibited), the ILA has offered to exchange that land with refugee land previously expropriated within the village.

The crux of this practice has been the rate of land exchange, which in the period between 1965 and 1980 (for which data were available) stood at 1:5.3, with village residents exchanging 158.6 *dunams* of agricultural land for 30.1 *dunams* of land within the village building zone (see Yiftachel 1993: 17). Significantly, even after the exchange, the ILA would normally retain a small joint ownership of the land parcel within the village (ranging from 10 to 25 per cent). This joint ownership means that the entire lot is jointly owned, thereby insuring a continuing ILA control over building activity in the village.

Interviews with village and ILA officials revealed that this practice has been taking place for some 30 years and has continued (albeit at a slower pace) since 1980. It is not difficult to see how it has caused a major shift of land resources from Arab household, starved for residential land, to the Israeli Land Authority.

This process has also suited the ILA and the Israeli government, whose main objective has been to maximize Jewish control over land in Israel (see also Kimmerling 1983; Carmon et al. 1991: chapter 1). Accordingly, large tracts of agricultural land have been more valuable for the authorities than small, fragmented pieces of residential land. The fragmentation of residential land within the village has also had a particularly degrading human aspect: several families had to exchange land to gain control over residential lots previously belonging to a family member, often a father or an uncle! The exchange practice (which is common in most Muslim Arab villages in the Galilee) is likely to continue for some time because, as shown in figure 15.3, large tracts of village land are still owned by the ILA.

Jewish Settlement Programmes

The third main method of territorial control has been the establishment of Jewish settlements near Majd el Krum. Jewish settlement programmes have assumed different forms since Israel's independence, but have always pursued a goal of containing the spatial development of Arab villages in general, and Majd el Krum in particular (see Kipnis 1984, 1987). As mentioned, the town of Carmiel was built in the 1960s on agricultural land expropriated from several villages, including Majd el Krum (figure 15.1).

A more explicit control of village expansion and development was embodied in the settlement programmes of the late 1970s and early 1980s, when 60 small Jewish settlements (often called *mitzpim*) were built in strategic sites around the Galilee. These sites were selected so as to create wedges between clusters of Arab villages and physically observe Arab building and agricultural activity in the region (Carmon et al. 1991; Newman 1984). As figure 15.2 shows, four such settlements – Lavon, Tuval, Gillon and Tzurit – were built so as to encircle and contain Majd el Krum. The first two settlements are also topographically placed immediately above the village. Despite the fact that later studies revealed that some 92 per cent of Jewish settlers in the Galilee moved to the new settlements for reasons other than assisting the control of state land, and that Arabs in the Galilee have had only a negligible rate of illegal use of state land (Carmon et al. 1991), the Jewish presence in small settlements around the village has had a marked psychological effect through the continuous observation and surveillance of everyday Arab life.

Administrative Boundaries

Another powerful means of territorial control has been the manipulation of administrative boundaries. As can be noted from figure 15.4, village residents have had to deal with a maze of boundaries, which have kept changing according to incremental decision-making by a range of Israeli authorities. This may sound like a normal case of adminis-

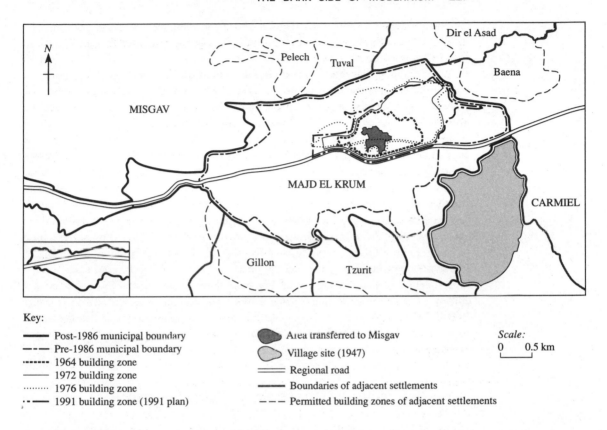

Key:

——— Post-1986 municipal boundary
– – – Pre-1986 municipal boundary
▪▪▪▪▪▪▪ 1964 building zone
——— 1972 building zone
·········· 1976 building zone
·–·– 1991 building zone (1991 plan)

⬤ Area transferred to Misgav
⬭ Village site (1947)
═══ Regional road
——— Boundaries of adjacent settlements
– – – Permitted building zones of adjacent settlements

Scale:
0   0.5 km

trative inefficiency, but in the case at hand it has been repeatedly used by the authorities as an additional avenue to impose bureaucratic control over the village residents. Here, two types of boundary stand out as effective tools of minority control: the extent of the village's permitted building zone and the municipal boundary of adjacent Jewish settlements.

The village's permitted building zone is demarcated by what is often known as 'the blue line', beyond which housing construction is illegal, and no state infrastructure is provided. In 1964 the Northern District Planning committee approved what was then thought to be a 'temporary blue line', to be in force until a statutory outline plan was prepared. However, it took much longer than expected for the village outline plan to be initiated by the government-appointed local planning committee. Due to the fast rate of natural increase of the village population (3.5–4 per cent per annum) and unacceptable levels of household densities (at times reaching 20–5 people per dwelling), pressures were mounting to allow the construction of new dwellings beyond the temporary building line. With official approval processes suffering lengthy bureaucratic delays, some families decided to build new dwellings (usually on their own land) outside the permitted zone,

Figure 15.4 Majd el Krum: administrative boundaries and outline plans. The insert shows the area immediately to the west Source: Majd el Krum Council and the Ministry of the Interior

thereby creating a sizeable problem of 'illegal' housing in the village. Usually, the authorities would eventually expand the village's building zone several years *after* illegal construction had begun.

This cycle of events repeated itself several times in Majd el Krum, with extensions of the permitted building zone in 1972, 1976, 1986 and 1991, meaning that at any particular point in time there were many houses classified as 'illegal'. The village's outline plan was finally gazetted in 1991 (27 years after the statutory planning process had begun) but, needless to say, is now seriously outdated. What is important for the present discussion is the use of this cyclical sequence of events for control purposes by the authorities: quite often, demolition orders would be issued for unauthorized dwellings, fines for 'illegal construction' imposed, and in some (rare) cases the houses demolished. Coupled with the associated hardship of living without basic infrastructure (which would not be provided by the state without a building permit), the constant existence of unauthorized dwellings in the village has allowed the district (mainly Jewish) planning authorities to exert a continuous level of control over the village's residents. Although the authorities have only rarely used the option of demolition, it can be seen that the very basic function of constructing family homes on private land had become a risky and uncertain venture for many of the village residents (see also Khameissi 1990; Yiftachel 1991b). In general, then, territorial policies have worked persistently to *contain* the spatial expansion of the village, to impose *surveillance* over the life of its residents and to *segregate* Arabs from Jews in the Galilee region.

PROCEDURAL CONTROL: EXCLUSION AND MARGINALIZATION

The procedural dimension of planning policies has influenced the residents of Majd el Krum through the level of their participation in the planning process, and their treatment by the authorities on procedural planning matters. Majd el Krum lies within the boundaries of the Galil Merkazi Local Planning Committee, which decides on most local planning matters, such as application for concessions, building permits, land-use change and the like. Until 1991, this committee included 23 Arab villages and six Jewish settlements in the Galilee. In 1988 the committee was responsible for the planning matters of some 133,000 people, making it the largest non-urban local planning committee in Israel. In comparison, other local committees in the Galilee, such as Misgav and Mate Asher, are responsible for only 5,000 or 7,500 people, respectively. Needless to say, the accessibility to residents from Majd el Krum of services offered by the committee has been difficult, and their potential influence on its decisions negligible (Interviews 1988–92).

The issue of a smaller and more accessible local planning committee has been a subject of continued struggle by leaders of Arab villages in the Galilee, including Majd el Krum. The five large villages in Bet Hakerem valley – Rame, Nahef, Dir el Asad, Baena and Majd el Krum (figure 15.2) – have been most active in this campaign and were led by the Majd el Krum mayor. In a letter to the Minister of the Interior, dated 4 January 1979, the mayors of the five councils state:

We wish to raise the problem of planning in the Arab sector in general and in our region in particular. . . . As the population of our five villages totals 23,000 people, a Local Committee is appropriate and will streamline the process of applying for building permits by our residents, which is currently lengthy and frustrating. It will also enable the five councils to better control development in our villages. Despite being turned down in previous meetings and correspondence we have great hope that your honour will agree to the establishment of a local planning and building committee in our region.

This request was referred to the Northern District Committee, which decided in its April 1980 meeting to refuse it because 'it was unrealistic.' The issue, which aggrieved many other Galilee villages in a similar situation to Majd el Krum, continued to appear in Arab publications and press releases throughout the 1980s and early 1990s. The issue was prominently included in the official manifesto of the Arab National Committee (which amounts to a long-term political agenda of Israeli Arabs) adopted in 1987, which called for the creation of Arab-managed local building committees for groups of villages totalling 10,000 people or more.

Finally, in 1991, the authorities responded to the problem by creating a new local planning committee in the northern portion of the Galil Merkazi area. However, the new Mevo'ot Naftali Committee includes only six Druze and two Jewish settlements, leaving Galil Merkazi as a large and cumbersome committee, still responsible for 15 large urbanizing (and predominantly Muslim) Arab villages, and a total population of 118,000 people. Interviews revealed that the improvement in the operation of this over-loaded committee has been minimal, if there has been any. Majd el Krum actually benefited from the changes more than other villages, with its mayor appointed as a member of the revamped Galil Merkazi Committee. However, the position is a rotating one, and the long-term problem of *exclusion* of the villagers from planning decision making is likely to remain in place. This is particularly significant because the local planning committee is the very planning authority which is supposed to be most accessible to local residents.

Another important procedural issue is the process of plan initiation and the on-going relations between planner and community. As mentioned, Israel's Planning and Building Law (1965) charges local planning comittees with the initiation of outline plans. This does not preclude the possibility of local communities and councils initiating plans, but the lack of professional expertise in most Arab villages during the 1960s and 1970s meant that in 79 per cent of cases, plans were not initiated by Arab local authorities (Khameissi 1990). In most cases they were initiated by the relevant local planning committees, which have been perceived by villagers as totally *dependent* on Israel's central government. Plan initiation by the government-appointed committees meant that village planners were also appointed by these committees. The capacity both to initiate the preparation of plans and to oversee the appointment of village planners gave the authorities a powerful tool for controlling the content of plans and the pace of their progress. This has not diminished over the years, because even though Arabs have awakened to the problems of the committee-controlled process, the slow pace of plan approvals in Israel stopped them from initiating new village plans, due to the fear of further delays to their gazettal, which is a prerequisite for receiving basic services.

This was the case in Majd el Krum. The local council entered into a contract with the Galil Merkazi Local Planning Committee and a Haifa-based (Jewish) planner in November 1978, to prepare an outline plan for the village within a year. The plan approval process suffered a lengthy series of delays, which occurred partially due to 'objective' planning problems, such as illegal construction, or problems associated with the widening of narrow roads in dense neighbourhoods, and difficulties in complying with district planning standards.

A critical contribution to these delays, however, was made by the alienation between the planner and the community. In 1985 and 1986, for example, seven letters were received by the appropriate planning authorities from the mayor of Majd el Krum, accusing the planner of a lack of ethics and professional incompetence, and blaming him for the distortion of facts and dates. Some of these letters were answered by the planner who, in turn, accused the council of lack of control over its 'law breaking residents' and the distortion of facts. In January 1988 the Majd el Krum Council resolved to ask the Galil Merkazi Local Committee to replace the appointed planner with another, a request later refused by the committee's chairman. After 1988, however, all work on the plan was carried out by the local council itself (or by professionals it hired on an ad-hoc basis) in clear defiance of the local committee's decision.

The conflict between the planner and the village is not in itself of particular interest, but the consequences of this lengthy stalemate are. They included: (1) a steady increase in illegal dwelling construction in the village (due to the lack of an approved plan); and (2) a bizarre situation where a planner who in principle should have helped the community was perceived by villagers as working against their interests and needs (Interviews 1988–92). To illustrate, a letter by the village mayor to the Israeli Ministry of the Interior dated 18 January 1988 states: 'I wish to stress that the planning of our village (by the appointed planner) as expressed in the outline plan is done in a shoddy manner . . . the appointed planner acts on his own accord without considering the needs of the village and its people.'

Most significantly for this discussion, the lengthy approval process caused by the alienation between the local authority and the planner has given the authorities an effective tool of control: in the absence of an approved plan, every single application needs to be processed by both (government-appointed) local and district committees, thereby *marginalizing* the legitimate wishes of the local community. Overall, procedural policies and practices have been used by Israel's planning authorities as a method of effective control over the Arabs by *excluding* the villagers from planning decision making, and by *marginalizing* their needs and aspirations.

SOCIOECONOMIC CONTROL: DEPRIVATION AND DEPENDENCE

In general, little attention has been paid by Israel's planning authorities to economic and social policies in Majd el Krum. The most discernible social and economic impact on the residents of Majd el Krum has been indirect, as a result of policies which targeted other areas, or as a consequence of neglect and inaction. In economic terms, the residents of Majd el Krum have benefited quite substantially from the establishment of Carmiel – a Jewish city of some 28,000 residents, four kilometres east of the village (figure 15.1). The main benefit has been the availability of employment. A survey conducted in 1989 among all industries in the Carmiel industrial area revealed that 211 employees were from Majd el Krum, constituting 12 per cent of the village workforce (Yiftachel 1991a). More employment is found by villagers in Carmiel in most menial service areas (such as cleaning and car servicing), retail, food outlets and some low-skilled white-collar jobs. It has been estimated by council officials that some 25 per cent of the village's workforce is employed in Carmiel.

Another indirect influence on the economy of the village has been the large-scale building activity in the Galilee during the last 15 years. A quarter of the village's workforce is employed in the building industry, with considerable work obtained in building projects tied to Jewish settlement in the Galilee. Yet the indirect benefit of available employment in Jewish enterprises has come at a considerable cost: the village economy has been stagnant since 1948. It was estimated by council officers that in mid-1992, 90 per cent of the workforce was employed outside the village. This has occurred because government policies have indirectly worked to retard the local economy, because the previously agrarian village economy lacked an industrial foundation, and because Arab entrepreneurship has been very limited (Czamanski and Taylor 1986). In short, the village economy became nearly totally *dependent* on external (mainly Jewish) sources.

In particular, two key policies have impeded economic development in the village: (1) the seizure of most agricultural land, as referred to earlier, drastically reduced local agricultural employment; this has been augmented by severe restriction on the supply of water for irrigation (Falah 1990); (2) unlike the case of the heavily supported Jewish settlements and enterprises in the Galilee, there has been a total lack of incentives for local economic development in Arab villages in general, and Majd el Krum in particular; this has occurred despite the surrounding region being declared as a priority development zone by Israel's Ministry of Industry. The above policies have worked to reinforce the *deprivation* of Arabs in the region, especially when compared to its Jewish inhabitants (see Haidar 1990; Semyonov and Levi Epstein 1987).

The local council, like most Arab municipalities, has suffered continuous financial problems, which seriously hampered its ability to supply the village community with the basic services it is responsible for: education, internal roads, public health facilities, recreation and local planning. These services tend to be of low standards in the village, especially when compared to the modern and well-serviced Jewish settlements in the vicinity. Two main factors underpin the funding and servicing problem of the local authority: (1) a chronic shortage of government financial assistance, which amounts to only a third of the funding given to Jewish local authorities (on a per capita basis – see al Haj and Rosenfeld 1990); (2) internal social tensions and problems associated with tax levy within the village, which restrict the revenue-raising powers of the local authority through local taxes and charges (for more details, see: al Haj and Rosenfeld 1990; Haidar 1991). (Significantly, Majd el Krum's servicing problems are not related to council inefficiencies and improper conduct, which have plagued many other Arab local authorities. In 1991, the local council received 'the efficiency prize' from Israel's Ministry of the Interior.)

In general, however, government policies (together with a range of local factors) have led the village to become largely *dependent* on the Jewish sector for its economic and social needs. In economic terms, Majd el Krum has been turned into a large (and cheap) labour pool for Jewish entrepreneurs and government agencies. In social terms, the local community has been *deprived* of the level of services and facilities widely available to their Jewish neighbours. The result has been the addition of a distinct class dimension to the territorial and procedural tensions highlighted earlier in the essay.

THE CONSEQUENCES OF PLANNING CONTROL: POPULAR RESISTANCE

Having demonstrated the pervasive and systematic use of planning as a powerful method of control over an ethnic minority, it is important to examine the consequence of these policies on the politics of majority–minority relations. This is especially important in democratic regimes, such as Israel, where minorities enjoy a range of political and individual rights which enable them to react against unfavourable policies with relatively few legal constraints. Most theories of ethnic relations predict rising levels of resistance and social and political conflict in the case of persisting majority–minority disparities (see, for example: Gurr 1993; Gurr and Lichbach 1986; Lane and Ersson 1990). Poststructuralist theorists postulate that, increasingly, 'modernist'-rational social control methods 'from above' are likely to be met by resistance 'from below' (Foucault 1980). This process is intimately tied up with the restructuring of the world economy and intergroup politics during the last three decades (Friedmann 1987; Berry and Huxley 1992; Yiftachel and Alexander 1993).

Protest Activity

While several ways of resistance have been evident in the village of Majd el Krum (including electoral behaviour and expressions of regime illegitimacy), I will concentrate on the most pervasive and persistent form of resistance: popular protest against the Israeli government and its policies. In this analysis protest events were divided into three categories, according to the main issue around which action was organized: (1) against planning policies, (2) against other public policies, and (3) on National-Palestinian matters. Planning policies were defined as the combination of policies issued and implemented by the Israeli planning system, as described earlier.

Figure 15.5 displays the main temporal trends in anti-governmental protest and violence in Majd el Krum since 1975 (the date from which data were available). The analysis includes protest events which occurred entirely within the confines of the village, and regional and national events in which local residents have taken an active part. The graph shows that a general increase has occurred in protest activity by residents of

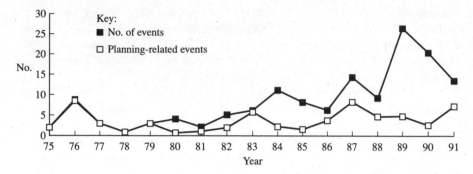

Figure 15.5 Trends in protest activity by Majd el Krum residents, 1975–91

Majd el Krum during the study period, indicating a growing level of resistance to Israel's control policies. Figure 15.5 shows that peaks in protest activity were recorded in four key periods: 1976–7, 1984, 1987 and 1989. These periods correspond with changes in Israeli policies in the region or the village, which usually entailed the introduction of new policies. The main policy events during these periods were as follows:

1 In 1976, large tracts of village land were expropriated for the expansion of the nearby Jewish town of Carmiel, and in 1977 two unauthorized dwellings were demolished in the village.
2 In 1984, an organized Arab campaign took place to modify the boundaries of the newly created (Jewish) Misgav regional council, which incorporated vast areas of private Arab land.
3 In 1987, the Arabs in Israel intensified their campaign for civil equality, culminating in several general strikes and large demonstrations; in late 1987, the outbreak of the Intifada (uprising in the occupied territories) also caused several large-scale protest activities across the country and in Majd el Krum.
4 In 1989, two main events dominated: the continuing Intifada which received wide verbal and political (but generally not violent) support in the Galilee, and another crackdown on unauthorized dwellings by the government, under which 15 houses were demolished in one day in another Arab village.

Figure 15.5 also shows that the volume of protest against planning policies has remained relatively steady over the study period, with notable peaks during civic struggle against the government's main planning initiatives discussed earlier. In addition, since the mid-1980s, the campaign to close the gap between Arab and Jewish municipal budgets has played a major role in Arab protest activity, especially during periods of concerted efforts on the matter, such as 1984–5 and 1990–1. While reaction to Israeli policies has played a key role in generating Arab protest, other factors have contributed to its steady rise. These have included the general rise of protest activity in Israel as a whole (Lehman-Wiltzig 1990) and a growing level of politicization among Arabs in Israel (Smooha 1992).

Equally significant are the 'troughs' in figure 15.5, which represent the periods of relative calm. During the early 1980s, for example, the village enjoyed a period of some progress, with a new high school being built and no immediate threats apparent for dwellings built without licence. Most importantly, during the 1985–6 period, protest and violence declined, mainly because a more liberal Labour-led government took office for a short period. That government paid particular attention to the needs of the Arab sector in general, and Galilee villages in particular.

A notable government initiative during that period was the return of 'Area 9' for the exclusive use of Arab farmers. Area 9 is an Arab-owned agricultural area some five kilometres south-east of Majd el Krum, which for years was used by the Israeli army for military exercises. Its return to exclusive Arab use was interpreted as a goodwill gesture by the government, and had a significant calming influence on Arab–Jewish relations in the Galilee during that period. In addition, 1986 was the year when Arab local authorities in the Galilee reached a compromise with the government on the issue of municipal boundaries, thereby further contributing to the lull in anti-government protest and violence. Also better representation of village leadership in some regional authorities and committees since 1990, and the gazettal of the village outline plan in 1991, relaxed the level of protest intensity during 1990–1, against the context of continuing Israeli–Palestinian tension in the occupied territories (Interviews 1988–92).

A broad positive association can be discerned between Israel's policies in the region and the village (with a prominent role for planning policies) and changes in the nature of local resistance. Policies which emphasized control over the minority (such as land expropriation and house demolition) have triggered anti-governmental protest and violence, thereby increasing the long-term levels of Arab–Jewish conflict. Conversely, policies which advanced consultation and compromise affected a reduction in the level of anti-governmental protest.

Resistance and Policy Change

The steady campaign of resistance by the villagers against Israeli policies has not, by and large, caused major policy shifts or the initiation of new, more responsive government programmes. However, a gradual *decline in the level of control* over the village development and its people can be discerned in recent years, partially as a result of the growing local assertiveness. This change has been piecemeal and inconsistent, and is yet to be backed by comprehensive strategies. Nevertheless, it has appeared in several policy areas, as illustrated by the following examples:

1 *Territorial policies*. The large-scale land expropriation common in the 1950s, 1960s and 1970s has all but stopped; house demolitions have not occurred since 1979; and no new Jewish settlements have been established around the village since the early 1980s. Also, in 1986, as a response to well-organized Arab protest against the boundaries of the Misgav regional council mentioned above (figure 15.1), the authorities have enlarged the municipal boundaries of most Arab local authorities in the Galilee (including Majd el Krum) thereby increasing the extent of local territorial control.

2 *Procedural policies*. The voice of the local people is increasingly being taken into account, albeit mainly in an informal manner. Interviews with policy makers revealed

that the delays and exclusion used by the authorities to sidestep Arab input into the planning process are proving increasingly difficult. Local residents have become more familiar with Israel's planning system, with their legal rights, and with the intricacies of political lobbying and informal pressure on decision makers. Most recently, for example, in 1992 several villagers proposed a new southern route for the major Akko–Zefad road which bisects the village (figure 15.2). The proposed new southern route alleviated a demolition threat hanging over many dwellings situated within the statutory easement of that road. The proposal was adopted by the local council, which convinced the authorities to consider it seriously. This marks an initiative 'from below' which was virtually impossible in previous years.

3   *Socioeconomic policies.* The large gap between government funding of Arab and Jewish local authorities has been constantly declining (from a ratio of 1:12 in the 1950s to a ratio of 1:3 in the late 1980s: see al Haj and Rosenfeld 1990). Further progress has also been recently achieved in the implementation of plans to provide the village with a deep sewerage system, which is currently under construction. In early 1993, Arab settlements were included for the first time in the classification for priority settlements, with incentives for investors and residents. This has equalized their status with their neighbouring Jewish settlements, after decades of unequal treatment.

While these signs of policy change are undoubtedly linked to the Arab campaign of protest and resistance, other factors in this process should not be ignored. These include Israel's democratic structure which allows (and even facilitates) the expression of minority grievances; the state's welfare provision which enabled the Arabs to develop a respectable educational infrastructure and short-term pragmatic consideration by Israel's politicians, who often need Arab support in their respective levels of government. Finally, the 1992 election of the Labour government signalled a certain policy change, with the declaration of policy goals more responsive to Arab needs and aspirations than those of the previous Likud administration. Overall, grassroot resistance to control policies in Majd el Krum has had a notable mark on the gradual (partial) change in the direction of these policies.

CONCLUSIONS AND IMPLICATIONS

In this essay I have demonstrated in detail how planning policies, which were conceived by the early founders of planning as tools for *reform and modernization*, can be systematically used for the opposite purpose of *controlling* a minority population. The control of the Arabs in Majd el Krum was put into practice through the territorial, procedural and socioeconomic dimensions of planning policies. Planning policies were therefore an integral part of the repression of the Arabs, reinforcing patterns of spatial, procedural and socioeconomic inequalities and deprivation.

The analysis has also shown that there are limits to the control of minorities in a democratic system. In recent years, the residents of Majd el Krum, like other Palestinian-Arabs in Israel, have started to mount more assertive resistance to the policies described above. This has resulted in some (albeit minor) policy concessions, which started to challenge pre-existing patterns of Jewish domination and control. On the basis of the case studied here, it is clear that traditional centralist planning methods imposed 'from above' are likely to encounter increasing levels of resistance 'from below', thereby creating social conflicts and intergroup tension. As noted at the outset, much planning research has concentrated so far on studying how planning can (or cannot) contribute to a 'public good'. While this research agenda is commendable, it bears little relevance to the understanding of the regressive type of planning explored in this essay. Planning theorists need to devote their attention to the question of 'control', which is more prevalent than past research would let us believe (see also Huxley 1993).

This essay has made a tentative start in the task of studying the phenomenon of 'planning as control'. Much more theoretical, empirical and comparative research is needed to understand that phenomenon fully. The challenge is clear: we must broaden and deepen our understanding of the causes, consequences and use of (traditional, modernist) planning methods to control minority populations. Such understanding not only will help us to interpret social and spatial processes fully, but may also facilitate the transition towards more appropriate forms of shaping the built environment: from planning for control, containment, exclusion and deprivation, onto planning for emancipation, inclusion, empowerment and equity.

NOTES

1 Data for the study were collected from a variety of sources, most notably: the archives of the Majd el Krum local authority and the Northern District branch of Israel's Ministry of the Interior; an extensive search of local and national newspapers; interviews with local Arab leaders and decision makers in government and public authorities; aerial photographs; and field surveys. The main methods used for the study included analysis of: (1) the content and implementation of relevant policies; (2) public reactions to these policies, and (3) changes over time of these variables.

REFERENCES

Alterman, R. and Hill, M. 1986: 'Israel', in N.N. Patricios (ed.), *International Handbook on Land Use Planning*, London: Greenwood Press.

Badcock, B. 1984: *Unfairly Structured Cities*, London: Blackwell.

Benziman, U. and Mansur, A. 1992: *Sub-Tenants, Israeli Arabs: Their Status and Government Policies towards Them*, Jerusalem: Keter (Hebrew).

Berry, M. and Huxley, M. 1992: 'Big Build: Property Capital, the State and Urban Change in Australia', *International Journal of Urban and Regional Research*, 16, 1: 35–69.

Burgess, P. 1993: 'City Planning and the Planning of Cities: The Recent Historiography', *Journal of Planning Literature*, 7, 4: 314–27.

Carmon, N. (ed.) 1990: *Neighbourhood Policy and Programmes: Past and Present*, London: Macmillan.

Carmon, N., Czamanski, D., Amir, S., Law Yone, H., Kipnis, B. and Lipshitz, G. 1991: *The*

New Jewish Settlement in the Galilee: An Evaluation, Technion, Haifa: Center for Urban and Regional Research (Hebrew).

CBS (Central Bureau of Statistics), 1972–92: *Statistical Publications and Yearbooks on Israel,* Jerusalem: CBS.

Cherry, G. 1988: *Cities and Plans,* Oxford: Blackwell.

Chisholm, M. and Smith, D. (eds) 1990: *Shared Space, Divided Space: Essays in Conflict and Territorial Organisation,* Boston: Unwin Hyman.

Connor, W. 1987: 'Ethnonationalism', in E. Weiner and S. Huntington (eds), *Understanding Political Development,* Boston: Little, Brown.

Czamanski, D. and Taylor, P. 1986: 'Arab Entrepreneurship in the Galilee', *Ofakim Begeographia,* 17–18: 123–144 (Hebrew).

Dear, M. 1986: 'Planning and Postmodernism', *Environment and Planning D: Society and Space,* 4: 367–84.

Dear, M. and Scott, A. 1981: 'Introduction', in M. Dear and A. Scott (eds), *Urbanisation and Urban Planning under Capitalism,* New York: John Wiley.

Demaine, H. 1984: 'Furnivall Reconsidered: Plural Societies in South-East Asia in the Post-Colonial Era', in C. Clarke, D. Ley and C. Peach (eds), *Geography and Ethnic Pluralism,* Boston: George Allen & Unwin.

Esman, M. 1985: 'Two Dimensions of Ethnic Politics: Defence of Homeland and Immigrant Rights', *Ethnic and Racial Studies,* 8: 438–41.

Eyles, J. 1990: 'Group Identity and Urban Space: The North American Experience', in M. Chisholm and D. Smith (eds), *Shared Space, Divided Space,* London: Unwin Hyman.

Falah, G. 1989: 'Israeli Judaisation Policy in Galilee and its Impact on Local Arab Urbanisation', *Political Geography Quarterly,* 8: 229–53.

Falah, G. 1990: 'Arabs Vs Jews in the Galilee: Competition over Resources', *Geojournal,* 21: 325–36.

Faludi, A. 1992: 'Dutch Growth Management: The Two Faces of Success', *Landscape and Urban Planning,* 22: 93–106.

Fincher, R. 1990: 'Women in the City', *Australian Geographical Studies,* 28: 29–37.

Forester, J. 1989: *Planning in the Face of Power,* Berkeley: University of California Press.

Forester, J. and Krumbholtz, N. 1990: *Making Equity Planning Work,* Philadelphia: Temple University Press.

Foucault, M. 1980: *Power/Knowledge,* New York: Pantheon.

Friedmann, J. 1987: *Planning in the Public Domain: From Knowledge to Action,* Princeton, NJ: Princeton University Press.

Friedmann, J. 1992: *Empowerment: The Politics of Alternative Development,* Oxford: Blackwell.

Gertel, S. and Law Yone, H. 1991: 'Participation Ideologies in Israeli Planning', *Environment and Planning C: Government and Policy,* 9: 173–88.

Gibson, K. and Watson, S. (eds) 1994: *Metropolis Now,* Pluto Press: Sydney.

G'naem, A. 1992: 'The Perceptions of the Muslim Movement in Israel on Regional Peace', in I. Pepe (ed.), *Islam and Peace,* Givaat Haviva: Institute of Arab Studies (Hebrew).

Gurr, T. 1993: *Minorities at Risk: A Global View of Ethnopolitical Conflict,* Arlington, VA: US Institute of Peace Press.

Gurr, T. and Lichbach, M. 1986: 'Forecasting Internal Conflict', *Comparative Political Studies,* 9: 3–38.

Haidar, A. 1990: *Arabs in the Israeli Economy*, Tel Aviv: International Centre for Peace in the Middle East (Hebrew).

Haidar, A. 1991: *Social Welfare Services for Israel's Arab Populations*, Boulder: Westview Press.

al Haj, M. 1988: 'The Socio-Political Structure of Arabs in Israel: External and Internal Orientations', in J. Hofman (ed.), *Arab–Jewish Relations in Israel – a Quest in Human Understanding*, Bristol, IN: Wyndham Hall Press.

al Haj, M. and Rosenfeld, H. 1990: *Arab Local Government in Israel*, Boulder, Tel Aviv: Westview Press.

Hall, P. 1988: *Cities of Tomorrow*, New York: Blackwell.

Harvey, D. 1973: *Social Justice and the City*, London: Edward Arnold.

Harvey, D. 1992: 'Social Justice, Postmodernism and the City', *International Journal of Urban and Regional Research*, 16: 588–601.

Healey, P. 1992: 'The Reorganisations of State and Markets in Planning', *Urban Studies*, 29: 411–34.

Hilali, A. 1983: 'Land Rights: An Historical and General Background to the Development of Land Ownership in Israel', in A. Shmueli, N. Kliot and A. Soffer (eds), *The Lands of Galilee, Vol. 2*, Haifa: Haifa University and the Ministry of Defence (Hebrew).

Hillier, J. 1993: 'To Boldly Go Where No Planner . . .', *Environment and Planning D: Society and Space*, 10: 377–92.

Huxley, M. 1993: 'Panoptica: Utilitarianism and Land Use Control', *Proceedings of the Conference on Postmodern Cities*, University of Sydney.

Huxley, M. 1994: 'Panoptica: Utilitarianism and Land Use Control', in K. Gibson and S. Watson (eds), *Metropolis Now*, Pluto Press: Sydney.

Interviews, 1988–92: In-depth interviews were conducted by Oren Yiftachel with 53 Arab leaders and 48 Israeli decision-makers in the Galilee.

Jackson, P. 1986: 'Social Geography: Race and Racism', *Progress in Human Geography*, 10: 99–110.

Jackson, P. (ed.) 1987: *Race and Racism*, London: Allen and Unwin.

Khameissi, R. 1990: *Planning and Housing among Arabs in Israel*, Tel Aviv: International Centre for Peace in the Middle East (Hebrew).

Kimmerling, B. 1983: *Zionism and Territory*, Berkeley: Institute of International Studies, University of California.

Kipnis, B. 1984: 'Minority Perceptions of Housing Needs and the Planning of a Housing Aid Policy: The Urbanising Arab Village in Israel', *Applied Geography*, 4: 145–9.

Kipnis, B. 1987: 'Geopolitical Ideologies and Regional Strategies in Israel', *Tijdchrift voor Economische en Sociale Geografie*, 78: 125–38.

Lane, J. and Ersson, S. 1990: *Politics and Society in Western Europe*, London: Sage.

Law Yone, H. and Vilknaski, R. 1984: 'From Consensus to Fragmentation: The Dynamics of Paradigm Change in Israel', *Socioeconomic Planning Sciences*, 18: 367–72.

Lehman-Wiltzig, S. 1990: *Stiff-Necked People in a Bottled-Necked System: The Evolution and Roots of Israeli Public Protest, 1949–86*, Bloomington: University of Indiana Press.

Lijphart, A. 1977: *Democracy in Plural Societies: A Comparative Exploration*, New Haven: Yale University Press.

Lijphart, A. 1984: *Democracies*, New Haven: Yale University Press.

Lindblom, C. 1977: *Politics and Markets*, New York: Basic Books.

Little, J. (in press): *Gender, Planning and the Policy Process*, Oxford: Pergamon.

Lustick, I. 1980: *Arabs in the Jewish States: Israel's Control over a National Minority*, Austin: University of Texas Press.

McLoughlin, B. 1992: *Shaping Melbourne's Future?*, Sydney: Cambridge University Press.

Meyer-Brodnitz, M. 1986: 'The Suburbanisation of Arab Settlements in Israel', *Ofakim Begeographia*, 17–18: 105–23 (Hebrew).

Mikessel, M. and Murphy, A. 1991: 'A Framework for Comparative Study of Minority-group Aspirations', *Annals of the Association of American Geographers*, 81: 581–604.

Newman, D. 1984: 'Ideological and Political Influences on Israeli Rurban Colonisation: The West Bank and Galilee Mountains', *Canadian Geographer*, 28: 142–55.

Pearce, B. 1992: 'The Effectiveness of the British Land Use Planning System', *Town Planning Review*, 63: 13–28.

Rumley, D. 1991: 'The Political Organisation of Space: A Reformist Conception', *Australian Geographical Studies*, 26: 329–36.

Sandercock, L. 1990: *Property, Politics and Urban Planning: A History of Australian Planning 1890–1990*, New Brunswick: Transactions.

Sandercock, L. and Forsythe, A. 1992: 'Gender: A New Agenda for Planning Theory', *Journal of the American Planning Association*, 58: 49–60.

Schaffer, D. (ed.) 1988: *Two Centuries of American Planning*, London: Mansell.

Semyonov, S. and Levin Epstein, N. 1987: *Hewers of Wood and Drawers of Water*, Ithaca, NY: CLR Press.

Smith, A. 1981: *The Ethnic Revival*, Cambridge: Cambridge University Press.

Smith, S. 1987: 'Residential Segregation: A Geography of English Racism?', in P. Jackson (ed.), *Race and Racism*, London: Allen and Unwin.

Smith, S. 1989: 'The Politics of Race and a New Segregationism', in J. Mohan (ed.), *The Political Geography of Contemporary Britain*, London: Macmillan.

Smooha, S. 1990: 'Minority Status in an Ethnic Democracy: The Arab Minority in Israel', *Ethnic and Racial Studies*, 13: 389–412.

Smooha, S. 1992: *Arabs and Jews in Israel: Continuity and Change in Mutual Tolerance, Vol. 2*, Boulder: Westview Press.

Thomas, J. 1988: 'Racial Crisis and the Fall of the Detroit City Plan Commission', *Journal of the American Planning Association*, 48: 150–61.

Thomas, H. and Krishnarayan, V. 1993: 'Race Equality and Planning', *The Planner*, 79: 17–21.

Williams, C.H. 1985: 'Minority Groups in the Modern State', in M. Pacione (ed.), *Progress in Political Geography*, London: Croom Helm.

Yiftachel, O. 1989: 'Towards a New Typology of Urban Planning Theories', *Environment and Planning B: Planning and Design*, 16: 23–39.

Yiftachel, O. 1991a: 'Industrial Development and Arab–Jewish Economic Gaps in the Galilee', *Professional Geographer*, 41: 161–77.

Yiftachel, O. 1991b: 'State Policies, Land Control and an Ethnic Minority: The Arabs in the Galilee, Israel', *Environment and Planning D: Society and Space*, 9: 329–52.

Yiftachel, O. 1992a: *Planning a Mixed Region in Israel: The Political Geography of Arab–Jewish Relations in the Galilee*, Aldershot: Avebury.

Yiftachel, O. 1992b: 'The State, Ethnic Relations and Democratic Stability: Lebanon, Cyprus and Israel', *Geojournal*, 21: 212–25.

Yiftachel, O. 1993: 'Planning as Control: Policy and Reaction in an Urbanising Arab Village in Israel', paper to the Postmodern Cities Conference, University of Sydney.

Yiftachel, O. and Alexander, I. 1993: 'Metropolitan Planning: Death or Restructuring?', paper to the Annual Conference of the Institute of Australian Geographers, Melbourne, September.

Zureik, E. 1993: 'Prospects for the Palestinians in Israel', *Journal of Palestine Studies*, 22 (Spring): 91–104.

16. Not Chaos, but Walls: Postmodernism and the Partitioned City

Peter Marcuse

A curious inversion has taken place in urban theory today. If the history of modern cities has been an attempt to impose order on the apparent chaos that is the individual experience of the impact of capitalism on urban form, an attempt Marshall Berman (1982) considers to be a defining characteristic of modernism,[1] then what is happening today may be considered the attempt to impose chaos on order, an attempt to cover with a cloak of visible (and visual) anarchy an increasingly pervasive and obtrusive order – to be more specific, to cover an increasingly pervasive pattern of hierarchical relationships among people and orderings of city space reflecting and reinforcing that hierarchical pattern with a cloak of calculated randomness. The inversion has a clearly conservative tendency embedded in it, for it can be used to tar with the brush of 'grand theory' and the 'ideology of progress' the argument that cities can be made better, more human places in which to live, with the tools of purposive action and public planning.[2]

The inversion is a reflection of practice, and supports practice. A perfect example is New York City's new interim plan for the 'rehabilitation' of Times Square,[3] which attempts 'to produce a street that looks unplanned,' with the help of a large and sophisticated team of planners and architects. Comments the *New York Times* architecture critic: 'the plan could easily pass for an apocalyptic preview of what things would look like if all public spaces succumbed to privatization.'[4] Such efforts can readily be interpreted as an attempt to use postmodern devices to defeat the 'project of modernism,' reflecting both an immediate effort to defend by concealing a prevailing order and a deeper fear about the inherent instability of that order. An immediate concern to solidify chaos by renaming it an orderless order, so it can be properly amortized, combines with a deeper and pathetic hope that what is today 'solid' will indeed not 'melt into air' for fear that nothing equally valorized will replace it. It is thus a reactionary practice, in the pejorative sense of that term, using the private market's goals to establish public objectives, hoping to use public instrumentalities for the apotheosis of private gain. And the language used to justify it speaks of the desirability of the unplanned, the spontaneous, the unordered.

But neither cities nor places in them are unordered, unplanned; the question is only whose order, whose planning, for what purpose, in whose interest. Those questions are not easy to answer. But that does not mean they have no answers. The market has an order as much as the state, social relations constitute an order as do economic ones. Different orders often conflict, contradict each other, change their patterns, break their molds, and the criticisms of over-simplifying theory and portrayals of a single logical order to the space of cities are well justified. Nevertheless, the effort to understand, and to influence, not just to describe, the patterns of space in cities remains a prime task of urban theory.

Cities are of course made up of parts, and those parts are of course connected to each other. Some divisions into parts are functional; the parts of a city used for transportation, for streets, cannot at the same time be used for residences, for buildings; the parts devoted to noisy or noxious manufacturing do not lend themselves to raising families. But other partitions of the city reflect (and reinforce) only the social relations which the functioning of the city produces; the separation of suburban-type housing tracts by quality, price and income is not a functional but a social separation that reflects a hierarchical consequence of a particular organization of functions. Still other partitions reflect some mix of both: Certain office uses may cluster together to achieve economies of scale, to share facilities they and only they use; but their particular location in a city, and their exclusion of other non-competitive uses in their neighborhoods, may reflect social rather than directly efficient or narrowly economic (production and distribution of goods and services) considerations.

In this essay, I want to focus on social divisions, although I want to make some reference to the relations of those social divisions to the economic organization of the city. I want to use walls — boundaries, partitions, borders, transitions — as both an embodiment and a metaphor for the nature of these social divisions, walls as both a reflection and a reinforcement of divisions. The trend such an examination reveals is, I think, ominous: an increasing social division, along increasingly sharp but double-edged and hence ambiguous lines, often buried in apparently chaotic or 'natural' spaces, divisions hierarchical in nature and of growing severity in impact. Obviously the full argument cannot be spelled out here; I hope only to present a coherent skeleton of it. At the end, I will try to draw some policy conclusions from the analysis.

To summarize the city as it has been in part for some time, and is increasingly becoming entirely: It appears chaotic and is fragmented, but underneath the chaos there are orders; the fragmentation is not random. It is divided, but not dual, or limitlessly plural. Quartered,[5] or five-parted, better captures reality. Its quarters are both walled in and walled out, but walls do not play equal roles for all quarters. Each quarter is thus separated from all others, but each is nevertheless intimately related to all others; they are mutually dependent. While the quarters are hierarchical in the power and wealth of their residents, all are dependent on forces beyond their separate control. Only a restructuring of the underlying dynamics of urban life, a restructuring that needs be local, but also national, and indeed international, can change this increasingly undemocratic pattern of urban life.

The causes of these phenomena are complex, but not hard to summarize in general terms. The societies in which our cities exist are, and have been for centuries, hierarchical; the inequalities among their residents are reflected in the inequalities in the spaces they occupy. With the advent of capitalism and the industrial revolution, those inequalities were more and more concentrated in cities. The growth of industries shaped the physical landscape of cities, spawning workers' quarters near industrial zones, separated from where the wealthy lived and where commerce was conducted. Casual workers and the unemployed were relegated to run-down districts at the edge. Increasing commerce and the growing importance of finance produced growing business quarters, centrally located. These and related tendencies are too well known to need repeating.

Much of what has happened in cities in the last twenty years is simply an extension of these long-term trends – probably more than we, who like novelty and get paid to explore it, want to admit. The division of cities between rich and poor is certainly nothing new; Plato described it and took it as an inescapable part of urban life more then two millennia ago.[6] The rigidly hierarchical spatial relationship between church, lord, city, and country in medieval times reflected social divisions sharply. But the divisions were different from those today; today's essentially developed with the rise of industrial capitalism in the eighteenth century, and were quite visible in the nineteenth. Engels's description of Manchester is, with the exception only of the development of major service sectors and their physical reflection in high-rise construction, remarkably applicable today.[7] The basic relationships of class, race and gender were certainly visible then.

But much is new. The development of the service sector and the technological advances that made skyscrapers, mass transit, and their corresponding city-shaping influences possible, date back to just before the turn of the century. In the period sometimes characterized as the postmodern, in any event the years commencing around 1970, other characteristics are new. Briefly,[8] they include displacement as the mechanism of spatial change; the intensity of turf allegiances and turf battles; the nature and extent of homelessness; the openness with which government supports the maximization of private business claims on city land and city infrastructure; and the political reorientations that have accompanied these changes. The context in which these new local and national trends take place is also quantitatively new: the internationalization of economic activity, and the decreasing possibilities of public control over them at national or local levels, paralleling the loss of meaning of local and even national considerations for business decisions.

As a result of the trends described above, we can find, at least in the typical large city of the technologically developed cities of today, a new pattern: five distinctive types of residential quarter. While each type is represented in multiple neighborhoods, giving a fragmented, mosaic-like appearance, those neighborhoods fall into an ordered pattern, which form separate but interdependent cities within the residential city:[9]

- a dominating city, with its luxury housing, not really part of the city but enclaves or isolated buildings, occupied by the top of the economic, social, and political hierarchy;
- a gentrified city, occupied by the professional-managerial-technical groups, whether yuppie or muppie without children;
- a suburban city, sometimes single-family housing in the outer city, other times apartments near the center, occupied by skilled workers, mid-range professionals, upper civil servants;
- a tenement city, sometimes cheaper single-family areas, most often rentals, occupied by lower-paid workers, blue- and white-collar, and generally (although less in the United States) including substantial social housing;
- an abandoned city, the end result of trickle-down, left for the poor, the unemployed, the excluded, where in the United States homeless housing is most frequently located.

Where people live is not likely to be where they work, for most people. While residential divisions largely parallel occupational and social divisions (Marcuse 1989; Mollenkopf and Castells 1991), the economic city is not congruent with the residential city. The dividing lines in the spatial patterns of economic activity define areas in which people of many occupations, classes, and status work in close proximity. Yet, if we define economic divisions by the primary activity taking place within them, one may again get a four- or five-part division.

The *controlling city*, the city of big decisions, includes a network of high-rise offices, brownstones or older mansions in prestigious locations, and is less and less locationally circumscribed. It includes yachts for some, the back seats of stretch limousines for others, airplanes and scattered residences for still others. But it is not spatially rootless. The controlling city is not spatially bounded, although the places where its activities at various times take place are of course located somewhere, and more secured by walls, barriers, and conditions to entry than any other part of the city.

Yet the controlling city tends to be located in (at the top of, physically and symbolically) the high-rise centers of advanced services, because those at the top of the chain of command wish to have at least those below them close at hand and responsive, and so it goes down the line.[10] Those locations, wherever they may be, are crucially tied together by communication and transportation channels which permit an existence insulated from all other parts of the city, if dependent on them. In that sense a 'space of flows,' or a 'space of movement,' is an apt, if metaphoric, phrase.

The *city of advanced services*, of professional offices tightly clustered in downtowns, with many ancillary services internalized in high-rise office towers, is heavily enmeshed in a wide and technologically advanced communicative network. The skyscraper center is the stereotypical pattern, but not the only possibility. Locations at the edge of the center of the city, as in Frankfurt, outside it, as in Paris at La Défense or outside Rome or at the Docklands in London, or scattered around both inside and outside a city with good transportation and communications, as in Amsterdam. Social, 'image' factors will also play a role; the 'address' as well as the location is important for business. Whether in only one location or in several in a given city, however, there will be strong clustering, and the city of advanced services will be recognizable at a glance.

The *city of direct production* includes not only manufacturing but also the production aspect of advanced services, in Saskia Sassen's phrase (1989), government offices, the back offices of major firms, whether adjacent to their front offices or not, located in clusters and with significant agglomerations but in varied locations within a metropolitan area. Varied, indeed, but not arbitrary or chaotic: where customers/clients (itself an interesting dichotomy!) wish to be in quick and easy contact, inner city locations are preferred (as in the industrial valley between midtown Manhattan and the financial district for the printing industry, or Chinatown and the garment district for textile production, in New York City).

For mass production, locations will be different. Here the pattern has changed dramatically since the beginning of the industrial revolution. At first factories were near the center of the city; indeed, to a large extent they led to the growth of the city around them, as in the manufacturing cities of New England or the mid-west, or the industrial cities of England. But more modern manufacturing methods require more single-story space, vastly more, with parking for automotive access rather than paths for workers coming on foot, and many more operations are internalized; so land costs become more important than local agglomeration economies, and suburban or rural locations are preferred.

The *city of unskilled work and the informal economy*, small-scale manufacturing, warehousing, sweatshops, technically unskilled consumer services, immigrant industries, is closely intertwined with the cities of production and advanced services and thus located near them, but separately and in scattered clusters,[11] locations often determined in part by economic relations, in part by the patterns of the residential city. Because the nature of the labor supply determines the profitability of these activities, the residential location of workers willing to do low-paid and/or unskilled work has a major influence. Thus in New York City sweatshops locate in Chinatown or the Dominican areas of Washington Heights, in Miami in the Cuban enclave, or in the slums of cities throughout the world.

The *residual city* is the city of the less legal portions of the informal economy, the city of storage where otherwise undesired (NIMBY) facilities are located, the location of abandoned manufacturing buildings, generally also congruent with the abandoned residential city. But for political protest many of the most polluting and environmentally detrimental components of the urban infrastructure, necessary for its economic survival but not directly tied to any one economic activity, are located here: sewage disposal plants, incinerators, bus garages, AIDS residences, housing for the homeless, juvenile detention centers, jails. New York City's recently adopted Fair Share regulations are a reflection of both the extent of the problem and its political volatility.

As one progresses down the scale in the quarters both of the residential city and of the economic city, in the United States the proportion of black and Hispanic and immigrant households increases, and so does the proportion of women heading households. Race, class, and gender create overlapping patterns of differentiation – invidious differentiation, for there is no doubt that the differences are not simply of 'life-styles' or 'special needs,' but reflect positions in a hierarchy of power and wealth in which some decide and others are decided for.

Walls define the quarters of the city – define, not surround; since the ghettos of medieval Europe were built, it has been rare that physical walls in fact circumscribe a delimited and homogeneous quarter of the city. Yet the walls existing within each quarter define the nature of that quarter and the position of its residents within the hierarchy of quarters, the hierarchy of cities within the city. Sometimes the walls are symbolic boundaries, often they enclose similar individual units within one quarter and define its character.

One might define five types of wall, related to the five types of city within our contemporary partitioned cities:

1 prison walls, walls defining ghettos and places of confinement, walls built for the control and re-education of those forced to live behind them – the walls of the ancient ghettos, the social and economic walls surrounding the modern ghettos, the physical walls of Andrew Cuomo's transitional homeless housing in New York City; walls defining the Abandoned City;

2 barricades, walls for protection, cohesion and solidarity, sometimes defined, as for immigrant quarters, simply by the language of street signs and spoken words, sometimes by the color of the skins of the residents, sometimes by the age and limited pretensions of the housing, sometimes by the social symbolism of the sign that says 'public housing' or the architecture of unornamented blank walls that spells 'project;' walls defining the Tenement City;

3 stockades, walls of aggression, symbolically walls of pointed stakes such as used by army troops in the conquering of the American West from native Americans, walls similar in function to the Roman walls built around the settlements created by the Roman empire in the lands of the 'barbarians,' walls of superiority, both protecting pioneers and securing their invasion, the analogy suggested by Neil Smith (1992) as appropriate for the process creating the Gentrified City;

4 stucco walls, sheltering gated and exclusive communities, where walls exclude for reasons of (and often in reality by means of, since physically they can be breached) status and social control, protecting privilege and wealth from the threat of physical intrusion, but necessarily coupled with other forms of selection and control of those admitted, since their presence is in fact necessary, at least during the daytime, to do the dirty work of maintenance and repair necessary for the continued comfort and convenience of the Suburban City;

5 ramparts, castle walls, the fortifications surrounding the citadels[12] in their literal meaning: according to the Oxford English Dictionary, a 'little city... a fortress commanding a city, which it serves both to protect and to keep in subjection'. Walls of domination, expressing superiority, typically today physically represented by superior height in the skyscraper apartments and penthouses that have replaced the

mansions of the upper class in the city, protected by technologically developed walls, gates, and security devices; walls defining the Dominating City.

How are we to evaluate these very different types of wall? A variety of distinctions is possible, but certain differences are particularly relevant for policy purposes:

- What is the wall's purpose: protection or confinement, insulation or limitation? Walls can insulate: against weather, rain, cold, most obviously, but also against the intrusion of threatening strangers as well. They can, for the individual, provide privacy, for a group, identity, and a chance at cohesion and mutual reinforcement. But walls can also be made to limit others, behind prison bars, to segregated ghettos, to exposed hillsides and river valleys, in overcrowded tenements or squatter settlements.
- What is the form of the wall: tangible or intangible, physically effective or physically symbolic of social and economic barriers? Walls can be of concrete or barbed wire; but they can be of price and status, of rule and prejudice, as well – more effectively, perhaps, for intangible walls can be internalized, by force and custom, and their causes and functions hidden, the maintenance costs reduced, in the process.
- Whom does the wall serve? Does the wall perpetuate the power of the powerful, or does it defend the powerless; does it protect domination, or shield vulnerability? Which part of the quartered city does it surround, which part exclude; whom is it for, and whom against? Morally, in terms of human rights and urban life, perhaps the most important distinction of all. As Robert Frost asked decades ago in 'Mending Wall,' 'Before I built a wall I'd ask to know/What I was walling in or walling out . . .' It is the crucial question indeed; for the lower-class residents of the Lower East Side of Manhattan, of Kreuzberg in Berlin, of the area around the University of Southern California in Los Angeles wish to keep the gentrifiers out as much as the residents of the suburbs and luxury housing of Manhattan, Berlin, Los Angeles want to keep them out; yet the two desires are not equivalent morally. One represents the desire of those poorer to insulate themselves from losses to the more powerful; the other represents the force of the more powerful insulating themselves from the necessity of sharing with, or having exposure to, those poorer. One wall defends survival, the other protects privilege.

It is one of the contributions of the postmodernist critique that it undermines the conception that walls are rigid, that they each have one and only one clear purpose. Boundary lines are dynamic; at the extreme case, as perhaps in Los Angeles, they may move from block to block, street to street, as one group moves in and another moves on or out, and only social or ethnic characteristics may separate one ethnic quarter from the other. But if the Koreatowns and the Watts and the barrios of Los Angeles are taken as separated ethnically, but all components of a city ranging from abandoned to tenement, the boundaries are easier to see.

For all but the cases at the extreme ends of the spectrum, walls will be ambivalent. Barbed wire protects, but it imprisons; stockades protect the invader, but confine as well;

stucco walls and wrought iron fences provide a sense of identity, but may increase feelings of insecurity, reveal vulnerability, as well.

These ambivalences, ambiguities, are not accidental. Most people are neither at the top nor at the bottom of the hierarchy of power, but in between. They are in daily contact with some above them and some below them in the ladder of wealth and influence; they need both, and are needed by both. Thus people may at different times defend and attack, need protection and want to aggress, wish to exclude but wish not to be excluded. Those are the inevitable results of living in a society which is hierarchically ordered; one's position in the hierarchy needs to be continually established, reinforced, in all directions. Hence the creation of walls that reflect such hierarchical status.

One tendency within postmodernism, what I would call its critical tendency, highlights precisely these ambiguities, together with the walls that at the same time contradict and embody them. In its rejection of rigid grand theories, of the effort to impose rational patterns on all human activity, in its revelation of the complexities of urban life and the insufficiency of any attempt to find single solutions for multiple problems, in its attention to the many layers that constitute social and economic relationships, in its emphasis on the cultural components of the activities that go on in cities, in its reflections on the ambiguities of the concept of progress and its doubts as to any unilinear or inevitable progression, postmodernist theory has made significant contributions to dealing with the problems of partitioned cities and the walls within them.

But postmodernism also has another side; it is at least as ambiguous as its subject-matter. To quote Edward Soja in a summation of Los Angeles which I would like to give as a summation of the postmodern approach to urban analysis as a whole: he says, in a political vein which needs more emphasis than it has received:

> [In Los Angeles] there remains an economic order . . . an essentially exploitative spatial division of labour, . . . more continuously productive than almost any other in the world. But it has also been increasingly obscured from view, imaginatively mystified in an environment more specialized in the production of encompassing mystifications than practically any other you can name. . . . this conservative deconstruction is accompanied by a numbing depoliticization of fundamental class and gender relations and conflicts. When all that is seen is so fragmented and filled with whimsy and pastiches, the hard edges of the capitalist, racist and patriarchal landscape seem to disappear, melt into air. (Soja 1989: 246)

Those hard edges are, in fact, very solid, if also complex. They are increasingly represented by walls within the city, walls both physical and symbolic, two-sided, ambiguous but real. Whether created directly by public actions or by those market forces that dominate public actions, they can be addressed, reformed, even destroyed, by public action.

Planning can be part of that remedial public action. Like postmodernism, like modernism, planning is ambiguous, many-faceted, contradictory; critical postmodernism itself should tell us so. Planning has indeed contributed substantially to the erection of many of the hierarchical walls that need to come down, and has perhaps interfered substantially with the preservation of the defensive walls necessary for the protection of vulnerable groups, alternate cultures. It has done so as much by abdication as by action, allowing the market to build walls where they do not belong, permitting the processes of gentrification and abandonment, displacement and over-building, to run out of social control. The consequences of ill-planned, but planned, actions can be seen from Columbus circle in New York to the West Bank in Palestine, from Johannesburg to Chicago, from the San Fernando Valley to Berlin.

But planning can also, following the other strand of its tradition, be used to reduce inequalities, open gates, level walls, permit free and non-hierarchical relations among the residents of a city. The historic buildings of Paris, the transit connections of most German cities, Roosevelt Island in New York, Harbor Point in Boston are all examples. Particular forms of political action are necessary to have planning contribute to these positive results. But it can be done.

For hierarchy is not an inevitable part of social organization. We live in a society in which the prosperity of one is often based on the poverty of the other. That need not be so; we have today the resources, the skills, the room, to be able to combine justice with prosperity, mutual respect with efficient organization. Physical rearrangements, restructuring, can help achieve such a society; attacking walls of domination, walls of confinement, will help. But they need to be part of a broader effort to build a better society, physically, economically, socially, politically.

Till then, even the best of walls will provide only a temporary refuge, the worst of walls are likely to remain. Let me end by quoting Thomas Hobbes (1983: 154), in yet another use of the word 'quarter': 'that which men do, when they demand . . . quarter . . . taking alive, is to evade the present fury of the victor, by submission, and to compound for their life, with ransom, or service: and there he that hath quarter, hath not his life given, but deferred till farther deliberation; for it is not a yielding on condition of life, but to discretion.'

We need cities that will be conditions of life, of full and free and unfragmented lives, not cities of discretion and domination; we need walls that welcome and shelter, not walls that exclude and oppress.

NOTES

1 Both 'modern' and 'postmodern' are elusive terms; each has been used to encompass a tendency to chaos and fragmentation (see, for instance, Wilson 1991), but the attempt to impose order on the chaos is certainly a feature of modernism largely rejected by postmodernism.

2 I return to the point at the end of this essay.

3 The plan was only developed as a reaction to a downturn in the market which, presumably only temporarily, prevented a proposal for four block-buster office towers being erected at the location, but what is temporary may well turn out to be permanent, and the approach was already reflected in the guidelines for the office towers. For a discussion of the politics of the situation, see Fainstein 1993.

4 The *New York Times*, September 19, 1993: 33.
5 The term was introduced in Marcuse (1989). The term may not be logically perfect, but seems to me to be appropriately vivid.
6 Plato, *The Republic*, IV, 422B. I owe the reference to Mollenkopf and Castells (1991).
7 For a good discussion, and a comparison with other contemporaneous accounts of English industrial cities, see Marcus (1974).
8 For a fuller discussion, see Marcuse (1993: 355–65).
9 I have discussed the concept of the 'Quartered City' in several other pieces (1989, 1991). 'Quartered' is used both in the sense of 'drawn and quartered' and of residential 'quarters;' there are essentially four such quarters, the very wealthy not being bound by any specific spatial configuration as to where they live. See also Mollenkopf and Castells (1991), especially the introduction and conclusion, and Wallock (1987).
10 Our interviews with those responsible for planning the then new high-rise office tower for the Bank für Gemeinwirtschaft in Frankfurt revealed professionals who had concluded that a separation of functions, with top executives downtown but all others in back office locations, was the most efficient pattern for the bank, but were over-ruled by their superiors, with only the advantage cited above as their reasoning. By the same token, Citibank in New York City wants its next level of professionals directly accessible to its top decision-makers; credit card data entry operations may move to South Dakota, but not banking activities that require the exercise of discretion.
11 See, for instance, Sassen (1989) whose brief but provocative comments on the spatial aspects of the trends she describes deserve further development.
12 The term was first used in the juxtaposition suggested here by John Friedmann (Friedmann and Goetz 1982: 309–44).

REFERENCES

Berman, M. 1982: *All That is Solid Melts into Air: The Experience of Modernity*, New York: Simon and Schuster.
Fainstein, S. 1993: *The City Builders*, Oxford: Blackwell.
Friedmann, J. and Goetz, W. 1982: 'World City Formation: An Agenda for Research and Action', *International Journal of Urban and Regional Research*, 6: 309–44.
Hobbes, T. 1983: *Leviathan*, London: Fount.
Marcus, S. 1974: *Engels, Manchester and the Working Class*, New York: Random House.
Marcuse, P. 1989: ' "Dual City": A Muddy Metaphor for a Quartered City', *International Journal of Urban and Regional Research*, 13, 4: 697–708.
Marcuse, P. 1991: 'Housing Markets and Labour Markets in the Quartered City', in J. Allen and C. Hamnett (eds), *Housing and Labour Markets: Building the Connections*, London: Unwin Hyman.
Marcuse, P. 1993: 'What's New about Divided Cities', *International Journal of Urban and Regional Research*, 17, 3: 355–65.
Mollenkopf, J.H. and Castells, M. (eds) 1991: *Dual City: Restructuring New York*, New York: Russell Sage Foundation.
Sassen, S. 1989: 'New Trends in the Sociospatial Organization of the New York City Economy', in R.A. Beauregard (ed.), *Economic Restructuring and Political Response*, Newbury Park, CA: Sage.

Smith, N. 1992: 'New City, New Frontier: The Lower East Side as Wild Wild West', in M. Sorkin (ed.), *Variations on a Theme Park: The New American City and the End of Public Space*, New York: Farrar, Straus and Giroux.

Soja, E.W. 1989: *Postmodern Geographies: The Reassertion of Space in Critical Social Theory*, London: Verso.

Wallock, L. 1987: 'Tales of Two Cities: Gentrification and Displacement in Contemporary New York', in M.B. Campbell and M. Rollins (eds), *Begetting Images*, New York: Peter Lang.

Wilson, E. 1991: *The Sphinx in the City*, London: Virago.

17. Postmodern Politics and Planning: A Postscript

Sophie Watson and Katherine Gibson

It is on the political terrain that perhaps the greatest ire has been expressed by those who are concerned about where postmodern (and poststructural) theory is taking us. Images of the relativist abyss, where no stand is ever taken, are deployed to undermine many of the useful insights and formulations that postmodern theory has provided (Hartsock 1990; Harvey 1992). The death of the subject, particularly of specific subject positions such as women and blacks, is a frightening prospect for many. Increasingly debates are leading us back in a full circle. The earlier certainties are being reasserted. Just as postmodern analysis has tended to caricature and simplify 'modernist' or 'structural analysis' and failed to acknowledge the complexity within Marxist literature, so those reclaiming a modernist politics, ethics and set of values caricature postmodern politics as amoral, directionless, fragmented and ignorant of political economic and global forces and powers.

But need postmodernist politics always be represented as the lack of, the other to, the subordinate of, modernist politics? For some writers a postmodern politics is about choosing marginality as a 'site of resistance, as a location of radical openness and possibility' (hooks 1990: 149). Others also include a celebration of fragmentation, discontinuities and ruptures in so far as they can be 'transformed from liability and weakness to opportunity and strength' (Soja and Hooper 1993: 193). What interests us is how heroic visions of modernist politics, that is of mass mobilization and emancipation of the oppressed, have eclipsed our view of the many possibilities of a postmodern politics.

What is interesting about the collection of essays in this book is the way in which the usual polarization in postmoderism and politics has been sidestepped. All the authors seem to be explicitly interested, despite some misgivings, in what a postmodern politics *might be* and not what it *is not*. We trace this positive interest to a shared concern among contributors for creating some form of active statement in the world. All of the chapters are concerned in one way or another with imagining and constructing new spaces, buildings and cities, and ways of living. They are also concerned with identifying the limits placed upon our imaginaries and constructions by established ways of thinking.

The LA and Bombay riots represent one face of postmodern political action, one which many of the critics of postmodernism dwell upon. The violence and fragmentation of such riotous images are used to provide a salutory warning to those who might be enticed by the playfulness and *jouissance* of postmodern theory. But as the chapters in this book illustrate, riot is only one of the faces of a postmodern politics. Other faces abound. John Lechte argues, for example, that if postmodern science is about undecidability and indeterminacy, this is not to say that it is not about action. A positive politics has not been abandoned by the postmodern. Indeed, what could be a more active and positive statement than to design and build postmodern spaces such as La Grande Arche or La Place de la Villette? What distinguishes this action from that associated with modernist building (and politics) is the belief that along with such action, use and outcome might possibly be determined/prescribed. In our postscript we draw out some of the contours of these other shadowy faces of postmodern politics alluded to in the preceding chapters.

THE POLITICS OF REPRESENTATION

One of the projects of a postmodern politics is to challenge established representations of the organization and nature of space and to trace how these representations affect the ways we live in and experience the world. With the ascendency of space in social theory, Foucault's notion of *heterotopia* and Plato's notion of *chora* have lent themselves to new interpretations of both discursive and extra-discursive space. Soja finds the identification and description of heterotopias a 'brilliant guidebook to unmasking the "other spaces" concealed in this modernist landscape of hidden signifiers', but ends by doubting whether it 'really' is possible to construct a postmodern politics of resistance which does not lead to immobility or playing with words.

Genocchio, on the other hand, suggests that the political strategy of deploying a notion of heterotopia to allow different strategies of spatial interpretation to be applied to any 'real' place is problematic. The pitfall, as he sees it, is that in setting up and naming the category of an absolutely other and differentiated space it already 'to some degree flattens or precludes, by definition, the very possibility of its arrival as such'. The same problem arises when the term is deployed more discursively. Despite the difficulties, Genocchio suggests that heterotopia is an important *idea* about space which insists that the ordering of spatial systems is arbitrary and subjective in that we know nothing of the totality it might presuppose, and as such it makes us contest, question and confront habitual spatial experience and uses. The performance of activities (he mentions an environmental installation) which challenge existing uses of space and highlight the ways in which spaces and their use are closely regulated is, for Genocchio, one form of an urban postmodern politics.

Plato's notion of *chora*, more recently developed in Julia Kristeva's work, is also found to be useful by writers in this volume. For Lechte *chora* is an unordered space which is prior to the ordering of time. It is a harbinger of pure chance, and an 'uncertain and indeterminate articulation'. What might be the political implications of *chora* as a space of indeterminacy and chance?

Lechte argues that the 'structure of modernism in the city that postmodern theory is concerned to elaborate' is that of a 'city of indetermination' rather than the heralded city of form, reform, function and intention. The notion of *chora* inspires us to think of postmodern politics and planning as the project of elaborating the indeterminate and unexpected outcomes of political movements and planning schemas designed around goals (the better good) and determinacy. Soja's heterotopologies might be one result.

For Grosz *chora* is the 'place where place is made possible, the chasm for the passage of spaceless forms into a spatialized reality, a dimensionless tunnel opening itself to spatialization, obliterating itself to make others possible and actual'. She reveals connections with femininity in that attributes of *chora* are those culturally bestowed on women. In her chapter she draws on Irigaray's writing on the dwelling to suggest that feminist readings of *chora* may reappropriate the implied maternal dimensions and thus 'reorient ways in which spatiality is conceived, lived and used'. The political project, she suggests, is for women to reoccupy places from which they have been re/displaced or expelled and to expose men's appropriation of the whole of space. Wilson and Swanson take up the former project in different ways, one suggesting strategies in which women might envision new ways of living in the physical space of the city and the other pointing to strategic feminist interventions into spaces of consumption.

There is much to be explored in the relationships between planning new places or building new spaces, and planning and building a postmodern politics of action. How might postmodern architecture and postmodern theorization of abstract spaces inform a postmodern politics? Can we see a positive politics of indeterminacy emerging? How might we reclaim spaces of exclusion?

Of course these questions pose the issue of how we currently conceive of spaces, especially city spaces, as ordered. Marcuse argues that cities today are increasingly fragmented and chaotic, yet behind the chaos there are patterns. In his chapter he suggests it is useful to think in terms of quartered cities, or five-parted ones, where the quarters are intricately interlinked, walled in and walled out, hierarchical in power, and dependent on outside social forces.

Diversity and difference are intricately linked with polarization and divisions. Individuals constituting themselves as groups because they have little economic, social or political power is not the same as the spatial separation of the rich. Thus the residential areas of Los Angeles where houses cost upwards of $A1,000,000, and security passes are needed to enter an estate which is protected by armed guards and elaborate electronic surveillance mechanisms (Davis 1990), cannot be usefully compared with Cabramatta in Sydney, which is inhabited by a large number of Vietnamese. Notwithstanding the positive representations of this area, the term 'ghetto' is deployed to describe the latter kinds of space (*Sydney Morning Herald*, 6 September 1993: 3), with their racial, crime and drug-linked connotations, and never the former. What draws the two groups together, however, is common interests. In Cabramatta it is shared culture, business opportunities and shared financial and family concerns. In the Los Angeles suburb it is wealth, the desire for a salubrious environment and fear of incursions by the poor. Similarly, gays inhabit specific areas of cities not only to assert a defined cultural identity (Wotherspoon 1991), but also to enjoy the cultural and economic opportunities which are generated by a critical mass of people with at least some shared concerns.

In contrast, where difference from the cultural norm is combined with a lack of economic or political power, spatial concentration may represent lack of either opportunity or choice – as in the case of many single parents, who are often consigned to poorly serviced and badly located suburbs through lack of an alternative (Watson 1988). Or, and in addition, concentrations of marginalized individuals and groups may represent resistance and solidarity against a hostile world; for example, in the case of racial minorities who have high rates of unemployment or who are subject to hostility from the dominant culture. Here the walls of protection or of exclusion are of another order.

In Bombay, Masselos describes the colonization of unused space, often street space, by new immigrants to the city who then create temporary shelters, which over time assume more and more permanence. As the permanence of the site grows, so the control by landlords increases, as does the intervention by governments in the provision of services. What was once a neutral, unbounded space becomes a space defined by both those within, as a space to be protected, and those without, as a space which can be used for the extraction of money and votes.

Difference implies power. Some groups have economic and social power to have their needs met in the urban system while others do not. Public participation is meaningless if only the more powerful sections of the community are involved. 'Walls' – or bounded spaces – occupied by specific groups may offer protection or places of resistance. These may be necessary for minorities to establish themselves. But even these spaces can quickly shift into places open to attack or abuse or lack of opportunity. Walls can, on the other hand, represent exclusion and domination – a space where those with power exclude those without. So walls or bounded spaces can have different meanings which shift all the time. Planners need to be aware of how these different meanings are constituted spatially and across time if space is to become more democratic.

A notion of democratic public spaces and cities implies a notion of planning for diversity and difference. But how is this possible without creating areas of exclusion, marginalization, ghettoization or Marcuse's quartered city, the partitioned city or the city of walls? To ask the question a different way, when does the concentration of a specific group in a circumscribed and well-defined location represent empowerment and possibilities and when is it symbolic of powerlessness or exclusion?

Are spaces of exclusion the appropriate focus of postmodern political action? How might we conceive of or build different spaces without reproducing just different patterns of segregation and exclusion? This raises the difficult question of whether there can be postmodern planning for postmodern cities.

RETHINKING PLANNING

This question resonates with the concerns of many of the chapters in this volume. Planning is, as Yiftachel, Marcuse and Mabin point out, an expressive and positive act born of a movement which held dearly to reform, emancipation and rational intervention into social life. Indeed, urban planning has been an influential form of modernist politics which has accompanied all social revolutionary and reformist movements of the twentieth century, whether guided by philosophies of welfare capitalism, socialism, anarchism or fascism (Wilson 1991).

Yiftachel's account of planning in post-colonial societies shows that it has been used as an instrument of control and repression. He defines three specific dimensions to planning policy of this kind. The territorial dimension includes planning policies which spatially contain minorities. The procedural dimension covers the formulation and implementation of processes of planning where minorities are denied access to decision making. The socioeconomic dimension is where planning acts to maintain and widen socioeconomic gaps through the location of development costs and benefits which privilege dominant groups. Yiftachel's account of an urbanizing village in Israel shows how planning, far from promoting reform and redistribution of resources, can often be a regressive force.

One important postmodern political intervention is precisely this exposure of the underlying assumptions of the traditional planning framework. Under question are the shibboleths of modernist planning; the notion that cities can be made better, that outcomes are knowable, that order and rationality should and can replace chaos and irrationality; the ideology of progress, and some notion of the better good (Dear 1986; Hillier 1993; Hooper 1992; O'Brien 1994). Criticism of the lack of recognition of cultural, racial or gendered/sexed differences, of the masculinist assumptions, and of the construction of universal principles are now destabilizing the established belief that planners can act in the 'public or common good' and the 'public interest' (Flathman 1966; Altshuler 1965).

Poststructuralist and feminist critiques have pointed out how universal principles are imbued with normative social relations and deny sex/gender difference and embodiment. The latter notions assume a political ideal of community, which, as Iris Young (1990) suggests, implies unity and subsumes difference. Social homogeneity is regarded as a good thing and cultural diversity is not encouraged because it makes no positive contribution to 'the public good'. The validity of the notion that planners act in the public interest has also been criticized by various theorists who recognize the diversity of competing interests in the planning arena (for example Simmie 1974: 121–4). A liberal democratic perspective of the state underpins this public interest ethos, where the state is seen to respond to and mediate the diverse interests of the population. There is thus assumed a public whose interests can be met, whose interests are knowable and known, existing in a prior and coherent form to be represented by planners. It also assumes a coherent and unified notion of the state within which planning fits and plays a defined part. Both these notions have been challenged by poststructuralist critiques (Pringle and Watson 1992).

Planning in a postmodern environment implies a different kind of planning process which seeks to respond to different interests, recognizing that interests are not fixed at any one time and will be continually contested. It means engaging with new forms of democracy which address notions of difference and power. Mechanisms to allow for a state of flux as well as addressing the ebbs and flows of power need to be incorporated into the planning process. It means confronting the uncomfortable relationship between the state and the market rather than allowing the market to dictate terms.

Foucault's notion of the micropolitics of power, where power is seen as operating in a capillary network throughout society, rather than being concentrated in one agency or institution such as the state, is useful here. Foucault sees space as fundamental to any exercise of power (Rabinow 1984: 252), where power necessarily implies resistance. This resistance can take any number of forms including discursive practices which challenge dominant meanings, metaphors and arguments. Hillier (1993: 110) argues for a discursive democracy which 'accepts the inevitability of conflict and obstacles to transparent decisionmaking such as hierarchy, inequality in the inability to make and challenge arguments, political strategising, deception, the exercise of manipulation, entrenched ideas, and self deception'.

Planning for difference, where difference is constructed as a threat to social order, means recognizing that planning as a tool for reform can shift to planning as a tool for control and repression. Yiftachel demonstrates how in post-colonial societies dominant ethnic groups use planning to maintain and strengthen their domination. Alan Mabin in his chapter addresses related issues in the southern African context. He suggests that in the postmodern, postfordist phase of southern African cities new approaches are emerging in planning. One of the most significant of these is the compact city, where the official segregation of widely separated areas sanctioned by the planning system is replaced by 'the good (integrated) city' where the totality of urban functions co-exists within walking distances. Where the forces of fragmentation have been so powerful, the notion of fragments has been closely associated with segregation and carries none of the positive associations of diversity/fragments within postmodern discourse. Here also the politics and planning practices of a modernist past are inappropriate to the contemporary changes being wrought in the cities.

So bound up in the belief in determinate outcomes, planning (and, indeed, the politics of which it is born) almost seems impossible from a postmodern perspective. Yet if we switch to the idea of planning as action without determination, what do we lose? If indeterminacy is at the core of the social, is planning any less possible?

POSTMODERN URBAN POLITICS

In political terms over the last two decades we have seen a shift from the notion of class alliances as the primary political alignment to a growing uncertainty as to what exactly constitutes a class position on the one hand, and an assertion of multiple forms of resistances and alliances, which are argued to be irreducible to class, on the other. Identity politics, where groups organize around the speficities of gender, race, sexuality and other forms of 'oppression' defined by lack of power, have increasingly taken the place of a politics of class. Yet identity politics have shared with class politics a binary structuring of relations – man/woman, black/white, straight/gay – which falls into the same traps of homogenizing categories, fixing difference along rigid lines, failing to recognize the interplays and complexities of powers, and disallowing a multiplicity of subject positions. A postmodern politics implies a more textured and complex understanding of power and difference.

As global processes of capital and new forms of communication have erased national boundaries, so the local has been increasingly asserted as a place of significant political resistance. And as the collapse of regimes based on communist ideologies has decimated old certainties and beliefs as to an imagined future overthrow of capitalism in the West by the oppressed classes, so also scepticism about political formulations deriving from Marx and later Marxist writers have spawned new political formulations and imagined futures.

Central to these have been, first, a critique of notions of community and an assertion of a politics of difference, and second, a deconstruction of assumed notions of justice, needs, interests and other categories deployed in the political terrain to justify certain actions, policy responses or alliances. In response, writers such as Harvey (1989, 1993) have been adamant that earlier values and principles must be reclaimed and asserted.

To look first at some of the insights gained from postmodern theory: amongst others, Young (1990) suggests that the political ideal of community, which subsumes and delimits difference, should be replaced by the political ideal of the unoppressive city. In her view, city life is the 'being together' of strangers. Strangers encounter one another, often remaining strangers and yet acknowledging their contiguity in living and the contributions each makes to others. In such encountering, people are not 'internally' related, as the community theorists would have it, and do not understand one another from within their own perspective. They are externally related, they experience each other as other, different, from different groups, histories, professions, cultures, which they do not understand (1990: 319).

In this formulation public spaces are both an image of the relationships of city life and also an important way that those relationships are lived out. In theatres, on the street, in restaurants, the diverse people of the city come together sometimes interacting, sometimes not, and then depart as strangers. Young sees the social differentiation of the city as providing a positive inexhaustibility of human relations. The unoppressive city is thus defined as 'openness to unassimilated otherness' (Young 1990:319). Paul Patton develops this notion in his chapter in this collection.

A politics of difference needs to lay down the institutional and ideological means by which differently identifying groups can be recognized and affirmed by giving political representation to group interests and by celebrating the distinctive cultures and attributes of different groups. New ways of thinking about public space offer a way into thinking a politics of difference (Watson 1994). Richard Sennett's (1974) work provides a useful conceptualization of public space with its retrieval and celebration of a public space and culture. Watson suggests that for cities to be more democratic, space needs to become less privatized so that individuals can interact in the open, expressing both their differences and their commonalities. These are spaces which are not bounded by walls of exclusion or inclusion – they are spaces without walls.

A more active reassertion of the public will be necessary for a democratic public space to be created. Many contemporary analysts (Howell 1993) are attracted to Habermas's realm of the public sphere, where the ideals of critical rational debate and genuine political participation act as an authoritative basis for political action (Howell 1993: 309). Yet this notion of the impartial public sphere, like many other formulations, lays itself open to a critique of universalism which ignores specificity and difference (Young 1990).

These ideas tie in with the notion of planning for a 'multiple public' (Hooper 1992: 72). Hooper argues for a planning theory and practice that must become decentralized and radically democratic. Beauregard (1989: 393) suggests that planners need to address more directly conflicts within society and its social and cultural heterogeneity. As Mabin suggests, the difficulties of such strategies in the context of deeply divided societies, where riotous and disorganized political behaviour is likely to threaten new planning practices, are immense.

A postmodern politics of identity takes up related themes. Recent collections such as Keith and Pile's *Place and the Politics of Identity* are grappling with similar questions to those which concern us here. In their introduction Keith and Pile write that they want to move away from a position of privileging positionality to one of acknowledging spatiality. Such a move takes us towards an understanding of identities as always contingent and incomplete processes rather than determined outcomes, and of epistemologies as situated and ambivalent rather than abstract and universal (1993: 34).

Within this they are concerned to hold on to notions of social justice as part of their ethical and political agenda, but this is, they say, 'a justice that radically contextualises the various forms of oppression to find the ground on which progressive action can be taken' (p. 36). Thus the book addresses a number of questions such as whether there should be one organizing principle of struggle (a return to modernist politics?), whether there should be multiple sites of resistances where one or more is prioritized according to context, and whether the powerful should join the oppressed at the centre or vice versa (p. 37).

Harvey (1989: 302) reminds us that most social movements, particularly disempowered minorities – racial minorities, women and colonized peoples – command place better than space. Making the connection between place, security and social identity, he suggests that 'In clinging to a place bound identity – often of necessity, such oppositional movements become part of the very fragmentation which a mobile capitalism and flexible accumulation can feed on. Regional resistances, place bound organisation, though excellent bases for political action, cannot bear the burden of radical historical change alone' (1989: 303). There is some common ground here with Jameson

(1991), who is similarly concerned about the immense strategic difficulties involved in coordinating local struggles with national or international ones (1991: 351).

Harvey himself is appealing for some return to notions of social justice. First, in *The Condition of Postmodernity*, he suggests that the very possibility of a rainbow coalition defines a unified politics 'which inevitably speaks the tacit language of class because this is precisely what defines the common experience within the differences' (p. 358). By 1993 we find him proposing a multi-dimensional conception of social justice which implicitly is universal but which must be construed in a dialectical relation to particularity and context (p. 63) and constantly open to negotiation. Ultimately, he is suggesting that a pursuit of identity politics *per se* may simply end up perpetuating the very processes which gave rise to the identities in the first place (p. 64).

In the new conceptualization of identity politics the old binary oppositions of class and gender and race are disrupted and dispersed, and new formations and alliances come together in different forms to erupt in new places and new forms. Instead of assuming single subject positions it is now commonplace to recognize that people represent several groups at once and occupy multiple subject positions and identities which shift and change all the time.

The concept of a diasporic politics is deployed with increasing force (Gilroy 1993; Hesse 1993). This is a notion which challenges place-bound identities by invoking an 'imagined geography, a spatiality that draws connections across oceans and continents and yet unifies the Black (Jewish etc.) experience inside a shared *territory*' (Keith and Pile 1993: 18).

CONCLUSION

A postmodern politics suggests many possibilities. It defines an end to simplistic notions of class alliances or urban social movements. It also defines an end to a politics which assumes a linearity of progress or the inevitability of revolution. No one political solution will emerge which will be universally just. Power will be continually contested, and new and different strategic alliances will emerge at each point of resistance. Rather than such a formulation implying the death of politics or the impossibility of change, reform or 'things for the better', what a postmodern politics recognizes is that there never can be one solution which will benefit all people in all places for all time. Such an ideal can only lead to disappointment. Rather, postmodern politics allows for optimism and possibility, since it celebrates struggles and new possibilities at many sites – both marginal and mainstream – recognizing that victories are only ever partial, temporary and contested. This does not mean passivity and inaction; it means strategic interventions and alliances which are capable of shifting with the fast-changing circumstances of cities today.

What we have argued in this chapter also, is that the division between discursive and non-discursive terrains and between the 'imaginary' and the 'real' needs to be crossed.

Different notions of the political, particularly spatial interpretations of the political, can inform each other. At the very least what postmodern theory has done is to open up a plethora of ways of thinking and acting politically.

REFERENCES

Altshuler, A. 1965: *The City Planning Process: Political Analysis*, Ithaca: Cornell University Press.

Anderson, K. and Gale, F. 1992: *Inventing Places*, Melbourne: Longman Cheshire.

Beauregard, R. 1989: 'Between Modernity and Postmodernity: The Ambiguous Position of US Planning', *Environment and Planning D: Society and Space*, 7: 381–96.

Benjamin, W. 1979: *One Way Street and Other Writings*, London: New Left Books.

Davis, M. 1990: *City of Quartz*, London: Verso.

Dear, M. 1986: 'Postmodernism and Planning', *Environment and Planning D: Society and Space*, 4: 367–84

Dietz, M. 1991: 'Hannah Arendt and Feminist Politics', in M.L. Shanley and C. Pateman (eds), *Feminist Interpretations and Political Theory*, London: Polity Press.

Duncan, J. and Duncan, N. 1988: '(Re)reading the Landscape', *Environment and Planning D: Society and Space*, 6: 117–26.

Flathman, R. 1966: *The Public Interest: An Essay concerning the Normative Discourse of Politics*, New York: John Wiley

Game, A. and Pringle, R. 1983: 'The Making of the Modern Family', in A. Burns (ed.), *Family in the Modern World: Australian Perspectives*, Sydney: Allen and Unwin.

Gibson, K. and Watson, S. 1994: *Metropolis Now: Planning and the Urban in Contemporary Australia*, Sydney: Pluto Press.

Gilroy, P. 1993: *The Black Atlantic: Modernity and Double Consciousness*, London: Verso.

Habermas, J. 1989: *The Structural Transformation of the Public Sphere: An Inquiry into a Category of Bourgeois Society*, Cambridge: Polity Press.

Hartsock, N. 1990: 'Foucault on Power: A Theory for Women?', in L. Nicholson (ed.), *Feminism/Postmodernism*, NY and London: Routledge.

Harvey, D. 1989: *The Condition of Postmodernity*, London: Verso.

Harvey, D. 1992: 'Social Justice, Postmodernism and the City', *International Journal of Urban and Regional Research*, 16, 4.

Harvey, D. 1993: 'Class Relations, Social Justice and the Politics of Difference', in M. Keith and S. Pile (eds), *Place and the Politics of Identity*, London: Routledge.

Healey, P. 1991: 'Debates in Planning Thought', in H. Thomas and P. Healey (eds), *Dilemmas of Planning Practice*, Aldershot: Avebury.

Hesse, B. 1993: 'Black to Front and Black Again: Racialisation through Contested Times and Spaces', in M. Keith and S. Pile (eds), *Place and the Politics of Identity*, London: Routledge.

Hillier, J. 1993: 'To Boldly Go where no Planners Have Ever . . .', *Environment and Planning D: Society and Space*, 11: 89–113.

Hillier, J. and McManus, P. 1993: 'Pull Up the Drawbridge: Fortress Mentality in the Suburbs', in *Postmodern Cities*, Sydney: Department of Urban and Regional Planning, University of Sydney.

hooks, b. 1990: *Yearnings: Race, Gender and Cultural Politics*, Boston: South End Press.

Hooper, B. 1992: 'Split at the Roots: A Critique of Modern Planning Doctrine', *Frontiers*, XIII, 1: 45–80.

Howell, P. 1993: 'Public Space and the Public Sphere: Political Theory and the Historical Geography of Modernity', *Environment and Planning D: Society and Space*, 11: 303–22.

Jameson, F. 1991: *Postmodernism or the Cultural Logic of Late Capitalism*, London: Verso.

Keith, M. and Pile, S. (eds) 1993: *Place and the Politics of Identity*, London: Routledge.

Lefebvre, H. 1991: *The Production of Space*, Oxford: Blackwell.

O'Brien, M. 1981: *The Politics of Reproduction*, London: Routledge and Kegan Paul.

O'Brien, B. 1994: 'Postmodern Planning – A Need for Strategies of Intervention', in K. Gibson and S. Watson (eds), *Metropolis Now: Planning and the Urban in Contemporary Australia*, Sydney: Pluto Press.

Pateman, C. and Gross, 1986: *Feminist Challenges*, Sydney: Allen and Unwin.

Pringle, R. and Watson, S. 1992: 'Constructing Interests', in M. Barrett and A. Phillips (eds), *Destabilising Theory*, Oxford: Polity Press.

Rabinow, P. 1984: *The Foucault Reader*, New York: Pantheon Books.

Rich, A. 1979: *On Lies, Secrets and Silence: Selected Prose 1966–1978*, New York: W.W. Norton.

Sennett, R. 1990: *The Conscience of the Eye*, New York: Alfred A. Knopf.

Sennett, R. 1974: *The Fall of Public Man*, New York: Alfred A. Knopf.

Sibley, D. 1992: 'Outsiders in Society and Space', in K. Anderson and F. Gale, *Inventing Places*, Melbourne: Longman Cheshire.

Simmie, J. 1974: *Citizens in Conflict: The Sociology of Town Planning*, London: Hutchinson.

Smith, M.P. 1992: 'Postmodernism, Urban Ethnograophy, and the New Social Space of Ethnic Identity', *Theory, Culture and Society*, 21, 4.

Soja, E. 1989: *Postmodern Geographies*, London: Verso.

Soja, E. and Hooper, B. 1993: 'The Spaces That Difference Make: Some Notes on The Geograsphical Margins of New Cultural Politics', in M. Keith and S. Pile (eds), *Place and the Politics of Identity*, London: Routledge.

Young, I. 1990: 'The Ideal of Community and the Politics of Difference', in L. Nicholson (ed.), *Feminism/Postmodernism*, London: Routledge.

Watson, S. 1988: *Accommodating Inequality: Gender and Housing*, Sydney: Allen and Unwin.

Watson, S. 1994: 'Re-creating Democratic Public Space – Planning for Difference', Working Paper, Department of Urban and Regional Planning, University of Sydney.

Wilson, E. 1991: *The Sphinx and the City*, London: Virago.

Wotherspoon, G. 1991: *'City of the Plains': History of a Gay Subculture*, Sydney: Hale and Iremonger.

Index

in South Africa, 188, 191–2
  see also chora
hyper-reality, 135–6, 141
hyperspace, 21, 113, 127

identity, 15, 117–18, 179, 181, 261
  cultural, 116, 127, 168, 169, 170, 175,
    176
  national, 171–3
  politics, 260
  see also subjectivity
ideology, 66–7, 71
imaginary, the, 5, 24, 37, 38, 42, 83, 104,
    112–20, 134–5, 161, 255, 262
indeterminacy, 5, 4, 48, 100–2, 103,
    104–5, 106, 108, 110, 255, 256, 259
insanity, 86–7
Irigaray, Luce, 48–9, 53, 54, 256

Jameson, Frederic, 20, 21, 22, 30, 36,
    112–15, 119, 174, 261
Jencks, Charles, 100, 117, 146
Johannesburg, 187–98
Joyce, James, 102–6, 109

Keith, Michael, 261
Kingston, 7, 149–62
knowledge, 28, 29, 39, 40, 43, 48, 99,
    101, 109, 110, 175
  see also power
Kracauer, Siegfried, 63–4, 91
Kristeva, Julia, 48, 100–1, 256

Laqueur, Thomas, 84
late modern, 20, 30, 100, 127, 128, 130,
    151, 179
  and cities, 130, 133
Lea, John, 7
Lechte, John, 5, 255, 256
Lefebvre, Henri, 21, 22–3, 29, 30, 33
London, 61, 67
Los Angeles, 2, 5, 6, 8, 13, 17–19, 21–31,
    112, 113, 125–37, 208, 249, 250,
    256–7
Lyotard, Jean-François, 119

Mabin, Alan, 8, 258, 259, 261

Marcuse, Peter, 9, 256, 258
Marx, Karl, 109, 260
Marxism, 63, 127, 128, 144
Masselos, Jim, 8, 257
maternal, the, 52, 54, 55, 256
men, 50, 55–7, 61–6, 68–9
  male gaze, 65, 68–9, 72
  masculine thought, 55
  masculinity, 85–6, 88–9, 93
migration, 153–4, 156, 160
  rural, 166, 167, 170, 192, 210
modernism, 106, 113, 127, 141
  and architecture, 187
  and planning, 191, 216, 243, 258
  and politics, 254, 261
Morris, William, 70
multiculturalism, 131, 132, 147, 166
Museum of Contemporary Art, 25

Nietzsche, Friedrich, 117
non-government organizations (NGOs),
    188–9
novels, 81–2, 109
  see also writing

palimpsest, 26–8, 30, 105
panopticon, 3, 23, 28–9, 30, 134
Papua New Guinea, 165–81
Parc de la Villette, 109–10, 255
Paris, 2–3, 5, 17–19, 26, 32, 61, 63–4,
    67, 72, 88, 103, 106
Patton, Paul, 5, 96, 260
phallocentric, 55, 57
philanthropy, 60–1, 70, 95
Pile, Stephen, 261
place, 55, 57, 134, 160, 174, 261
Plato, 48, 49, 50, 51, 57, 104, 117, 245,
    255, 256
polarization, 133
  see also segregation
politics, 7–9, 22, 27, 29, 42, 64, 112,
    119–20, 126–7, 147, 174, 254–63
  in India, 200
  in Jamaica, 156
  of place, 134
  in PNG, 177
  in South Africa, 193